★ ★

FEDERALIZING THE MUSE

★ ★

Federalizing the MUSE

UNITED STATES ARTS POLICY AND THE
NATIONAL ENDOWMENT FOR THE ARTS,
1965–1980 ★ DONNA M. BINKIEWICZ

The

University

of North

Carolina

Press

Chapel Hill

and

London

© 2004
The University of North Carolina Press
All rights reserved
Set in Minion and Castellar
by Keystone Typesetting, Inc.
Manufactured in the United States of America

An earlier version of Chapter 2 appeared as "Culture from Camelot:
The Origins and Goals of Arts Policy in the Kennedy Administration,"
UCLA Historical Journal 16 (1966): 103–30.

Library of Congress Cataloging-in-Publication Data
Binkiewicz, Donna M.
Federalizing the muse : United States arts policy and the National Endowment
for the Arts, 1965–1980 / Donna M. Binkiewicz.
    p. cm.
Includes bibliographical references and index.
ISBN 0-8078-2878-5 (cloth: alk. paper)—ISBN 0-8078-5546-4 (pbk.: alk. paper)
1. Federal aid to the arts—United States—History—20th century. 2. National
Endowment for the Arts—History. 3. Art and state—United States. I. Title.
NX735.B56   2004
700'.1'03097309045—dc22   2004001718

cloth   08 07 06 05 04   5 4 3 2 1
paper   08 07 06 05 04   5 4 3 2 1

Dedicated to the memory of my parents,

Louis J. Lochs and Margaret B. Lochs,

and to my family,

especially Paul, David, Daniel, and Mark.

ILLUSTRATIONS

ACKNOWLEDGMENTS

Over the years many people and institutions have supported my work; I extend my gratitude to all of them. I would like to thank the members of my dissertation committee at UCLA who first launched me on this project a decade ago. Richard Weiss worked with me on the Master's thesis from which this book originated and has provided much support along the way. Cecile Whiting furnished expertise in art historical analysis. Robert Wohl enlightened my work with cultural theories and studies of art and the state in modern Europe. Bruce J. Schulman has generously offered his insights throughout the years and across the miles. His constructive critiques have greatly improved this book, and his sound advice and encouragement have sustained me through its completion.

I would also like to acknowledge my UCLA dissertation group. Ingrid Fey, Chris Gold, Jennifer Kalish, Shirley Lim, Michelle Moravec, and Rumi Yasutake read drafts of these chapters. They also offered an atmosphere of collegiality, support, and friendship that I will long remember and appreciate.

Many others have read all or parts of this manuscript along the way. I thank Casey Nelson Blake, Logan Dalla-Betta, Marc Dollinger, Janice Reiff, Richard Candida Smith, and Jessica Wang for their suggestions.

I undertook much of the research for this study in Washington, D.C., where I served as an Arts Administration Fellow at the National Endowment for the Arts. I would like to acknowledge several people who aided me there: Judith O'Brien, Anya Nykyforiak, Jeanne McConnell, Ana Steele, Tom Bradshaw, Olive Moser, Karen Elian, Gary O. Larson, Bert Kubli, Michael Faubion, Brian O'Doherty, Paul Carlson, Edythe Jacobs, Silvio Lim, and Daniel Sheehy. I also reaped needed support from my fellowship colleagues, especially Kim Buchheit.

The course of my research required several trips to archives around the United States. I am grateful for grants from the John F. Kennedy Memorial Foundation and the Lyndon Baines Johnson Presidential Library that enabled me to travel to Boston, Massachusetts, and Austin, Texas, to review materials in the presidential libraries. The archivists at both institutions were most helpful. I also appreciate the UCLA History Department's travel grant, which allowed me to return to Washington, D.C., to work at the National Archives, the Archives of American Arts, and the Library of Congress and to interview several important people for this project.

Personal accounts have refined my knowledge and added depth to this study. I thank the following people for contributing their time and wisdom: Livingston Biddle, Bess Lomax Hawes, August Heckscher, Alan Jabbour, Senator Claiborne Pell, Roland Reiss, Pièrre Salinger, Arthur Schlesinger Jr., and Ana Steele.

I owe so much to my family. My mother always encouraged me to follow my dreams, while she and my Dad provided an example of discipline and hard work that have carried me through my academic journey. I would not be where I am today without the love and support of my parents and my family. I endeavor to follow their example while raising my own children. My son Daniel has already grown into toddlerhood watching his Mommy with her books and computer. I hope he will understand how much I appreciated his sharing me with my academic pursuits and that he and his new little brother, Mark, will be inspired to a lifelong love of reading and learning. Finally, I am most indebted to my husband, Paul, for his endless patience, encouragement, and love.

ABBREVIATIONS

AFI	American Film Institute
CWA	Civil Works Administration
FERA	Federal Emergency Relief Administration
FDR	Franklin Delano Roosevelt
GNP	Gross National Product
HUAC	House Un-American Activities Committee
JFK	John Fitzgerald Kennedy
LBJ	Lyndon Baines Johnson
Met	Metropolitan Museum of Art
MOMA	Museum of Modern Art
NCA	National Council on the Arts
NEA	National Endowment for the Arts
NEH	National Endowment for the Humanities
OMB	Office of Management and Budget
PWAP	Public Works of Art Projects
UNESCO	United Nations Educational, Scientific, and Cultural Organization
USIA	United States Information Agency
USSR	Union of Soviet Socialist Republics
WPA	Works Progress Administration

★ ★

FEDERALIZING THE MUSE

Introduction

*Art is our nation's most precious heritage, [for] it is in our works of
art that we reveal to ourselves and to others the inner vision which
guides us as a nation.*
—Lyndon Baines Johnson, "Remarks at the Signing of the Arts and
  Humanities Bill," September 24, 1965

*Art is created by man's imagination in relation to his time. When art
exists, it becomes tradition.*
—David Smith, "Statements and Writings (1947–1952)"

★ ★

In 1995 Congress cut budget allocations for the National Endowment for the Arts (NEA) and slashed funding for individual artists. The
aftermath of budget reductions forced the NEA to eliminate thirteen of its
seventeen programs, including the Visual Arts Program.[1] That the bill man-
dating these cuts passed without significant debate reflects not only the conservative political and fiscal climate of the 1990s but also Congress's lingering
unease over a few "objectionable" art displays. The spate of controversies
erupted in 1989 when the Corcoran Gallery opened a show of Robert Mapplethorpe's photographs, including shots of flowers, portraits, and homo-
erotic images. Disgust over Mapplethorpe's "perverted" representations soon
spread to another artist, Andres Serrano, whose *Piss Christ* had been displayed at North Carolina's Southeastern Center for Contemporary Art the
previous year. Although both exhibits had been mounted without funds
from the NEA directly earmarked for the Mapplethorpe or Serrano works, the
NEA had supported these well-respected museums with grants for their sea-
sonal operations. The arts agency took the brunt of the attack for its allegedly
"inappropriate" use of taxpayer funds.[2] Leading the assault, staunchly conservative arts foe Sen. Jesse Helms (R-N.C.) at first proposed eliminating the Endowment altogether, then attempted to insert language into the appropriation bills that called for a ban on all funding for art depicting sexually explicit
activities or denigrating religion. While these recommendations failed, Congress inserted a "decency clause" into NEA guidelines and mandated that
"obscenity is without artistic merit, is not protected speech, and shall not be
funded."[3] The outcry against degeneracy drowned out the agency's weak

attempts at self-defense; over the next several years, critics continued to hound federal arts employees while Congress dramatically downsized NEA appropriations and curtailed its operations. Because of these high-profile disputes, many Americans came to associate the NEA with controversial art and assumed that it was the plaything of ultra-liberals out to undermine common decency with degraded aesthetics.[4]

This conventional wisdom, so little supported by historical evidence, suggested the need for a balanced historical analysis of the Endowment. Such a study offers insight into the relationship between politics and culture in contemporary U.S. history. The NEA has served not merely as the focal point for the history of twentieth-century American arts funding but also as a window through which to view art historical developments, the intellectual milieu of the 1950s and 1960s, American domestic and international politics, and interpretations of culture and power in the post–World War II period. The NEA's history is rich with connections to the broad historical tendencies of our time. It offers crucial insight into the ways the national government sought to construct, and reconstruct, American national identity. The agency's administration of art funding illustrates what American political and cultural leaders chose to celebrate or to dismiss about American culture.

This study examines the intellectual and political origins of federal arts policy that led to the establishment of the National Endowment for the Arts in 1965. It also explores the administration of national arts policy between 1965 and 1980. The early period of the agency's history, which scholars have all too often ignored, proved critical in the formation of NEA policies. Understanding the events and context of this formative period is essential to comprehending NEA operations. Ideological and political influences of the Cold War era significantly affected the development of arts policy and the NEA. Politicians and social science advisers committed to a consensus liberal philosophy and political agenda crafted arts policy. They followed the progressive liberal tradition, believing in positive, problem-solving action by the federal government in economic and social policy combined with anticommunism.[5] Later many Americans rejected modern liberal practices and came to believe that arts funding signified an out-of-control government spending taxpayers' money on the most avant-garde and offensive aesthetic styles. Yet, history proved otherwise. The NEA was founded with a much more moderate undertone; and the agency has been unfairly maligned despite its many achievements.

While recounting the history of the NEA, *Federalizing the Muse* examines a series of important questions. Historically, how have American leaders defined the relationship between the arts and public policy? To what extent did the Cold War provide the impetus for the creation of a federal arts policy? Why did the nation implement no such policy before 1965? Did national politics guide the NEA, or did the agency enjoy administrative autonomy in arts funding? Which forms of art were promoted and why? How and why did the NEA and American policy makers draw a dichotomy between "high" and "popular" art and culture?

This study comprises seven chapters organized into two parts. Part I examines the unprecedented transformation of America from a nation maintaining staunch opposition to full-fledged federal sponsorship of the arts to one upholding its art as symbolic of American democracy, freedom, and cultural prowess. Chapter 1 elucidates the background to American art and arts policy prior to 1960. The next two chapters assess cultural policy development and implementation during the Kennedy and Johnson presidential administrations, the era when American leaders federalized the arts to promote domestic social uplift and further international Cold War posturing.

Part II examines the actual experience of federal arts policy from the creation of the NEA to the Reagan era, analyzing which art forms received federal support. Chapter 4 assesses the leadership and policies of the National Council on the Arts and the origins of the NEA's Visual Arts Program. Chapter 5 details the program's art funding awards and juxtaposes them with an analysis of dominant aesthetic trends and cultural criticism of the 1960s and early 1970s. Chapter 6 assesses arts policies and funding advanced under the administration of President Richard Nixon. The final chapter details arts funding in the Ford and Carter years as the NEA widened its funding categories to include greater varieties of arts and artists.

After the demise of the New Deal Works Progress Administration (WPA) art projects, the federal government retreated from active sponsorship of the arts. At the same time, in the decade and a half following World War II, American abstraction emerged as the foremost modernist art form. Both of these historical streams converged in the development of the NEA as Kennedy and Johnson sought to develop an unprecedented federal arts program that would promote the best of American art—which NEA officials continued to believe was the modernist abstraction that had reached its zenith of influence by the early 1960s.

Two distinct rationales for establishing a national arts policy motivated both the Kennedy and Johnson administrations. One focused on domestic policy and began as a reaction to 1950s cultural criticism that accused the United States of having become conformist, materialist, complacent, and aesthetically deplorable. In response to such reproaches American intellectuals and leaders decided to enlist the arts as a means of social uplift. Stimulating and showcasing aesthetic excellence, they believed, would reinvigorate creative ingenuity, beautify the cultural landscape, and remind Americans of what true civilization embraced. The second rationale for arts policy extended beyond American domestic policy to include a larger international mission. Presidential papers and congressional records demonstrate that the Cold War proved an important impetus in arts policy development during the Kennedy, Johnson, and Nixon presidencies. American leaders endeavored to outshine the Soviets in cultural displays and by so doing entice developing nations away from the lures of communist culture. Moreover, U.S. officials embraced the argument that America was the protector of Western culture after World War II and the cradle of even greater aesthetic achievements in the prosperous postwar decades. Administrative records and grant histories at the NEA and the National Archives suggest that this Cold War mind-set encouraged NEA funding of predominantly classical Western arts during the agency's first years.

The actual administration of the arts endowment reinforced these political and aesthetic objectives. Because the National Council on the Arts and Visual Arts Program were comprised primarily of modernist abstract artists, they supported high culture, and modern art, more specifically, rather than promoting the prevailing pop and postmodern art forms most popular at the time. While American art in the 1960s was moving into pop, performance, conceptual, feminist, and ethnic arts that were more critical of American society, federal art support continued to favor older modernist abstract forms. The self-imposed focus on high modernist arts underlying the Visual Arts Program made it impossible for the NEA to fulfill it dual mission to both promote aesthetic excellence and make art more accessible to the national public.

The NEA matured significantly during the Nixon administration. The size and scope of the agency expanded, and Chair Nancy Hanks opened wider avenues for arts funding and received higher congressional appropriations than anyone previously thought possible. Ironically, the agency became more liberal in terms of grant-making—both in dollar amounts and types of art funded—under Nixon than during the "liberal" administrations of both Kennedy and Johnson. Adjusting to art world trends of the 1960s and to criticism of its own elitism, the NEA incorporated more populist art forms, although it still lagged behind the avant-garde trends of the 1970s. Central themes of promoting excellence in and access to art and displaying American freedom in a cultural Cold War remained. Yet Nixon also used the agency to promote his administration domestically as one in tune with the needs of American youth and able to provide it positive cultural expression at a time when the Vietnam war seriously divided the country and threatened a breakdown of Cold War ideology.

During the 1970s Presidents Gerald Ford and Jimmy Carter vowed to continue support for the NEA but also pledged to open its doors to more populist art forms. NEA officials appointed during the Carter years widened its mandate to include augmented funding of representational, feminist, ethnic, and folk art in addition to high modernist forms, although modernism remained dominant. Ironically, just as the NEA improved its advocacy of pluralist arts that its leaders deemed more representative of American culture, the agency ran up against a growing current of budget limitations and questions about its legitimacy.

The study ends in 1980, when Ronald Reagan ushered in a period of federal cutbacks and instigated a drive to end federal art funding. The conclusion briefly addresses subsequent arts controversies resulting in diminished budget allocations for the NEA after the 1980s.[6] That much of the recent strife over arts funding occurred after the end of the Cold War era reinforces the significance of the conflict as a powerful influence in generating bipartisan support for the arts. The breakdown of its ideological underpinnings suggests that a rethinking of the agency's justifications will be needed if arts funding is to survive and flourish in the twenty-first century. The decline of the Endowment also parallels the political shift away from the Cold War liberal paradigm toward a much more conservative fiscal and social agenda that triumphed in the 1994 election of the 104th Republican-controlled Congress and its "Contract with America." The Endowment's future depends on its answering the conservatives' renewed challenge to federal support for the arts and defending its actions. Historical perspective is a crucial and all too often neglected factor in these culture wars.

Federalizing the Muse employs an interdisciplinary approach drawing on the fields of intellectual and cultural history, art history, and American political history to situate the National Endowment for the Arts within the cultural and political framework of the 1960s and 1970s. A few art historical and cultural monographs have studied portions of the NEA's administration; however, accounts of the agency too often focus either on politics *or* on specific cultural programs, thus remaining largely incomplete.[7]

Much of the "cultural turn" in historical studies began with European history, where many fascinating books have interwoven analyses of political experiences and aesthetic change. Thus, I began my work by absorbing accounts of art and the state in Europe with the goal of applying similar methodologies to my study. Deborah Silverman's *Art Nouveau in Fin-de-Siècle France* proved a most worthy example, as she found that French officials and the avant-garde worked together to promote art nouveau and uplift French nationalism during the 1890s.[8] Other accounts demonstrated the opposite dynamic. Carl Schorske and Peter Paret have illustrated how conflicting agendas underlay the relationship between the Austrian and German governments and artists, as officials promoted a more traditional style and the status quo while modern artists attempted to break free of those constraints.[9] My study of politics and culture in the United States delves into similar concerns. In America, arts policy was developed as a national response to the United States' stature as a superpower and as a means of illustrating American cultural preeminence to the world. Ideology and politics not only significantly affected the development of arts policy, but also influenced the selection of aesthetic styles for national arts awards.

Several art historians have combined art historical and political analyses to document a relationship between American art and politics during the 1950s. Max Kozloff, Eva Cockcroft, and Serge Guilbaut have all demonstrated how abstract expressionist painting was used as a propaganda tool during the Cold War to highlight American cultural freedom in contrast to communist repression—with each scholar incrementally strengthening the links of cooperation between politicians and artists.[10] I argue that the National Endowment for the Arts formalized and extended the relationship between politics and culture. Government officials used art for political purposes while artists either agreed or conveniently looked the other way. Those artists who protested openly were not usually rewarded with NEA grants.

A number of European studies have also identified generational conflict as a crucial factor in the evolving relationship between modern art and the twentieth-century state.[11] In the United States that generational conflict often marked the relationship between the prominent 1950s politicians and artists who founded the NEA and the generation of the 1960s and 1970s who began to break from the older generation's political and aesthetic ideals. Because so many younger artists, critics, and intellectuals of the 1960s and 1970s represented what cultural theorists have labeled "postmodern" developments, this study also draws on recent cultural theories.[12] Writings by theorists Pièrre Bourdieu, Michel Foucault, and Antonio Gramsci and works by historians Lynn Hunt and John Toews have proposed that power is implicit in language and that elite culture perpetuates itself in language and representation.[13] My work assesses how language and aesthetics established a particular standard of excellence in federal arts funding which political leaders and art officials used to achieve their agendas of political and cultural power. The rise and dominance of high modernist aesthetics at the NEA and federal officials' goals of using modern art to perpetuate their ideal brand of American politics and culture illustrate this dynamic.[14]

Beyond cultural studies, *Federalizing the Muse* also engages recent scholarship in American political history and contributes to recent historiographic reevaluations of presidential politics and programs. The NEA was a product of the New Frontier and Great Society and, thus, the liberal American state of the 1960s. However, like recent political historians who have found the Kennedy and Johnson administrations to be less "liberal" ideologically than previously thought, I will argue that a recognizable strain of conservatism underlined Kennedy's and Johnson's plans.[15]

Nixon's great expansion of NEA funding testifies to the potency of that conservative strain in federal arts policy. Many scholars have previously observed that Kennedy and Nixon in 1960 were probably more alike than different politically. Both were staunch cold warriors as well as fiscal and social conservatives, and their partisan differences were more a matter of degree than of substance.[16] Although Johnson and Nixon seemed worlds apart in 1968, they were actually far closer than they may have appeared in ideology as well. Both remained committed to anticommunism and winning the war in Vietnam, and both worried about radicalism among American youth; yet while Johnson's social policies were far reaching but fell short, Nixon's were more extensive and long lasting than he was given credit for after Watergate. In an analysis of Nixon's presidency, I argue that Nixon needs to be considered in a broader context outside of Watergate.[17] His impact on domestic policy, including art policy, was significant; it represented some of the best and worst tendencies in contemporary American politics.

My evaluation of Jimmy Carter's stewardship of the NEA also sheds new light on the achievements and failures of his presidency and the larger political challenges of the 1970s. Carter did not simply mirror or extend the liberal-

ism of his democratic predecessors; rather, he anticipated the fiscal conservatism that would become the dominant feature of the political landscape
during the 1980s and 1990s. The National Endowment for the Arts offers a
compelling case study of the political landscape of the 1960s and 1970s, high-
lighting continuities that persisted across vastly different presidencies.

To chart these long-term trends in the day-to-day decisions of the NEA,
this study focuses on the agency's most celebrated and controversial endeavor, the Visual Arts Program. Because visual arts grants have generated
much of the recent controversy about NEA funding, studying the history of
this program is the best way to investigate whether or not NEA policies were
progressive and in step with contemporary aesthetic developments or if the
Visual Arts Program actually advanced more conservative social and political
agendas. Arts manager Edward Arian's study of the NEA argues that music,
theater, and museum funding was highly conservative.[18] That theory turns
out to apply to the Visual Arts Program in an even more dramatic fashion,
because while visual arts trends change more rapidly than those in classical
music, theater, and performing arts, NEA funding did not keep apace of the
most contemporary aesthetic developments. Moreover, it becomes clear that
abstract visual arts were used to represent American freedom of expression
during the Cold War in the 1950s and continued to perform that function
into the 1960s and 1970s.

In the end, a historically balanced evaluation of the Visual Arts Program
reveals more than significant developments in the arts and their funding. It
also provides insight into the heart of American society and politics. The
history of the NEA highlights the fundamental ways in which Americans
interpret not only the importance of art and culture, but also the role of the
government. Over the course of American history, liberals and conservatives
have construed the issue of federal action differently; nevertheless, the issue
remains crucial to understanding American ideals. The history of the NEA
represents one aspect of this ongoing saga in defining American identity.

I

* *

FEDERALIZING THE MUSE

Prelude to Policy

*I must study politics and war, that my sons may have the liberty
to study mathematics, philosophy, geography, natural history and
naval architecture, navigation, commerce and agriculture in order
to give their children the right to study painting, poetry, music, and
architecture.*
—John Adams, "Letter to Abigail Adams, 1780"

1

★ ★

Throughout most of its history the United States stood apart
in the realm of national arts policies. Other nations routinely spent large percentages of their gross national products on cultural endeavors. The French
and Austrian monarchies generously patronized the arts for centuries, while
modern constitutional states also supported culture. They did so as a matter
of course, not only during prosperous eras but in difficult times as well. Even
in the depths of World War II's Battle of Britain, British Prime Minister
Winston Churchill set aside funds to maintain art and culture rather than
shifting those funds to military budgets. Churchill believed that art was essential to morale and that the nation's cultural heritage represented the essence of what the war effort aimed to preserve. By the middle of the twentieth
century, European countries were spending between twenty and forty times
what the United States allocated for arts support, and they considered it a
source of national pride.[1]

The United States historically shied away from such action. Social and
political obstacles long prevented the American government from instituting
a national arts policy. Important factors, including national and international
prestige, presidential support for arts policy, and congressional backing, only
converged during the 1960s to enable the establishment of a permanent
federal arts policy.

★ *The U.S. Government and the Arts, 1776–1932*

Until the twentieth century, the United States government possessed no
official arts policy. This stand was rooted deep in the nation's history, stem-
ming from religious and social traditions in early American culture. Puritan

founders in Britain had condemned the lavish decorations and expenditures on art of the royal European courts and the church. Puritan New Englanders feared that indulging in the arts would distract colonists from industrious pursuits and foster idle ones instead. In the colonial period, little art existed in America, and colonists were limited to enjoying art in the forms of hand-crafted furniture and costume. They remained indifferent to arts policy.[2] Southern colonists enjoyed the arts to a greater extent, although they recognized that higher forms of music and theater were limited to the elite planter class who could afford such leisurely activities. Throughout the colonies, people fashioned distinctly American folk art forms; and, although enjoyed by "middling and lower sorts," these remained relegated to an inferior aesthetic status. Americans from various regions and social classes did not expect or desire their colonial governments to institute arts programs and no federal government yet existed to consider a national policy.[3]

American leaders also reflected the attitudes of the American population in the eighteenth and nineteenth centuries. Most governing elites believed that the federal government's first concerns in the early national period were to establish a workable form of democratic government and to achieve basic political, economic, and social stability. The arts had to be deferred for the time being. As John Adams stated, "I must study politics and war, that my sons may have the liberty to study mathematics, philosophy, geography, natural history and naval architecture, navigation, commerce and agriculture in order to give their children the right to study painting, poetry, music, and architecture."[4] Moreover, many in Congress believed that federal support for the arts would result either in the elitist control of artistic freedom that marred European art patronage or the encouragement of frivolous luxury.[5] Even Thomas Jefferson, who greatly admired European art and enjoyed French culture while he served as the U.S. minister to France, considered the court of Louis XVI at once authoritarian and licentious. Upon his return to the United States and election as president, Jefferson pursued U.S. economic and geographic growth with the Louisiana Purchase but otherwise maintained a low level of U.S. involvement in international affairs and advocated minimal federal expansion. He never advocated national encouragement of the arts.[6]

During the Jacksonian period, Americans' celebration of the common man and sense of self-sufficiency were powerful forces that kept American leaders away from formal artistic pursuits or European-style patronage. Indeed, the element of anti-intellectualism that emerged in the Jacksonian era actively hindered arts support as Congress raised tariffs on importation of art, and Jackson's antielitist rhetoric widened the gap between "cultured" society and the democratic masses.[7]

In this early period, the federal government only supported the arts through occasional architectural projects. As construction of federal buildings proceeded, the government often commissioned architects, sculptors, muralists, and painters to embellish such structures, including the Capitol.[8] During the nineteenth century, federal agencies began to commission statuary more frequently. Still, the results hardly encouraged future arts support. In 1832, Congress hired Horatio Greenough to design a statue of George Washington for the Capitol rotunda.[9] When completed in 1843, the piece depicted Washington dressed in a Roman toga and sandals, seated on a throne, holding a sword in his extended hand.[10] Few were ready to accept such an imperial image of their beloved republican President, so the statue was ridiculed and, eventually, removed.[11] Although Greenough's *George Washington* proved less than successful, Congress continued to hire artists to adorn the nation's capital, generally with historical paintings and sculptures which they considered more acceptable.

Some congressmen called for support for the arts by various additional means in the late nineteenth and early twentieth centuries when the United States sought a larger role in international affairs and worked to bolster its national status. In the 1870s, Rep. Samuel Cox (R-N.Y.) sponsored a bill for the establishment of a Federal Arts Council.[12] Later in 1891, Congress passed a bill creating a National Conservatory of Music but failed to appropriate funds for its support.[13] While these attempts at arts policy indicated concern for the arts by some in the national legislature, their failures demonstrated that the majority in Congress remained unconvinced that the arts were worthy of national support. Most considered financial support for such purposes impractical or out of their jurisdiction. While America busied itself with expansion and industrialization, they maintained that the nation had little time for leisurely artifice.[14]

Early in the twentieth century, the federal government demonstrated an increased readiness to engage in arts support. President Theodore Roosevelt became one of the most recognized advocates of art and culture, inviting artists to the White House and patronizing art performances.[15] He was also noticeably interested in the United States' relative position in the world—both as a political and military power and as an advanced "civilization." His concerns reflected leading Americans' desire in this period to show that amid proliferating urbanization, industrialization, bureaucratization, specialization, and consumerization, American culture remained both democratic and highly civilized.[16] Roosevelt, who had already expanded government action in a variety of areas during his administration, issued an executive order in 1909 to create a Council on the Fine Arts—a thirty-member body that would, upon request, advise the president and Congress on the aesthetics for public buildings, monuments, and parks in Washington, D.C., and on other arts issues. The council met only once before Roosevelt left office, recommending an extension of the Mall from the Capitol beyond the Washington Monument to the Potomac River with a new memorial to Lincoln to be constructed near the water's edge.[17]

William Howard Taft took control of the Executive Office only a month later and abolished the council. Taft objected not to the council's mission but to the way it had been implemented. He believed that legislation rather than presidential action was the proper avenue for public policy. Therefore, in 1910, he asked Congress to approve a Commission on the Fine Arts. After some discussion, including opposition to "experts" who some congressmen feared would move beyond a mere advisory role, Congress ultimately authorized the commission with a paltry annual budget of $10,000.[18] The Progressive faith in expertise and desire to use government for the betterment of American society at this point outweighed opposition to federal involvement in the arts. The Commission on the Fine Arts remained in place until the 1970s. Its founding demonstrated the power of presidential attention to arts policy both by Roosevelt and Taft, whose interest was a significant factor in winning its approval in Congress. The commission operated quietly for decades securing projects ranging from the Lincoln Memorial to the Watergate Complex. Nevertheless, the commission fell far short of a national arts policy. It remained a small advisory committee concerned with the capital city alone.

★ Government Art Projects during the New Deal

The first significant action by the federal government to create a national arts policy came in the 1930s under the auspices of the New Deal Works Progress Administration. The rationale for the 1930s programs and their ultimate successes and shortcomings provides the essential background for the founding of the National Endowment for the Arts in the 1960s. Many arguments in favor of U.S. government involvement in the arts, as well as protests against such affiliation, carried over from the 1930s into the 1960s.

Taking office in the midst of the Great Depression, President Franklin

Delano Roosevelt implemented new monetary, commercial, industrial, and agricultural policies to spur renewed economic activity in the country and stimulate greater employment. In May of 1933, FDR signed the order creating the Federal Emergency Relief Administration (FERA) and assigned Harry Hopkins its director.[19] Under this policy federal art programs commenced.

Ten thousand artists were unemployed in March of 1933, as compared to fifteen million unemployed Americans overall. Prior to the establishment of the WPA, most artists were forced to choose between their calling or a more practical line of work that could provide a steady income.[20] During the depression the arts were considered an unaffordable luxury, which made it difficult for artists to support themselves through the sale of their work. Those who wished to continue as artists without taking on another form of work were left with the culturally disgraceful option of accepting handouts for unemployment.[21]

Hopkins, head of the new FERA, acknowledged this cultural assumption that the dole was degrading for the recipient; he also understood that the government had limited funds and that federal relief seemed to extend the unsavory handout principle. In the face of congressional opposition to subsidies and to further economic reconstruction, Hopkins called for the development of a work relief program. Along with other agency heads, principally Harold Ickes of the Public Works Projects Administration and Edward Bruce of the Treasury Department, Hopkins asserted that artists were like any other American worker who paid rent, bought groceries, and had family obligations and, therefore, that they should merit employment relief for their professions just as other unemployed workers did.

Congress granted this wish in November of 1933 by creating the Civil Works Administration (CWA), which included artists as part of the white collar work force. Artists' work fell under the control of the Treasury Department, which had commissioned art for government buildings in the past. Secretary of the Treasury Henry Morgenthau then created the Public Works of Art Projects (PWAP) and appointed Edward Bruce as its director. The arts projects under the PWAP were divided into sixteen regional divisions and granted a budget of $1,039,000 from Hopkins; it provided work relief for approximately 25 percent of needy artists in 1933.[22]

After the elimination of the PWAP in 1934, heated debates and negotiations over implementing the WPA art programs exposed major congressional concerns over the necessity of government involvement in the arts. Especially in the midst of the Great Depression, congressional leaders often considered art to be a luxury that the federal government could ill afford. They believed arts funding would be a misuse of taxpayers' money. Furthermore, during the 1930s Keynesian economics remained in its formative stages, and the majority of leaders believed in fiscal conservatism.[23]

Partisan politics also arose as a major issue. The Republicans in Congress opposed government aid to art because they rejected liberal fiscal policies, but they also used this budgetary conservatism as an excuse to thwart Roosevelt and to block Democratic programs in Congress. Likewise, Democrats sometimes called for the placement of loyal Democrats on art committees and attempted to control art management. After Roosevelt lost his once powerful sway with Congress as a result of his attempt at packing the Supreme Court in 1937, passage of his arts programs became ever more difficult in the face of partisan fighting and opposition to increasing control by the chief executive.[24]

After the demise of the PWAP arts programs, the Treasury Section of Painting and Sculpture retained control of public building art projects, functioning more as an art commission program than as a relief program. Traditionally, the treasury had received 1 percent of the congressional funds for public buildings, and it continued to do so during the depression. By contrast, the WPA art programs relied on annual congressional appropriations. The Treasury Relief Art Program, another division of the Treasury Department art projects, was a subsidiary of the WPA and received its funds through the WPA until its elimination in 1938.[25] Scholars note that the divisions and subdivisions of the arts programs both on a national and state level contributed to bureaucratic difficulties, and artists were often discouraged from applying for WPA work because of the amount of paperwork and governmental procedures involved.[26]

In response to continuing opposition to the dole, Congress organized the 1935 Works Progress Administration differently than the PWAP programs. The new form of the WPA was less a relief aid policy than a more rigorous work program, with artists among one of the many groups its extensive work programs were designed to employ. The goals of the WPA art projects were twofold: first, to provide work for the unemployed and, second, to depict "the American Scene." Its projects were divided into four major sections: music, drama, literature, and visual art. Historians agree that the WPA succeeded in achieving its first goal. Ninety percent of the artists employed by the WPA were hired from the relief rolls, with only 10 percent nonrelief artists hired. (These were usually master artists whose skills were necessary for proper direction of large art projects. Conservative critics of WPA funding consistently used the administration's employment of these skilled artists to justify criticism of the WPA for funding non-needy workers.) Artists were classified and paid on a scale of professional, skilled, intermediate, or un-skilled and received between $69 and $103 per month for 96 hours of work.[27] The funds came entirely from the federal government until 1939, when con-gressional debates over appropriations demanded supplementary funding from local and private institutions. In 1939, Congress amended the enabling legislation requiring the states to supply 25 percent of the costs.

The second goal of the WPA—to depict the American scene—proved a memorable triumph, but it also provoked concerns about how politicians and artists linked aesthetics and ideology. One of the issues most often dis-cussed by Congress and artists alike when considering the appropriation of funds for art projects was whether Congress, as the fiscal provider, would be able to exert control over artistic creativity and dictate content to any extent. Karal Ann Marling has acknowledged that "to fulfill the economic demands of the patron, the artist had to agree, tacitly if not publicly, to curtail his or her choice of both style and subject matter."[28] Marling chronicles numerous instances in which government money stifled the expression of modernist painting as conservative political views clashed with creative expression. Art-ists generally steered away from abstract themes to portray figurative, histori-cal, and patriotic ones. The majority of WPA murals were executed in an American-scene realist style like that typically illustrated in Grant Wood and Thomas Hart Benton paintings. Marling concludes that WPA artists were not as creatively free as many now nostalgically depict them, because depression-era Americans wanted to find in the works reassurances of a serene and bright tomorrow rather than new questions and problems. This desire, she argues, resulted in "poor art for poor people."[29] The WPA suppressed art that depicted provocative or politically challenging themes. For example, painters Anton Refregier and Victor Arnautoff were asked to paint over communist symbols in their infamous Coit Tower murals in San Francisco.[30] Artist Lorser Feitelson complained that federal aid was "burdened with too many non-art considerations and limitations."[31] Thus, the party holding the purse strings exerted control, and ideological views of what constituted the American scene were not divorced from aesthetic tastes.[32]

The Federal Theater Project proved far more controversial: So offensive to Congress was this federally supported endeavor that the House Un-American Activities Committee (HUAC) investigated the project, which eventually lost its funding. Not only did Congress deem the content of many plays subversive, anticapitalist, and unworthy of federal support, but allegations of communist activities by theater members led to the demise of the theater project.[33]

Despite questions regarding funding and control of the arts during the 1930s, the WPA established the model for national arts policy. The WPA constituted the largest government-run arts program in U.S. history. At its peak, the Federal Art Project employed 5,000 artists and created 108,000 paintings, 2,500 murals, 18,000 sculptures, 200,000 prints, and 35,000 posters. The Federal Theater Project employed 13,000 people and produced 850 plays.[34] Many artists who later became masters of their field in the 1950s and 1960s were able to maintain their status as professional artists through support from the WPA. Yet, as a work-relief program, and one that never shook its association with the dole, the WPA ceased to be a major concern of the American government when attention turned from domestic problems to the frightening outbreak of aggression in Europe in 1939. At that time the economy began to improve and cutbacks in the art programs began in earnest. After the United States entered the Second World War, the WPA art program became part of the Graphic Section of the War Services Program, and art projects, especially poster projects, concentrated on the advancement of the war effort. Workers at a Philadelphia art project dubbed it an "Artsenal for Defense" after they silk-screened thousands of rear rifle-sights charts.[35] Less creativity was tolerated and service to the War Department became the primary function of art. Even these modest war activities were finally abolished in 1943. The basis of work relief was no longer deemed necessary once the war economy took off and dispelled the rampant unemployment of the depression era.[36] Thus ended what until that time had been the most widespread federal arts program of the twentieth century. While America was occupied with World War II, the arts garnered little federal attention.

★ *Art and Politics in the 1950s*

During the 1940s and 1950s, a generational shift occurred in the art world. Many American artists turned away from the regionalist and realist illustrations typical of the 1930s to develop a new abstract expressionist style. Art historians have asserted that this aesthetic transformation stemmed from the artists' efforts to reconcile their painting style with the overwhelming changes in the world order brought on by World War II and the Cold War. It also became an important element in the increasing interaction between American art and politics during the late 1950s and early 1960s that culminated in the establishment of the NEA.

Abstract expressionist art took several different forms. The movement included the gestural painting of nonfigurative scenes originated by artists such as Jackson Pollock, Willem de Kooning, Franz Kline, and Robert Motherwell (who later became a consultant for the NEA) and the abstract color-field painting of artists such as Mark Rothko and Barnett Newman.[37] Pollock's work exemplified the gestural branch of abstract expressionism with lines and drips of various colors on monumentally sized canvases. Pollock produced these large-scale paintings by laying the canvas on the ground then pouring, dripping, and splattering paint on it from all sides until he achieved a thick network of texture and colors.[38] Pollock broke from the traditional smaller, easel-sized canvases to produce paintings that dominated the wall. Spectators were meant to feel absorbed in the work. As Pollock explained:

> [Viewers] should try to receive what the painting has to offer and not bring a subject matter or preconceived idea of what they are to be looking for. . . . Modern artists have found new means of making their statements. It seems to me the modern painter cannot express this age, the airplane, the atom bomb, the radio, in the old forms . . . new needs new techniques. . . . Most of the paint I use is a liquid, flowing kind of paint. . . . I am able to be more free. . . . painting today certainly seems very vibrant. . . . Modern art to me is nothing more than the expression of contemporary aims of the age that we're living in.[39]

Pollock and other abstract expressionists' art turned from painting realistic life scenes to explorations of paint, form, color, and individual stylization. Artists used abstraction to voice mankind's anxiety and to display their freedom without trying to depict the overwhelming realities of life during the Cold War.[40]

Art critics Clement Greenberg, Harold Rosenberg, and Irving Sandler heralded abstract expressionists as heroes of the American art scene and considered their work the triumph of modern painting.[41] As early as 1949 a *Life* magazine article posed the question, "Jackson Pollock: Is He the Greatest Living Painter in the United States?"[42] The art world began to celebrate abstract expressionists' emphasis on risk-taking, freedom, and personal discovery. American painters who broke from the tradition of realistic depictions succeeded in establishing an American art style that surpassed the previously dominant trends historically centered in Europe.

Abstract expressionism also gained the attention of American politicians interested in support for the arts. Abstract expressionists had demonstrated that American artists could not only compete with but also outshine their European counterparts. They had elevated American art to a level of international prominence. Some politicians appreciated this symbol of American triumph and were aided by the art and artists themselves in their use of abstract art to promote the message that American art best symbolized freedom and democracy's triumph in the post–World War II era.[43] The abstract nature of the art and many of the artists' reluctance to explain its content allowed art institutions and American politicians to promote whatever message they wished in association with abstract expressionist works—nothing in the paintings would contradict them. They chose to promote such works as "demonstrating freedom in a world in which freedom connotes a political attitude."[44] American officials used these artists' work to promote the hegemony of American culture in international exhibitions and a specific brand of excellence in American art within the United States.

The successful marriage of art and politics did not occur immediately. In the late 1940s and early 1950s the arts remained primarily under private patronage, although the interconnections between private and public institutional support for the arts gained importance with increasing American involvement in international affairs. While serving as FDR's coordinator of inter-American affairs, Nelson Rockefeller offered exchanges of artwork from the Museum of Modern Art (MOMA, of which he became president in 1936) to Latin America as part of a larger effort to improve relations between the United States and countries in that region. As the Cold War heated up during the late 1940s, Rockefeller became very enthusiastic about expanding such aid and cultural exchanges, arguing that the United States could maintain its preeminence only if Third World nations understood that "their best interests and opportunity for the future are identified with our country and our way of life" rather than that of the Soviet Union.[45] When President Harry Truman and the federal government proceeded too slowly for his taste, Rockefeller moved to win the confidence of Latin America on his own. He pressured oil companies to donate funds to Latin American governments, and the Rockefeller Foundation began to support art exhibitions and exchanges between Latin America and the United States. Surely Rockefeller and other American businessmen viewed these actions as helpful not only to Latin America but to themselves. By giving back a portion of their profits, American corporations could counter their image as greedy capitalists, exploiting the region's resources purely for their own benefit. Aid to Latin America proved a useful measure to protect their investments and expand their operations in the future. The Ford Foundation, established in 1957, joined the Rockefeller effort to promote overseas programs and cultural exchange. Links between such organizations and the State Department developed over the course of the 1950s, as the State Department also sponsored American art exhibits overseas—although the government did not publicize this type of arts support and made no attempt to institute a national program within the United States.

Inspired by such efforts and motivated by similar concerns, a few members of Congress attempted, unsuccessfully, to promote federal arts support during the 1950s. Still, a lack of executive leadership hampered their efforts. Whereas President Taft helped to establish the Commission on the Fine Arts in 1910, President Dwight D. Eisenhower's reluctance to provide significant leadership on arts policy during his administration encouraged the Republican-controlled Congress to block passage of a bill for an arts foundation. Had they been confronted with a strong stand in favor of the arts by a president from their own party, congressional Republicans might have been persuaded otherwise, but the president's inaction played an important role in undermining potential support. By contrast to the Eisenhower years, when arts legislation languished in Congress, presidential leadership would play a key role in the eventual establishment of the NEA by Congress when Lyndon Johnson came out in favor of the arts on Capitol Hill.

In keeping with his general belief in limited government responsibilities, Eisenhower rejected a prominent role for the federal government in arts funding.[46] However, over time, as he recognized that the United States lagged behind other governments' cultural sponsorship, he began to adopt the more moderate position that the United States could provide some symbolic support for cultural endeavors short of a national arts foundation.[47] Eisenhower appointed Nelson Rockefeller to a post as coordinator of international programs and entertained his advice on America's cultural and psychological warfare efforts. However, when Rockefeller proposed augmenting cultural exchange and training programs for Third World leaders to the tune of $420 million, including $150 million for the United States Information Agency (USIA), Eisenhower rejected his plan as too expensive. Many Republican leaders perceived Rockefeller as tainted by his former association with the New Deal and his seemingly liberal spending habits.[48] Eisenhower proceeded more conservatively even as congressional hearings and the *New York Times* reported in 1956 that Soviet cultural efforts far outweighed meager American efforts. The Soviet Union allocated $8,750,000 per year for art museums and traveling exhibits, and between 1954 and 1955 sent out 385 cultural and trade delegations, compared to only 37 sponsored by the United States. Indeed, USIA and State Department programs had been cut in the aftermath of congressional opposition to "pink," or allegedly socialist, abstract art, and no American painting exhibitions were sent abroad between 1947 and 1953. Eisenhower eventually supported increases for cultural exchange programs, establishing an arts advisory council to the president, and building a national cultural center, provided it would be funded predominantly by the private sector.[49] His acceptance of these steps encouraged other, more conservative government officials to support government aid to the arts, which led to the passage of a bill authorizing a national cultural center in 1958 (later named the John F. Kennedy Center for the Performing Arts). This increasing Republican interest would eventually become crucial to the emergence of solid bipartisan support for arts policy in Congress during the Kennedy and Johnson administrations. Nevertheless, Eisenhower did little in response to a commissioned study on national goals that recommended further action to cultivate the arts.[50] The author of the study, August Heckscher, would have to wait until after Kennedy's election for more substantive action from the president. In the interim, Eisenhower's reticence reinforced that of the majority in Congress who were not anxious to support the arts.

The culture of the Cold War also subdued congressional actions toward a national arts policy because of McCarthy-era tensions and the specter of Soviet-style art censorship. In the post–World War II period, Americans in general and Congress in particular expressed an unusually heightened dread of communism and of the Soviet Union. This fear affected the arts since many artists and intellectuals had supported socialism or communism during the 1930s and were often suspected of harboring radical sentiments. Investigations of motion picture producers and the resulting blacklist attested to the power anticommunist crusaders held over American artists. Many members of Congress feared that subversives would undermine the U.S. government and the American way of life. Moreover, they also worried that any hint of support for arts policy would invite attack by McCarthyites and investigation by the House Un-American Activities Committee. The fate of Alger Hiss and other prominent government officials gave sufficient pause to anyone who questioned anticommunism's power.[51]

Second, many Americans had considered arts funding a tool for dictators to manipulate culture and serve their own political purposes. In this light, Congress rejected development of an arts policy that could be used for partisan purposes to destroy artistic freedom. Again, the prime source of this fear was the Soviet Union. Congressmen frequently argued against a national art policy by evoking the image of Josef Stalin's censorship of artists' freedom in the Soviet Union and his exploitation of social realist painting to promote his regime. If the Soviets and old-world dictators proved that the purity of art would be undermined by the institution of government policy, the United States should not follow a similar path and risk a similar fate.

★ *Congressional Opposition to and Advocacy of Art Policy*

Rep. George Dondero (R-Mich.) mobilized these arguments to mount the most vociferous opposition to modern abstract art and to government art funding during the 1950s. He considered modern art un-American because it was dominated by "foreignisms," and he often railed against modern art as communistic. (This accusation is particularly ironic since Stalin himself denounced abstract modern art as degenerate.)[52] Dondero vowed to oppose any support of radical artists on the grounds that they were part of a larger conspiracy. He warned his colleagues on one occasion not to forget that "communism is a hydra headed serpent that attacks the true democracies on all fronts, political, social, economic, scientific, cultural."[53] He depicted artists fighting for art support as a sinister force—art served as a means of propaganda for communism and government art support was part of a larger revolutionary plot that should be thwarted. Dondero considered it his duty to expose the "throttling dictatorship of this Red cultural monopoly" and to ward off artistic treason in the federal government by the "cultural fifth column."[54] Although Dondero's extreme view hardly represented the majority opinion, his efforts fueled a successful effort to block serious arts policy initiatives. Proposals presented in the Senate in 1948 and 1952 by Jacob Javits (R-N.Y.) and Charles Howell (D-N.J.) for the establishment of an arts agency were easily thrust aside.

Congress also did little to advance the cause of American arts during the 1950s because of what it considered the disappointments of the 1930s federal art projects under the Works Progress Administration. Reluctance to repeat government errors thwarted the many efforts by former WPA painter and prominent art patron George Biddle to rejoin art and federal policy during the 1940s.[55] In essence, criticism of the WPA revolved around two issues, economic responsibility and control of the arts by the federal government. On the first matter, many officials opposed support for the arts on the grounds that government had no mandate for using taxpayer money to fund artists. They maintained that the government had no jurisdiction in aesthetic endeavors and should not provide subsidies; rather, it should retain a laissez-faire stance in this area. The WPA projects had been a rare short-term work-relief effort that only happened to include artists as one set of employees. Since the economy of the 1950s had vastly improved and unemployment had declined, working men's conditions no longer warranted any such relief.

The second and more widespread argument against the WPA asserted that government funds necessarily imposed standards and curtailed the freedom of artists. Critics asserted that officials in the WPA projects had stymied artistic freedom. Moreover, artists trying to please their audiences, not to mention federal patrons, produced material that was palatable to the masses but not necessarily aesthetically excellent. Henry Allen Moe of the Guggenheim Foundation (who later became a chairman of the National Endowment for the Humanities), criticized the WPA for inflating its art projects and employing "artists" where there were none. He believed that the work-relief programs had undermined the quality of American art.[56]

Since many enjoyed the regionalist styles of such WPA artists as Thomas Hart Benton and even the somewhat abstract renditions of Stuart Davis, arguments about the poor quality of WPA art held less sway among many congressmen than did the implications of government control. The very hint of federal bureaucrats dictating the content and uses of art conjured parallels to Nazi or Soviet dictatorships, which congressmen of the 1950s vigorously sought to avoid. The WPA projects seemed only to prove that the United States was capable of creating a similarly restrictive environment, because there had been several instances in which government officials questioned the content and rendition of paintings and destroyed controversial pieces. Thus, government control of art had an established and bitter history in the not-so-distant past.[57]

★ *The Congressional Arts Coalition*

Despite considerable opposition to federal arts support, a few dedicated arts advocates began laying the foundation in the 1950s for future legislation. Rep. Frank Thompson (D-N.J.) and Senator Javits were two of the most vocal. In the late 1950s and early 1960s, Senators Hubert Humphrey (D-

Minn.) and Claiborne Pell (D-R.I.) and Rep. John Brademas (D-Ind.) joined them. Together, they developed stronger arts bills and advanced the cause as far as they could on Capitol Hill before Presidents Kennedy and Johnson succeeded in securing arts legislation.

Thompson joined the fight for the arts upon entering Congress in 1955 as a replacement for outgoing representative Charles Howell, who had also supported an arts policy. Thompson had been born to a newspaperman's family and acquired a flair for politics early in his life. Moreover, he shared common interests and connections to other high-ranking government officials. His uncle served as an adviser to New York governor Nelson Rockefeller, another prominent cultural enthusiast whose assistant, Nancy Hanks, later became chair of the NEA. Thompson served as a naval officer in the 1940s and during the Korean War, experiences that later enhanced the camaraderie between the congressman and fellow arts supporter and former naval officer, John Kennedy. Indeed, White House correspondence shows that he developed a comfortable working relationship with both the president and Mrs. Kennedy on arts policy.

Capitol Hill colleagues sometimes called Thompson the "culture vulture" because of his unfailing efforts on behalf of art policy and his great interest in music. Soon after his election, Thompson introduced several bills in the House, advocating a congressional charter for the National Music Council, the creation of an advisory committee on cultural exchange, the repeal of federal taxes on concert and theater tickets, the creation of a federal advisory committee on the arts, the building of a national cultural center, the protection of historic buildings and the establishment of a permanent site for the National Collection of Fine Arts, and federal medals for distinguished civilian service in twelve fields including the arts. One *Washington Post* article noted that Thompson introduced no fewer than eight cultural measures in Congress in 1956 alone.[58] In addition, he attempted to include a cultural plank in the Democratic Party platform in 1956.

Thompson was also an ardent internationalist and civil rights champion. He supported measures to increase world trade, mutual security programs, and U.S. subscriptions to the International Monetary Fund and the International Bank for Reconstruction and Development. On the domestic front, he worked for the passage of civil rights legislation, public housing laws, and the expansion of social security.[59]

In the context of his liberal leanings, Thompson wrote a number of articles linking his arts advocacy to broader national and international concerns and was one of the first to overturn unsophisticated equations of modern art with leftist politics. He stoutly delineated the benefits that a national arts policy could bestow on the country, arguing that by increasing the value of the arts in the United States, the nation could foster a cultural presence that would attract international attention. Thompson directly linked his assertions to Cold War ideology. In an article entitled "Are the Communists Right in Calling Us Cultural Barbarians?" he asserted that making Washington the "cultural center of the world would be one of the best and most effective ways to answer Russian lies and defeat their heavily financed effort to have communism take over the world."[60] American cultural policy was a must, in his opinion, and he encouraged others to join the fight to achieve it.

In the Senate, one of Thompson's most important counterparts was Jacob Javits. Elected to the upper house in 1956, Javits served previously in the lower house and as New York's attorney general. Unlike many of his colleagues, Javits had working-class origins. He grew up in Manhattan's Lower East Side, the son of a Jewish immigrant father who worked in the garment industry and later as a tenement house janitor. His mother had sold dry goods from a pushcart to help support the family. His father, a one-time rabbinical student in Austria, instilled in Javits the values of education and culture that would become a central part of his political life. Javits worked his way through school and became a trial lawyer in New York before serving in the Army during World War II. Through his involvement in Republican Party politics during the 1940s, Javits created a blend of liberal and conservative politics that attracted bipartisan interest and allowed him to become a powerful bridge builder between partisan factions on Capitol Hill.[61] Javits was supported by kindred spirit Nelson Rockefeller, progenitor of the "Rockefeller Republican"–style of support for big government action (and spending) on social and cultural policy and hawkish internationalism. Indeed by the late 1950s, this blend of an activist, problem-solving approach to national issues and a cold warrior stance in foreign affairs was increasingly common among both Democrats and Republicans.[62]

During his years in Congress, Javits displayed a commitment to international as well as domestic concerns. He served as a member of the House Foreign Affairs Committee, supporting foreign aid and trade policies, and he voted against Congress's action to limit funds for the USIA, one of the arms of government most active in touring American art abroad.[63] Javits cautioned against an American return to isolationist policies and urged Congress to show the world that "we intend to push forward with the responsibilities of free world leadership more vigorously than ever" because isolationism is "as dangerous to our own security as it would be to the whole free world."[64]

Domestically, he often supported more liberal policies than many of his fellow Republicans. He endorsed civil rights and civil liberties legislation and opposed appropriations for HUAC in 1948. As a member of the Rules and Administration Committee, he had the most influence on arts legislation. Javits worked to eliminate the tariff on the import of art for exhibitions and to liberalize art policies in the United States. He believed that if State Department and USIA touring art exhibits were to promote the best image of American culture, more emphasis would first have to be concentrated on raising the cultural level in the United States to a higher level of excellence. He supported arts advisory councils, the funding of artists through a national arts foundation, and the building of a permanent national cultural center to help achieve these goals. The coalition of arts supporters, including Thompson, Javits, Rockefeller, and Pell, shared a certain cosmopolitan outlook and concern for how the United States compared culturally to Europe. Most came from the Northeast and held elitist notions about promoting high art.

Javits's dedication to arts policy intertwined with a growing concern about cultural uplift that permeated American intellectual discourse during the 1950s. In Senate subcommittee hearings Javits lamented the bleak picture of American art fostered by mass media and directed at the popular masses. He argued that although true culture could be found in major cities, it "has been dying off in the rest of the country at an alarming rate . . . which I think is harmful to our national cultural pattern."[65] While many disagreed with Javits that culture was dying out and cited a growth in the arts, they often defined culture broadly. Javits focused more on a dearth of high culture rather than an abundance of mass culture. In this respect, he echoed the concerns of such cultural critics as Henry Seidel Canby in the 1920s and Dwight Macdonald and others writing during the 1950s who feared that lower forms of mass culture or "midcult" would supplant more sophisticated forms of high culture (see Chapter 2 for more detailed discussion).[66] The efforts of many cultural advocates on Capitol Hill began to converge during the late 1950s as cultural policy concerns mounted. Promoters increasingly drew on intellectual writings about American culture and the need to elevate it during the 1950s. Their fear of pervasive mass culture drove their call for the formation of a national arts foundation to combat debasement. However, a more solid political coalition with the executive office would not form until the 1960s.

Another senator influential in the fight for a national arts foundation was

Hubert Humphrey, who was elected in 1948. Like Javits, Humphrey also came from humble origins and carried a deep appreciation for the values of education and liberal social policies. Humphrey was influenced in this regard by his father, a pharmacist and, later, South Dakota state legislator, who imbued him with a sense of compassion and moral responsibility.[67]

In his youth, Humphrey was also affected by the Great Depression, which cost his parents their family farm and forced him to postpone college to help his father in the family business. Humphrey idolized Franklin D. Roosevelt and later completed his master's thesis at Louisiana State University on New Deal philosophies. He also worked as a teaching superintendent for the WPA's Workers Education Service in Minnesota. He remained committed to advancing education and worked to promote education bills throughout his tenure in Congress. Many of his aid-to-education proposals became part of the National Defense Education Act that Humphrey's colleague Lyndon Johnson pushed through Congress in 1958.[68]

Humphrey also worked to expand federal action to aid those less privileged members of American society, which was an important legacy of the New Deal and a central part of Johnson's Great Society as well. He steadily supported such measures as increased welfare programs, public housing, unemployment benefits, social security, urban renewal, and civil rights. Indeed, Humphrey first gained national attention by successfully lobbying at the Democratic National Convention in 1948 for a civil rights plank in the Democratic platform.

Upon his election to the Senate, Humphrey joined the Committee on Labor and Public Welfare and later the Appropriations and Foreign Relations Committee, where he worked with Senators Javits and Pell. In these positions he found a means to advance his interests in social policy and express his international commitments not only to anticommunism but also to reducing Cold War dangers by supporting arms reductions and promoting peace initiatives.

Humphrey began supporting arts policy along with Javits and Thompson in the early 1950s, and he gained increasing influence in Congress throughout the decade. He called for a national arts commission in 1952 and by 1956 was advocating an advisory council and a venue to showcase the arts in the capital. Both of these approaches were important strategies used by arts advocates in later congressional sessions. Moreover, believing that the State Department programs and President Eisenhower were not doing enough to

promote American art abroad, Humphrey defended art touring and supported expanded cultural exchanges despite Dondero's antiart outcries.[69] In
conjunction with Thompson, he also voted for appropriations for an art
exhibit in Brussels in 1958 and for establishing a medal for distinguished
civilian service for the arts.

Sen. Claiborne Pell rounded out the congressional coalition on arts legislation. Elected in 1960, Pell came from a wealthy and prestigious New England family with a long history of public service. While growing up, he
attended private schools in New York and Rhode Island and later gradu-
ated from Princeton University. He served as a Coast Guard seaman during
the Second World War and later taught government at a military school in
Princeton before taking posts in federal service.

Like many of his colleagues, Pell displayed a keen interest in foreign affairs
and worked for the U.S. embassy in Prague and, later, the State Department.
After being elected to Congress, Pell found a seat on the powerful Senate
Foreign Relations Committee. Unlike many staunch cold warriors of the
early 1960s, he often argued against treating communist nations as a mono-
lithic bloc and encouraged a toning down of militaristic anticommunist
rhetoric and policies. This stance ultimately aligned him with President Kennedy's own adoption of less hard-line Cold War policies, and both men
worked together to foster international cultural exchanges.

Pell's first assignment in Congress was on the Labor and Public Welfare
Committee, which allowed him access to legislative agendas for both education and the arts. He also found a place on the Rules and Administration
Committee, where he learned about and influenced Senate administration. It
is a mark of Pell's importance to the Democratic Party and of his ability to
work with influential members of Congress that he was able to serve on so
many powerful committees during such a short tenure in office. Moreover,
Pell's personal friendship with fellow New Englander and sailor President
John Kennedy enhanced his prestige.[70] Pell's backing aided the advance of
arts legislation initiatives once he was established as a force in the Senate.[71]

Pell joined with Jacob Javits, Hubert Humphrey, and Frank Thompson in
drafting bills that would later serve as the foundation for the National Endowment for the Arts. Pell considered the federal government a branch of
society that should exert its power to advance the arts. Moreover, he believed
that the arts "should be political," because politicians in touch with constituents' interests could advance the interests of the American public in cultural

endeavors, unlike councils of arts experts that were less concerned with the public than with aesthetics.[72] His desires to place arts policy directly in the federal arena were a powerful force in subsequent legislative successes.

Pell gained an influential position in the Senate when Sen. Lister Hill (D-Ala.), who chaired the Committee on Labor and Public Welfare, agreed to create a Special Subcommittee on the Arts.[73] This committee was chosen because the arts were deemed a part of the "general welfare" referred to in the Preamble to the Constitution, and arts measures were increasingly linked to public welfare and education committees as they made their way through Congress. The creation of this subcommittee was a key factor that united arts supporters in a more substantial base.

In the late 1950s and early 1960s, Thompson, Javits, Humphrey, and Pell successfully challenged some of the obstacles that had generated long-standing opposition to arts legislation. Among these matters were the nature of federal jurisdiction in the arts, the necessity and cost of federal involvement in the arts, and the level of government control or censorship of federally supported art content. Arts backers' efforts gained recognition as the Cold War context began to shift. By 1954, Americans had begun to stand up against the excesses of McCarthyism and McCarthy himself was censured by Congress. Anticommunist sentiments previously centered on accusations and prosecutions turned toward competing with the Soviet Union by improving American military and cultural achievements. This element of competition would become a larger factor in congressional arts policy debates under the leadership of President Kennedy.

Arts supporters recognized that before Congress could proceed with appropriate legislation, federal authorization in this new area would have to be established. They realized that their opposition in Congress did not believe such authorization existed. Sen. Strom Thurmond (D-S.C.) spoke for many of his colleagues when he questioned Pell by asking, "[under] what provision of the Constitution does the Senator from Rhode Island feel that the national Government has jurisdiction to set in legislation of this kind?" Pell responded, "In the Constitution itself, in article I, section 8, there is a specific reference . . . for the arts. The provision reads: 'To promote the progress of science and useful arts.'. . . But in direct answer to the Senator's query, I can only read from the Preamble of the Constitution, a part of the intent of which is 'to promote the general welfare.' To my mind, the bill falls directly within the confines of general welfare."[74]

Generally, opponents of arts legislation were conservative Republican congressmen who did not believe the U.S. government had any jurisdiction in artistic matters. Strom Thurmond, still a Democrat in 1963, was already showing his own conservative tendencies and would join Republican ranks the following year. On the other hand, supporters found precedent not only in the Constitutional mandate to "promote the general welfare" but also in past government proposals. Sen. Hubert Humphrey concurred with Pell and went on to cite a series of previous government supports for the arts. He included among these a statement by President George Washington recognizing the importance of the arts as "essential to the prosperity of the state and . . . the happiness of human life," the implementation of the L'Enfant Plan for the development of the capital, the WPA projects of the 1930s, and the State Department's cultural exchange programs of the 1950s.[75] Although much of this federal involvement had been haphazard or temporary policy rather than institutional government support, it did provide grounds for government involvement. By this time more members of Congress agreed. Pell, Humphrey, Javits, Rockefeller, and Thompson formed part of a growing cadre who advocated a more expansive role for the federal government; their broad interpretation of government's jurisdiction embraced not only the arts but federal aid to education, science, parks and recreation, highways, and housing, among other causes.

Once federal jurisdiction was established, several representatives argued that the arts did not require federal aid. Historical precedent was on the side of the fiscal conservatives in this respect. They consistently opposed the development of an arts endowment on the grounds that such programs simply would be too expensive for a government in debt. Rep. Howard Gross (R-Iowa) presented their case, "We are more than $290 billion in the red in this country. . . . I am sure that spending $100,000 each year for this purpose, for culture, can very well wait until we have a balanced budget in this country and start retiring the Federal debt. I just do not see any necessity for this kind of business at this time."[76]

His concerns continued to come up in each year's sessions, though with decreasing frequency until the actual passage of arts legislation. On the other hand, Javits and his colleagues were better able to advance their argument that the establishment of a federal arts program would incur only limited costs to the federal government. Javits asserted that, "the elimination of the theater tax would reduce the federal revenue by only .0007 percent. Grants to individual states would be measured in thousands of dollars. The program to bring the arts to outlying sections of the country is estimated to cost about

$10 million a year—half the cost of a jet bomber."[77] His assessment gained supporters because U.S. economic growth during the 1950s and early 1960s was sufficiently strong to quiet the loudest cries against government spending on the arts.

Eventually, lingering opposition to providing financial support to artists and arts programs was also overcome. Rep. William Fitts Ryan (D-N.Y.) countered opposition arguments by saying, "I doubt if economic success is a proper or meaningful test of the value of the arts, and especially the fine arts. . . . [The] danger . . . is that those art forms without commercial value lead a precarious existence." He concluded that art was "essential to a free society . . . [and] must be supported and encouraged."[78] Senator Javits also demonstrated that the principle of government subsidy was well established, with many successful industries receiving government funds to support their business. Why could this same principle not be applied to the arts?[79]

In addition, Rep. John E. Fogarty (D-R.I.) acknowledged the widespread emergence of arts centers across the country but asserted that this rapid expansion also resulted in a lack of needed funds to provide for all Americans interested in participating. He argued that many artists could not support themselves on their meager salaries, citing that "in 1960 the average player in one of our 26 major symphonies was employed only 27 weeks that year and he earned a mere $3,900 before taxes." He went on to purport that while it may be reasonable to expect such a man to go out an find another musical job, the facts indicated that "30 percent of these people could not find other employment as musicians and had to work at whatever part-time jobs they could find."[80] Such conditions would deprive American culture of its best talents. Fogarty believed that the creation of a national arts foundation to fund creative artists in need would not only prevent their demise but assure that American culture would flourish.

The issue of government control also permeated the debates on arts funding. Many opposed to the arts programs held that, just as it had in the 1930s, government funding for the arts would necessarily be given with strings attached. Therefore, the artist supported by the government would not be free to reach the full potential of his or her creativity. Taking an opposite tack, others argued against arts funding because the bills that had been proposed did not allow Congress enough power over the art produced. Many wished to control the art forms made and thus dictate a certain aesthetic. Arts policy supporters attempted to walk the fine line between these issues by supporting freedom of expression but also by maintaining that it would not be abused.

They were not able to fully overcome this issue until the 1960s, when the final drafts of art legislation included clauses that allowed for some congressional oversight but also upheld the ideal of artistic freedom.

Increasingly, congressional leaders turned to the notion of extending American cultural programs as part of a wider effort to uplift American talent and use it as an international example of freedom and democracy during the Cold War. While the ideas were debated in Congress during the 1950s, they effected little substantive policy until the following decade under the leadership of the Kennedy and Johnson administrations.

Prior to the 1960s, the American government made no substantive attempts to institute a national arts policy for the United States. Support for the arts was generally limited to architecture, sculpture, and painting commissions. Most arts support remained in private hands, as federal officials believed the government had more pressing political, economic, and social concerns. By the early twentieth century, greater attention was given to the realm of culture as Taft oversaw the establishment of the Commission on the Fine Arts and FDR instituted federal art projects under the auspices of the WPA. While both institutions had the potential to grow into permanent, national programs, each ultimately failed as federal attention turned elsewhere.

The 1950s marked an increase in debates over national culture in the context of the Cold War. As the United States vied with the USSR, Americans scrutinized their cultural achievements. Many in Congress advanced the idea that a national cultural policy would help provide a positive image of American society to other countries during the Cold War. However, this notion still had to contend with more powerful fiscal and social conservatism and a lack of presidential leadership in favor of national arts policy.

The election of 1960 marked a significant shift in America. During the 1950s, the sociopolitical context promoted an ideology of conservatism in American society and politics that inhibited the implementation of federal arts support. However, the new Kennedy administration tapped into and fanned Americans' desire for change and brought greater urgency to cultural policy and to improving American society. The efforts undertaken toward arts policy during Kennedy's presidency set in motion an upsurge of interest in cultural advance and support for arts policy that would eventually lead to the establishment of the NEA under President Johnson.

Let Us Begin

Arts Policy during the Kennedy Administration

> *I look forward to an America which commands respect throughout the world not only for its strength but for its civilization as well.*
> —John F. Kennedy, "Remarks at Amherst College upon Receiving an Honorary Degree," October 26, 1963

★ ★

"Babbittry is behind us. We live in an era of impressive artistic achievement. Our painters, sculptors, musicians, dancers and dramatists are the envy of the world."[1] Such was John F. Kennedy's assessment of the arts during the 1960 presidential campaign. His reference to Babbitt was pointed. It immediately drew attention to the United States' artistic success during the post–World War II era. Kennedy's remarks signaled his pride in the highest achievements in American culture and his pleasure at the worldwide attention they generated.[2]

Yet much more than idle praise for the arts resounded in Kennedy's response to a questionnaire from the publication *Musical America*. Beneath the overt commendation lay a subtle challenge for American culture. The reference to Sinclair Lewis's landmark 1925 novel *Babbitt* evoked images of early twentieth-century American nouveaux riches who believed they had achieved a certain level of prominence. However, these arrivistes were more interested in wealth and social climbing than in genuine cultural progress. On this level Kennedy's reference may be taken as criticism of perceived growth in American materialism and complacency during the 1950s. Kennedy promised to reinvigorate America, and he selected the arts as one means to raise the level of American civilization. His remarks to the magazine went on to explain the purposes art could serve in both domestic and foreign arenas to elevate America's image and culture.[3]

Kennedy's letter to *Musical America* revealed his desire to improve the quality of life in the United States through increased intellectual and cultural achievement, which he believed a federal arts policy could encourage. He pointed out historic eras in which great advances were made in politics and culture and expressed hope that his tenure as president would inspire similar results. Musing on the interconnections between success in public life and artistic progress, Kennedy pointed out that the age of Elizabeth was also the age of Shakespeare. He then maintained, "the New Frontier for which I campaign in public life, can also be a New Frontier for American art. For what I descry is a lift for our country: a surge of economic growth, a burst of activity in rebuilding and cleansing our cities . . . an age of Discovery in science and space; and an openness toward what is new that will banish the suspicion and misgiving that have tarnished our prestige abroad. . . . For we stand, I believe, on the verge of a period of sustained cultural brilliance."[4] Kennedy recognized that to attain long-lasting international recognition as a great culture, America would first have to raise its own level of sophistication. He believed that the arts could play a part in programs designed to reengage American ingenuity in combating domestic problems. By their very nature, the arts could instill a higher sense of purpose to American endeavors and inspire superior achievements. This effort would, ultimately, produce an American culture worthy of world acclaim.

Not only were the arts important for domestic welfare, but they also promoted foreign policy interests by showcasing American leadership and freedom. Indeed, these applications would become a vital selling point for later arts policy. In 1960, Kennedy asserted that the American government should support the arts, "for art . . . speaks a language without words, and is thus a chief means for proclaiming America's message to the world over the heads of dictators."[5] He reiterated these sentiments in a *Saturday Review* article advocating expanded international exchange programs and State Department cultural programs. "[If] every student of the USSR and the satellites could tour the United States and compare what they see with what they have been told," he wrote, "I would have little fear of future wars."[6]

As a candidate and as president-elect, Kennedy acknowledged the importance of culture in his drive to make the United States the leader of advanced civilization. During his campaign he frequently argued that America needed to be first. Kennedy railed one day in frustration that the first vehicle in space was *Sputnik*, rather than the American *Vanguard*, and the first passengers to return safely from outer space were dogs named Strelka and Belka, rather than Rover or Fido. Kennedy vowed that he wanted to become the president who "not only held back the Communist tide but who also advanced the cause of freedom and rebuilt American prestige."[7] His competitive attitude was well known throughout the Cold War world and drove many aspects of his campaign and administration. Eventually, he would elevate the arts to a level of national importance linked to military and political measures. Indeed, these domestic and foreign policy applications of the arts would become a vital selling point for the formation of the National Endowment for the Arts.

John F. Kennedy's administration brought unprecedented attention to the arts. The president and First Lady Jacqueline Kennedy transformed the White House into a theater and museum that focused a spotlight on the arts brighter than at any previous time. The Kennedy's basked in their reputation as cultural sophisticates, although Jacqueline Kennedy often deserved more accolades than her husband. Kennedy has been critiqued as a shrewd social climber and arriviste, not unlike those he himself referenced in his comments to *Musical America* about Babbitt, who disingenuously masked his personal tastes and ambitions behind claims of refinement. Kennedy privately acknowledged that image was key and that sometimes "it's not what you are, it's what people think you are that counts."[8] Kennedy believed that developing a mystique of elegance could help advance cultural policy. Moreover, he saw Nelson Rockefeller's patrician background and art patronage and the Rockefeller wing of the Republican Party as an ever-present challenge with which to contend. Rockefeller himself had been a candidate for the Republican nomination in 1960 and continued to loom as a formidable presence on the political scene, influencing not only Kennedy's but also Nixon's attitude toward the arts.

While some of his motivations were certainly self-serving, Kennedy nevertheless used his administration to push for an institutionalized arts policy. Ultimately, he developed and maneuvered such a policy through the executive office, and subsequently, Lyndon Johnson drove it through Congress. The arts policy struggle that emerged during the Kennedy years set the tone for federal arts administration in the future. Unlike the governmental forays into arts policy before the 1960s, the National Endowments for the Arts and Humanities achieved a scope and permanence previously unknown in the nation's history.[9]

★ The Intellectual Milieu

During the 1950s developments in the intellectual and cultural milieu had transformed American painting, politics, and culture. Not surprisingly, this presaged much of the evolution in these areas during the following decade. Specifically, Kennedy's cultivation of the arts during the early 1960s manifested the central ideologies of prominent 1950s thinkers, some of whom were closely involved with his political administration, including Arthur Schlesinger Jr. and John Kenneth Galbraith. A consensus emerged in support of liberal pluralism and capitalism, allowing critics' attention to shift away from the economic realm to the cultural realm. Economists such as Galbraith successfully demonstrated that the country was thriving economically; while at the same time, critics such as Dwight Macdonald, Paul Goodman, and Schlesinger argued that prosperity appeared to breed mediocrity in culture. In their view, arts policy was no longer a minor issue but a crucial one to redefine and enrich America.

American intellectuals during the 1950s had in large part coalesced around two ideological frameworks that became central to the Kennedy vision: the Cold War consensus and an urge to uplift the quality of American life in an age of abundance. Many intellectuals who had espoused Marxist or socialist utopian ideals during the 1930s were subsequently horrified by Stalinist totalitarianism. During the late 1940s and 1950s, they found themselves discarding their former ideas and becoming defenders of American-style capitalist democracy. Leftist intellectuals' turn away from socialist politics was also accelerated by Joseph McCarthy's anticommunist crusade, which demanded support of American democracy and capitalism.

Dwight Macdonald was one prominent 1950s thinker who had renounced his Marxism and lashed out against Soviet dictatorship and censorship in articles for the *Partisan Review* and *Politics*. In "Why I Chose the West," he acknowledged dissatisfaction with America's political and economic systems, yet argued that they allowed for freedom and growth for intellectuals and ordinary citizens. In "a predominantly private-capitalist society like our own, there are crannies in which the artist and intellectual can survive," Macdonald conceded. In the Soviet Union, however, dictatorship required "mediocrity and lifeless conformism."[10] Artists and intellectuals in the United States had the potential to ignore the commercial market and produce decent work; whereas in the USSR "there are no loopholes—the artist cannot create independently of the Central Committee's directives since the State controls the art galleries, the orchestras and concert halls, the theatres and the publishers."[11] In comparison to this fettered existence, the liberty enjoyed by intellectuals in the United States appeared enviable. Macdonald, who continued to be a radical and anarchist politically, still managed to defend the American system during the Cold War before he began to focus his writings more on cultural issues rather than political ones.

Emerging from the anticommunist, rather than radical, liberal tradition, Arthur Schlesinger's *The Vital Center* played a pivotal role in expounding the new intellectual consensus that became an integral part of both Kennedy's and Johnson's political philosophy. Schlesinger called for intellectuals to "discard Marx" since he no longer inspired realistic ideals. Recognizing the complexity and dark side of humankind exposed especially during World War II, Schlesinger believed that rather than dream of utopias, intellectuals should strive for political action that would improve society. He posited the New Deal as one successful model of practical action that had done much to balance powerful forces in American political and economic spheres. In the prosperous postwar economy, he argued, intellectuals should not be antagonistic to business but should celebrate pluralist society. Furthermore, he urged support for American policies of containment and of aid to progressive regimes to ensure the continued strength of anticommunist forces.[12]

According to historian Christopher Lasch, Schlesinger's views represented a new brand of liberal pragmatism that combined realism with calls for political action.[13] Schlesinger believed intellectuals had an important role to play in advancing American-style freedom. He hoped to elevate political discussion to the level of philosophical debate and encouraged Kennedy's adoption of a similar style. Interestingly, both Macdonald and Schlesinger attended the inaugural conference of the Congress for Cultural Freedom in Berlin in 1950, where they and other prominent thinkers expressed the values of American intellectual life and culture in hopes of wooing Europeans into full agreement that the American system surpassed the Soviets'. Their ideas were well received.[14]

A realization that American capitalism was not going to self-destruct lay at the heart of consensus liberal thinking. Intellectuals came to terms with American economic success during and after World War II and stopped worrying that capitalism would fail as a system. John Kenneth Galbraith had articulated this notion in *American Capitalism*, which defended the stability of the American economy. He argued that, after all, with corporate power checked by government and unions, the economy virtually regulated itself. The Gross National Product grew at an unprecedented annual rate of 3.9 percent and ordinary citizens prospered.[15]

Yet something seemed amiss. Amid the affluence of the 1950s, American intellectuals began to comment on certain undesirable undercurrents they detected within American society—and their suggested correctives would influence Kennedy's and, later, Johnson's developing political programs.

The trouble, as cultural critics saw it, centered on the increasing conformity that resulted from a loss of individual freedom in the workplace and new suburban housing, as well as the American public's misuse of its expanding leisure time.[16] In essence, they became preoccupied with analyzing Americans use of their free time outside of the workplace—which was increasing as work hours decreased in the prosperous economy. Leisure time figured prominently in the writings of William Whyte and David Riesman, who assessed American society in their works, *The Organization Man* and *The Lonely Crowd*. Each found that conformist work environments were constraining American men. In Whyte's account, the modern workplace demanded that employees gauge their activity according to the needs of the company rather than their own. Such action ultimately restricted individuality and resulted in the production of managerial drones rather than creative operatives. Even though Whyte argued that people could choose whether or not to conform, and thus retained personal freedom in theory, he clearly demonstrated that society expected people to choose to conform and was, therefore, stifling. He warned Americans that the "peace of mind offered by the Organization remains a surrender, and no less so for being offered in benevolence," and he encouraged Americans to resist the tyranny of the community.[17]

Evaluating the workplace and beyond, Riesman's text traced a developing shift in American character types from the "inner-directed" man, who worked independently, attuned to an internalized set of goals and without social direction, to an "other-directed" man, who worked as part of a group sensitized to the expectations and preferences of others. The growth of the other-directed man focused attention on the development of personality skills rather than on the production of materials and, more importantly, the production of individual character. Riesman expressed the fear of many Americans in the 1950s when he stated "today it is the 'softness' of men rather than the hardness of material that calls on talent and opens new channels of social mobility."[18] Riesman believed that not only would this "soft," other-directedness eventually restrict ingenuity on the job, it would have detrimental effects on the overall American social character and culture. He feared that as the economy shifted from production to consumption and from the rewards of work to the pursuit of image, Americans would be left empty.

Both Whyte and Riesman argued that modern Americans would have to turn to play or leisure time to find the independence lacking on the job. Yet to achieve this autonomy, leisure would have to be more than undirected play or conspicuous but hollow consumption. Rather, it must create a meaningful style of life and sound character by "uplifting the mind."[19] Education was deemed a crucial arena in this respect. Cultural critics noted that schools were focusing ever more attention on technological and personal skills and less on the humanities and pure intellectual activity to develop the mind. Whyte noted that students' questions in school centered only on technological points but never "the what, or why."[20] While this served the immediate goals of specialized training, critics found that it set a disturbing trend in the ultimate achievements of American civilization. They feared that the dilution of learning and lack of student creativity would leave a future America bereft of the capacity and dynamism to cope with problems and survive as a worthy nation.

The disturbing trends exposed in the works of Whyte and Riesman continued to influence other intellectuals' writings throughout the 1950s. In *The Affluent Society*, a monograph devoted to broad economic developments, liberal economist John Kenneth Galbraith also explored the dark side of affluence. The paradox of postwar prosperity, Galbraith argued, lay in its simultaneous creation of both economic abundance and a low quality of life among Americans, which, in essence, left "the bland leading the bland."[21] Galbraith traced the problem to the false assumption that sound economic and cultural health relied upon an ever-expanding rate of production and increased economic growth based on consumer spending. While he noted that Americans did indeed live amid abundance, he found this "success" due to the production of "manufactured want" rather than necessities. He argued that businesses' encouragement of consumer spending created imbalances in American culture—supporting a counterproductive idea that private spending on consumer goods was positive but public expenditures on services was unsound. It allowed for families with beautiful, "air-conditioned, power-steered and power-braked automobiles" to take drives through cities that are "badly paved, made hideous by litter, blighted by buildings, billboards, and posts for wire that should long since have been put underground" to a countryside where they may picnic on "packaged food from a portable icebox by a polluted stream" and camp in a park that is "a menace to public health and morals."[22] In such a scenario consumer products coupled with lack of public policy created a less than ideal situation. It revealed a society lacking in thoughtful goals, long-range cultural health, and even the fundamentals for long-term economic prosperity.

Galbraith proposed that the state should step in to halt the potentially destructive downward spiral of American culture, just as it had worked to regulate the economy in modern times. By expanding investment in research beyond military development and encouraging civilian goals, the government could create a healthier society. Specifically, increased education could redress the moral and economic loss seen in declining work hours and could enable Americans to learn the skills necessary to make the best use of leisure time and improve the overall quality of American life.[23] The ultimate test would be "less the effectiveness of our material investment than the effectiveness of our investment in men" who would be called upon to apply their intelligence and creativity to solving American problems, thus advancing American civilization in the future.[24] Galbraith weaved a well-supported economic appeal for increased investment in social and cultural programs, which echoed other cultural critics' arguments and laid the initiative at government's doorstep. His arguments, moreover, held sway with President Kennedy, who frequently consulted with Galbraith and other intellectuals for advice while planning his political endeavors.

While Galbraith's ideas pointed out the perils of prosperity, they remained more general than substantive. Arthur Schlesinger Jr. went a step further to form such criticism into objectives for an active government to achieve a viable welfare state. He believed government should use its powers to extend the virtues and rewards of American life to all its citizens and to others in the developing world. Indeed, Schlesinger was only one among many intellectuals who believed social scientists could—and should—actively identify the forces of social and economic change and aid government in developing public policy to manipulate progress.[25] Expressing commitment to the public interest in "The Challenge of Abundance," Schlesinger called for "qualitative liberalism . . . to improve schools, hospitals, cities . . . the public domain," which included cultural activities.[26] He specifically called for a greater role for the federal government in arts policy, since he believed the arts lent value and thoughtfulness to true civilization.[27] As an adviser to Kennedy, Schlesinger was able to lobby for the implementation of such plans and made his mark as one of the more influential White House cultural advisers in the development of arts policy.

Other intellectuals addressed cultural problems more directly. Clement Greenberg and Dwight Macdonald claimed that American leisure was increasingly dominated by a mass media that promoted mediocre products and deplorable aesthetics. Greenberg railed against "kitsch" in his essays for the *Partisan Review* and *Commentary* while defending the achievements of modernism and the avant-garde.[28] Macdonald noted that, on the one hand, the rise of mass culture was "desirable politically" because it was democratic and closed the gap between the wealthy and the common people. On the other hand, however, it caused "unfortunate results culturally" by destroying our sense of community and encouraging the production and consumption of "junk."[29]

Paul Goodman asserted similar ideas in *Growing Up Absurd*, in which he declared that American conformity and mass consumption produced a society devoid of any respectable culture. He argued for concrete action to promote higher cultural standards in the United States, calling for patriotic peer pressure to achieve such uplift. He purported that nationalism and patriotism nourished great statesmanship and that serving one's country could inspire artists to produce masterpieces above their usual capacity. Goodman criticized the American leadership in the late 1950s for reneging on its responsibility to stimulate artistic excellence. "Our present President (Mr. Eisenhower) is an unusually uncultivated man," Goodman lamented, "It is said that he has invited no real writer, no artist, no philosopher to the White House. Presumably he has no intellectual friends; that is his privilege. But recently he invited the chief of the Russian government (Mr. Khrushchev) to a banquet and musicale. And the formal music of that musicale was provided by a Fred Waring band playing 'Oh, What a Beautiful Morning' and such other numbers. This is disgraceful."[30] Goodman, like other intellectuals, advocated federal leadership in cultural affairs and action to elevate the level of American culture as a whole. The foreign policy benefits of this approach were also implied in his writing. As he noted the national disgrace brought upon the United States before a Soviet audience by a dearth of true culture, Goodman stressed the potential prestige America could gain with a display of high cultural achievement.

The chorus of challenges by American intellectuals coincided with a series of disconcerting events for the United States. The first occurred in 1957 when the Soviet Union launched the satellite *Sputnik*. American rocket scientist Werner von Braun had prophetically warned that "it would be a blow to U.S. prestige if we did not do it first."[31] As a second Soviet satellite orbited the earth, Khrushchev boasted that the USSR would surpass the United States in economic output within fifteen years to become the world's leader. *Life* magazine printed "Arguing the Case for Being Panicky," Arthur Trace published *What Ivan Knows and Johnny Doesn't*, and Americans from all walks of society feared that the United States was losing the race with the Russians. Lyndon Johnson, then senate majority leader, blamed the problems of American affluence and complacency for the failure to match the Soviets and quipped, with a reference to Detroit auto manufacturers, "It is not very reassuring to be told that next year we will put a better satellite in the air. Perhaps it will even have chrome trim and automatic windshield wipers."[32] Such cumulative reproach helped to shock Americans out of their self-satisfaction and renewed their interest in achievement—not only in military terms but also in intellectual and cultural endeavors. While preparing his bid for the presidency in 1960, Kennedy joined the call to action.

★ Toward Promoting the Arts

John Kennedy's campaign pledge to "get the country moving again" referred not only to closing the perceived missile gap and containing communism, it also included a vow to promote intellectual values and renew the nation's commitment to cultural excellence. As he courted academics and sought their advice, Kennedy embraced the ideals of consensus liberalism. Once elected, he brought many intellectuals directly into his new administration, including social scientists Walt Rostow, Lincoln Gordon, David Bell, Max Millikan, Lucian Pye, Samuel Hayes, and Eugene Staley.[33] Frequently consulted as an economic policy adviser, Galbraith became the American ambassador to India. Schlesinger, a White House speech writer and presidential aide, served as a link to the intellectual community and continued to shape Kennedy's rhetoric and programs. Schlesinger noted that Kennedy's collection of the "best and the brightest" thought that "the world was plastic and the future was unlimited."[34] Their enthusiasm and belief that they could change the world matched the president's.

The Kennedy administration's efforts to recharge the tone of American politics and invigorate American culture began as soon as the new president took office. In January 1961, Robert Frost, unofficial poet laureate of the United States, stood at the podium in an unusually cold capital city and began to read the poem he had written for John F. Kennedy's inauguration. He began, "Summoning artists to participate / In the august occasions of the state / Seems something for us all to celebrate." Unfortunately, even with Lyndon Johnson trying to shield the lectern, glaring winter sunlight prevented Frost from completing his reading and forced him to conclude by reciting from memory "The Gift Outright," a poem with a similar theme of pioneering and promise. The text of Frost's original poem was to continue, "It makes the prophet in us all presage / The glory of a next Augustan age . . . /

A golden age of poetry and power / Of which this noonday's the beginning hour."[35] His verse voiced hope for a new beginning for the country and for the arts in the new administration.

After Frost's recitation, the new president took his oath of office and stood to speak. Kennedy delivered his now well-known oration vowing American military strength in the face of a worldwide communist threat and calling upon Americans to join their "energy, faith, and devotion" in a struggle to redefine the United States as the world leader not only in military force but also in scientific progress and aesthetic excellence. Mitigating the direct challenge to the Soviet Union, Kennedy invited cooperation with the U.S. to "invoke the wonders of science instead of its terrors . . . explore the stars, conquer the deserts, eradicate disease . . . and encourage the arts."[36] Yet he also left no doubt that he believed Americans could triumph in any contest and thereby provide the world with the best example of freedom and democratic success.

Kennedy's inaugural address expressed themes that would characterize his presidency. First, it stated his concern for foreign policy and his dedication to the preservation of American democracy and world freedom in a continuing Cold War struggle. At the same time, his speech professed a belief in change and announced a new approach to world conflict—that of joining social and cultural advancement to the single-minded militarism of the Cold War. His call to work with the Soviets toward scientific and artistic advancement also marked an attempt to instill a calmer tone in the Cold War that would be carried throughout his administration, evidenced by his bilateral test ban treaties and his repudiation of any lingering effects of domestic McCarthyism. Kennedy's faith in America's potential for energetic cultural progress would also serve as a good omen for the arts.

Among the thousands gathered to hear these words proclaimed were fifty-eight artists, including first generation abstract expressionist painters Mark Rothko and Franz Kline, and MOMA directors Alfred Barr and René d'Harnoncourt.[37] That so many invitations went out to artists and intellectuals was another hallmark, for never before had so many been included in the usual crowd of inaugural-day dignitaries. The president-elect and Mrs. Kennedy wished to showcase individuals representing the quality and excellence of American culture, especially in art and music, and to recognize representatives of leading cultural institutions. Their effort at the inauguration launched what Kennedy had only hinted during his campaign, that "the New Frontier . . . [would] be a New Frontier for American art."[38]

Kay Halle, a Kennedy friend, drew up the list of inaugural guests in consultation with Arthur Schlesinger Jr. She arranged for the invited artists and cultural institution heads to be officially greeted on the morning of the event and to receive instructions, credentials, and tickets for the ceremonies. Those assembled were also asked to inscribe their sentiments in a book to be presented to the president and first lady.[39] Their expressions recorded on that morning were overwhelmingly laudatory and supportive of the new administration, as were the numerous telegrams and letters received from the art world. Declaring his pride and pleasure in Kennedy's recognition of artists and the hopeful tone of the inauguration, Archibald MacLeish wrote that the address "left me proud and hopeful to be an American—something I have not felt for almost twenty years. I owe you and send you my deepest gratitude." John Steinbeck sent an even more politically enthusiastic messages. Recalling that artists had been attacked in the past for their leftist politics, he wrote to Kennedy, "What a joy that literacy is no longer prima facie evidence of treason."[40] The reintegration of artists into the good favor of the federal government was, indeed, a significant move by Kennedy to alter what had become burdensome social and cultural constraints imposed by the Cold War. Defying a McCarthyite mentality under which artists suspected of communist sympathies were blacklisted, Kennedy boldly invited artists to participate fully as citizens along with government in raising American culture to new heights.[41] Kennedy's actions, more than his public speeches, expressed his desires to diffuse the accusatorial tendencies in government's dealings with those who criticized U.S. social and economic policies and to infuse politics and culture with a higher purpose.

However, Kennedy initially conceived of his gesture to invite prominent artists to his inauguration as more symbolic than substantive. August Heckscher later recalled that when the artists attended, "I don't think he [Kennedy] had any idea of the stir it would cause."[42] Indeed, the public recognition of artists generated great expectations in the artistic community, and many hoped that Kennedy would truly support the arts on a national level. This hope was shared by key Kennedy staff members, including Schlesinger, Stuart Udall, and Pièrre Salinger. Press Secretary Salinger moved a step further after the inauguration and solicited ideas on arts policy, which he later gave to special art consultant Heckscher. Commenting on the first steps on the path toward an official arts policy, Heckscher said, "it was the inauguration which really had begun everything."[43]

Kennedy advisers have agreed that the president generally moved forward in a series of small, trial steps. He would test the waters with a modest gesture, gauge the response, and then, if it was positive, proceed in a somewhat bolder fashion. Such was the case with the arts. Kennedy began with a gesture of recognition for artists, rather than a clearly orchestrated plan for arts policy, but soon determined to take advantage of the positive reception that had greeted this gesture. The president and Jacqueline Kennedy were delighted with the admiration and support showered upon them by the art world after the inauguration. They were also genuinely pleased with the book of messages compiled by Kay Halle and responded with a personal letter of thanks to each artist. As in most presidential letters, the chief executive began in perfunctory prose, "Mrs. Kennedy and I have had extraordinary pleasure in going through these volumes. . . . I am hopeful that this collaboration between government and scholarship will continue and prosper." He continued, however, with a plea for concrete ideas, "I would be particularly interested in any suggestions you may have in the future about the possible contributions the national government might make to the arts and scholarship in America."[44] After finding the test waters warm, Kennedy moved toward more significant action.

Kennedy made the most of his background as a man groomed to high culture and intellectual achievement. His education at Choate and Harvard as well as his European tours instilled in the future president a familiarity with the fine arts and an appreciation of their place in a sophisticated lifestyle or an advanced national culture. Kennedy played up his reputation as a fine arts patron, although it is now clear that his own artistic preferences were less lofty than publicized at the time.[45] Kennedy mostly enjoyed reading history and classical novels or viewing eye-catching Broadway musicals, ancient Greek or Roman sculpture, and seascape paintings.[46] While such tastes served as common ground between the president and mainstream American arts audiences, Kennedy's admiration of individualism and desire for cultural advance also fostered his appreciation of more avant-garde modern art styles, however little he personally enjoyed them. Kennedy believed that exposure to excellence in arts and culture were important means to elevate one's own cultural level as well as that of American society as a whole, and he was willing to go out of his way to support highbrow culture.[47]

He was certainly encouraged in this regard by his wife. Surprisingly little notice has been given to the role of First Lady Jacqueline Kennedy in focusing on the arts. It was she, however, who was responsible for suggesting the invitation of artists to the inauguration. Mrs. Kennedy, more so than the president, kept her eye on setting a tone of style and grace for the new administration and encouraging the development of arts events and policy. She channeled many of her ideas through Pièrre Salinger, who, as a formally trained classical pianist, shared her tastes and ambitions, and later through August Heckscher, the president's special consultant on the arts.[48]

Without a doubt, Jacqueline Bouvier Kennedy exerted a great deal of pressure on her husband to patronize the fine arts and, by so doing, set an example of American cultural maturity. Her education at Vassar and the Sorbonne, and her exposure to the art collection of her stepfather, Hugh Auchincloss, imbued Mrs. Kennedy with a wide familiarity and affinity for the high culture of ballet, symphony, and chamber music as well as an appreciation for modern art. She was particularly fond of seventeenth- and eighteenth-century antiques and of impressionism, postimpressionism, and abstraction in the visual arts.[49] Thus, the first couple shared a certain cultural breeding and were both long-standing patrons of the arts. Among their most frequent private dinner guests at the White House was painter Bill Walton, whose own aesthetic style had evolved from representational to abstract by 1960 and influenced the Kennedys' tastes. Moreover, the first people invited to the mansion were poet Robert Frost and New York City Ballet director George Balanchine. Mrs. Kennedy also lunched with Isaac Stern, who would later serve on the National Council on the Arts, to confer with him about potential arts policies. Indeed, it was her initiative that transformed the White House into a showcase for art and artists during the Kennedy administration. Mrs. Kennedy encouraged the president to replace stodgy state receptions with elegant cultural soirées in the executive mansion. During the Kennedys' tenure at the White House a stage was built that could be stored and erected on short notice. Pages of handwritten memos attest to her detailed planning of White House events and her careful cultivation of the president's and America's public image.[50] Fully understanding the importance of image as well as example, President Kennedy, as the head of state, liberally patronized culture. As Thomas Reeves has pointed out, this made for both "good theater and excellent politics."[51]

★ Kennedy White House Events

Following the positive public reaction to the participation of artists in the inauguration, the Kennedys began to showcase the arts in a series of dinners and performances and in Jacqueline Kennedy's now-famous televised tour of

2.1. *President Kennedy introducing Pablo Casals.*
(Photo courtesy of the John F. Kennedy Library)

the newly redecorated White House. One of the most famous occasions was a November 1961 evening honoring Puerto Rican governor Muñoz Marín that included a performance by Spanish musician Pablo Casals, who had been refusing to play his cello publicly in the United States in protest of the nation's recognition of Spanish dictator Francisco Franco (fig. 2.1). Introducing Casals, Kennedy announced, "[We] believe that an artist, in order to be true to himself and his work, must be a free man."[52] By graciously acknowledging Casals's freedom to criticize U.S. policy toward Spain, the president demonstrated his belief in the importance of freedom in the relationship between the arts and politics. He continued, "I think it is most important not that we regard artistic achievement and action as a part of our armor in these difficult days, but rather as an integral part of our free society."[53] Kennedy's frequent references to freedom and democracy reinforced the United States' position in the Cold War. Thus, despite Kennedy's effort to detach overt political value from the occasion, it is nevertheless clear that the arts were meant not only for beauty and entertainment but for political purposes as well. The Casals recital drew very positive responses from a national audience, and the *New York Times* announced that, in the area of culture, "the White House is rising to its responsibilities and—in one respect at least—coming of age."[54] Such praise encouraged Kennedy's growing endorsement of artistic excellence.

★ *Jacqueline Kennedy's Role*

The Casals concert almost instantly gave the president a reputation as a serious classical music lover, a perception that demonstrated the Kennedys' successful management of their refined image. But the irony of this reputation was not lost on the first lady, who was the true classical music devotee. Jacqueline Kennedy soon tired of the misplaced admiration for her husband and quipped to a friend: "The only music he likes is 'Hail to the Chief.' "[55] Nevertheless, her remarks remained private and much of her work to orchestrate the event went quietly unknown; although records and interviews reveal that Mrs. Kennedy played a prominent role in conceiving and arranging the Casals concert and other events—with her influence extending all the way from the large-scale program planning and publicity down to the details of flower and seating arrangements. Mrs. Kennedy chose to remain behind the scenes because she believed that her husband, as president, should claim the spotlight. In fact she feared being seen as seeking public acclaim for herself and distracting attention from her husband's public work, and she preferred to place her priorities on her family role. As she had professed in a campaign interview, if John Kennedy were elected, "I'd be a wife and a mother first, then First Lady."[56]

Like many women of her generation, Jacqueline Kennedy considered the proper place of women in public to be secondary to that of men. As Elaine Tyler May suggested in *Homeward Bound*, an intense desire for security during the Cold War era translated into an idealized vision of home and family that subordinated women and contained them within the domestic sphere.[57] Unwilling to publicly challenge the status quo and draw criticism to the White House, Mrs. Kennedy eschewed a more public role in arts policy development, instead encouraging the arts from her position as first lady and enlarging her stewardship of the White House.

The most time-consuming of Jacqueline Kennedy's aesthetic endeavors proved to be the restoration of the White House. Mrs. Kennedy formed a Committee of Fine Arts to officially oversee the project and devoted untold hours to researching and reacquiring, or copying, historic furnishings and artwork for the mansion. In this respect, Mrs. Kennedy resembled certain early twentieth-century women whom historians of culture have celebrated for gaining a prominent role in cultural institution building.[58] Like Museum of Modern Art founder Abby Rockefeller, Jacqueline Kennedy appointed prominent men to head the cultural projects, while she herself played a less visible though nonetheless significant role. Even her habit of corresponding personally with commission members and staff via handwritten memos helped disguise the scale of Mrs. Kennedy's contributions by diminishing the paper trail on the White House projects.

But the first lady's labors gained national attention in a televised tour of the White House broadcast in prime time by all three television networks in February 1962. The one-hour program included a narrated history of the White House and a room-by-room tour. Dressed in her trademark two-piece wool suit with a three-strand pearl necklace, the first lady walked slowly through each room detailing the history and recovery of each piece of furniture, painting, and work of art. In her soft, breathy voice she described who originally purchased each piece, in what style and when the piece was made, how it was copied or reacquired, and who contributed to its restoration. It is evident that she was very aware of and made somewhat uncomfortable by the camera following her around the mansion, yet her excitement about the art and her pride in her achievement were clear. In one particularly revealing moment, the CBS commentator noted the special place the arts had achieved in the Kennedy administration and inquired as to whether she felt that there should be a particular connection between the arts and the national government. Mrs. Kennedy smiled and replied, "Oh that's so complicated. I don't know. I just think everything in the White House should be the best."[59] Then she casually moved on to describe the East Room candelabra. By deliberately shunning an opportunity to remark on political matters, the first lady relegated herself to the private arena and presented an image of herself as apolitical, leaving the public and political realm to her husband. President Kennedy arrived at the end of the television program to bestow his blessing on his wife's project and to remark on the importance of reclaiming history and American culture. He ended the program by encouraging children to visit the White House so that they might be excited by history and perhaps even inspired to live there themselves one day. "Even the girls," he said with a grin. In this closing scene the president essentially stole the show and presented himself as firmly in charge and looking to the future. Television viewers saw him as a man ready to mold policy and shape American cultural sensibilities while his wife preserved tradition and the first home—exactly the image the Kennedys wished them to see.

The Kennedys specifically emphasized culture rather than the traditional diplomatic focus of state dinners at a reception for French minister of culture André Malraux. Jacqueline Kennedy had toured French art galleries with Malraux on the Kennedys' state visit to France in 1961, and the Kennedys wished to impress the minister of culture with an American show of talent on his visit to the White House in May of 1962. Guests for the evening included painter Andrew Wyeth; poet Robert Lowell; playwrights Arthur Miller, S. N. Behrman, and Tennessee Williams; actress Geraldine Page; ballet director George Balanchine; Metropolitan Museum of Art curator James Rorimer; White House arts consultant August Heckscher; and business and culture magnates John Loeb and David Rockefeller, in addition to a retinue of government officials. Guests were treated to a French dinner and a recital of Schubert's Trio in B-flat Major, op. 99, performed by Eugene Istomin on piano, Isaac Stern on violin, and Leonard Rose on cello. In his remarks, John Kennedy scoffed at the idea that the life of an artist was "soft," borrowing a word from Riesman's critique of American society in the 1950s. "Actually," the president asserted, "creativity is the hardest life there is."[60] His statements once again provide insight into his admiration of artists as hardworking individuals who must devote hours of difficult and often lonely and unrewarded practice to perfect their talents. Kennedy believed such dedication to be an important component of individual accomplishment and a quality society should value.

Following this glamorous dinner, Malraux endorsed an unprecedented cultural exchange between France and the United States. In 1963 he helped arrange a tour of Leonardo da Vinci's *Mona Lisa* from the Louvre to the National Gallery of Art in Washington and the Met in New York. The painting was designated a "guest" of the president and traveled under his personal protection. At a reception for the president and Mrs. Kennedy held at the French Embassy prior to the exhibition of the *Mona Lisa* in Washington, Kennedy expressed his gratitude to France as the "leading artistic country" for its loan of the priceless portrait. Moreover, he used this occasion to argue that the United States would "continue to press ahead to develop an independent, artistic force of its own."[61] Not coincidentally, the Kennedy administration was orchestrating U.S. State Department support for the American painting exhibition at the 1964 Venice Biennale, whose prizes historically had been France's domain. Kennedy hoped that American success there would announce the United States' cultural presence on the European continent.[62] Kennedy's calculated encounters with the arts were amounting to more than image-making opportunities, and the president soon took the lead in creating a new federal policy concerning the arts.

★ Conceptualizing a Federal Arts Policy

With the encouragement of his advisers, Kennedy had already begun taking determined steps toward devising a federal policy on the arts. In July of 1961, Pièrre Salinger, Arthur Schlesinger Jr., Max Isenberg, and Phillip Coombs met for a lunch to discuss art policy. The meeting centered on Isenberg's policy paper, "A Strategy for Cultural Advancement."[63] A State Department official interested in American cultural expansion, Isenberg proposed that Kennedy evaluate the realm of government and the arts and examine the possible improvement of existing government art programs and expansion of federal efforts into new cultural areas both at home and abroad. Reminding the president of his inaugural commitment to cultural advancement, Isenberg called for fulfilling this pledge for two reasons. First, he believed it would improve the quality of life in the United States. He argued that the "pursuit of happiness" should be restored to its proper place in American thought—people should be reminded through aesthetic endeavors that striving for peace and material well-being were not ends in themselves but means to a higher quality of life. Remembering this would "do no less than transform the national character and open, for the whole world to see, an exhilarating new chapter in the American Revolution for the nineteen sixties."[64]

Underlying Isenberg's ideas on American life were equally salient concerns about how it would be perceived abroad. His second reason for promoting arts policy explicitly stated that "[It] would make the less developed nations think better of us as a model; and to the nations of the Soviet bloc, it would show devotion on our part to a humanism transcending political differences, a demonstration which holds more promise than any other approach tried thus far of bringing forth affirmative, even conciliatory, response from their side."[65] Kennedy staff duly noted the potential for arts as a foreign policy tool. Moreover, the timing of this proposal was significant, for it came on the heels of tense international incidents at the Bay of Pigs in Cuba and in Berlin, Germany.[66]

The Bay of Pigs invasion resulted in a great deal of public criticism of the

Kennedy administration. Among those denouncing the president's assault against a small, independent country were a number of American artists who gathered at a demonstration in Washington and carried protest signs against repression. One young poet directed her outcry to the first lady with a placard reading, "Jacqueline: *vous avez perdu vos artistes!*" (You have lost your artists), appealing to Mrs. Kennedy's cultured persona and signaling these artists' rejection of strong-arm tactics.[67] The painful experience taught Kennedy to back away from uniquely hard-line military means to secure U.S. power and to carefully consider how U.S. actions would be perceived around the world, especially by small, third world countries caught in the struggles between the United States and the USSR.

In his assessment of the Berlin Wall crisis, Henry Kissinger advised President Kennedy that firmness should not be proven by shying away from diplomacy until only military options remained.[68] Kennedy agreed that more flexibility was necessary in Cold War confrontations to avoid total warfare; therefore, he increased his options by abandoning Eisenhower's policy of massive retaliation in favor of flexible response military tactics.[69] His approach to world crisis came to include not only a military arsenal that included nuclear weapons, but also Special Forces recruits and Peace Corps volunteers enlisted to out perform the Soviets around the world. With the president's concern for total mobilization militarily and socially, it would take only a short time for him to incorporate cultural endeavors.[70]

By the fall of 1961, the unofficial Isenberg paper became the basis for the next step toward developing an official arts policy, as Kennedy's advisers recommended the appointment of a special White House consultant. Arthur Schlesinger Jr. suggested an old friend from the Twentieth Century Fund, August Heckscher. Heckscher had been closely tied to Nelson Rockefeller's pursuit to advance American culture and had been recruited by him to write a paper for Eisenhower's Commission on National Goals titled "The Quality of American Culture," which called for a federal arts policy. At the time Kennedy staff members approached him, Heckscher was working on a book proposing involvement in the arts as an antidote to the alienation of modern life—a philosophy akin to both Schlesinger's and Kennedy's beliefs.[71] Kennedy also liked the idea of appointing a moderate who had close ties to the Rockefeller Republicans so that his work would carry greater weight as a bipartisan effort. Assured by Schlesinger in November that "no editorial writer has used the Casals dinner to accuse you of fiddling while Berlin burns," Kennedy was ready to act.[72] He wrote to Heckscher in December 1961

2.2. *President Kennedy with his special consultant on the arts, August Heckscher, and Heckscher's son. (Photo courtesy of the John F. Kennedy Library)*

that the time had come for "a more systematic approach" to addressing the arts and asked him to come to Washington to conduct a survey and recommend presidential actions on matters of culture. Yet to downplay the expectations of the artistic community and leave his options open, Kennedy requested that Heckscher execute his duties quietly and "without fanfare."[73] Heckscher, recruited to work on a part-time basis for six months, soon found his place among the busy and ambitious full-time White House staff.

★ *The First White House Arts Post*

The first official "Special Consultant on the Arts to the President" took on responsibilities more important than simply maintaining the first cultural office in the White House. Although Heckscher communicated with the president mainly through Schlesinger, Salinger, and White House assistant Kenneth O'Donnell, he understood the significance of his position. Heckscher knew that Kennedy considered the cultural effort of his administration to be far more encompassing than the creation of the office of the special consultant; Kennedy's manner, speeches, and contacts with scholars all hinted at his wider interest in the arts. Having placed a qualified man in the special consultant's chair, the president was not interested in the daily routine of the office as much as in its ultimate impact on national policy. The very appointment of a special consultant on the arts indicated a new interest on the part of the federal government. Heckscher believed "all he had to do was ask me down there and then that set in motion waves which carried quite far."[74] Indeed, Heckscher's arrival made the front page of the *New York Times* and received nationwide attention. Soon, the office was busy addressing Americans' cultural concerns, responding to letters from across the country and writing articles and delivering speeches on the relationship of the government and the arts.

Upon assuming his position in March of 1962, however, Heckscher's main goal was to assess the relationship of government and the arts and to report to the president on means to improve federal policy. In May of 1963, after more than a year of conducting work and research, he submitted his report, "The Arts and the National Government," to the president. Heckscher's introduction reiterated the philosophy on culture that Kennedy had adopted from the academic community—that the sixties would be a decade in which Americans would need to address the issue of increasing leisure time, acknowledge the growing importance of the cities, and recognize that there was far more to American life than the acquisition of material goods. Heckscher's opening lines asserted, "The United States will be judged and its place in history ultimately assessed—not alone by its military and economic power—but by the quality of its civilization." Evoking the foreign policy applications underlying his work, Heckscher also noted "the evident desirability of sending the best examples of America's artistic endeavors abroad." Significantly, he recognized that this aim had forced American leaders to reexamine U.S. achievements in the field of aesthetic creativity and to realize that more needed to be done at home to cultivate the excellence desired both within American culture and for its representation abroad. The time was ripe for a domestic arts policy to preserve the American cultural assets and promote "an environment within which cultural values can be realized."[75]

Heckscher's commitment to elevating the best of American culture was apparent in his statements on the arts prior to his official report. In a speech before the Conference on Aesthetic Responsibility in 1962, for example, Heckscher commended the widespread interest in the arts developing in the United States at that time. Still, he warned that Americans must beware of blurring the distinction between "the excellent and the second-rate, between the genuine and the spurious, between the artist and the amateur." Only by striving for excellence in the arts (including painting and sculpture in addition to architecture) could the United States hope to attain outward beauty and fulfillment akin to that of Athens in the Classical Age. With Greece as his model of civic and aesthetic achievement, Heckscher advised American officials to "make sure, as we build for ourselves, that men and their cities prove of equal worth. It is not, after all only beauty itself, but the striving for beauty that lifts up men and makes a civilization."[76] These words resurfaced often in congressional debates over arts policy and became a mantra among those advocating aesthetics as a responsible means to uplift society.

Heckscher's report addressed the critical question of how this cultural goal should be achieved. The report began by pointing out the recent history of inadequate government support for the arts and the existence of policies impinging upon their development. It emphasized the importance of government research and interagency cooperation in matters of culture and recommended that the federal government take up a number of wide-ranging actions. Heckscher's research, in large part corroborated by the Bureau of the Budget, first indicated that there was already varied and extensive government involvement in the arts through the uncoordinated efforts of numerous agencies. He counseled a categorical assessment of agencies' use of art and a streamlining of separate efforts under a defined federal policy. His recommendations included the following: increased government acquisition of art, including purchasing more visual arts for the Smithsonian Museums, the National Gallery, and the Library of Congress; the commissioning of more art for public buildings under the General Services Administration; the exhibition of art in American embassies; the elevation of design standards for government posters, bulletins, and stamps; historic preservation; increased urban renewal efforts under the Public Housing Administration; the development of a National Cultural Center (for which Congress had passed legislation in 1958 and Kennedy had appointed Roger Stevens chairman of the board in September 1962); increased funds for international exhibitions; beautification of Washington, D.C. (for which Kennedy established the Pennsylvania Avenue Advisory Council in May 1962); greater funding for arts and humanities education; the recognition of artists with national merit awards; and the rewriting of tax laws to lighten the burden on artists.

Heckscher's three most explicit recommendations proved more fundamental than these overall concerns. First, he advised the appointment of a full-time, permanent special consultant on the arts, who would be available to advise the president on all matters pertaining to the arts in addition to carrying out the policy-making, planning, and review functions of the original assignment. Second, he favored the establishment of an Advisory Council on the Arts reporting directly to the president. He argued that its function would be to expand the duties of the special consultant. As part of the federal government apparatus, the council would be responsible for gathering information about the arts, reviewing federal policies and making recommendations for improving design and long-range programs, and encouraging the active participation of the artistic community in the government effort.[77] Third, Heckscher called for the establishment of a National Arts Foundation. This agency would administer grants, generally on a matching basis, to states and for projects proposed by artists or cultural organizations. Thus, it would be able to support "experiments designed to increase attendance, to foster creativity and introduce contemporary works to new audiences, or to offer services on an experimental basis."[78] The arts foundation would be commissioned to encourage the artistic innovation and excellence that both Heckscher and the president so esteemed. Upon submission of the report, Heckscher resigned his post as special consultant to the president so he could resume his duties at the Twentieth Century Fund. He agreed to remain, however, until a successor was named and to serve on the advisory council once that body was established.[79]

Kennedy considered the report "a milestone" that would open up "a new and fruitful relationship between the government and the arts."[80] He embraced the suggested exemplary role of the federal government in aesthetic achievement and its responsibility in promoting the pursuit of happiness.[81] Heckscher's report provided a constructive outlet for the Kennedy administration to join the battle against the decadence many feared was accompanying increased leisure time in what Galbraith had termed an "affluent society."[82] Economic growth was a major factor enabling arts policy implementation, but the Kennedy circle envisioned the arts as something more than products to be enjoyed. Kennedy's remarks at a dinner promoting the National Cultural Center and an article he wrote for *Look* magazine both reiterated that in a time of growth and abundance, "with peace too often comes an exclusive preoccupation with material progress and private pleasures." Kennedy extolled the artist—who worked amid deprivation and loneliness to hone his skills and realize his vision—as a virtuous individual and the alternative to decadent materialists. He admired the discipline, willingness to take risks, and pursuit of excellence displayed by artists and believed his government should encourage such qualities. Kennedy believed these values would enrich the lives of American audiences as well as those of the artists. He wrote "[the] suburban housewife harassed by numerous children, the husband weary after the day's work, young people bent on having a good time—these might not appear to enjoy a very high level of intellectual pursuit. Yet . . . the appreciation of cultural and intellectual values has a place. To further this appreciation of the arts among all the people, to increase respect for the creative individual and to stimulate participation by those of even modest gifts, is one of the great and fascinating challenges of these days."[83] Always willing to accept a challenge, Kennedy prepared to implement the Heckscher report recommendations.

★ Arts Advisory Council by Executive Order

First, a long-standing debate between JFK and his advisers over exactly how to act would have to be addressed. Essentially, the dilemma was whether the president should wait for congressional legislation or exert executive action. Kennedy had called upon Congress to act on a bill to establish the arts council in the name of national prestige, saying, "If we are to be among the leaders of the world in every sense of the word this sector of our national life cannot be neglected or treated with indifference. . . . A bill (H.R. 4172) already reported out of the House would make this possible."[84] When Congress proved slow to act, the president resolved the issue by signing Executive Order 11112 in June of 1963. This order established the President's Advisory Council on the Arts, giving the United States for the first time a formal government body to survey the arts across the nation and to recommend to the president ways to encourage them.[85]

In a statement accompanying the release of the executive order, Kennedy expressed the value he placed on excellence in art and culture. He began by sharing his discontent that many American children were growing up without ever having seen a professionally acted play, which he felt deprived them of important cultural opportunities. Then, echoing Heckscher's public statements, he emphasized the importance of the professional artist, because "without the professional performer and the creative artist, the amateur spirit declines and the vast audience is only partially served. . . . The concept of the public welfare should reflect cultural as well as physical values."[86] Kennedy's advocacy of professional excellence in his promotion of American culture exhibits elitist predilections; yet it also expresses an interest in promoting the arts for all Americans as part of the "public welfare." This constitutional reference was a deliberate way to legitimize federal arts policy and make it more palatable for congressional opponents who did not see its relevance for their constituents, while at the same time aiding Kennedy's promotion of high culture.

★ Kennedy and Congress

Ultimately, although he had exerted presidential initiative by organizing an Advisory Council on the Arts, Kennedy resisted establishing an arts foundation without congressional approval. Presidential historians have observed Kennedy's reluctance to press his adversaries on domestic issues. His narrow electoral victory had not given him the political clout he would have hoped for, which kept him from risking his prestige on bills that were uncertain of passage on Capitol Hill.[87] In addition, his hands-off style and aristocratic airs clashed at times with the manners of career congressmen, making it difficult for him to negotiate legislative measures. One down-to-earth representative from Tennessee who found the president distant pronounced, "[All] that Mozart string music and ballet dancing down there [at the White House] and all that fox hunting and London clothes. He's too elegant for me. I can't talk to him."[88] Thus, to avoid seeming to impose his will and to assure a strong base of support for a federal policy, Kennedy insisted that Congress give arts policy a statutory basis.

The president and Mrs. Kennedy labored to cultivate a positive image of American culture and to press ahead quietly with the development of arts policy until the atmosphere would be friendly to its legal implementation. Jacqueline Kennedy was not only responsible for planning White House events but proved a crucial behind-the-scenes figure in discussions of government cultural programs. Senator Pell spoke directly to the first lady rather than to the president about the Advisory Council on the Arts and about who might be appointed as its first chair, and congressional leaders diverted letters concerning legislative proposals about cultural policy to her office.[89] Clearly,

Jacqueline Kennedy took great interest in and responsibility for keeping talks alive between the White House and Capitol Hill, especially while President Kennedy was more preoccupied with foreign affairs and the Cuban Missile crisis in 1962.

The Kennedys' advances toward arts policy rejuvenated the efforts of its advocates in Congress. Sen. Jacob Javits and Rep. Frank Thompson had been leading an effort to obtain federal aid for the arts throughout the 1950s. With support from the White House they joined forces with Sen. Hubert Humphrey on the Committee on Labor and Public Welfare and Claiborne Pell on its Special Subcommittee on the Arts. Together they proposed arts measures designed to establish a federal advisory council on the arts, provide financial aid to state arts projects, and fund a national arts foundation. These proposals were combined into a single bill in 1963, to which Kennedy gave his explicit endorsement.[90]

★ Arts Policy in Congress

Between 1960 and 1963, with the blessing of the Kennedy administration, congressional arts policy advocates were able to advance their proposals in Congress. Their efforts repeatedly encountered certain concerns regarding the establishment of a national arts foundation, including questions about funding mechanisms, government interference with freedom of expression, democracy, and, especially, foreign policy implications. In fact, over the course of the Kennedy administration, the debate increasingly focused on the use of American cultural development as a foreign policy tool to win the cultural aspect of the Cold War.

Javits's and Humphrey's cogent arguments had largely set aside complaints against federal jurisdiction and costs by the end of the 1950s. Such issues no longer formed a stumbling block for arts policy; federal jurisdiction was accepted under the public welfare clause of the Constitution, and the booming economy enabled Congress to feel less constrained in its spending. This notwithstanding, Congress still expressed concerns over the nature of federal involvement in a national arts foundation, prompting arts supporters to write arts policy legislation that addressed the opposition's concerns.

The 1963 bill to establish a national cultural foundation set limits on federal support and upheld the principle of freedom of expression. Senator Humphrey proposed that the government divide funds into small sums shared by federal programs, the states, and local governments, thus providing for each region (and congressional district). Such a disbursement of funds appealed to those interested in democratizing arts policy. More importantly, Humphrey characterized this government money as, in essence, "seed money" that would generate further funds. He estimated that "for every dollar appropriated there is a multiplier of 5, thus producing $50 million of cultural activity for every $10 million appropriated."[91] The extra funds would, in fact, come from private foundations and art benefactors, as assured by the matching-grant status of the federal funds proposed in the arts foundation bill.[92] The policy of acquiring most of the funding for arts programs from nonfederal sources ultimately won the approval of many critics.

Not only did tightfisted attitudes dissipate once members were convinced that matching grants would produce funds from private sources, members also became more supportive when the legislation handed them more control. As Congressman Horace Seely-Brown (R-Conn.) reminded his associates, the bill for an arts foundation called for money to be appropriated annually, "thus assuring Congress control of the dimensions of the programs," if not the actual selection of art.[93] The final bill eventually also gave Congress the power of reviewing and renewing the entire arts program every five years. Congressional opposition to the use of federal funds for the support of the arts, which had been a crucial factor in the demise of arts legislation during the 1950s, evaporated.

Another important obstacle overcome during the 1960s was the long-term issue of government censorship in arts funding. Opponents of the arts programs persisted in their complaints that government funding would have strings attached, constraining artistic freedom and creativity. Congressman Bruce Alger (R-Tex.) bemoaned that the long arm of the Kennedy administration might reach into every aspect of American life. Alger illustrated artists' fear of control by quoting an article demonstrating that the Royal Academy of Arts in London, out of fear that the British government would control their art through a subsidy program, sold a precious Leonardo da Vinci sketch to remain self-supporting.[94] Fears of federal domination could be detrimental to cultural organizations if they behaved in a similar manner. Still, most refused to believe that such a scenario would be possible in the United States. Senator Javits asserted that there "is no reason to assume a danger in this respect than in any other part of our economy." He emphasized that under the terms of the proposal the federal government's "position will not in any way endanger the traditional freedom of the artist and his form of expression and that the legislation . . . does not in any way infringe upon this time-honored prerogative of the artist."[95] In fact, President Kennedy invoked this ideal of artistic freedom in his remarks at Amherst College, pronouncing, "[If] art is to nourish the roots of our culture, society must set the artist free to follow his vision wherever it takes him. We must never forget that art is not a form of propaganda; it is a form of truth."[96] Kennedy professed that the free expression of the artist both symbolized and uplifted American culture.

The final bill, drafted by Pell's aide Livingston Biddle, removed government officials and even NEA directors from the direct selection of artistic grantees by instituting peer panel review of grants and by requiring art council approval for grants. However the arts would ultimately be defined and funded (and as Chapters 4 and 5 reveal, these decisions would be heavily influenced by executive policy), the argument in favor of demonstrating freedom through arts policy was quite powerful in rallying both Democrats and Republicans in Congress around arts legislation.

Supporters also argued that arts policy would express American democracy. In his Senate speeches Javits envisioned a renaissance in American art during the early 1960s that would cause theaters and arts groups to crop up all across the country. By supporting art, the government would truly be championing what the people had already shown they wanted. "Is that not the role of government in a democracy?" he asked.[97]

The proposed foundation would encourage the growth of arts throughout the United States; by promoting equal opportunity for all Americans to view art, it would democratize access to high culture. Arts supporters, like President Kennedy, voiced concern that children in smaller American towns had never actually seen a theater production.[98] Javits argued in favor of spreading the arts more evenly throughout the country by contending:

> [Support] for the visual and performing arts now comes in large part from private benefactors. . . . This situation has . . . tended to concentrate the development of cultural programs in centers of wealth, leaving wide areas of the country without opportunity to enjoy and participate in the visual and performing arts.
>
> The U.S. National Arts Foundation would encourage by matching grants and subvention to nonprofit groups the distribution of live performances and exhibits in cities and towns which could not otherwise receive and support them . . . and make it possible for many more people in many more places to see and hear the best in American culture.[99]

In Javits's view only a national arts foundation could ensure that the arts would be more evenly distributed throughout the United States. Sen. Mike Mansfield (D-Mont.) agreed, asserting that "in the days of the Medicis, culture was for the privileged few. . . . In 20th century America, however, music and art, ballet and drama should be available to all."[100] Thus, congressmen wanted arts policy to symbolize and advance the cherished American ideal of democracy.

The argument that art policy would express American freedom and democracy resounded deeply amid the heightened Cold War tensions of the early 1960s, when the United States' and Soviet Union's brinkmanship brought the world to the verge of nuclear war. A high proportion of the art legislation debates in Congress during the Kennedy administration contained direct references to foreign policy. Congressmen became convinced, as Kennedy had, that the arts could prove a useful weapon in garnering world support for the United States. They supported arts funding as a nonmilitary means to counter the Soviet and communist threats.

Moreover, many of the congressmen advocating the arts programs sandwiched their discussions of the arts in between their introductions of other Cold War measures. Nearly half of all arts discussions preceded or followed discussion of such Cold War issues as military strength, funding for the war in Vietnam, or Soviet transgressions. For example, the discussion following Senator Javits's argument for establishing a national arts foundation included Javits himself praising the U.S. forces fighting communism in Vietnam and another congressman commemorating the deportation of Baltic citizens to Siberia by the Soviets, deploring the lack of freedom in the Communist Bloc. Numerous instances of similar rhetoric may be found throughout the congressional records.[101]

Such Cold War references appeared early on in the arts debates and grew in intensity and frequency as the passage of the bill for the U.S. arts foundation appeared imminent in late 1963. When introducing the Federal Advisory Council Bill in January of 1961, Senator Humphrey called for the "advancement of the arts in the United States, as well as the expanded use of the arts in our Nation's foreign policy . . . to preserve our own way of life now under attack."[102] Senator Javits stressed that "the Russians have gotten more benefit from sending Oistrakh, their violinist, the Bolshoi Ballet and the Moiseyev Ballet to the United States than they have from Sputnik I." He chastised the Senate for remaining mired in thinking from the eighteenth and nineteenth centuries and believing that the United States should not be involved in arts support. He argued that by doing so Congress was "deliberately forgoing by archaic . . . ideas one of the most effective instruments in the hands of mankind today, first to assert the efficacy and the virtues of our free institutions, and second, to make human beings throughout the world feel that we are people who deserve to be followed."[103] Thus, Javits recognized the Soviets' use of art as a foreign policy measure to successfully promote their way of life. He believed the United States should follow the same course to better compete with the Russians.

Many others agreed. Rep. John Monagan (D-Conn.), for example, endorsed a stronger cultural exchange program as a weapon in the ideological Cold War:

> In the current contest with the Communists, guns and bombs are not the only weapons that are employed. We are also waging a war of ideas.
>
> One of the insidious tactics of the Communist powers has been to create in the minds of uninformed people an image of the United States . . . as a country of crass, worldly and mercenary culture. In the struggle for survival, it is, therefore, our problem to dispel this misinformation and to make clear to the world the fundamentals upon which this Nation is based and to demonstrate the unique and profound culture that is characteristic of the United States.[104]

Monagan echoed Kennedy advisers such as Coombs, Isenberg, and Heckscher in arguing that international cultural policies would effectively expand foreign policy beyond simple military terms and would extend U.S. prestige. Bolstering America's image would also counter other nations' old perception of the United States as culturally backward by illustrating the nation's cultural achievement and demonstrating the desirability of the American way of life.

Rep. Harris McDowell (D-Pa.) explained in greater detail just how such a scheme should work. He believed that American artistic talent sent abroad would wow the surprised communists. He posited that young artists would "not only astound the world with their cultural proficiency . . . they are quick to make friends and give intelligent answers offstage. . . . This is the way to show how democracy works, to send young America with its verve and skills and interest and intelligence. . . . In the field of performing arts . . . we have a huge potential which is just beginning to be recognized. . . . When the Michigan University Symphonic Band went to Moscow last spring, young Russian students mobbed them with enthusiasm . . . asking them questions about the United States."[105] Young artists and performers were America's best ambassadors of democracy and freedom, according to McDowell.

Nearly three decades later, historian Reinhold Wagnleitner would reiterate McDowell's idea of young artists as ambassadors of democracy, although not exactly as McDowell had argued. In his study of American cultural diplomacy in Austria, Wagnleitner demonstrated that Europeans, particularly the young, embraced American jazz music, films, and popular culture more readily than "high culture" classical music and theater, for which they still maintained a preference for European performances. However, abstract expressionist painting and avant-garde art were one form of high culture that Europeans did accept from the United States.[106] Many in Congress agreed with McDowell that exporting American culture was essential to advancing U.S. policy goals, although sending American artists abroad was only one goal of the arts bills introduced into Congress during the early 1960s.

In fact, arts policy emphasized American art at home; cultural achievement might become a symbol of American democracy's ability to produce art as beautiful as the Soviets' Bolshoi Ballet and significantly more free. Noting that support in the United States for art legislation was long overdue, Rep. Seymour Halpern (R-N.Y.) called for a strong arts bill to remedy the situation, arguing that "[a] dynamic, free society, such as ours, needs an equally dynamic and free expression of creativity." Halpern emphasized that an arts council "would act as a potent weapon on our struggles against atheistic, materialistic communism, for it would prove that creativity—as well as economic and political-social development—can be encouraged and flourish in a free society."[107]

Underneath all the flag waving, however, lay a note of concern. The Cold War era witnessed widespread soul-searching and intellectual criticism of Americans as complacent. Writings such as "Arguing the Case for Being Panicky" and *What Ivan Knows and Johnny Doesn't* compared the nation unfavorably with its rivals. Thus, Americans grew increasingly worried about how such disparities could be redressed.[108]

With fears of failure in mind, the perceived need to catch the Soviets appeared more urgently in arts legislation debates during the winter of 1962. Representative Carroll Kearns (R-Pa.) inserted the arguments of the "Johnny and Ivan" books into art issues by pronouncing, "Ivan and European children are exposed from their earliest days to the finest cultural expressions, to the greatest classics of our Western cultural heritage, to the opera, the theater, and to great art in all fields. Little Johnny, on the other hand, sees the Three

Stooges, and all kinds of trash on the TV programs at home, and when he goes to the movies he is not any better off."[109] Like cultural critics Macdonald and Goodman, who lamented the low level of popular culture and promoted an elitist version of high culture, Kearns used the disparity between European high culture and American mass culture to demonstrate the need for more advanced cultural programs in the United States. He called for government support for the arts to challenge and inspire Americans to acquire greater sophistication and an ability to compete in international culture. Such elitist arguments shaped arts advocates' drive for the founding of the NEA and would later influence its administration of visual arts grants as much as, if not more so, than the seemingly ever-present Cold War fears.

The opening remarks about art legislation in the 1963 congressional session expressed a greater concern for winning a Cold War on all fronts. In reintroducing his revised bill for creating a U.S. arts foundation, giving states funding for the arts, and establishing an advisory council for the arts, Senator Javits remarked, "I introduce this bill with a greater sense of urgency derived from increasingly sharp cultural competition abroad which the United States faces from the Soviet bloc countries."[110] Senator Pell further stressed that the United States must keep pace with the Soviets. He explained that the Soviet's Central Party journal *Kommunist* pronounced that the Soviet Union had a mission to bring the "light of an advanced culture to the peoples of the whole world." Americans should not be like the Soviets in their use of art as propaganda, Pell argued, but should fight to keep hold of the cultural realm "which has been the domain of free societies."[111] Hitting on the concerns of arts opponents about the possible "waste" of money on the arts—and reminding his colleagues how much money many of them had voted to direct to the space programs—Pell later added, "Our scientific research, for which we spend billions annually . . . to maintain the posture of strength . . . will mean very little, if the culture of our people . . . is allowed to erode. . . . We must contribute to the world something better than [materialism], something more lofty, something that is in tune with free men . . . so we will demonstrate still another failure of communism."[112]

In what would be his last call for arts legislation, Kennedy asserted in a speech dedicating a memorial to the late poet Robert Frost, "The artist, however faithful to his personal vision of reality, becomes the last champion of the individual mind and sensibility against an intrusive society and an officious state. . . . I look forward to an America which will steadily raise the standards of artistic accomplishment and which will steadily enlarge cultural opportunities for all of our citizens. And I look forward to an America which commands respect throughout the world not only for its strength but for its civilization as well."[113] Kennedy wanted this speech to serve as a manifesto on federal arts policy. He had clearly concluded that in the Cold War era the freedom of artists represented a fundamental American value posing an alternative to totalitarianism. Kennedy intended to refer directly to Soviet control in this speech. His original draft read, "In Soviet Russia, Chairman Khrushchev had informed us, 'It is the highest duty of the Soviet writer, artist and composer, of every creative worker, to be in the ranks of the builders of communism . . . to fight for the triumph of the ideas of Marxism-Leninism.' " Kennedy deleted this line on the plane to Massachusetts, Schlesinger recalled, because he did not wish to appear too antagonistic just before impending arms talks with the Soviet Union.[114] Nonetheless, his point was made. Americans recalling *New York Times* articles on recent Soviet denunciations of abstract art exhibits in Moscow would further draw the conclusion that American modern artists were to be praised for their style and Americans were to be congratulated for their tolerance and vision.[115]

Although President Kennedy created an atmosphere of acceptance for the arts unparalleled by any other chief executive, he would not see the passage of arts legislation before the fateful morning of November 22, 1963. In October of that year, the Senate debated a bill for the establishment of the U.S. arts foundation for which Javits, Humphrey, Pell, and Thompson had pressed. Javits and his wife Marion enlisted artists including modernist painters Robert Rauschenberg, Andy Warhol, Jasper Johns and a host of other arts enthusiasts as lobbyists who recommended the bill's passage by Congress.[116] Yet, the legislation failed at the end of the 1963 Senate session and would not be considered again by the House until the following spring. Fiscal restraint, political conservatism, and the absence of direct presidential pressure once again combined to halt arts progress on the Hill. The appointments of Arts Council members would also be postponed in the wake of Kennedy's assassination. In the long run, though, Kennedy's death became a contributing factor in Lyndon Johnson's achievement of a federal arts agency as Jacqueline Kennedy and Kennedy supporters successful engaged the image of "Camelot" to encourage Johnson and Congress to fulfill the wishes of the martyred president. Americans' undeniable embrace of the Camelot myth testifies to the power of imagery and its potential to influence public policy. Kennedy understood this and would have been proud of its impact while at the same time rejecting the maudlin romanticism the myth of Camelot bestowed upon him.[117]

Although not yet incorporated as a full-fledged federal program, the arts were given unprecedented recognition by the Kennedy administration. They were displayed prominently in the Kennedy White House and hailed as a mark of American civilization worthy of national support. Kennedy's art policies grew through a series of successful trial steps into an administrative program intended to institutionalize arts support at the federal level, thereby cementing the value of artistic achievement in American culture. These policies reflected a desire to celebrate American artistic excellence and success as victories in the cultural Cold War. In accordance with prevailing liberal ideology, Kennedy officials believed government should act to improve the quality of American life. Domestically the arts would be an effective tool to raise aesthetic standards and stimulate intellectual activity, which would counterbalance popular acceptance of more mundane and material commodities. Internationally, this achievement would then demonstrate the success and desirability of American democracy and cultural freedom. The ideal of high cultural achievement so valued as part of the New Frontier was instrumental in setting the stage for the ideological and administrative development of the National Endowment for the Arts. The basic contour and purpose of Kennedy's arts policy remained in Johnson's Great Society program and were ultimately manifested in the mission statement of the Endowment. The goals of Kennedy's art policy and the ideological consensus behind them thus outlasted his tenure in the White House.

Let Us Continue

Arts Policy during the Johnson Administration

The pursuit of artistic achievement, and making the fruits of that achievement available to all its people, is among the hallmarks of a Great Society.
—Lyndon Baines Johnson, "Statement to Congress Accompanying the Bill to Establish the National Foundation on the Arts and Humanities," March 10, 1965

★ ★

In December 1963, Johnson presented the Fermi Prize for achievements in nuclear energy research to J. Robert Oppenheimer and showered the renowned scientist with words of praise.[1] The event was no ordinary recognition of a famous scientist by an American president. For despite Oppenheimer's achievements, the celebrated director of the top-secret Manhattan Project during World War II had renounced the end results of his work and declared his opposition to the development of the hydrogen bomb. In 1953, the Atomic Energy Commission labeled him a security risk and the Eisenhower administration revoked his security clearance. At a time when Americans displayed rampant anticommunist sentiments and attacked Oppenheimer's stance as un-American, such federal censure cast a pall over Oppenheimer that followed him throughout the 1950s. By the early 1960s however, President Kennedy had eschewed such hard-line practices and intended to resurrect the scientist's reputation. Lyndon Johnson's decision to follow through with the prize ceremony following Kennedy's assassination reinforced the shift in American politics away from the excesses of McCarthyite assaults to more measured, though staunchly anticommunist, policies. This action also indicated the continuity between the Kennedy and Johnson administrations; both were committed to winning the Cold War, to expressions of American freedom, and to using government action to encourage social uplift.[2]

Realizing the magnitude of the trauma Kennedy's murder had caused, Lyndon Johnson believed his first priority was to ensure stability before embarking on any new course of action. He initially upheld Kennedy's plans and policies, and, in fact, saw many Kennedy initiatives through to fruition. Nevertheless, Johnson sought to impose his own personal stamp upon the presidency and to emerge from Kennedy's shadow. As time passed, Johnson hired his own staff and set his own agenda, moving firmly toward greater commitments to domestic affairs and the populist flavor that would distinguish his Great Society.[3] Johnson's belief in activist government and leadership skills proved crucial to the establishment of a national arts institution.[]

★ *Inheriting the White House*

Upon assuming the presidency, Johnson inherited a set of policies and legislative initiatives as well as a staff dedicated to carrying out Kennedy's ideals. A smooth transition of power remained his top priority, an effort to reassure both the country and the world that his administration would sustain American standards and strength. With this in mind, Johnson immediately expressed his determination to honor Kennedy's commitments at home and abroad. In his first speech to Congress, Johnson reminded members that Kennedy had asked them to begin along a path toward much progressive legislation. "Let us continue" along that path, Johnson urged, "[for] no memorial oration or eulogy could more honor President Kennedy's memory."[4] He also invited all staff members to stay on at the White House. Many of Kennedy's primary speech writers and policy analysts remained, including Theodore Sorensen, Arthur Schlesinger Jr., and staff member Lawrence O'Brien.

While carrying on the Kennedy legacy, Johnson quietly but firmly imposed his own mark on the presidency. Shortly after his arrival at the White House, he summoned Princeton historian Eric Goldman and asked him to join the White House staff as a special presidential adviser for cultural and intellectual affairs. Goldman found Johnson to be truly interested in ideas and believed he was destined to be a "great liberal President."[5] Goldman was assured in no uncertain terms that he was neither a replacement for nor Johnson's version of Arthur Schlesinger Jr., although he was exactly that. Johnson simply hoped to avoid any comparisons with Kennedy by which he would suffer as an intellectual interloper.

Still, both presidents shared concerns about elevating the quality of life for Americans through social and cultural policy. Kennedy had first drawn upon the ideas of intellectuals such as Schlesinger and Galbraith, and Johnson continued to do so, if in a less direct manner. When Schlesinger himself moved from the Johnson White House, Goldman and various staff members, including Bill Moyers and Richard Goodwin, filled his shoes. Moreover, Schlesinger's and Galbraith's convictions remained an important influence on Johnson policy development.

LBJ secretly assigned Goldman to formulate a "brain trust" of intellectuals to serve as informal presidential advisers. Abe Fortas, Johnson's confidant and legal adviser who was also highly interested in cultural matters, was available to Goldman for advice on this assignment, since Fortas was extremely well connected and intimately involved in White House recruitment of qualified men to serve in all levels of government.[6] Goldman was most interested in those he called "metroamericans"—generally upper-class, educated, suburbanites who were more public spirited and cultivated than materialistic and who held sway in American culture because of their influence in books, magazines, radio, and television. Goldman maintained contact with numerous academics and knowledgeable individuals on an informal basis, including Richard Hofstadter, Margaret Mead, David Riesman, Norman Podhoretz, and John Kenneth Galbraith.[7]

While their assessments of national needs covered many areas, these intellectuals all sounded a common theme. They noted that the president was more than a political leader and the guardian of national security. He was the leader of national welfare. Through Goldman, the group urged Johnson to use the White House to influence American values—to reinstate moral emphases rather than material ones. Echoing previous concerns with what many perceived as rampant materialism and a downward spiral of American culture, intellectuals advocated for a substantive reordering of priorities. *Commentary* editor Norman Podhoretz argued that it was necessary to "effect a spiritual revolution in the American character in order to cope with affluence and automation." In similar terms, Robert Heilbroner also argued the need for a change. He explained, "The conquest of commercialism strikes me as perhaps the acid test that America must undergo in this period of its national existence—the test that will determine whether it survives not merely as a nation but as a meaningful society."[8] His statements expressed the urgency many intellectuals thought underlay the United States' need to counter the forces of commercialism.

The intellectuals' preoccupation with Americans' ability to transcend the material and renew their moral obligations to social and cultural progress reasserted the issues that 1950s intellectuals such as Riesman, Galbraith, and Schlesinger had broached. Intellectuals continued to bemoan the demise of individualism in an assembly-line, organization-man society and the corrosive effects of postwar affluence that allowed Americans to squander their leisure time consuming the latest products rather than building their minds and characters.[9]

Moving beyond scholarly identifications of social and cultural ills, Johnson's brain trust recommended that the administration take direct action to improve society. In discussions of policy formation, many echoed Schlesinger's call to action in *The Vital Center* and "The Challenge of Abundance." They urged Johnson to act on antipoverty policies and civil rights and also to join in a national effort to raise critical, aesthetic, and moral standards in the country.[10] Goldman translated such desires into support for cultural activity in the Johnson White House and urged the president to move forward on the cultural front as Kennedy had done.

Johnson's own public statements attested to his assimilation of these ideas in his proposals for more activist government policies. In a commencement address at Swarthmore College, Johnson acknowledged fears that America was mired in an age dominated by the oversized organization in which the individual was "smothered by senseless urban sprawl, and enfeebled by the material gadgets of success." Yet he argued that Americans could rise above these problems if the federal government rewarded individual accomplishment through higher learning and the appreciation of excellence, including nourishing artistic talent in painting and sculpture. Johnson asserted that greater government involvement was not something to fear by contrasting big government to big corporations; "far from crushing the individual, government at its best liberates him from the enslaving forces of his environment. For as Thomas Jefferson said, 'the care of human life and happiness is the first and only legitimate object of good government.'"[11] Thus, the president poised himself to use government in combating what many had identified as an unhealthy conformity, materialism, and malaise in American society.

★ Continuing Arts Policy Measures

A number of advisers and government officials encouraged Johnson to move forward with arts policy as rapidly as possible. During the first days of his administration, Johnson received urgent letters from August Heckscher and Sen. Jacob Javits. Heckscher expressed concern that Johnson would neglect the arts legislation he had worked toward under Kennedy. Through Fortas, he urged the president to take up the standard for the arts.[12] Similarly,

Javits noted his past legislative progress on arts policy and the great care which had been taken under the Kennedy administration to organize a National Council on the Arts. "I feel that I bespeak the hope of many of my constituents . . . that you will shortly announce the appointment of the members of the President's Advisory Council on the Arts."[13] Johnson assistant Larry O'Brien replied that the president would give these concerns his full attention in the near future.[14]

In fact, Abe Fortas, Lucius Battle, Isaac Stern, and Pièrre Salinger were already reviewing the Heckscher report and deciding how to incorporate it into the new administration. After some debate, they left the report intact and forwarded it to Johnson along with a recommendation by Fortas to continue where Kennedy had left off. Subsequently, Bill Moyers sent a letter of thanks to Heckscher for his work on arts policy development and solicited his recommendations for presidential advisers on the arts. Although he had already submitted a letter of resignation to Kennedy, Heckscher agreed to maintain his post as special consultant on the arts until his successor was named; therefore, he was still affiliated with the Johnson White House.

Kennedy had planned to name Richard Goodwin as Heckscher's replacement. With the change of administration, however, Goodwin was dropped from consideration as Johnson sought his own man. Goodwin eventually became a prominent speech writer and special assistant to Johnson. For the post as special consultant on the arts, Johnson's longtime friend and legal consultant Abe Fortas suggested Roger Stevens, a prominent theater producer and real estate mogul. Stevens had already been appointed chair of the planned Kennedy Center as well, so Fortas considered him more acceptable to the arts establishment than another outsider. When it appeared that Stevens's appointment might be abandoned because of a news leak (a phenomenon that Johnson despised), Fortas wrote, "with fiddle in hand, I implore the President to appoint Roger. . . . It is absolutely right that he should also be Chairman of the Trustees of the Kennedy Center so that there can be centralized loyal and dedicated direction of the two institutions."[15] Stevens was officially appointed in April and, at his own request, worked without salary out of the Old Executive Office Building. His office had been slated to move elsewhere, but it remained where it was after Stevens argued successfully that such a move before arts legislation was passed might signal a lessening of interest by the president.[16]

In addition to recommending Stevens, Fortas also served as an arts patron for the White House. As a violin player and classical music devotee, he encouraged Johnson to continue the after-dinner entertainment that the Kennedys had so adroitly used to enhance their reputation as cultural sophisticates. Fortas had been involved in arranging the Casals concert in 1962 because of his acquaintance and support of both the musician and the evening's guest, Puerto Rican governor Muñoz Marín. Expanding on his role that evening, Fortas procured a list of musicians from Carnegie Hall's Julius Bloom and forwarded it to the Johnson White House for future recruitment purposes.[17]

Johnson's victory in the 1964 presidential election provided the support he needed for the ambitious legislative agenda that he wished to achieve. Unquestionably, the landslide that kept him in the White House was more than a fulfillment of his dreams. Johnson took over 61 percent of the vote, a more resounding victory than any other president had won in the twentieth century. Moreover, the widespread gains by Democratic Party candidates had Johnson presiding over a Congress that was overwhelmingly behind him. A month after the election, Johnson also recorded a 69 percent approval rate in the popularity polls.[18] Johnson basked in the glory of such overwhelming support and was satisfied that he now had the mandate he needed to proceed with his agenda.

A number of advisers, including Eric Goldman and Douglas Cater, suggested that Johnson invite prominent American and international artists to his inauguration, as Kennedy had in 1961.[19] Johnson resisted doing so on a large scale and quietly rejected a proposed reading at the ceremony by John Steinbeck. Instead, fifty artists were invited to a reception at the home of Roger Stevens. Thus, Johnson once again sidestepped direct comparisons to the cultured Kennedy administration while still endorsing the arts. He soon began to make more deliberate distinctions.

★ *The Great Society*

In what became a hallmark of his administration, Johnson pointed out that he was not an advocate for artists, per se, but for the people. He did not want to single out any group for distinction, but to use his office to elevate all Americans. President Johnson's populism manifested itself in the vast range of his policies, including the arts policy he eventually advocated; although his belief in consensus politics and anticommunism also influenced his actions.[20]

Johnson searched for a distinctive statement to characterize the goals of his administration. He set numerous advisers to work on the task, including

Theodore Sorensen, Abe Fortas, Richard Goodwin, and Eric Goldman, who ultimately coined the phrase Johnson would select to distinguish his presidency. According to Goldman, the writers wished to convey the idea that with the Johnson administration Americans were entering the new era of a post-affluent society—one that had overcome the problems of the 1950s and could see to the qualitative as well as quantitative needs of its citizens. Goodwin christened this vision of America "the Great Society." Johnson first employed the phrase in a speech at the University of Michigan, when he asserted that national wealth should be used to advance the qualities of American life beyond material well-being. The president affirmed, "The challenge of the next half-century is whether we have the wisdom to use that wealth to enrich and elevate our national life, and to advance the quality of our American civilization. . . . The Great Society . . . is a place where men are more concerned with the quality of their goals than the quantity of their goods."[21] Johnson presented his Great Society ideals for the advancement of American society to the entire country in his State of the Union address in 1965, pronouncing, "Today we can turn increased attention to the character of American life. . . . The Great Society asks not how much, but how good; not only how to create wealth, but how to use it; not only how fast we are going, but where we are headed."[22] At the heart of Johnson's vision lay a desire to uplift the general populace through an array of welfare-state legislation. He believed that the government could afford and should expand social programs to provide the best life possible for the most people. In his address, Johnson proposed to improve the quality of life in American society through a number of specific social programs designed to show action and unity. The president specifically announced his intention to form a National Endowment for the Arts to recognize and encourage those who could be "pathfinders for the nation's imagination and understanding."[23]

Johnson's leadership was essential to the passage of arts legislation. His proposals and tactics not only encompassed the Cold War concerns so central during the 1950s and the Kennedy era but also encouraged a marriage of arts issues with the national push for the human welfare of the Great Society. This approach struck a chord with Congress, which facilitated Johnson's efforts on behalf of the arts.

The president's personal lobbying also proved crucial. Johnson sent messages to congressional leaders and committees on the arts to urge the passage of art proposals and, more importantly, demonstrated his concern for the issues by referring his own versions of the arts bills to those committees for their consideration. He praised those congressmen who worked for the passage of art programs and invited them to special White House functions honoring the arts. Significantly, such functions were timed to coincide with the impending votes in Congress on legislation such as the 1965 National Foundation for the Arts and Humanities bill.

In contrast to Kennedy, Johnson had a wealth of experience in Congress, having spent twenty-four years learning the inner workings of the committee rooms and the floor. As a congressional leader and again as president, he kept fully abreast of Capitol Hill politics and asserted his influence on the members of Congress through friendship and arm-twisting to gain the passage of proposals he favored. He understood and expressed in no uncertain terms that the presidency was not only "a center of action and administration" but also, "perhaps more importantly, a wellspring of leadership."[24] Johnson used his leadership skills with Congress to secure a great variety of domestic policy proposals that historians agree another president might not have been able to win. Among these was the unprecedented passage of legislation to establish the National Foundation for the Arts and Humanities.

Johnson also succeeded because of his emphasis on pursuing policy proposals very early on in his administration. He operated under a belief that "[You've] got to give it all you can, that first year. . . . It doesn't matter what kind of majority you come in with. You've got just one year when they treat you right."[25] Political scientists have dubbed this the honeymoon period and contended that presidents' proposals are most accepted in Washington during the first months of the first term.[26] In accepting and employing this idea, Johnson was able to pass the most comprehensive package of legislation, outpacing even New Deal policies. He successfully obtained not only legislation that had been pending, such as the art foundation proposal, Medicare, and immigration reform, but a flurry of new bills such as the Civil Rights Act, a centerpiece of his Great Society.[27]

The common belief that America had entered a period of stability and growth enabled lawmakers to consider legislation that fiscal conservatives had traditionally called frivolous. In 1964, the economy showed gains in jobs, family income, and the GNP. The unemployment rate fell four-tenths of a percent to 5.25 percent, and inflation remained in check. Economic experts generally agreed that the United States had been experiencing a long-term bull market and that, despite temporary downturns, economic growth would continue.[28] Johnson believed, and helped to persuade the American public and Congress, that the nation's economic strength warranted the implementation of ambitious social programs.

Yet prosperity alone was an insufficient motivator. In contrast to the 1950s, when America experienced a booming economy but refused to legislate, arts policy became law in 1965 because of Johnson's desire to achieve it. The president pressed his views among influential figures on Capitol Hill, telling Speaker of the House John McCormack that although private initiative was important the arts were "also of vital concern to the federal government."[29] He also stressed that the government's role would be to "enlarge access of all our people to creation."[30] In keeping with the overall goal of the Great Society, Johnson's emphasis in arts policy was more on the general welfare of the public than of artists in particular.

Congressional supporters of arts legislation during the Johnson administration continued their struggle for the arts in an atmosphere of greater cooperation with the president. Moreover, they saw one of their own move into a prominent position of influence as Hubert Humphrey was selected as vice president. Humphrey not only took on the traditional vice presidential duties of presiding over the Senate but also actively promoted legislation in Congress.[31] Thus, the White House became a force for cultural policy with ever increasing influence on Capitol Hill.

As congressional art supporters worked more closely with allies in the administration, they remodeled their proposals to conform to the broader goals of Great Society legislation. Eventually, the foreign policy emphasis of the Kennedy administration receded.

The debate over arts policy reflected long-standing concerns, but also revealed new, important twists in the arguments over federal support for the arts. Economic feasibility, control, fostering excellence and democracy in American art, and the Cold War remained important concerns. Fiscal conservatives consistently raised objections but the economic boom, rising support for funding of the arts, and the matching grant proposals in the legislation eventually muted them. Similarly, the anticontrol provisions of the bills under consideration countered forebodings about government interference that may have arisen out of federal funding for the arts. Many congressmen agreed with Rep. Thomas Pelly (R-Wash.), who declared, "I support the underlying policy of this legislation: namely that the arts depend upon freedom and individual initiative. . . . I refer to the provision that . . . no department, agency, officer, or employee of the Federal Government shall exercise any control or direction over the policy of any group or State agency involved in the arts."[32] Such assertions were offered countless times throughout the legislative debates.

Significantly, the arguments demonstrating the freedom of artists and defining art as an expression of American democracy also contained pleas for the promotion of artistic "excellence." While this in itself was not unusual, the types of arts then defined as "excellent" revealed a certain bias on the part of legislators. Many of them endorsed the free development of a variety of arts, but their calls generally included support for symphony orchestras, ballet companies, classical theater, and opera companies. One art supporter went so far as to complain, "[It] is most unlikely that the works of Riley or Kipling . . . or even the 'Pennsylvania Polka' by Lawrence Welk could be heard above the din of ear-splitting toots and screeches that taunt youth with unbarbered manes to perform jungle gyrations, but America must plan beyond the generation-a-go-go. When young children are exposed to good music, poetry, and plays, the impression will carry through into adult life and bring a better appreciation of the arts."[33] A colleague countered him by questioning whether anyone in the government should "say that the patrons of the Beatles are any less the patrons of art than those culturally minded citizens who donate to the support of symphony orchestras."[34] Nevertheless, favoring of certain forms of art dominated discussions throughout the congressional records and in the presidential papers. This proclivity again demonstrates the arts supporters' powerful critique of mass culture and their belief that a nation arts institution should celebrate high culture. No small amount of irony underlines arguments calling for artistic freedom while at the same time promoting mostly elite forms of art. Later chapters will explore how difficult it became for the NEA to translate the freedom of expression guaranteed in the arts legislation into sincere promotion of all art forms, not just high art.

The Cold War struggle against communism also demanded consideration. Rep. Silvio Conte (R-Mass.) directed congressional attention to the link between the Cold War and the arts in no uncertain terms. "The cold war," he asserted, "is . . . an ideological war. . . . We must win men's minds. The encouragement which this proposal would provide in this area should perhaps be all the argument necessary in its behalf."[35] Such remarks attested to the continuing preoccupation with the Cold War that dominated congressional thought during the Kennedy presidency.

The new emphasis on domestic policy led legislators to frame their proposals in a different language. The rhetoric of the Great Society began to play a much larger role in congressional debates on the arts. Rep. William Fitts Ryan, for example, supported a national art foundation by asking, "[Are] not the arts, just as libraries and schools, necessary for the improvement of our way of life and for the development of the great society which President Johnson seeks for America?"[36] Rep. Philip Philbin (D-Mass.) later embraced this same emphasis when he avowed that the arts and humanities foundation would "provide the impetus for culture that must be the cornerstone of the Great Society."[37]

★ The Arts Joined with the Humanities

The proposal for an arts endowment gained momentum because it became more firmly linked to Johnson's effort to improve American educational institutions and increase congressional interest in American scholarship. In this new atmosphere proposals to fund the arts merged with efforts to support the humanities. Dillon Ripley of the Smithsonian (who would later struggle unsuccessfully with Stevens over control of the arts foundation) and Barnaby Keeney of Brown University (future chairman of the National Endowment for the Humanities) received widespread attention in the summer of 1964 with the publication of the Commission on Humanities report urging the establishment of a national humanities foundation. The first direct incorporation of the humanities into arts legislation came from the White House version of the arts bill presented to Congress on March 10, 1965, although internal memos suggest that the idea had already been under consideration for some time.[38] Johnson's statement accompanying the bill draft underlined his belief that the "pursuit of artistic achievement, and making the fruits of that achievement available to all its people is among the hallmarks of a Great Society."[39] Johnson found it easier to promote the arts not as an abstract concept but as part of a legislative package to enrich the minds of the American public. Combining the arts and humanities provided a means of linking the arts more directly to national education as well as securing greater support for the proposal in a Congress historically opposed to federal funds being used for the arts alone.

This inclusion of the humanities marked another departure from past arts proposals. The Eighty-Ninth Congress embraced Johnson's Great Society, especially its call for better and more balanced education in American society. Arts proponents then rationalized the need for the arts under the rubric of the general need for education. They did so both by proposing a dual arts and humanities foundation, thus directly linking the arts with liberal education, and by demonstrating the need for a balance between studies of science and studies of the arts and humanities.

Representative Ryan first introduced the initiative for a dual arts and humanities foundation during House debates over the National Council on the Arts bill. While calling for its passage, Ryan innovatively linked the arts proposal to the necessity of all education by advocating both an arts and humanities foundation and joining it to Johnson's Great Society package.[40] In time this issue gained greater strength and support.

Actually, education and culture advocates had tossed around the idea of creating a national humanities foundation for some time. In 1964 the American Council on Learned Societies published a widely read report recommending such a foundation. Senator William Moorhead (D-Pa.) and Rep. Ernest Gruening (D-Alaska) introduced legislation of this nature in the Senate and the House, respectively, at the opening of the Eighty-Ninth Congress's second session on January 4, 1965. Rep. Frank Horton (R-N.Y.) cited an "urgent need to discover human values" along with scientific research and development. His bill modeled the humanities foundation after the National Science Foundation created in 1950. In the following months, a host of other senators and representatives would join in Horton's cries for a redress of the imbalance between the sciences and the humanities. Horton demonstrated that the sciences, and the military in particular, got a great boost after the launch of *Sputnik* and were developed "to the point where we may now turn our attention . . . to defense of our beliefs and ideals."[41] He asserted that his bill for the humanities foundation would make that possible.

Seizing the opportunity to associate the arts proposals he had long sought after with the rising interest in education, Senator Javits reintroduced into the Senate a bill for the institution of a national foundation for the arts (S. 310). Meanwhile Senator Pell kept in touch with the White House about consideration for both arts and humanities proposals, and the Johnson Administration closely followed the debates on the Hill.[42] Pell then brought before the Senate dual bills: the National Arts Foundation Act of 1965 (S. 315) and the National Humanities Foundation Act of 1965 (S. 316). On the same day, Rep. John Fogarty (D-R.I.), with the support of Rep. Frank Thompson, introduced comparable bills into the House.[43] Arts supporters believed that the time was ripe for these bills in 1965, since the economy was booming, national defense had been bolstered, and the sciences were flourishing with the developments in the space program. It also became clear that the inclusion of the humanities would draw support that legislation for the arts alone had not garnered. Rep. Albert H. Quie (R-Minn.) was one among a number of congressmen who had previously opposed subsidy for the arts but favored support for the humanities. The combined bill significantly increased the numbers of those who were willing to vote for its passage.

Congressional arts advocates received a significant boost in March of 1965 when the Johnson administration submitted its own arts bill to Congress. The White House bill, like the Javits, Pell, and Thompson measures, called for the establishment of equal endowments for the arts and the humanities under the umbrella of one federal agency and rejected proposals for a humanities agency with the arts as merely one of its responsibilities.

The White House bill also included other elements that aided the progress of arts policy. First, taking a page from earlier versions of legislation that had been introduced in Congress during the Kennedy years, it called for private sector matching funds on an equal basis with government outlays. This requirement of outside moneys would essentially limit both the funds and any element of direct federal control over projects. Second, the bill called for a special program for the arts to be established within the Office of Education. Such an arrangement would help spread the arts to students in U.S. schools and was closely tied to Johnson's interest in expanding educational opportunities.[44] To ensure maximum publicity, Johnson also delayed submitting his bill to Congress until a day after a well-publicized crime measure dominated the press. With one stroke, this bill adeptly molded a number of longstanding debates into a stronger legislative measure that would overcome prior problems and garner widespread support. It breathed new life into ideas that had been languishing in Congress and gave them the powerful executive support needed to succeed.

Pell and Thompson immediately introduced the measure in the two congressional chambers for a final debate. Arguments in favor of the arts and humanities bill suggested that while the sciences had flourished in the Cold War era, as most believed they should have, the arts and humanities had been unduly neglected. Moreover, this imbalance would need to be corrected if the United States wished to become the leader of the free world in more than military and materialistic endeavors. Rep. Richard Fulton (D-Tenn.) proffered statistics demonstrating the rise in government funding for scientific research, revealing that fellowships given to the National Science Foundation had increased from 2,155 in 1960 to 8,040 in 1966. In fact, more than 70 percent of federal research funds went to the physical sciences, and nine times as many postdoctoral fellowships were available in the sciences as in the humanities.[45] In light of such evidence of where the U.S. government placed its emphasis in education, Rep. Adam Clayton Powell (D-N.Y.) groaned, "Socrates in 1965 would have ended up as a researcher at the National Institute of Mental Health."[46]

Having illustrated the significance attached by the federal government to science, congressmen then argued for similar treatment for the arts and humanities—endeavors they believed would heighten American cultural achievement and further demonstrate American ideals of freedom. According to Rep. Lloyd Meeds (D-Wash.), science would help us " 'get there' faster but we [would] ultimately fail for lack of having a meaningful place to go" should we neglect the spirit in favor of the material.[47] Such arguments progressed to demonstrate the increasingly dominant congressional belief that "democracy, freedom and man himself [depend] upon maintaining and developing the creative and imaginative abilities of mankind . . . to unite mankind and shape its destiny."[48] The arts and humanities together would be a potent force with which to temper unabashed power and rampant materialism.

Intellectuals and educators had been pressing this point since the mid-1950s. One of the more strident cries for redressing the imbalances between the sciences and the humanities came from the physicist, writer, and educator C. P. Snow, who argued that a gulf of misunderstanding existed between scientists and humanists that threatened intellectual life in the whole of western society if cooperation could not be reached.[49] Snow might well have been reacting to such extremists as George Tichenor of the Massachusetts Institute of Technology who had argued that study of the humanities "watered down" engineers' training and should be eliminated. Cultural critic William Whyte also took Tichenor to task.[50] Many intellectuals lamented the seeming rule that, as President Johnson put it, "somehow the scientists always seem to get the penthouse, while the arts and humanities get the basement."[51] By 1965, appeals to heal the cultural divide were gaining strength not only in academic circles but also in the federal government as efforts to establish funding for the arts and humanities mounted.

Support for increased attention to the humanities also came from many prominent American scientists. Glenn T. Seaborg of the Atomic Energy Commission testified before Congress that the nation's neglect of the humanities had fostered an excessive concentration on practical achievements. He argued that "because of this preoccupation with 'means' . . . areas of study concerned with 'ends' are beginning to suffer." Seaborg asserted that humanities fields should be supported by the federal government. In a similar manner, Leland J. Haworth of the National Science Foundation wrote to Senator Pell in favor of establishing an arts and humanities foundation, insisting that scientists would also benefit from the strengthening of teaching and research in the humanities.[52]

★ Arts Events at the Johnson White House

To demonstrate personal support for the arts, President Johnson held two major events at the White House during the spring and summer of 1965. In March, Johnson officially named Roger Stevens the first chair of the National Council on the Arts. Then on April 9, the first meeting of the Council took place in the Cabinet Room of the White House. President Johnson personally welcomed the Council members and presided over a swearing-in ceremony for them (fig. 3.1). Johnson then discussed arts policy with the group, cautioning them that the stakes of their endeavors could well be the "survival of our entire society" and urging them to contact their friends and representatives on Capitol Hill to support the arts legislation then pending in Congress.[53]

Later in June, while Congress debated the arts legislation, Johnson convened a Festival of the Arts at the White House to call attention to the arts measure. It became the pet project of Eric Goldman, who viewed it as an opportunity to enhance Johnson's relationship with American intellectuals. Goldman solicited art from museums to be displayed in and around the White House and invited a representative group of recognized artists in the fields of literature, music, dance, film, and the visual arts. In the midst of planning the affair, enthusiasm ran high among the White House cultural advisers for this national tribute to American culture.

The mood soon soured, however. On June 3, the *New York Times* published a letter from poet Robert Lowell to President Johnson rescinding what had been his initial and very public acceptance to attend the festival. Alluding to the war in Vietnam and the recent invasion of the Dominican Republic, Lowell described his fears that the United States was becoming chauvinistic and drifting closer to nuclear war. Although he expressed pleasure that Johnson was hosting an arts festival, Lowell concluded that "every serious artist knows that he cannot enjoy public celebration without making subtle public commitments. . . . I have decided that I am conscience-bound to refuse

3.1. *President Johnson swearing in the National Council on the Arts, April 9, 1965.*
(Photo courtesy of the Lyndon Baines Johnson Library)

your courteous invitation."[54] Johnson was livid. He ordered Goldman to simply acknowledge the letter without further comment.[55] Meanwhile, the president considered extending a trip to Texas to avoid returning in time for the festival.

The potential for a severe public rift between the president and the invited artists and intellectuals increased as others expressed their support for Lowell's position and maneuvered to provoke a response. Most notable among these were authors John Hersey and Dwight Macdonald, who contributed to the tensions on the day of the festival. Before the guests, including the first lady in a front-row seat, Hersey recited a powerful antiwar reading from *Hiroshima* in lieu of a representative piece of his literature. At the same time, Macdonald brazenly circulated a petition on which guests could indicate that their presence at the festival in no way repudiated Lowell's position, although he procured only six signatures.[56]

With all this continuing controversy, aides feared that their angry president might destroy his new relationship with American artists and intellectuals by lashing out against what he considered an affront to his hospitality. Johnson, however, refused to be so provoked and carried on with the festival as planned, although he did restrict media coverage. Despite full prior knowledge of Hersey's planned reading and Macdonald's intent to openly support Lowell and stir up trouble, Johnson did nothing to block their actions. Moreover, he prominently displayed paintings by artists who had also protested his Vietnam policies and refused to attend the festival, including Mark Rothko's *Ochre and Red on Red* and Peter Volkous's *5,000 Feet*.[57]

Throughout the event, Johnson and his staff maintained that their selection of artwork and of artists invited was not made with regard to political affiliations or opinions, which they believed were irrelevant to the goals of the occasion—honoring that which was noteworthy in American culture. To this end the White House was arranged in gallery style, with paintings borrowed from the nation's top museums hung throughout its halls and on nearly every wall surface, sculptures interspersed throughout the indoor and outdoor spaces, and stages erected in various rooms where live music and theater performances were held (figs. 3.2, 3.3, and 3.4). In his remarks at the festival, Johnson acknowledged, "art is not a political weapon. Yet much of what you do is political." Having expressed some dissatisfaction with dissenters, he continued on a conciliatory note, reaffirming his position on the separation of artistic achievement from political controversy. "Art flourishes most abundantly when it is fully free," he began and went on to assert that artists should always describe life as they saw it, without interference from public officials. Johnson concluded that "by honoring artists . . . we not only reflect, but we help to mold the values of this country. . . . American culture is a great achievement. But with it comes great responsibilities . . . to lift and to strengthen . . . a nation."[58] He argued that art was no frill and that American art was influential around the world. Thus, Johnson reiterated his belief that artists and exhibition of the arts at home and abroad should be upheld and also considered a serious means to express American achievements and freedom. In the end, those attending the White House Festival of the Arts had received the acknowledgement they came for and the potential for public discord was averted.

The *New York Times* proclaimed the next morning that the undercurrents of protest did not distract from the "proud celebration."[59] The newspaper

3.2. White House Festival of the Arts, June 1965: Mrs. Johnson and contralto Marian Anderson touring the art installations in the White House. (Photo courtesy of the Lyndon Baines Johnson Library)

also concluded that "by tolerating dissent within its own precincts, the White House raised its own and the nation's stature. For here was proof that democracy could practice what it preached."[60] Certainly, this was just the message that Johnson and the arts supporters in Congress wanted to express not only to the nation but to the entire world during the Cold War. The event concluded as a successful display of Johnson's interest in America's free and democratic culture.[61] However, it also foreshadowed rifts between artists and youth culture on the one hand and the nation's Cold War–era, consensus-generation politicians on the other that would deepen as the Vietnam war grew larger and more unpopular.

In addition to his concern for social and cultural policy, Johnson's legisla-

3.3. *White House Festival of the Arts: Mrs. Johnson and guests viewing paintings.*
(Photo courtesy of the Lyndon Baines Johnson Library)

tive ambitions contributed to the final passage of arts policy measures in
Congress in the fall of 1965. As he began the final push for this legislation,
Johnson swore that the establishment of the National Endowment for the
Arts and Humanities would be "one of the most historic enactments of
Congress in this century" and argued that it was time for the arts to be given
proper recognition and encouraged actively.[62] To achieve his goals, Johnson
employed his considerable political prowess. Contending that presidents accomplish the vast majority of their work within their first two years in office,
the president strove hard to achieve desired legislation as soon as he could.
Indeed, Johnson courted and cajoled Congress with all his persuasive powers
and achieved an unprecedented legislative record overall. He would apply his
skills to the arts bill during the fall of 1965.[63]

3.4. *White House Festival of the Arts: reception in temporary sculpture garden.*
(*Photo courtesy of the Lyndon Baines Johnson Library*)

Johnson pressed Congress to apply the twenty-one-day rule to the legislative package for the arts that had been mulling in Congress that summer (this
rule allowed the speaker of the house to call on a committee member who
had introduced the bill to call a vote after twenty-one days), thereby circumventing House Rules Committee Chairman Howard Smith (D-Va.), who had
the power and the desire to kill the bill.[64] After Smith stalled this bill and
others, President Johnson called Speaker John McCormack to invoke the rule
and call up the bill. Although only three bills were scheduled for action at that
late hour, Johnson insisted on adding the fourth for the NEA. Charles Mark,
assistant to special art consultant Roger Stevens, later recalled his belief that
without Johnson's support, "it is unlikely we would have had the arts program."[65] With Johnson's pressure the bill reached the House for debate on
September 15 and was passed on a voice vote before proceeding to the Senate
and passing there the following day.[66]

In a ceremony in the White House rose garden on a sunny September 29, 1965, President Johnson signed the bill into law before 278 invited guests, including future NEA chairs Roger Stevens, Livingston Biddle, and Nancy Hanks, policy supporters Abe Fortas and August Heckscher, the entire National Council on the Arts, over 100 members of Congress, and many artists, including Willem de Kooning, Ansel Adams, and Robert Rauschenberg. To the delight and surprise of much of the audience, Johnson added a dramatic flourish to the usual speeches and signatures by proposing to create prominent national institutions to showcase American art, including a National Repertory Theater, National Opera Company, National Ballet Company, and an American Film Institute. (Only the AFI actually came to be a part of the NEA agenda.) Yet in keeping with his own emphasis, he stressed the importance of federal partnership with the states and local governments, private institutions, and schools that would make the arts more accessible to the national public. Johnson spoke of the arts as an institution for the people but also a hallmark of American culture. "Art is our nation's most precious heritage," he asserted, "[for] it is in our works of art that we reveal to ourselves and to others the inner vision which guides us as a nation. And where there is no vision, people perish."[67] His words and signature that day established the vision of arts policy developed during the Kennedy administration and completed during his own—to promote artistic excellence and its appreciation among the American people, as well as, it was hoped, to illustrate American cultural success to the world.

II

★ ★

THE ENDOWMENT

Creating an Agency

The National Council on the Arts and Its Agenda

With increased leisure, and our widespread education, it is
imperative that the federal government support the arts more
actively, and provide leadership and resources to advance the
arts to a point where our national inner life may be continuously
expressed and defined. . . .

In a society which has always been marked by that special
disorder which comes of vast spaces, a highly diversified people,
great natural and technical resources, and a rapid tempo of
historical change, the arts are here of utmost importance—not only
as a moral force, but as a celebration of the American experience
which encourages, clarifies and points to the next direction in our
struggle to achieve the promise of our democracy. . . .

The Council is discussing many projects in the arts which can be
readily accomplished. . . .

The Council is convinced that the arts, at the highest level of
excellence, must become an enriching part of the daily life of the
American people.
—Policy Statement of the National Council on the Arts, 1966

★ ★

The inaugural policy statement of the National Council on the
Arts both reflected the NEA's ideological origins and foreshadowed future
developments. The Council's insistence that the national government provide leadership in the arts at a time of increasing leisure relied heavily upon
arguments from the Kennedy and Johnson administrations. In addition, calls
for mustering federal resources to advance the promise of American democracy echoed Great Society aims.[1]

The National Council on the Arts served as the NEA's administrative body
and was responsible for implementing the agency's mission by setting policy
and organizing program functions. The individuals appointed to the original
council proved crucial in creating an agenda for the NEA as a whole and for
the Visual Arts Program in particular. They determined whether federal

support for the visual arts set in place unnecessary bureaucracy, as many had feared it would, or whether it promoted free and democratic artistic expression, as its founders desired. Arts Council members struggled to translate abstract intellectual goals of achieving social uplift, expressing the benefits of American freedom and democracy, and increasing access to artistic excellence into tangible federal programs. Their faith in abstract aesthetics and their acceptance of 1950s consensus politics influenced the organization of the Visual Arts Program and its mission. The first Arts Council revealed that political and cultural leaders preferred to promote a distinctly modernist aesthetic vision.[2]

★ Background

The federal government had drafted bills for the establishment of an advisory council on the arts on numerous occasions during the twentieth century, with some of the most vigorous support for such a body coming from Senator Jacob Javits in the Congress of 1949. Nevertheless, none of the bills even reached the floor for debate until the early 1960s. During the Kennedy administration, Congress began to consider the arts with greater interest, although passage of national arts legislation was not immediately forthcoming. Realizing this legislative hesitancy yet hoping to secure a permanent basis for arts policy development, John F. Kennedy established the President's Advisory Council on the Arts by executive order in 1963. But while the Kennedy administration had discussed the Council's possible membership, no one had yet been appointed by the time of Kennedy's death in November of that year.

Like his predecessor, Lyndon Johnson sought congressional approval of, and thus a stronger mandate for, the Arts Council. For this reason, he hesitated to appoint its members at the beginning of his presidency. Congress debated and finally passed a bill approving the National Council on the Arts in August of 1964 (PL-579), marking the first time the federal government established a permanent body to promote the arts throughout the United States.[3] Meanwhile, Johnson reviewed and revised Kennedy's recommendations for Council membership. Ultimately, little differed between the two presidents' lists; yet Johnson took some time to name the Council's membership. True to his political nature, he announced the appointment of the advisory body's members on the very day congressional hearings opened on the national arts and humanities legislation; the president thus maneuvered to achieve maximum attention for his announcement while simultaneously expressing support for the arts foundation bill. Some arts administrators described the announcement in particularly dramatic fashion, recalling that the list of appointees was whisked into the congressional meeting room just as Senator Javits began urging that the White House move more quickly to appoint the Council.[4]

★ The Council

After the passage of the National Arts and Humanities Act in September of 1965, the Council became the administrative body for the newly formed National Endowment for the Arts and assumed responsibility for organizing and setting the agenda for the agency during its quarterly meetings. The chair of the Endowment also assumed leadership of the Council. On April 9, 1965, President Johnson swore in the first National Council on the Arts, and its members conducted their first meeting at the White House that weekend.[5]

The first Arts Council assembled an illustrious collection of prestigious artists representing multiple fields and art administrators from around the country who united to develop a federal arts policy. Special consultant to the president on the arts and acting NEA chair Roger Stevens served as the first NCA chair. Council members, who were appointed in staggered six-year terms, included prominent figures from all branches of the American art world (table 1). (See on-line Appendix 1 for a comprehensive list of Council members.) The prestige of its artist members made the first Council extraordinary, as did its mandate to create the new agency and set its mission and goals.

Authorizing legislation called for the National Council on the Arts to meet at least twice per year to conduct studies and make recommendations on methods by which "creative activity and high standards and increased opportunities in the arts may be encouraged and promoted in the best interests of the Nation's artistic and cultural progress, and a greater appreciation and enjoyment of the arts by our citizens can be encouraged and developed."[6] In this important section of the law, Congress set forth the Council's primary responsibilities as the promotion of both high standards for and public access to the arts. The Council incorporated these ideas directly into the NEA's mission statement and set out to determine how best to accomplish these goals.

From the beginning the Council established the practice of gathering four

TABLE 1. THE FIRST NATIONAL COUNCIL ON THE ARTS

Class of 1966

Elizabeth Ashley; actress; Los Angeles, Calif.

Agnes de Mille; choreographer; New York, N.Y.

Ralph Ellison; writer, lecturer, teacher; New York, N.Y.

Fr. Gilbert Hartke; clergyman, theatrical educator; Washington, D.C.

Eleanor Lambert; fashion designer; New York, N.Y.

Gregory Peck; actor; Los Angeles, Calif.

Otto Wittman; art museum director; Toledo, Ohio

Stanley Young; author, publisher, executive director of American National Theater
and Academy; New York, N.Y.

S. Dillon Ripley; secretary, Smithsonian Institution (ex-officio); Washington, D.C.

Class of 1968

Leonard Bernstein; composer, conductor; New York, N.Y.

Anthony A. Bliss; president, Metropolitan Opera; New York, N.Y.

David Brinkley; newscaster; Washington, D.C.

Warner Lawson; musician, educator; Washington, D.C.

William Pereira; architect; Los Angeles, Calif.

Richard Rodgers; composer, producer, writer; Southport, Conn.

David Smith; sculptor; Bolton Landing, N.Y.

James Johnson Sweeney; writer, museum director; Houston, Tex.

Class of 1970

Albert Bush-Brown; president, Rhode Island School of Design; Providence, R.I.

Paul Engle; poet, writer, teacher; Cedar Rapids, Iowa

R. Philip Hanes; president, Community Arts Council; Winston-Salem, N.C.

René d'Harnoncourt; director, Museum of Modern Art; New York, N.Y.

Oliver Smith; scenic designer, producer, painter; New York, N.Y.

Isaac Stern; musician; New York, N.Y.

George Stevens Sr.; film director; Los Angeles, Calif.

Minoru Yamasaki; architect; Seattle, Wash., and Detroit, Mich.

Source: "List of those commissioned for the National Council on the Arts,"
March 2, 1965, WHCF, FG 11–12/A, box 123, LBJ Library.

Note: David Smith was killed in a car accident in 1965, and David Brinkley resigned in
1966 because of pressing duties in broadcast news. Herman Kenin, president of the
American Federation of Musicians, replaced Smith; and John Steinbeck replaced
Brinkley. Painter Richard Diebenkorn joined the council in 1966.

times annually for intensive three-day sessions, then designating committees with assigned tasks to complete in the interim periods. After the first rendezvous at the White House, the Council convened frequently in closed meetings at an estate in Tarrytown, New York, owned by the Biddle family, who were long-time supporters of federal arts policy and whose descendant, Livingston Biddle, served as the NEA's first deputy chairman.[7] This location afforded members the atmosphere of a private retreat, in which they could freely discuss their ideas and avoid outside influence or criticism while conceptualizing the new arts endowment. Essentially, such privacy was meant to guard the NEA from political control and guarantee the aesthetic quality of its developing programs by leaving them in the hands of leading artists and fulfilling the legislative decree that no one in the federal government should exercise any "control, over the policy and program determination . . . in the arts."[8]

Over the course of meetings in 1965, the Council set the tone for future NEA policy. Taking their cue from the congressional mandate but embossing it with elements from Kennedy's and Johnson's plans, the Council established aesthetic excellence and audience enhancement as their foremost goals. First, experts from each artistic field on the Council, and eventually outside panels of expert consultants, would determine criteria for aesthetic excellence. Second, audience enhancement would be developed through complex systems of supporting artists and institutions of quality as well as finding new ways to increase the availability and visibility of their arts to the general public. To this end, the Council asserted that "the continuing and significant flowering of the arts in America today will depend largely on education."[9] It resolved to cooperate with the U.S. Office of Education and to study means of increasing students' exposure to the arts in schools. The Council also implied, however, that its vision of education encompassed more than what went on within school walls.

The Council perceived itself as leader of the federal effort to raise the level of American culture and enrich the lives of the American people. As its mission statement first attested, the Council considered the arts a moral force in an age of affluence.[10] Through promoting the appreciation of excellence in the arts, the NEA would be aiding the American public in making use of "knowledgeable leisure time" and thus participating in the "revitalization of [the] . . . national environment."[11] In essence, the Endowment would be carrying out both the Kennedy and the Johnson administrations' efforts to address what they and their intellectual advisers considered the overly materialistic and culturally underdeveloped nature of the mass public. The Council hoped to delineate specific means to achieve these ends.

During its opening meetings, the Council decided to concentrate its efforts on a few noticeable projects that it hoped would gain positive attention for the new federal arts agency and make the most out of its limited financial resources—$5 million for its first year. The first Endowment undertakings included a theater project, an emergency grant to the American Ballet, the development of an American Film Institute, and the establishment of its practice of granting funds to individual artists. Council members' initial ad hoc approach allowed them to experiment and analyze which types of programs would best achieve their goals.[12] And ultimately, their original actions and policy discussions emerged into established programs for the various art forms supported by the NEA.

★ The Visual Arts Contingent

The Visual Arts Program vividly illustrated the subtle biases in NEA policies. They were not in step with contemporary aesthetic developments but were actually more conservative.[13] Moreover, abstract visual arts had been used to represent American freedom of expression during the Cold War in the 1950s.[14] During the 1960s, leaders of the Arts Council and later of the Visual Arts Program carried over their older generation, art establishment and political notions about abstract expressionist and monumental art styles as the best in American culture. The backgrounds and aesthetic tastes of chair Roger Stevens and members René d'Harnoncourt, Oliver Smith, David Smith (until his death in 1965), Richard Hunt, and Richard Diebenkorn, along with frequent guest Robert Motherwell and the Visual Arts Program directors Henry Geldzahler and later Brian O'Doherty gave prestige to the Council and shaped its enduring preferences in arts policy.

These individuals' work and reputations in the field were critical in gaining President Kennedy's and Johnson's attention and contributed to their selection for Council membership in the first place. Their appointment, then, reveals much about the aesthetic preferences of the White House and the president's vision for visual arts administration. Once chosen for the Council these men set the tone for NEA Visual Arts Program development and artist and museum grant selection. In both respects their interests and influence in American modernist painting and sculpture were pivotal. "Modernism" and "excellence" were the ideals that united these cultural leaders and the political leaders who developed arts policy. These terms became the standard that enabled political and cultural ideology to be transformed into a tangible visual arts program.

It is also worth noting the styles and interests of those rejected for Council membership, as the exclusion of certain artists also factored into political leaders' visions for national cultural policy and exacerbated the marginalization of art outside the modernist high-art model. Kennedy administration recommendations for arts advisory council membership were initially more wide-ranging than the final form of the Arts Council would suggest. Original White House files on Arts Council appointment lists reveal that Kennedy had been considering the appointment of highly regarded artists Andrew Wyeth and Ben Shahn.[15] Both were primarily representational painters. Wyeth was best known for his figurative scenes and portraits and for being one of the best-known American painters who did not embrace the abstract style that dominated the American scene after the 1940s.[16] While this proved popular with much of the public who viewed his works, Wyeth was not considered a high-ranking master among art connoisseurs. (See Fig. 6.2 for examples of Wyeth's work.)

Likewise, Shahn, one of the notable social realist painters who gained attention during the 1930s for their figurative works, often depicted social scenes with an unmistakable political commentary.[17] His series *The Passion of Sacco and Vanzetti*, 1931–32, for example, presented sympathetic illustrations of the two executed anarchists in their coffins, implying a critique of the American legal system that condemned them.[18] Popular in the New Deal era, social realism began to be viewed suspiciously during and after World War II as Nazis and Soviets put this style to use for propaganda, and American anticommunism swelled.

The bulk of Kennedy's Arts Council considerations were abstract artists, however. Among those considered were Kennedy friend and abstract painter, Bill Walton, and the more widely known Philip Guston of the abstract expressionist school.[19] Guston's interest lay in working with color in geometric shapes, exploring coloration, and painting multiple conflicting shapes and studies of their relation to the space and shape of the canvas. His 1956 painting *Dial* presents one example of Guston's explorations of geometric shapes of color in abstract design—with thick, splotchy rectangles of red, pink, black, green, and blue forming a larger rectangular shape at the center of the canvas. This style placed him firmly within the abstract expressionists interests in formalism.[20]

Foremost on Kennedy's list of potential Arts Council members were sculptor David Smith and painter Richard Diebenkorn. Smith had first been tapped as a possible member of Mrs. Kennedy's White House Commission on Fine Arts. Though he did not work at the White House, his philosophy of art and politics corresponded with Kennedy's, as Smith claimed, "progress in art, progress by society, one accompanies the other and both are decried by Babbitt reactionaries. The government needs to . . . [create] a ministry of fine arts."[21] Ultimately, both Smith and Diebenkorn became members of the first Arts Council.[22]

Under President Johnson, Kennedy's final list remained the basis of Arts Council appointments, and the contours of the Kennedy vision were also maintained. The Kennedy list suggested a preference for abstract artists as visual art delegates to the Council, even though consideration of representational painters offered the potential for more balance among painting genres. This possibility declined as the Johnson administration reconfigured the list of potential Arts Council members.

Johnson administration lists included some of the most recognized abstract artists in American painting.[23] Among them was Willem de Kooning, whose work contained some figuration, as seen in his "Woman" paintings, which presented variations of female figures as sex symbols, fertility goddesses, and threatening or caricatured forms (see figs. 4.1 and 3.2).[24] Even among these paintings the abstract expressionist mode of vigorous brush strokes, layers of color, and abstract designs were prominent. And many of de Kooning's other works were even more abstract.

Abstract painters Helen Frankenthaler and Robert Motherwell (then husband and wife) were also featured on the Johnson Arts Council appointment list. Frankenthaler's work retained a clear focus on abstract color and design, exhibiting few of the gestural tendencies of earlier abstract expressionists. Frankenthaler applied multiple layers of thin paint washes to her canvases, usually with a central design motif. This technique identified her as a transitional figure between the original abstract expressionists and the later color-field painters.[25] Although not initially chosen for Arts Council membership, she eventually served on the Council in 1984.[26]

Motherwell, for his part, mixed gestural tendencies with color-field painting, as some of his paintings contained gestural lines and splotches of paint while others featured stains and layers of color. His work in the "elegies" series, which included *Elegy to the Spanish Republic #70* (fig. 4.2), featured large, oblong shapes on vertical, rectangular canvases.[27] Despite his eventual

4.1. *Willem De Kooning,* Two Women in the Country, *1954. (© 2002 Willem de Kooning Revocable Trust/Artists Rights Society [ARS], New York; Hirshhorn Museum and Sculpture Garden, Smithsonian Institution, Gift of Joseph H. Hirshhorn, 1966 [66.1200])*

elimination from consideration for Council membership, Motherwell maintained a close relationship with his best friend David Smith and other Council members as well as with NEA chair Roger Stevens. Motherwell was among the first to testify before Congress on behalf of the legislation formulating the National Endowment for the Arts and Humanities and staunchly argued that artists should administer cultural institutions. Motherwell believed modern art had an important place in society, because art was not an abstract concept but a concrete means to express human contact and to depict feelings univer-

4.2. *Robert Motherwell,* Elegy to the Spanish Republic #70, *1961.*
(© Dedalus Foundation, Inc./Licensed by VAGA, New York, N.Y.;
Metropolitan Museum of Art, anonymous gift, 1965 [65.247])

sal to modern man.[28] He donated the first artwork to the offices of the NEA to enhance its aesthetics and aura of distinction as an arts agency. Thus, Motherwell remained an important influence on the visual arts aspects of the NEA in its nascent stages.[29] He eventually was appointed as a special adviser to the Arts Council in 1969.[30]

Clearly, Johnson's appointments reflected a preponderance of American modernist painters, with abstract expressionists dominating the list. Johnson also demonstrated an interest in abstract sculpture. In addition to those nominated for Council membership during the Kennedy years, Johnson considered sculptor Richard Hunt. Although not enlisted for the first Council, Hunt joined in 1968. He studied at the School of the Art Institute of Chicago and later taught there and at the University of Illinois at Chicago, the Chouinard Art Institute in Los Angeles, and Northwestern University. In 1958 his works were displayed in a one-man show in New York, where they drew a great deal of attention. Hunt's sculptures, like David Smith's, were metallic abstractions. Hunt demonstrated an interest in prefabricated and often discarded materials that he welded into new artistic forms, thus combining

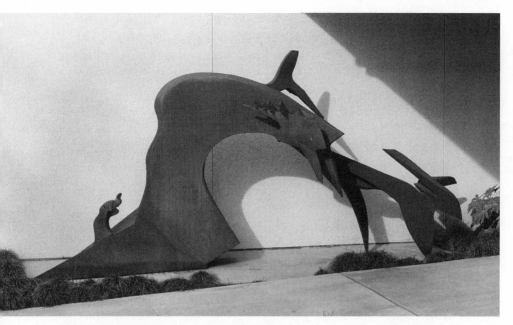

4.3. *Richard Howard Hunt,* Extended Forms, *1975. (Art © Richard Hunt; courtesy New Leaf Gallery/Sculpturesite.com, Los Angeles County Museum of Art, purchased with funds provided by the Ahmanson Foundation, the League of Allied Arts, the Charles R. Drew Medical Society Auxiliary, and the Los Angeles Chapter of Links, Inc.; photo © 2000 Museum Associates/LACMA [M.80.24])*

metalworking with industrial technology. Hunt liked to compose mixtures of opposites from "the organic and the geometric, the organic and the abstract . . . the traditional and the contemporary." His sculpture *Extended Forms* (1975) contrasts geometric lines and volume at the base with a curvilinear abstract shape arching up and over into several jutting points and curvilinear shapes (fig. 4.3).[31] An organic figure climbing up the pyramid base heightens the contrast between soft, organic motion and firm, abstract structure. The piece was also situated outdoors to draw upon natural surroundings and light to extend its effect even further.[32] Hunt shared much of his abstract aesthetic with other Arts Council nominees.

Hunt was also one of the first (and few) African American Arts Council nominees, and Hunt's selection reflected Johnson's interest in achieving a fair race and gender balance among Council appointees. Thus, the president's vision of the NEA paralleled other respects of his Great Society. Johnson worked within accepted parameters (including aesthetic ones in the case of the arts), however, he pressed for advances in what he hoped to accomplish. Johnson remained committed to Cold War politics and militarism but also moved toward civil rights and elevated social policy. His Council appointments reflected these multiple agendas.[33]

One important figure originally considered for Arts Council membership but then dropped was art critic and writer Susan Sontag. Sontag's appointment would have helped to remedy the low representation of women on the Council. She accepted modernism as well as newer avant-garde and popular arts and appreciated the interplay between multiple aesthetics and interpretations, and thus could have expanded the aesthetic sensibilities of the Council.[34] Nevertheless, an FBI background check revealed her vehement opposition to the Johnson administration's escalation of the Vietnam war.[35] Although her aesthetics were not consistent with the modernist makeup of the Council preferred by the president, and presumably that could have been reason enough for her exclusion, that argument did not hold true for Henry Geldzahler, who also displayed interests in contemporary art and was selected as the first Visual Arts Program director at the NEA. Therefore, it seems that political factors counted more than Johnson would have liked to admit.

After a long period of consideration extending through the Kennedy and early Johnson administrations, the original NCA leaders were selected. Not surprisingly, they represented a modernist aesthetic typical of that which had dominated the art world during the late 1950s and early 1960s, when most Council members had achieved prominence in their respective fields and gained the attention of the White House for their endeavors. Selected as representatives of artistic excellence, they were to serve as role models and use their expertise to construct a federal arts program designed to promote artistic achievement and foster art appreciation—with the hopes that these ends would raise the level of American culture and illustrate its accomplishments to the world. Council members' aesthetic sensibilities and their acceptance of this broadly defined mission would ultimately influence their development of the Visual Arts Program and the distribution of grants.

As the first visual arts representative on the National Council of the Arts, René d'Harnoncourt was a critical figure. Born in Vienna, Austria, Count d'Harnoncourt came from a French aristocratic family. He became interested in painting and art collecting as a teenager but went to college to study chemical engineering. In 1924 he was forced to leave school when his inheritance was expropriated by Czechoslovakia following the dissolution of the Austro-Hungarian Empire.

The following year d'Harnoncourt moved to Mexico and supported himself as an artist and antique collector. He soon received a commission from the Mexican government to collect and lecture on folk art. In this capacity he met the American ambassador to Mexico, Dwight Morrow, who suggested him to the American Federation of Arts and the Carnegie Foundation to prepare an exhibition of Mexican fine art to be shown at New York's Metropolitan Museum of Art in 1930. Two years later, d'Harnoncourt applied for American citizenship and took posts as art historian and lecturer at Sarah Lawrence College and the New School for Social Research.

Beginning his affiliations with the U.S. government in 1938, d'Harnoncourt became general manager for the Indian Arts and Crafts Board of the U.S. Department of the Interior, promoting the work of Native American artists. Later, in 1943, he served as the acting director of the arts section of the office of the coordinator of inter-American affairs, and he helped organize exhibition exchanges throughout South America. D'Harnoncourt also worked on the Advisory Committee on Art of the Department of State, and, in 1946, as a senior counselor of visual arts for the United Nations Educational, Scientific, and Cultural Organization (UNESCO). Thus, his travels and international interests became intertwined with the growth of U.S. government forays into arts exhibition and promotion in the international arena during the late 1940s and 1950s.

While he remained affiliated with U.S. government and international arts exchanges, d'Harnoncourt moved into a position as the director of the Museum of Modern Art's Department of Manual Industries, where he oversaw a study of the potential contribution of manual industry to the world. Simultaneously, he took charge of MOMA's foreign affairs activities and, with the encouragement of Nelson Rockefeller, devoted attention to expanding the museum's participation in touring exhibitions of American art to Central and South America.[36]

D'Harnoncourt achieved prominence rapidly at MOMA. Two years after joining its staff, he became the director of curatorial departments and in another two years was elected director of the museum as a whole.[37] At the time of his appointment to the National Council on the Arts, he was serving as the head of an art institution containing what is considered one of the most comprehensive collections of twentieth-century art in the world. The museum also operated with an ongoing directive to collect modern works by the most important contemporary masters. D'Harnoncourt's distinguished career, demonstrated preference for modernist art, and past affiliation with the federal government's promotion of American arts made him a clear choice for Council leadership.

Like d'Harnoncourt, Henry Geldzahler also came to the Council as a museum curator and contemporary art aficionado with an interest in federal government art sponsorship; he also had a personal connection to international affairs. Geldzahler shared a European background with d'Harnoncourt. He was born in Antwerp, Belgium, but immigrated to New York as a young child when his Jewish family fled the German invasion of Belgium in 1940. Geldzahler decided on a career in art collecting while in high school when he viewed an Arshile Gorky show at the Whitney Museum. He recalled that after the exhibit, "I came home and threw up, then slept for eighteen hours. I was completely knocked out, and that's when I first realized that art could be that moving."[38] Two years later he began studies in art history at Yale. While in college, Geldzahler volunteered at the Metropolitan Museum of Art then spent a year abroad at the Sorbonne's Institut d'Art et d'Archéologie and at the École du Louvre in Paris. In 1957 he began graduate studies at Harvard but left his Ph.D. program to accept a job as curatorial assistant in contemporary art at the Metropolitan Museum.[39]

Geldzahler's career at the Met would prove both accomplished and controversial. Geldzahler spent his first two years frequenting artists' studios, galleries, and "happenings" in New York to identify current trends in American art and suggest purchases for the Met. While this nontraditional approach marked him as a maverick, Geldzahler believed he was still working from a background in classical training. He explained, "I was associated with the avant-garde, but . . . had a strong background in art history and could relate whatever I was seeing to traditional art . . . [and could] legitimize . . . things that freaked a lot of people out," describing his defense of purchase proposals to more conservative museum directors at the Met.[40]

In his position at the Met, Geldzahler consistently promoted modernist, abstract, and pop artists and aided in the rise of contemporary artists such as Jules Olitski, Kenneth Noland, James Rosenquist (who would eventually serve on the Arts Council in 1978), Roy Lichtenstein, Frank Stella, Claes Oldenburg, and Jasper Johns. Soon after joining the Council, he praised Helen Frankenthaler's painting in an *Artforum* interview.[41] Geldzahler himself participated in several Oldenburg "happenings" and became the subject of an Andy Warhol film that featured him smoking a cigar for ninety minutes. Ultimately, Geldzahler concluded that pop was "interesting" but not a major movement. On the other hand, he remained committed to what he considered more timeless and generative movements, such as abstract expressionism, color-field art, and monumental sculpture.[42]

In a 1969 *Newsweek* interview, Geldzahler defended his choices of abstract expressionists for special consideration in his exhibition, asserting their noteworthiness because "no period, not even the Renaissance, has ever had forty-three major artists." Geldzahler's argument placed him firmly in the company of established American art critics and museum directors, yet he drew criticism from some reviewers who assailed his selections. *New York* magazine critic Barbara Goldsmith claimed that the show was "simply Geldzahler's choice, and he could have called it 'Painters I Like.'" *Newsday* magazine dismissed it as a predictable assemblage compiled by Geldzahler and his "coterie of taste-and-value-makers."[43] Unmoved by such criticism, Geldzahler securely maintained his position, considering the show a resounding success. However, his personal conviction and controversial action in promoting his vision of modern art eventually led to his departure from the Metropolitan Museum. This occurred after he participated in a secret trade of six paintings by Modigliani, Bonnard, Juan Grises, Picasso, and Renoir for two contemporary works by David Smith and Richard Diebenkorn. (Interestingly, both were members of the National Council on the Arts along with Geldzahler.) In addition, Geldzahler was further isolated from other Met officials after he refused to organize what later became a highly popular Andrew Wyeth exhibit. He left in 1977 to become the New York City cultural affairs commissioner.

Geldzahler's quick rise to prominence at the Metropolitan Museum, recognized influence as a contemporary art curator, and well-known defense of those he considered the best representatives of modern American art gained him notice as a confident voice in the field of visual arts. This earned him a position on the National Council on the Arts, where he worked with other prominent museum directors and proponents of modern art.

The new Arts Council also relied on the talents of Broadway scenic designer and theater producer Oliver Smith, one of the more prolific and innovative theater figures of his time. Smith began his career as a student of architecture at Pennsylvania State University and a painter whose works were shown at such places as MOMA, the Chicago Art Institute, and Yale.

After moving to New York, Smith joined the Scenic Designers Union and began designing sets. His first professional sets were for the Ballet Russe de Monte Carlo's production of Massine's *Saratoga* and Agnes de Mille's *Rodeo*. (De Mille and Smith later served together on the NCA.) In 1945, Smith also began a long codirectorship (with Lucia Chase) of the American Ballet Theater while continuing to design decor for numerous ballets, operettas, and musicals. Among his most notable scenic designs were those he created on Broadway for *Miss Liberty* (1949), *Paint Your Wagon* (1952), *Will Success Spoil Rock Hunter?* (1955), and *The Sound of Music* (1959). His sets for *My Fair Lady* won him an Antoinette Perry (Tony) Award in 1956.[44]

Smith considered himself a designer who blended painting with architecture, mediums for which he believed he possessed a natural affinity. He enjoyed the abstract quality of the architectural drawings he used to create sets and generally used these types of drawings rather than scene sketches. Yet he felt that due to its collaborative essence, scenic design could not "reach the intensity of a painting."[45] His interest in painting clearly influenced his style, as evident in a 1946 *Theater Arts* review: Smith's work "reflects a painter's understanding of how to use bright colors against shades . . . and of how to outline theatrical space with delicate clear lines . . . within a convention that is especially suited to music-drama and to ballet."[46] The reviewer's comments on color, line, and outline in Smith's scenic designs echo painterly interests and the language associated with abstract art. Smith's involvement in theater thus reveals a close affiliation not only with Broadway theater production but also to modern art. These interests coincided with those of National Council on the Arts and NEA chair Roger Stevens, who was also a Broadway theater producer, as well as with those of Council members affiliated with American abstract painting and sculpture through museum and artistic careers.

At the time of his appointment to the Council, David Smith had achieved worldwide success as a sculptor. He began as a student of painting at the New York Art Students League, where he became heavily influenced by Picasso's surrealist painting and occasional metal sculpture. During the 1930s Smith produced a series of figurative, realist paintings and sculptures. He also painted with Stuart Davis and began to study abstraction and to experiment with constructed sculpture.

His early studies gave way to increasingly abstract forms for which Smith received acclaim in the 1950s. He perfected his welding and metalwork techniques first at an automobile factory then at a locomotive factory job during World War II and became convinced that metal was the best material to symbolize the twentieth century and industrialism. Strikingly, steel work was also emblematic of American power and hegemony in modern times. Smith emerged from the 1940s with a greater interest in large, monumental works and embarked upon what would be a career-long fascination with metal sculpture, particularly iron and steel, which he considered "beautiful because

4.4. *David Smith*, Cubi XII, *1963. (Art © Estate of David Smith/Licensed by VAGA, New York, N.Y.; Hirshhorn Museum and Sculpture Garden, Smithsonian Institution, Gift of the Joseph H. Hirshhorn Foundation, 1972 [72.268])*

of all its strengths and functions."[47] Smith constructed his modernist works in a linear mode, often producing series of sculptures focused on line and form modifications.[48] An example of his style may be seen in *Cubi XII*, 1963, one of a series of variations on cube and linear constructions in stainless steel (fig. 4.4).

Smith was highly regarded by the art world. Indeed, Clement Greenberg considered Smith "the best sculptor of his generation" and called the *Cubi* series "the very essence of what . . . [monumental] truly means."[49] Smith saw major exhibitions of his work shown around the United States and internationally, most notably in a MOMA retrospective in 1957 and at the Venice and Sao Paulo Biennales of 1954, 1958, and 1959. Thus, his painting was already quite familiar to Council members d'Harnoncourt and Geldzahler through their New York museum careers.

Smith's ideology also made him an attractive choice for the Arts Council. He considered the monumental American painting and sculpture of his time the "most important in the world." He asserted, "Present day contemporary America is producing masterpieces. Art . . . is created by man's imagination in relation to his time. I feel raw freedom and my own identity. . . . The freedom of man's mind to celebrate his own feeling by a work of art parallels his social revolt from bondage."[50] Smith's expression of individual freedom in American abstract art agreed with a sentiment common to many in both cultural and political arenas in the 1950s and early 1960s who believed abstract painting and sculpture were universally important and expressed freedom in the postwar age. Smith also shared with culture brokers, as well as with Kennedy and Johnson administration officials, a strong belief in the importance of federal sponsorship of the arts and increased public arts education. He argued on many occasions that "[there] should be a state project to encourage the production of art of all kinds, and the best of its kind. The public can be helped to understand it through an aggressive program of popularization."[51] Clearly, not only Smith's artistic reputation but also his expression of similar ideology to arts policy organizers placed him in an influential position as the first practicing visual artist selected to the National Council on the Arts.

After Smith's sudden and premature death, Richard Diebenkorn joined the Council in 1966, essentially serving as a visual arts replacement for the late Smith. Diebenkorn also represented the West Coast arts community. He began his career painting in the abstract expressionist style he learned from Mark Rothko and Clyfford Still at the California School of Fine Arts, where he studied in 1946 and later joined the faculty in 1948 after attending Stanford and the University of California at Berkeley. Like others of his generation, Diebenkorn was interested in aesthetic formalism and in exploring fields of color and geometric design in relation to the flatness and rectangular shape of the canvas. In the mid-1950s, he shifted from pure abstraction to figurative painting containing images of people in representational settings; even so, he

4.5. *Richard Diebenkorn,* Berkeley No. 22, *1954. (Courtesy Estate of
Richard Diebenkorn; Hirshhorn Museum and Sculpture Garden,
Smithsonian Institution, Regents Collections Acquisition Program, 1986 [86.5886])*

maintained his explorations of formal lines and color in the structure of the
work, subordinating the figuration in his painting to the overall abstract
construction of the piece.[52] At nearly the same time he was appointed to serve
on the National Council on the Arts, Diebenkorn had returned to painting
abstract series, which he found most "free" since they liberated both painter
and viewer from the weight of association normally carried by representational pieces. (For an example of Diebenkorn's work, his *Berkeley No. 22,* see
fig. 4.5.) The large canvas and abstract designs of his work in many ways
paralleled in painting the same modernist style David Smith had constructed
in sculpture. On the whole, Diebenkorn worked within the abstract expres-

sionist tradition that most critics considered the finest of American art during the 1950s and 1960s and that the visual arts representatives on the Council favored.

Clearly, the visual arts representatives chosen for the National Council on the Arts reflected the dominant aesthetic preference of the political and cultural leaders formulating the NEA's administrative body. Abstract expressionists predominated because they were thought to best represent not only aesthetic excellence but also the free expression symbolic of American society, especially during the Cold War. Those few artists and museum leaders known to prefer representational or emerging pop and postmodern sensibilities were considered only briefly then passed over for Council membership. Moreover, folk artists and craftspeople were never even considered. The original Council, and its replacement members in following years, demonstrated a distinctly modernist and abstractionist orientation in the fields of painting and sculpture. Unquestionably, they carried such aesthetic taste into their discussions as NEA Council members and were consciously and unconsciously governed by them while developing the policies and structures of NEA visual arts administration.

★ *Visual Arts Policy and Program Development*

The Arts Council determined during its first meetings that individual departments would be developed for each major art form—with support for painting, sculpture, and the purchase of modern American art by museums administered under a Visual Arts Program. This program was officially organized by 1967 under the direction of Henry Geldzahler. Before establishing the now-familiar structure of grant applications and peer panel reviews, the Council itself had a great deal of influence over art grants. Members determined the parameters of all artistic endeavors they would or would not fund and solicited applications from artists and organizations they considered worthy of support. Indeed, during the first year it was possible for artists to be considered for money for which they had not applied. Yet the number of applications that began to pour in soon overwhelmed the Council, obliging them to formalize a method to deal with the work load.

During their second meeting, the Council reviewed legislation that authorized the NEA to convene panels of experts from time to time to aid them in selecting the most qualified artists for recognition and concluded that this method should become standardized. Motherwell had argued in his pleas for government support that artists' agency was crucial to determining aesthetic excellence, because critics or civil servants were removed from artistic creation and unqualified to judge it.[53] Others shared his view. D'Harnoncourt advocated most strongly for expert panels, which he believed would aid the Council in selecting only artists of the highest quality.[54] By 1967 the peer panels were firmly in place—with Council members recommending experts in their fields to the NEA chair for approval. Panel members met to review grant applications then submitted their list of recommended grantees for approval up the line to the program, the Council, and, ultimately, the NEA chair. Again, visual arts Council members exerted a significant influence over the selection of panelists, thus ensuring a consistent standard of taste through each level of the Visual Arts Program.[55] (More detail on the panelists and their work appear in Chapter 5.)

The Council's first consideration of the shape the Visual Arts Program was to take occurred during the spring of 1966 in subcommittee meetings, results of which were later presented to the general Council by d'Harnoncourt, Geldzahler, Diebenkorn, and guest participant Robert Motherwell. As it was originally conceived the Visual Arts Program—concentrating on painting, sculpture, and photography—was to put into practice the NEA's overarching mission to recognize individual achievement and disseminate knowledge and opportunities to enjoy the arts. This was done in a number of specific ways.

First and most important, Richard Diebenkorn proposed direct assistance to individual artists in the form of grants that would encourage them to advance their work.[56] These grants were not to be allocated to commission a specifically proposed art piece but were to be given to the artists to use as they saw fit—whether it be the production of new work or time off to travel or study. The point was to honor artists and to allow them to pursue their work free from fears of government control. The Council felt that individual artist support was best administered on a national level and held such promise that it should be expanded indefinitely as funds allowed. The first official grants to individual painters and sculptors were awarded in 1967, while photographers received funds at a later date. (The nature of these grants will be analyzed in the following chapter.)

Additional grants were provided to artists through other program activities. As part of the Council's overarching educational plans, some artists were given funds to provide for sabbaticals from their regular work so they could take up residence in schools where they worked and taught students through personal example and classes. This fulfilled the NEA's didactic goals "to increase awareness of the visual arts and instill knowledgeable leisure time . . . in the new generation, future citizens in our great society."[57]

Artists also benefited indirectly from a number of short-term grants awarded by the Council. First, members authorized a study of new materials for artwork, particularly sculpture, and made it available to artists. The Council also commissioned an analysis of artists' legal rights and a larger review of community art resources so that they could assess the needs of state agencies and museums for exhibitions, touring, and cooperating with educational institutions in their areas. In addition, the Council instituted a project in conjunction with the J. Kaplan Fund of New York that provided a matching grant to develop housing and studio space in Manhattan where artists could live and work in a cooperative atmosphere.

The Council also approved a museum purchase plan, which granted funds to museums to buy works by living American artists; it supported print and drawing workshops to reproduce modern artwork and distribute it to smaller museums and schools. To publicize and attract participants in the developmental stages of the museum purchase program the NEA mailed applications to museums around the country inviting them to apply for funding.[58] These grants sought both to funnel money to contemporary American artists and to encourage the display of modern artwork—called "didactic materials"—to more of the American public.[59] One Council member asserted that this was essential as "one of the ways to build up an audience for contemporary art is to improve the level and taste and standards of the American public."[60]

Indeed, disseminating slides or prints to schools and museums would aid in the aesthetic education of more Americans and could provide the "key to mass art appreciation" and cultural education.[61] Just what kind of an education the Council aimed to provide can be seen in the final form of the approved reproductions. Among those whose work was considered acceptable were such modern artists as Robert Motherwell, Willem de Kooning, Louise Nevelson, Helen Frankenthaler, and Philip Guston. At a later meeting some finished prints by Joseph Albers, Jasper Johns, and Robert Rauschenberg were provided to the Council.[62] Although the inclusion of Johns and Rauschenberg indicates that the Council supported a few figurative pop artists, the preference for modernist abstract art was clear from the collection of approved prints. This aesthetic preference also applied to the panel selection for the museum purchases, as the following museum panel leaders were chosen to select the 1967 grants: Walter Hopps of the Washington, D.C.,

Gallery of Modern Art, Jan van der Marck of the Chicago Museum of Contemporary Art, and Maurice Tuchman of the Los Angeles County Museum of Art.[63] Leaders on the Council and those chosen for the museum program pursued the idealized goal of public education, but they were no doubt also aware of the potential financial benefits and increased status for modernist artists and museum officials whose work would be celebrated.

In addition to expanding museum and school art and art slide collections, the Council considered other proposals to create more widespread viewing opportunities of modern art, including an "artmobile" and support for international exhibitions. The artmobile was designed to utilize several railroad cars set up as a mobile museum that could reach areas lacking museum facilities of their own. Council member James Sweeney argued that the "artmobile [would be] good for didactic ends . . . bringing real contemporary production, actual works of art, to people throughout the country." His idea elicited a resounding second from d'Harnoncourt.[64] It would both showcase aesthetic achievement and realize the NEA's (and Great Society's) goal of promoting more democratic access to the arts. Artrain was eventually founded in 1971 by the Michigan Council for the Arts and was touring around the United States by the mid-1970s with support from the NEA.

The Council had more ambitious ideas as well. Members carried on initial discussions of international exhibition support to fund both foreign artists' shows in the United States and the exhibition of American painting abroad. The first proposal was rejected because it would not support American artists. The second proved more difficult for members to dismiss. Council Chair Roger Stevens felt that sending American painting and sculpture abroad would not only support American art but also build the prestige of American culture worldwide. His attitude echoed that of American political leaders who had advocated art programs as a Cold War–era necessity and considered the touring of contemporary American art a demonstration of the United States' cultural freedom and achievement. D'Harnoncourt approved of the application of this idea through NEA funding for an exhibition of American artwork at the 1966 Venice International Biennale. Council member and MOMA curator Geldzahler took charge of selecting the artists to represent the United States, choosing modern abstract artists Helen Frankenthaler, Jules Olitski, and Ellsworth Kelly and pop artist Roy Lichtenstein. The Council approved $38,000 in funding for this exhibition.[65] This would be its only grant to such an international project, however. The Council then established a long-term policy of rejecting the funding of international exhibits by the

NEA because it did not wish to duplicate the efforts already underway by the State Department and USIA, both of which had been funding international touring of American art in the postwar period. Council members believed that bypassing support of international exhibits would not signal their rejection of these endeavors since they provided expert consultation for the projects. Such action would also allow the Council to reserve limited finances for other projects not yet under way.[66]

In a telling move, Council members also rejected a proposal from the National Folk Art Association for support of its festivals. The Council insisted that it did not have sufficient information about the group's plans to give it fair consideration, although records document a steady correspondence about the subject from the association's leader Sarah Knott to NEA Chair Roger Stevens, the Council, and even President Johnson.[67] The Council's discussion revealed that members were baffled by the idea of funding the folk arts and even had difficulty defining them sufficiently, indicating that little if any thought had been given to the genre. Even René d'Harnoncourt, who, ironically, had begun his career as a folk art collector in Mexico, seemed more intent on advancing the well-established high art forms with which the Council members were most familiar. Folk art was not in their area of expertise, and they viewed it as a second-rate genre produced by amateurs rather than classically trained artists. Such work was not deemed worthy of incorporation into the still-unfolding Visual Arts Program.

As early discussions of the visual arts continued, d'Harnoncourt urged the Council to approve commissions for two or three large-scale public works per year, advocating the development of what would become one of the NEA's most visible visual arts programs, called Art in Public Places. This proposal was considered the NEA's contribution to the Johnson administration urban renewal and beautification plans, as the NEA would work with cities and with other federal agencies to provide an artistic component to redevelopment projects, aiding in the "revitalization of our national environment."[68]

One business meeting between NEA visual arts leaders and Pennsylvania Railroad president Stuart Saunders illustrated much about how the NEA dealt with business leaders and the community and what they hoped to achieve through building prominent modernist sculpture in public places. In 1966 René d'Harnoncourt, Henry Geldzahler, and Livingston Biddle, the Endowment's deputy chairman, visited Saunders. Biddle explained that he was a representative from the new arts Endowment and was interested in a piece of land the railroad owned.

"You want to buy a piece of land?" asked Saunders.

"No, we want a right-of-way," replied Geldzahler, "so that we could put up a sculpture."

Saunders looked puzzled. "Sculpture? And who pays for that?"

Biddle replied, "The National Endowment for the Arts pays half and the City of Philadelphia pays half; and the railroad permits part of its property to be used."

"Well," Saunders inquired, "what would the art look like? Who would it be a statue of?"

"Oh it wouldn't be a statue at all," d'Harnoncourt responded, "it would be like a wonderful tree. Fragile. Full of light and shimmering. Catching the subtleties of sunlight and shadow."

"A tree?" Saunders questioned. "How big is this tree?"

"Oh maybe a hundred and sixty feet high . . . Or it could be smaller," d'Harnoncourt added, sensing disapproval, "sixty or seventy feet, tapering down from a very thin top to a wider bottom, supported by a small base of perhaps, no more than one square foot."

"I should think it would blow over," Saunders commented.

"Oh no, it would be very strongly anchored, and it would not be heavy at all for its size. It would be full of air. You see, it would be made of steel alloy, polished, little thin runners about as thick as a ruler, parts tied together that can move, shimmer. You see, the possibilities, I'm sure. A slender tower, a tree. Like symbols of different moods and mystery. Modern art always suggests a mystery that we can solve. . . . We want to bring this to new contexts and extend it to the public."

"Well, yes," said Saunders. "It's been very interesting meeting with you gentlemen. It's been a kind of an education. I will think it over."[69]

In the end, this tree never shimmered above Pennsylvania Railroad land, although the city of Philadelphia later received a public sculpture sponsored by the NEA. Nevertheless, this conversation illustrated the NEA's use of matching grants and its attempts to encourage business leaders to cooperate with their art projects. Significantly, it also revealed the modernist bent of the visual arts leaders and their goals of using public sculpture not only to beautify an area but to educate the public to higher aesthetic tastes.

Eventually, the Art in Public Places Program, under the direction of Geldzahler's Visual Arts Program, gave out the very first visual arts money ever granted by the Endowment. This grant for a public sculpture stemmed from

4.6. *Alexander Calder,* La Grande Vitesse, *1969.*
(Courtesy of the artist and the City of Grand Rapids)

a visit Geldzahler paid to the Grand Rapids Art Museum in 1967. While giving a lecture there, Geldzahler was introduced to the museum vice president, Nancy Mulnix, who later toured him through a large plaza area that was to become the center of the city's urban renewal efforts. Geldzahler mentioned the newly formed Art in Public Places Program and encouraged the city to apply for a grant to secure a sculpture for the plaza. A mere one month later the NEA awarded the city of Grand Rapids $45,000 for a public sculpture, provided the city could match the grant and would commission an American artist. Alexander Calder was then selected by a panel of NEA and city art consultants because of his reputation and because the panel wished to commission a large-scale, colorful piece that would dominate the plaza.[70]

The result was the 1969 installation of *La Grande Vitesse*—a massive iron sculpture in the monumental abstract style preferred by arts administrators and painted a bright red to announce its presence in the plaza (fig. 4.6). Remaining funds from the grant were used to purchase art, including a Richard Diebenkorn painting, for the Grand Rapids Art Museum.[71] At the dedication ceremony for *La Grande Vitesse*, then Michigan congressman Gerald Ford noted with pride, "This is a dramatic and significant moment in the life of our community because it illuminates our city in the eyes of all of us and ... those of the State, of the Nation, of the World."[72] The sculpture was celebrated by the federal government, the NEA, the state of Michigan, and the city of Grand Rapids, and undoubtedly by many of its citizens, as a great achievement and testament to the successful marriage of policy and aesthetics. Although some residents initially complained that it was too abstract and unrecognizable, and they simply did not understand it. There was only a minor controversy surrounding the Calder sculpture, but it foreshadowed similar arguments that would be made regarding other NEA projects that were primarily abstract and monumental. Eventually, congressmen hearing complaints about the dominance of abstract art funded by the NEA called for lists of the types of art funded by the Endowment's Visual Arts Program, which they reviewed while considering appropriations for the agency and its reauthorization.[73] Some congressmen wished to see a greater balance of representational and abstract artists funded by the NEA. However, no conflict materialized between the Congress and the NEA while all could agree that the arts—including abstract arts—did improve the quality of life in American cities.[74] Nevertheless, tiny seeds were planted that in the absence of bipartisan support for the arts would grow into heated controversy over art funding and result in its eventual cutbacks in the 1990s.

The Art Council's goals of promoting artistic excellence and encouraging the democratic enjoyment of the arts proved only partly attainable in the Endowment's early period. Council members defined artistic excellence as modernist abstraction. Not surprisingly, the NEA's Visual Arts Program promoted this style of aesthetics. In arts policy, political and cultural elites joined together to create a national arts institution and set a cultural standard for the achievement of high culture.[75] It was hoped this would raise the level of American culture and allow the United States to model and promote its achievement internationally. Nonetheless, celebration of one particular high modernist cultural vision also resulted in the marginalization of more avant-garde or popular arts.

In its formative stages, the NEA ignored pop art and folk art forms that were gaining widespread acceptance in the more populist era of the mid- to late-1960s. As later chapters document, the Endowment did not adjust to popular aesthetic trends in terms of grants until well into the 1970s and even then retained its dominant funding of more accepted classical and modernist art forms. The vision of the first Council was institutionalized early on, as the Visual Arts Program set out to promote the aesthetic excellence of modern abstract painting and sculpture and to spread the appreciation of that style to the American public. Ultimately, the goal was to educate the public in high art appreciation and thus promote a form of social uplift rather than to encourage public enjoyment of popular or mass culture. Finally, in light of the ideology behind its development, the Council proved true to its mission to recognize what it considered aesthetic excellence and to enhance audience development, yet the promise of democratic pluralism in arts funding remained elusive.

A Modernist Vision

Visual Arts Program Administration, 1967–1975

The art of the twentieth century has no collective style, not because it has divorced itself from contemporary society but because it is part of it. . . . We are terrified by the endless vistas and the responsibility of an infinite choice. This terror . . . can be solved only by an order which reconciles the freedom of the individual with the welfare of society and replaces yesterday's image of one unified civilization by a pattern in which many elements, while retaining their own individual qualities, join to form a new entity. The perfecting of this new order would unquestionably tax our abilities to the very limit, but would give us a society enriched beyond belief by the full development of the individual for the sake of the whole. I believe a good name for such a society is a democracy, and I also believe that modern art in its infinite variety and ceaseless exploration is its foremost symbol.

—René d'Harnoncourt, "Challenge and Promise: Modern Art and Society," November 1948

★ ★

René d'Harnoncourt envisioned art as a tool to combat the vast anonymity of modern life and the anxieties of the post–World War II nuclear age. He believed that modern artists could maintained their individuality while expressing universal principles that connected people in free societies.[1] D'Harnoncourt's celebration of modernist aesthetics as the embodiment of American democracy encapsulated what had become the canon of American art critics and culture brokers.[2] Furthermore, as the leading spokesman for the visual arts on the National Council on the Arts, d'Harnoncourt exerted a powerful influence on the development of the NEA's Visual Arts Program. His and fellow Arts Council member Henry Geldzahler's romanticizing of modernist abstract art became the driving force behind the earliest policies and grant allocations for the NEA in the visual arts.

During its first decade, the Visual Arts Program played an important role in the larger history of the NEA.[3] As the NEA's opera, music, theater, and museum programs supported traditional arts, so too did the Visual Arts Program, even though it funded painting and sculpture which were decades newer than many classical scores or dramas. The Visual Arts Program in the 1960s and 1970s funded modern abstract art of a nature that was politically acceptable and by then already long revered in the art world. While the American visual art scene in the 1960s embraced pop, minimalist, performance, feminist, black, and Chicano arts that were more critical of American society, federal art support continued to favor older modernist forms, such as those generated by abstract expressionist and color-field artists, who had dominated the art world in the 1950s and had earned a reputation as the best representatives of American freedom.

★ *Conceptualizing the Program*

The National Council on the Arts developed the original concept for the Visual Arts Program during a series of meetings between 1965 and 1967, most significantly in a gathering of a subcommittee on the visual arts in the spring of 1966. The subcommittee of d'Harnoncourt, Geldzahler, Diebenkorn, and Motherwell designed and won Council approval for a program of grants that would allow artists to work in schools to develop art programs and heighten students' awareness of the arts; underwrite the production and distribution of modern art prints; enable museums to purchase works by contemporary American artists; fund individual painters, sculptors, and photographers; and encourage cities to purchase and display sculptures on public property.

While programs for artists in schools and the museum purchase plan eventually developed into larger entities warranting their own programs, the major thrust of the Visual Arts Program centered on offering individual artists grants with which to advance their work as they wished. What follows will elaborate on the evolution of this vital part of the program, assessing the NEA rationale behind it and analyzing the nature of the grants awarded between 1967 and 1975.

At the heart of the program's development was the vision of its first director, Henry Geldzahler, and his staff. As illustrated by the discussion in Chapter 4 of the grant to the city of Grand Rapids for the placement of *La Grande Vitesse* by Alexander Calder, Geldzahler's personal direction of the program and solicitation of individual applications established the parameters of how the Visual Arts Program would function before it formalized the details of the application process, peer panel review, and awards. During the first two years of the NEA's existence, the National Council on the Arts was the most influential voice in selecting grants and organizing program functions. Thus, because of his place on the Council alongside other visual arts leaders d'Harnoncourt, David Smith, and Richard Diebenkorn, Geldzahler fashioned the primary structures of the Visual Arts Program. His influence became even more profound after the early deaths of Smith in 1966 and d'Harnoncourt in 1968, and when he was selected by the Council to head the Visual Arts Program in 1967.

As the Visual Arts Program became one of the NEA's major grant-making arms, Geldzahler followed the skeleton policies laid down by the National Council on the Arts but also relied on his own resources to develop detailed policies and procedures at the program level. At first, the program made awards to individual artists on the basis of "recognition of past contributions" to the field of visual arts, maintaining the course the Arts Council had originally proposed regarding the grants. Thus, when Geldzahler considered the initial round of awards, he drew upon what he and the established art critics and culture brokers considered to be the best in American art in the early 1960s—primarily abstract expressionist and color-field painting and abstract monumental and minimalist sculpture. Such a rationale underlay the Visual Arts Program's selection of Calder for the Grand Rapids award.

This rationale also influenced the development of the first awards to individual painters and sculptors in the form of visual arts fellowships. Aided by his program assistants, Devon Meade and Starke Meyer, Geldzahler developed and sorted through the first visual arts grant requests and applications. When the NEA was in its developmental phase artists had already begun to request funds for their work by writing directly to the Johnson White House or to NEA chair Roger Stevens. These artists discovered that application procedures had not yet been established and funds could not yet be disbursed at that point, however.[4] By 1967, such requests were forwarded to the Visual Arts Program to handle. Despite outside interest by artists in possible visual arts awards, the program was still relatively unknown and loosely organized during its first couple of years of operation. At first, fellowships were not awarded based upon letters and grant applications. Rather, selection was determined by nominations solicited from museum directors, art critics, art magazine editors, and artists.[5] Established art institution leaders who were approached by Geldzahler determined which aesthetic was best suited for recognition.

The first visual arts fellowships were awarded to individual painters and sculptors in 1967 on the basis of such nominations. This inaugural group of fellowships consisted of sixty awards of $5,000 each. They were given to artists to develop their careers by setting aside time and purchasing materials for their work. The artists could spend the funds as they saw fit. Thus, the grants were not awards for commissions of particular art pieces but instead resembled bonuses that affirmed the artists' achievements in their fields.

An analysis of this group of fellowships indicates that the solicitation and nomination process had a significant influence on which artists, in which fields, were deemed worthy of support by the small group of established arts leaders making the selections. The first group of grantees included Robert Goodnough, Gene Davis, Donald Judd, Agnes Martin, Richard Stankiewicz, Theodoros Stamos, and George Sugarman—all well-known painters and sculptors. Sugarman had worked at the Hunter Art College during the 1950s with Robert Motherwell and Helen Frankenthaler.[6]

These and many of the other grantees also conformed to a certain aesthetic. I have documented the styles of over 78 percent of the artists granted awards in 1967 by the Visual Arts Program.[7] Among these, 67 percent of the grants were given to abstract artists, while 7 percent went to artists whose work contains both abstraction and figuration, and only 5 percent went to purely representational artists.[8] In determining these art styles, I have defined abstraction as art that contains no realistic figuration but is primarily focused on formalistic designs of color, line, and form. Some abstract painting may contain figuration, such as Willem De Kooning's *Women*, although figures are not recognizable as realistic forms. Realist works, on the other hand, are recognizable, true-to-life images, such as Andrew Wyeth's portraits.

Typical of the kinds of work awarded funds in this first group was that of Robert Goodnough and Gene Davis. Goodnough had staked his claim in the world of abstract painting during the 1950s, developing works that incorporated analytical studies of form and color with expressions of motion. He drew on art historical traditions ranging from analytic cubism, such as that of Piet Mondrian, to American abstract expressionism, but added his own mark through his recognizable geometric shapes.[9] For example, his work *Movement of Horses B* combines a gray-toned color-field background with a flurry of colored, geometric shapes that signifies motion in the central portion of the canvas (fig. 5.1). In 1962 *Newsweek* magazine announced that Goodnough had "arrived" with the distinction of working in "two or three styles at once."[10] Not long afterward, *Art News* called him one of the more complex painters of his day.[11] Thus, Goodnough was a critically acclaimed abstractionist well before receiving his NEA visual arts award in 1967.

5.1. *Robert Goodnough,* Movement of Horses B, *1961. (Courtesy of the artist;*
Hirshhorn Museum and Sculpture Garden, Smithsonian Institution,
Gift of Joseph H. Hirshhorn, 1966 [66.2126])

Similarly, Gene Davis was one of the artists Clement Greenberg had identified as a major figure in "post-painterly abstraction." In part, this style of
painting represented a reaction to abstract expressionism, but it essentially
continued the explorations of openness of design and the formal, linear
qualities of a canvas. Rather than examining contrasts of light and dark as
abstract expressionists did, color-field artists usually painted with harder
edges and purer hues of lucid color that seemed more anonymous—meaning
their work did not reveal the painters' actions through the drips, splashes,
and heavy brush strokes common among abstract expressionists.[12] Davis's
work specifically dealt with the vertical color stripe repeated in various paintings with different color and width variations. Davis attributed his interest in
stripe painting to his admiration for Barnett Newman's now-famous "zip"

paintings as well as to a desire to embrace new subject matter when "it was heresy in 1958 to do a stripe." He also argued that his work developed out of an interest in studying intervals, which his stripes in various widths formally explored.[13]

Generally, the Visual Arts Program, the NEA, and the art world as a whole considered these first awards a great accomplishment. *Art News* lauded Stevens and Geldzahler's leadership and announced that the NEA's first awards were the "best list of grants (or prizes, or honors, call them what you will) that we have ever seen in the field."[14] Yet some people outside of the close-knit circle of abstract painters complained that the awards reflected too great an interest in abstract forms. Congressman Theodore Kupferman (R-N.Y.) brought to the House's attention the objections of Francis Vandeveer Kughler, a portrait painter and muralist, former president of the Salmagundi Club, and president of the Hotel Des Artistes in New York.[15] Kughler protested before Senator Claiborne Pell and the Senate Special Subcommittee on the Arts that NEA funds were being divided unfairly, with the vast majority given to modern artists rather than representational ones.[16] Others who appreciated more traditional forms joined his calls for a more equitable balance.[17]

In one Senate hearing, artist Michael Werboff captured congressional leaders' attention with his colorful objections to modern abstract art. He displayed a print of an abstract expressionist work done by Willem de Kooning as typical of modern art. Then he held up another canvas of indistinguishable forms and informed the committee that the second work had been done, not by a human artist, but by a monkey! This juxtaposition served as his proof that modernist forms were unworthy of federal support. Endowment officials reacted quickly to this attack, defending the intellectual and aesthetic validity of modernism. More tellingly, Deputy Chair Livingston Biddle quietly informed the committee that the artist who had spoken so disparagingly about modern art was in fact a Russian, and, of course, Russians were known for their distaste of abstract art. This news checked any further questioning of the art grants by the congressional leaders, who wished to avoid being goaded by a "communist" into curtailing American artistic freedom. Such a response would have been considered less than patriotic in the Cold War era while competition with the Soviet Union remained strong on all levels. In the end, while leaders such as Senator Pell listened sympathetically to the complaints, they ultimately defended the NEA policies and grants and upheld the congressional policy of noninterference in NEA procedures.[18] Their actions confirmed that it was more politically acceptable to support freedom of expression than their personal tastes—even though, ironically, that meant supporting the high modernist tastes of cultural officials at the time.

Thereafter Senator Pell would periodically ask the Endowment for a list of artists' awards by style, to indicate that he monitored the NEA's selections, and he encouraged the Endowment to maintain a balance of support for both modernist abstraction and more realist forms. The NEA complied fully to the request for a list. However, they prepared its content creatively. Any art style that contained recognizable elements was defined as "representational," so that the proportion of grants could be perceived as more equally distributed among the abstract and representational art forms.[19] A more objective analysis of the NEA Visual Arts grants reveals that such a balance was rarely achieved.

★ Formalizing the Program

A detailed assessment of NEA visual arts fellowships indicates that the aesthetic ideals held by the Arts Council and Visual Arts Program leaders and advisers were manifested in their selections of painters and sculptors, although this phenomenon became subtler over time. After the first couple of years, the Council members no longer nominated individual artists for awards. Formal application procedures were developed, and the Visual Arts Program advertised in major art magazines to solicit applications from artists.[20] Panels reviewed the applications, selected finalists for awards, then submitted their choices to the Arts Council for final approval.

Panelists for the Visual Arts Program became increasingly important in the selection process as the program grew in size and scope. The enabling legislation allowed the NEA to call upon "experts in the field" in identifying and rewarding artistic excellence. Each program ultimately developed a generally praiseworthy practice of consultation with artists and critics to determine who should receive NEA funds. In the Visual Arts Program, expert advice was solicited from among notable art critics, museum directors, and artists in different areas of the country. Panelists gathered in regional groups and later in Washington to review grant applications and recommend awards. Initially the panelists' names were not disclosed and panel meetings were kept private, so that members would be shielded from public pressures and could make selections according to their proven aesthetic judgment. By the 1970s, panelists' names were published in the NEA annual reports, although the panel meetings remained closed.

In 1967 visual arts panels convened in three regions: the East, which was the purview of Robert Motherwell, George Segal, and Barbara Rose, who often met with Henry Geldzahler; the Midwest, which was overseen by Richard Hunt, Edward Henning, and Martin Freidman; and the West, which was directed by John Humphrey, John Dinman, Walter Hopps, and Richard Diebenkorn.[21] Generally modernist-oriented artists, critics, and museum directors, these panelists selected grantees after viewing applications and sample slides of work by applying artists. As the number of applications grew, this became quite a formidable task, which augmented panelists' tendency to select artists whose work complemented their own taste and definitions of aesthetic excellence.[22] Panels expanded during the 1970s and were subdivided into groups according to the types of art under review as the Visual Arts Program created new categories of funding. For individual fellowships and public art, panelists included many of the above artists but also new additions such as Sam Gilliam, F. Van Deren Coke, James Melchert, Mel Edwards, Irving Sandler, George Segal, Wayne Tiebault, Roy Lichtenstein, Barbara Haskell, and James Rosati. Still overwhelmingly made up of modernists, the panels included a couple of pop, figurative artists by the mid-1970s, as well as an ever-enlarging cadre of arts managers and trustees rather than practicing artists.[23]

This greater number of panelists along with the increase of funds and the formalization of program procedures contributed to a basic change in awards policy. During its first year or two of administration, the Visual Arts Program had granted awards to artists primarily in recognition of past achievement. By 1969, individual fellowships were granted to artists for production of future work. This policy marked a return to the original Arts Council ideal of granting funds to artists to use as they saw fit to advance their careers. Artists still submitted portfolios of past work as part of their application resumé to be reviewed by the panels; however, individual painters and sculptors did not propose specific projects to which the award of funds would be applied. If chosen, they could use NEA funds however they wished.

Not only was this a reemphasis of Visual Arts Program goals to support artistic talent and individual creativity; it was also a coup in the program's efforts to protect itself against criticism for funding avant-garde art that might affront more conservative tastes such as those of the Senate subcommittee that questioned the disproportionate funding of abstract artists. Wishing to avoid potential conflict over awards, NEA Chair Nancy Hanks quietly advised the Visual Arts Program staff to delete proposals for specific projects from grant applications.[24] Thus, by having highly regarded artist panelists review an application and award funds based solely on an individual's noted talent, the Visual Arts Program fulfilled the NEA mission of advancing the careers of excellent artists without the risk of funding a proposal that could be criticized. The new Visual Arts Program director, Brian O'Doherty, considered this a brilliant move by Hanks in defending individual artists' freedom.[25]

O'Doherty took over the reigns as the director of the Visual Arts Program from Henry Geldzahler in 1969, and during the next five years he guided the expansion of the program while guarding its modernist vision. Like Geldzahler, O'Doherty came to the NEA from New York and, while working for the Endowment, retained a full-time job in the art world as the editor of *Art in America* magazine. Under his direction, much of the magazine's dealings with American modernists focused on abstract expressionist, color-field, and minimalist artworks of the 1950s, 1960s, and 1970s. Later, his critical work revealed his own enchantment with color-field, minimalist, conceptual, and process art that engaged a viewer's mind and sometimes challenged preconceived notions of self-contained canvases and gallery spaces as the proper location of art. In essays for *Artforum* magazine, O'Doherty argued that "context provides a large part of late modern and post-modern art's content" and, in such art, gallery space itself was "enlisted as a unit of esthetic discourse," or the artist staged a "quasi-revolution" by looking at new contexts for their work.[26] O'Doherty's regard for interactive contexts for modern art and for the use of alternative spaces contributed to his support for placing modern abstract art in public locations—because he felt that "social engagement was important"—and motivated him as director of the Visual Arts Program to encourage funding newer forms of minimalist and conceptual art.[27] Yet his more postmodern views did not develop until the mid-1970s and thus did not sway the NEA to dramatically change directions in its arts funding policies during his tenure as director of the Visual Arts Program.

O'Doherty was also an artist who practiced under the name Patrick Ireland. His aesthetic was abstract, primarily minimalist and conceptual. For example, in a series called *Rope Drawings*, O'Doherty suspended lengths of colored rope in gallery spaces and outdoor arenas to highlight the three-dimensional line's ability to construct and illustrate illusions of space and geometric forms. His early rope works were web-like formations or grids hung between walls and columns, while his later works often utilized almost invisible nylon threads to hold the ropes in place, creating the illusion of free-hanging geometric forms that could appear as multiple arrangements of color

5.2. *Patrick Ireland, view of the installation,* Omphalos, *from the exhibition,*
Patrick Ireland: Labyrinths, Language, Pyramids and Related Acts,
at the Elvehjem Museum of Art, University of Wisconsin–Madison, 1992–93.
(Courtesy of the artist and Elvehjem Museum of Art)

lines as the viewer moved about them.[28] (See fig. 5.2 for an example of Ireland's work, an installation entitled *Omphalos*.) Interestingly, these drawings
with rope resemble some of the minimalist forms and styles of other artists
who received awards from the NEA's Visual Arts Program under O'Doherty's
direction. As a practicing artist, O'Doherty was afforded respect in the artistic
community and was able to negotiate between the NEA as a federal agency
and younger artists who became disenchanted with the U.S. government over
its involvement in the Vietnam War in the early 1970s. He helped to ease
frustrations and foster continued cooperation between art and politics.

★ *Individual Artist Awards, 1967–1975*

The individual artist awards in the late 1960s and early 1970s reflected the
program's distinctly modernist orientation. I have documented 52 percent of

the artists' styles among all NEA grants to individual painters and sculptors between 1967 and 1975.[29] (See on-line Appendix 3 for detailed information on these fellowships.) Individual artists who displayed abstract expressionist, color-field, and geometric abstractionist aesthetics received the majority of the funds allocated by the NEA for painters and sculptors in all years (68 percent in 1967; 75 percent in 1968; 85 percent in 1969; 78 percent in 1971; 89 percent in 1973; 67 percent in 1974; and 83 percent in 1975). Second to these in the number of awards received were those artists who practiced figurative or conceptual work—styles that remained primarily abstract in execution while often incorporating recognizable elements into the overall scheme of the painting or sculpture (8 percent in 1967; 18 percent in 1968; 9 percent in 1969; 14 percent in 1971; 7 percent in 1973; 28 percent in 1974; and 14 percent in 1975). Finally, realists and neorealists consistently received the least number of awards (6 percent in 1967; 7 percent in 1968; 3 percent in 1969; 8 percent in 1971; 4 percent in 1973; 7 percent in 1974; and 1 percent in 1975).

Several of the artists who received grants were notable figures in the 1960s art scene, especially in the areas of abstract painting and minimalist sculpture. Edward Avedisian, Darby Bannard, Dan Christensen, Ron Davis, Friedel Dzubas, Al Held, Richard Pousette-Dart, Dorothea Rockburne, and Mary Miss were among the individual painters recognized for the excellence displayed in their abstract works. Henry Geldzahler had been following several of them and believed that these young artists out of the abstract tradition were growing in stature and accomplishment.[30] Many of Dan Christensen's paintings of the 1960s looked almost like minimalist versions of Jackson Pollock's work, with intersecting, colorful lines of paint swirled onto an otherwise barren canvas—although they also hint at other emerging artists' fascination with neon. Darby Bannard's work resembled more of a color-field than gestural style of abstract expressionism. His paintings showed a concern with distinct and overlapping triangular constructions washed onto the canvas in muted colors. Ron Davis, on the other hand, explored the cube form, and thus the formalism and construction of space on the canvas as well as in sculpture. Each of these artists emerged from the historical tradition of post–World War II American abstract painting and were rewarded for extending its life by some of the older-generation artistic figures who sat on the Arts Council and the visual arts panels.[31]

This is certainly true of Richard Pousette-Dart, who became one of the most acclaimed among this group. He was influenced by abstract expressionism and studies of American myths and symbols in the 1940s and 1950s as he began working with modernist abstract designs and forms. In fact, Geld-zahler considered him part of the abstract expressionist generation.[32] As Pousette-Dart's work matured, he synthesized his style into a purely abstract "sheer optical saturation" that provided "no forms, shapes, or images to serve as convenient points of reference."[33] His paintings concentrated his aesthetic vision into a focused area of space and demanded that the viewer consider it emotionally and subjectively, suspending comparisons of the art to material forms. These works have been described as spiritual and transcendental in the same way that Mark Rothko's works were considered expressions of an ageless and universal human understanding. Many cultural leaders, including NEA officials, believed such expressions perfectly represented universality and desires for beauty and truth rather than materialism and militarism in a nuclear age.[34] Pousette-Dart had his own full-scale retrospective at the Whit-ney in 1963 and was acclaimed as a giant in color-field painting, with close ties to his contemporaries in abstract expressionism in the early 1960s. His stature and the obscure but positively interpreted aspects of his painting made him an attractive visual arts program awardee.

The individual sculptors who received the NEA awards were an even more immediately recognizable group than the painters. Grantees included Dan Flavin, Donald Judd, Carl André, Mark di Suvero, Sol LeWitt, Robert Irwin, Charles Ginnever, Richard Serra, Tony Smith, Larry Bell, and Nancy Holt, among others. Almost all of the sculptors selected by the NEA for awards worked with monumental, abstract styles, often incorporating the use of nontraditional materials such as steel alloys, Plexiglas, environmental ele-ments, and neon. By and large they were also minimalists who streamlined the elements and concepts of their art into simple executions.

Mark di Suvero's work expressed many of the ideals that these NEA grant-ees sought to present through their art. His sculptures presented large-scale combinations of welded metal and natural elements such as wood, often painted brightly in reds or yellows. On occasion, he included recognizable man-made pieces such as a chair or a tire into his work and always strove to achieve a balance of natural, oppositional forces in his sculpture. His sculp-ture entitled *Are Years What? (for Marianne Moore)*, 1967, was a monumental steel piece architecturally employing long steel beams welded into a tall sup-port structure from which a large V-shaped section was suspended with wires and hooks (fig. 5.3).

Di Suvero's work has been described by some as the sculptural equivalent to the bold, linear strokes of a Franz Kline abstract expressionist painting.[35]

5.3. *Mark di Suvero,* Are Years What? (for Marianne Moore), *1967. (Courtesy of the artist and Spacetime C. C.; Hirshhorn Museum and Sculpture Garden, Smithsonian Institution, Joseph H. Hirshhorn Purchase Fund and Gift of the Institute of Scrap Recycling Industries, by exchange, 1999; photo by Lee Stalsworth [99.19])*

More aptly, he realized an aesthetic akin to that of Arts Council member David Smith, focusing on using a material that symbolized western technology and power—steel. After receiving his award, di Suvero told the NEA that it helped him to effectively advance his career by allowing him to purchase a crane that he used like "a paintbrush . . . to do what every modern sculptor has dreamed of: to use industrial scale and size in sculpture."[36] Yet he also appreciated "the edge of irony in using [steel] . . . to provoke memory and emotion; to express universal, primordial forms . . . in a state of gently precarious equilibrium."[37] He believed his art was a means of expressing modern human emotions in tangible form and, more importantly, linking mankind across space and time in new possibilities of cooperation.[38] For di Suvero, such connections were meant to express not just American national unity but the sense of international cooperation and understanding that his former residencies in China and France had instilled in him. He understood that these sensibilities and hopes were important in a modern, Cold War–era world. His hopeful expressions and abstract aesthetics were engaging to art critics and cultural leaders in the same way that abstract expressionism had been.

However, while his aesthetic lineage stemmed directly from the abstract expressionism that politicians and culture brokers used as a Cold War weapon, di Suvero was also a member of a younger generation of artists who began to challenge Cold War rhetoric by the late 1960s. Di Suvero so strongly advocated peace that he participated with other artists opposed to the Vietnam War in the building of the Peace Tower in Los Angeles in 1966, and he later left the United States between 1971 and 1975 after Nixon began the American bombing of Cambodia.[39] Amid these activities, he received his first NEA grant as an individual artist in 1967 and received commissions for sculptures under the Art in Public Places Program in 1971 and 1972. Thus, di Suvero's antiwar stance did not prevent his recognition by the federal arts agency. In fact, NEA officials struggled to maintain the principles of artistic freedom and nonpolitical awards that had been established in the Endowment's authorizing legislation and upheld by President Lyndon Johnson, even while artists were protesting under his roof during the White House Festival of the Arts in 1965.

Although most of the painting and sculpture funded by the Visual Arts Program consisted of high modernist abstract painting and monumental sculpture, minimalist art was also heavily represented. Minimalists stripped artwork down to its essential elements in their painting and sculpture, using only a few unadorned brush strokes in painting or bare primary shapes and structures in three-dimensional sculpture. In most cases abstract painting, monumental sculpture, and minimalist forms went hand in hand. This may be seen in Ron Davis's simple cube image paintings and Mark di Suvero's lean outdoor sculptures.

Minimalism founder Donald Judd received an individual artist's grant from the NEA in 1967 and additional grants in 1975 and 1976. His works highlighted various cube and rectangular shapes in their barest forms. Judd's sculpture *Untitled*, 1970, contained six rectangular structures made of stainless steel and purple Plexiglas (fig. 5.4). Each element stood alone, yet together they created a vertical series reminiscent of a straight ladder. The forms served the minimalist aesthetic, as did the lack of a title to suggest

5.4. *Donald Judd,* Untitled, *1970. (Art © Donald Judd Foundation/Licensed by VAGA, New York, N.Y.; photo by Rudy Burckhardt)*

any other references in the piece. Other works by Judd included similar rectangles arranged vertically or horizontally and in various colors. In a statement that captured the essence of minimalist art, Judd explained how three-dimensional works could rescue aesthetics from the problems of painting. He argued,

The main thing wrong with painting is that it is a rectangular plain placed flat against the wall. A rectangle is a shape itself; it is obviously the whole shape. . . . Three dimensions are real space. That gets rid of the problems of illusion and of literal space, space in and around marks and colors—which is riddance of one of the salient and most objectionable relics of European art. The several limits of painting are no longer present. A work can be as powerful as it can be thought to be. . . . Anything in three dimensions can be any shape, regular or irregular, and can have any relation to the wall, floor, ceiling, room, rooms or exterior or none at all. . . . [Artists may] use all sorts of materials and colors.[40]

Furthermore, he objected to those who called his work reductive, positing "if my work is reductionist it's because it doesn't have the elements that people thought should be there. But it has other elements." Rather than being composed of parts, "the whole's it."[41] Judd and other minimalists advanced the idea that less was indeed more.

In the work of a small number of the NEA grantees, minimalism and conceptual art styles overlapped. Conceptual art, which is based on the ideas behind the work, became another genre that received limited NEA funding by the mid-1970s. This style began to be popularized earlier in the American art scene, beginning with Allan Kaprow's "happenings" in 1959. Influenced by the work of composer John Cage, Kaprow combined elements of painting, three-dimensional objects, music, and light along with performance and audience participation to produce unique events that were both frivolous and thought provoking.[42] Kaprow defined a happening as "an assemblage of events performed or perceived in more than one time and place. Its material environments may be constructed, taken over directly from what is available, or altered slightly; just as its activities may be invented or commonplace. A Happening, unlike a stage play, may occur at a supermarket, driving along a highway, under a pile of rags, and in a friend's kitchen, either at once or sequentially. . . . The Happening is performed according to plan but without rehearsal, audience, or repetition. It is art but seems closer to life."[43] This kind of collage of art and life defined one happening in which Kaprow constructed two rooms in a warehouse. One was a brightly lit bedroom filled with yellow objects, while the other resembled an attic, lined with tar paper and cluttered with boxes, clothes, and junk. The audience was allowed to move through each, rearranging the objects into a mess. Then some women began to clean the mess and gradually returned the rooms to their original order. The event was conceptualized but not controlled by the artist, who allowed the audience to participate in action that reflected real-life housecleaning.[44]

Kaprow himself received an NEA individual artist's fellowship in 1974, long after his own work had been popularized and, ultimately, rendered virtually passé, although his encouragement of process art and real world connections thrived in the abstract environmental sculptures of such artists as Michael Heizer, Richard Serra, Mary Miss, and Nancy Holt.[45] Kaprow's happenings and other pop art appeared more frivolous as art forms and were not often recognized by the NEA through its visual arts awards.[46] Instead, NEA officials preferred "higher" modernist abstract forms such as abstract expressionist and color-field painting and minimalist, abstract sculptures.

One artist who combined both minimalist structures and conceptual ideas and was celebrated by the NEA was Sol LeWitt, who received an individual fellowship in 1971 and Art in Public Places funds in 1975. LeWitt has generally been credited with gaining attention for conceptual art as a movement through his publications, "Paragraphs on Conceptual Art" in 1967 and "Sentences on Conceptual Art" in 1969. In these writings, LeWitt compared language to other visual systems of art and justified incorporating language into his artworks, asserting that, "[the] idea of concept is the most important aspect of the work. . . . All of the planning and decisions are made beforehand and the execution is a perfunctory affair. . . . Conceptual art is made to engage the mind of the viewer rather than his eye or emotions."[47] His work, *Drawing Series 1968 (Fours)*, illustrated the artist's ideas for executing drawings and the drawings themselves, which were based upon variations of four squares subdivided into another four squares. In other works, LeWitt fabricated multiple types of square sculptures, extending his ideas on cube formations into three-dimensional figures. Although developed out of a concept series, on a smaller scale these sculptures were similar to many of the monumental abstract pieces constructed by other NEA-funded artists. Thus, LeWitt's aesthetic paralleled the heroic modernist forms usually deemed deserving of Endowment recognition.

Other types of art that were gaining popularity at the end of the 1960s and early 1970s when the NEA granted these individual fellowships were overlooked or marginalized in the award process. As with pop art, feminist, ethnic, folk, and performance art did not begin to garner individual visual arts awards until late in this period, although these genres were gaining increasing attention in the art world.[48] As will be documented in Chapter 6, craft awards began to be given out in 1973, and folk art was later recognized under its own program that served not only the visual arts but also music, dance, literature, and performances.[49] A very small number of new representational arts were recognized, including neorealist or hyperrealist works by artists such as Richard Estes or Philip Pearlstein, yet these awards were not significant enough in number to signal any shift in Visual Arts Program trends.

Thus, NEA visual arts awards were not as diverse initially as many have argued. Ann Galligan and Elaine King have celebrated the NEA as a democratic and pluralist art institution.[50] In his recent work *Visionaries and Outcasts*, Michael Brenson argues that the NEA focused on the "creative process," its fellowships "rewarded risk taking," and the "majority of panel members were attentive to the unfamiliar."[51] The record reveals the contrary. Far from being "outcasts," modernist artists and devotees were insiders at the NEA. In its first decade, the Endowment was more conservative in its visual arts funding than it later became in the late 1970s. Between 1967 and 1975, the Visual Arts Program awarded individual artists who carried on in the celebrated traditions of abstract expressionism, color-field painting, and minimalist, monumental sculpture that had been the proven champions both in the art world and in the successful cooperation between art and politics. Political leaders, cultural officials, and in many cases artists who belonged to the first generation of abstract expressionists, believed this genre best represented American freedom and used it to highlight the ideals of American democracy in international exhibitions.[52] Their outlook, which stemmed from the Cold War context of the 1950s, remained in place during the 1960s. This manifested itself in NEA policy as political leaders selected older generation cultural leaders for the Arts Council, and these Council members in turn chose like-minded artists and cultural leaders to head the Visual Arts Program. Evidence indicates that this program initially focused its attention on recognizing artists whose aesthetics continued to represent the tried-and-true marriage of abstract art and Cold War politics. Eventually, as Americans began to change their views and the Cold War consensus began to collapse, artists' styles also began to change and to incorporate increasingly figurative and sometimes controversial content. The NEA did little to keep apace with these transformations until well into the 1970s.

★ *Regional Distribution*

In addition to stylistic conservatism, individual artist fellowships also demonstrated the NEA's limited success in fostering the visual arts throughout the nation. Artists' residences at the time of their awards illustrate an uneven distribution of grants by region.[53] This was particularly evident in the first three years of the program's administration. In 1967, artists in New York received the bulk of the grants and not a single artist in the South received an award. Then, in 1968, only artists in the South and Midwest received grants in an apparent attempt to make up for the dominance of the East and West among the first year's awards. This change proved short-lived; in 1969 awards rushed back to New York artists, who received a whopping 95 percent of the grants that year. After 1971, the distribution of awards stabilized with nearly 50 percent of the awards going to artists in the East, although not always predominantly in New York, 30 percent to artists in the West, 10 percent to artists in the Midwest, and 7 percent to artists in the South.

Of course, the maldistribution of the visual artists' awards reflected the concentration of artists' centers in New York and on the East and West Coasts, where most successful artists resided. (And to be fair, many of them had relocated from other areas of the country.) The NEA's early policy of granting awards to already well-known artists contributed to its uneven distribution of awards to these centers. Nevertheless, the Endowment's mission was not only to reward aesthetic excellence but to enhance arts distribution and public access to the arts throughout the country. Presidents Johnson and Nixon emphasized this aspect of the NEA's policy through their populist rhetoric and encouraged the NEA to work toward more equitable allotments of its awards. During the 1970s, the agency attempted to distribute awards more evenly. Nevertheless, parity in the awards to artists by region was never achieved and perhaps never could be achieved.

★ Works of Art in Public Places

In addition to the individual fellowship awards, the Visual Arts Program oversaw grants to cities for public art displays. Its Works of Art in Public Places Program began rather informally in 1967 under the direct supervision of Henry Geldzahler. However, it became much larger and more formalized as the years progressed. From the Council's original conception of "Awards of Excellence" to major American sculptors, the program developed into one that was less controlled by the NEA officials and more of a collaboration between NEA and city representatives.[54] The Visual Arts Program initiated a joint panel system through which three NEA panel members and three city art professionals would review the site and select the artist for the commission.

Initially this new process changed little about the art selection trends but gave local officials and the public a greater sense of participation in the grant process, even if they often deferred to NEA Visual Arts representatives. Officially published guidelines for the program were not established until 1973. These then set in place the general parameters that were already under way and changed only slightly over the years with the addition of some smaller-scale grants for new artists and a short-lived public mural program.[55]

As it was originally conceived, the Art in Public Places Program was to focus on promoting three large-scale public sculptures per year. In its first three years, the program actually funded only one such sculpture annually. However, from this humble beginning it later grew into a division of the Visual Arts Program that awarded a significant number of grants for public art—sculptures, murals, and prints—twenty-two in 1973, thirty-one in 1974, and thirty-six in 1975. Many of the artists who received awards for site-specific sculptures selected under the Art in Public Places Program had also received individual artists fellowships from the NEA; therefore, the stylistic trends documented for individual sculptors also hold true in the public sculpture awards.

Between 1967 and 1975, the preponderance of the sculptures commissioned for public sites were abstract and monumental works. 95 percent were abstract, while only 5 percent of the pieces were figurative. Several artists received more than one award to prepare sculptures under the Works of Art in Public Places Program. Among these multiple-award winners were Isamu Noguchi (four awards), Mark di Suvero (four awards), National Council on the Arts member and Visual Arts Program regional panelist Richard Hunt (three awards), Tony Smith (three awards), David von Schlegell (three awards), Alexander Calder (two awards), Charles Ginnever (two awards), Michael Heizer (two awards), Louise Nevelson (two awards), George Rickey (two awards), Beverly Pepper (two awards), James Rosati (two awards), and Isaac Witkin (two awards).[56]

Isamu Noguchi was among the first and most frequently selected artists to produced site-specific sculptures for this program. He was American born of Japanese descent, spent his youth in Japan, then studied in the United States and Europe, where he completed two years of a Guggenheim fellowship in Paris studying sculpture with renowned artist Constantin Brancusi. Noguchi often supported himself on commissions for sculpting portrait heads of his patrons and designing sets and costumes for dance companies, including

Martha Graham's. Nevertheless, his primary aesthetic interest and style was abstract, biomorphic, and minimalist sculpture.

Noguchi considered his art a forum for the emotional and spiritual expression that he believed to be so desperately needed in the mechanical and war-torn world of the twentieth century. In this sense his art was not abstract to him but a symbol and means to help achieve order and harmony. He explained,

> When the very meaning of life becomes obscure and chaotic, how necessary is the order which with the practice of the arts leads to harmony, and without which there is only brutality. I think of sculpture especially as the art of order—the harmonizer and humanizer of spaces. . . . Even the purest geometry is not completely abstract, for the presence of geometric forms in nature evokes human responses and charges them with vital associations. . . . Rediscovery of the sculptor as a direct worker—plus the growing acceptance of the new reality of space, plus the imperative need of bringing order and meaning into a world menaced by chaos, plus the fact that this has always been sculpture's role—indicates the promise of sculpture's growing reintegration with society. . . . In it man may find surcease from mechanization, in the contemplation and enjoyment of a new spiritual freedom. It will be a time when the enjoyment of leisure will be the measure of a good life."[57]

Noguchi's belief in creating art to express both freedom and order and his desire to emphasize public enjoyment of the arts as a positive leisure pursuit reflected the ideals expressed about the arts by the creators and leaders of the NEA. As a member of the first generation of abstractionists, Noguchi embodied exactly the type of artist political and cultural officials upheld as symbolic of American excellence.

Noguchi's world-renowned stature as an artist also contributed to his popularity with NEA cultural arbiters. As early as 1949, art critic Clement Greenberg noted the contributions of Noguchi's art, and Hilton Kramer of the *New York Times* labeled him "the purest of living sculptors" in the 1970s.[58] Henry Geldzahler considered him a "genius for harmoniously expressing his work" and one of the artists of his time who could provide viewers with "a glimpse of the *numen*, the invisible essence that informs the universe and is as close to the apprehension of beauty as we can come."[59]

As he was in facilitating the Calder commission for the city of Grand

Rapids, Geldzahler was influential in the selection of Noguchi to create a public sculpture for Seattle when it received the second Art in Public Places award from the NEA in 1967. NEA Chair Roger Stevens announced the $45,000 matching grant to the city after the NCA approved the award at its November meeting. The work Noguchi executed for the site in Seattle's Volunteer Park was a large, circular, polished black granite sculpture entitled *Black Sun*. It contained irregularly shaped front and back sides with a slightly off-center circular hole that allowed viewers to peer through the sculpture into the sky or onto the park. As onlookers shifted their positions the view through the work and perceptions of its shaped sides also changed. Such interaction gave a role to the viewer and added depth to the piece.

When the sculpture was dedicated in 1969, the newly appointed NEA chair Nancy Hanks announced that the work allowed the Endowment to foster cooperation between government and private funding sources and between the artist and the community and to realize its task of "increasing the quality of every citizen's life." She asserted that the existence of such a work was "evidence of a community's basic health and of the fortunate direction of its energies. In this context a great work of art is not just a visual delight, but a moral force."[60] Thus, the work seemed to achieve Noguchi's sought-after connections between art and life as well as fulfill the federal government ideals for city beautification and public uplift.

City officials considered the sculpture a great success and moved to expand local art activities. In 1969, the Port of Seattle Commission voted to spend $300,000 of revenue bonds for art displays in the new Seattle-Tacoma Airport terminal. Then in 1973, the city enacted its One Percent for Art Ordinance that allocated funds from municipal construction projects for the acquisition and installation of art in public spaces.[61]

Although the response to the Seattle commission of Noguchi's *Black Sun* was positive, Washington State Arts Commission members suggested that the NEA should also consider distributing smaller awards to further more artists in a wider area, rather than continuing only with large awards such as those for the Calder and Noguchi sculptures. Grants of perhaps $10,000 to cities with populations under 200,000 would go a longer way, they argued, and a "national program of support to smaller cities and towns would have a great impact locally and nationally and would reach many people who ordinarily would not have the opportunity to view such works."[62] In fact, what this commission was suggesting had been part of the NEA's founding mission, although the Endowment was not entirely able to live up to this goal during its first few years of operation. The NEA partly embraced such advice as it expanded its programs during the 1970s, including more and smaller grants and a somewhat more expansive regional distribution of funds to artists and cities in the Works of Art in Public Places Program.[63]

Noguchi, though, continued to receive large-scale commissions for public sculptures. In 1974 and 1975, the artist was awarded commissions to create sculptures for the cities of Atlanta and Honolulu, both of which received $50,000 matching grants from the NEA for the projects. In each case, he produced monumental abstract sculptures. Atlanta received *Playscapes*, variously shaped and brightly painted elements in geometric forms that included bars, slides, and tubes on which neighborhood children could climb and play. This achieved Noguchi's goal of integrating art and social interaction and allowed the NEA to promote uplifting uses of public space and of youths' leisure time.[64] By contrast to this playful piece, Honolulu received *Sky Gate*, a large tubular structure that rose from three sides to meet in a curving crown open to the sky (fig. 5.5). This work was more typical of Noguchi's abstract style and was installed in a location symbolic of his East-meets-West aesthetic.[65] More importantly, Noguchi's four commissions through the NEA's public art program demonstrated the Visual Arts Program's continuing focus on large-scale, monumental abstract works as the best form for its public sculptures.

The Art in Public Places program also funded commissions for public mural projects, acquisitions of prints and paintings for public locations, and special projects for which cities applied for matching funds. These grants consisted of 40 percent of the program funding, 86 percent of which went to mural projects. My research in this area has been limited due to incomplete records and the frequent selection of lesser-known artists for many municipal mural projects. However, from the sources available, it is clear that mural projects included both abstract and figurative illustrations that reflected community life.

Unlike the large-scale public sculptures placed in one location, generally in a city center, mural projects often subdivided grants to several artists whose work could be spread out across a larger urban area. Such projects targeted inner cities, with the dual aims of community development and urban renewal. These goals had been emphasized by political leaders such as President Johnson under the rubric of his War on Poverty and community action programs and by the Arts Council. City planners and arts commissions reiterated them in their proposals to the NEA, indicating that local areas had

5.5. *Isamu Noguchi,* Sky Gate, *1975. (Published with permission of the Isamu Noguchi Foundation, Inc.; courtesy of the City and County of Honolulu, funded by the City and County of Honolulu and the National Endowment for the Arts; photo by Paul Picard)*

taken up the ideals expressed on a national level. The Boston Foundation's Summerthing Festival application for a mural grant argued that "art can make the city civilized again" by giving local minority artists means to express pent-up energy and a chance to "resist the bleakness and blind walls of decaying parts of the city." It was hoped that murals would visually transform run-down areas and "help to catalyze social change."[66]

To this end, the NEA awarded the foundation a $5,000 grant in 1970 and another $20,000 in 1971 with the agreement that half of the funds would be allocated to black artists in the Boston area. The Boston Foundation and the NEA also hoped that abstract artist Frank Stella would be commissioned for a mural but were disappointed that details for a contract with him could not be arranged in time. Instead, in 1970 the foundation granted several $500–$600 awards to local artists for various community murals. These included funds to Sharon Dunn, a black teacher, who constructed a frieze of pregnant women in front of a low-income housing project; an award to Keiko Prince, a Japanese artist, for executing a brilliantly colored abstract design on a North End Italian community area; and a grant to Maria Cordez to paint a mural in Fields Corner that, according to the foundation, "transformed a hideous Parks Department wall . . . [and provided] an alternative to outright destruction."[67]

Similar grants were awarded several times to the cities of New York, Chicago, and Los Angeles. Mural projects reached wider locations within municipal areas but received consistently smaller grants than those for large public works. On average, mural grants were for amounts between $5,000 and $10,000 while sculpture grants were between $25,000 and $50,000. In part, this was due to the less costly nature of mural art. Nonetheless, the thrust of public sculpture coincided more closely with NEA officials' aesthetic sensibilities and desires to promote modernist abstract art. Eventually the public mural movement lost some momentum in the late 1970s as community activism waned, and the Visual Arts Program cut back its mural project grants.

The Visual Arts Program accomplished much of what the National Council on the Arts and program directors organized it to achieve. Its leaders and expert consultants set a standard for excellence in contemporary painting and sculpture and rewarded hundreds of individual artists in many, if not all, areas of the country. In contrast to the now-widespread perception of the NEA and the Visual Arts Program in particular as a leader and radical supporter of an ultraliberal avant-garde, the agency generally favored conservative and traditional art forms. Just as in opera, music (classical), theater, and museums, which were its major funding programs, the NEA supported long-established forms of visual arts.[68]

Arts administration analyst Edward Arian claimed that the "cultural preferences of elites are hostile to modernism because their tastes are the result of a self-perpetuating circle of conservatism wherein traditional organizations . . . continue to satisfy elite demands for the tried-and-true repertoire."[69] On the contrary, the Visual Arts Program embraced modernism. Trends in the visual arts change at a more rapid rate than those for classical music, opera, and theater. Museums purchasing impressionist paintings support an art form that is one hundred years old and has been the staple of fine painting for at least a half-century, whereas classical music and opera remain focused on centuries-old standards. Seldom, and only very cautiously, do these arts accept newer genres. The Visual Arts Program clearly celebrated abstract expressionist and color-field painting and monumental abstract sculpture—

post–World War II modernist forms that by the 1960s had become "classical" and standard visual art forms.

By the time these modernist arts were supported by the NEA as the epitome of fine arts achievement, they no longer represented the most current and pathbreaking forms in the art world. Instead, the avant-garde genres of pop, postminimalism, performance, feminist, black, and ethnic arts, and even folk arts, were at the pinnacle of fashion in the late 1960s and 1970s. These were marginalized by the NEA's focus on the more conservative abstract forms which were considered symbolic of American individuality, risk-taking, and free expression. These qualities had been lauded in opposition to the conformity and control associated with totalitarianism during the 1950s, and American politicians continued to uphold them during the 1960s and early 1970s as part of their Cold War strategy. At the same time, American art forms returned to including more figuration, much of which could be read as political protest during the late 1960s and 1970s, when more of the American public began to question American policies during the Vietnam era. Not surprisingly, the NEA did not rush to keep pace with these styles, although the agency did pursue significant changes under the Nixon and Carter administrations.

The Improbable Patron
Richard Nixon and the Expansion of Arts Policy

I propose that Congress approve new funds for the National Foundation . . . [that] will virtually double the current year's level. . . . Few investments we could make would give us so great a return. . . . The arts have a rare capacity to help heal divisions among our own people and to vault some of the barriers that divide the world.
—Richard Nixon, Speech to Congress on Arts Policy, December 10, 1969

6

★ ★

2001: A Space Odyssey, a film tracing humans' evolution from violent prehistoric creatures to technologically advanced space explorers, served as the American entry to the 1969 International Film Festival in Moscow. The movie premiered on March 3, 1969, the same night that American astronauts rocketed toward the moon in *Apollo 9*. The careful timing dramatized American achievements to an international audience, but the Russian location of the festival also provided an added opportunity for Cold War one-upmanship. While the film played to 7,000 Russians in the Palace of the Soviets, American festival judge (and future NEA deputy chair) Michael Straight kept one eye on the film and the other on the audience. As the film drew to a close, Straight waited for what he believed would be an ovation from the audience but was met instead with stunned silence. Surprised by the lack of reaction, he sought out one of the high-ranking Soviets in the audience and began to explain the film. "I pointed out the anti-war sentiments in the film, thinking that she had missed them," Straight recounted. "I emphasized to her that it was the subordination of the computer to narrow, military objectives that led to its breakdown and destruction; . . . I offered to give an interpretive talk about it. . . . 'You don't understand,' she said bitterly. . . . 'Your film is a challenge to the imagination and we are not permitted to use our imaginations!' "[1]

This response reflected exactly what American politicians hoped their international cultural activities would evoke. The film itself demonstrated

American technological achievements, portending greater advances in the future, and provided an example of what peaceful attitudes and creative minds could attain. By screening the film in Moscow, American officials sent a message that the ingenuity and freedom of the American system produced desirable benefits and was vastly preferable to the confines of the Soviet system. The film's success delighted President Nixon and the White House International Cultural Planning Group, of which Straight was a member, and the White House did not hesitate to publicize it.[2] Furthermore, Nixon remembered Straight's involvement with the film festival and later pressed for his appointment as deputy chairman of the National Endowment for the Arts.

That Nixon was a staunch cold warrior is by now a tired fact. But the extension of his Cold War strategies to international cultural affairs and even domestic cultural endeavors has long been overlooked.[3] Arts policy represented one among several positive yet little-known accomplishments of Nixon's presidency. Indeed, Nixon propelled the largest expansion of federal arts funding, overseeing a nearly ten-fold increase in the NEA budget from just over $7 million in 1968 when he took office to over $64 million in 1974 when he resigned the presidency. Nixon made it possible for the NEA to enjoy a golden age during the 1970s.

How did Nixon—someone widely perceived as the spokesperson for fiscal and social conservatives during the post–World War II era—become the most liberal spender on the arts? In part, the answer lies in breaking down some continuing misperceptions of Nixon. On the one hand, Nixon was more liberal in his policies—and spending practices—than his opponents recognized. On the other hand, he cunningly manipulated events and policies for reasons that were just as likely to be self-serving as motivated by a desire to do the right thing. His arts policies were consistent with his overall character and agenda.

Nixon's approach to cultural policy reflected his frequently contradictory nature and was but one example in a host of unusual or unexpected actions by the Republican president. While he touted fiscal restraint and a limited role for the federal government, Nixon also expanded federal programs and instituted new ones. Among his more liberal policies were wage and price controls, health care initiatives, pollution regulations, and the establishment of the Environmental Protection Agency. Known as a hard-line anticommunist, Nixon secretly negotiated with the Soviets and Chinese to secure American interests in Third World arenas, reduce armaments, and open diplomatic and cultural ties to those nations. On occasion Nixon also reveled in actions that would outdo and foil the liberals, such as widening affirmative action to require the hiring of minorities and women by government contractors and proposing a national Voting Rights Act (since Johnson's 1965 law only applied to seven southern states). His motivation in this case was ostensibly to advance the cause of civil rights, yet Nixon also knew it would essentially let the South off the hot seat (in keeping with his southern strategy) and cast congressional liberals as status quo defenders if they opposed him (which they did). As Florida senator George Smathers once proclaimed, "[Nixon] was the most calculating man I ever knew."[4] Nixon's activities on behalf of American arts policy paralleled his actions in other domestic and foreign areas, and his motives were often laced with self-serving goals rather than a simple desire to patronize the arts.[5]

Furthermore, arts policies reflected Nixon's "new federalism." This concept was an attempt to redistribute certain functions back to state and local governments while retaining control at the national level for others. For the arts this meant increased decentralization in the form of more support for state and local programs, while the NEA retained overall policy management under the direction of the White House. Nixon's new federalism did indeed result in more spending to spread arts policy rather than in a cutback of the federal role, as it would under the more conservative new federalism of Ronald Reagan during the 1980s.

Arts policy under Nixon pursued varied goals. The expansion of the NEA reflected Nixon's continuing interest in Cold War competition, but it also expressed his desire to mitigate what he perceived as undesirable cultural outbursts in the United States. As his administration became more deeply involved in the divisive Vietnam War, and later when the Watergate investigations captured the nation's attention, Nixon hoped to quiet his critics and to instill more positive (and conservative) moral aims in domestic cultural programs. Of course, underlying this approach was also the desire to project a positive image of American society and culture at a time when Vietnam threatened a setback in Cold War strategy and domestic upheaval painted an unseemly picture of American values.

Nixon's art policy continued the theme of federal interest in preserving a high quality of life for the American people and showcasing it to the international community. Yet, Nixon became less interested than earlier presidents in encouraging the arts for the sake of social uplift and more concerned with using arts policy to appease or control discordant groups as well as present a more favorable image of himself.

★ *A Slow Start*

Nixon did not enter the White House with a commitment to multiply arts allocations or harness the positive publicity potential of arts policy. Rather, in his first year he moved sluggishly, or not at all, on the arts. Shortly after he entered the White House, Nixon allowed NEA Chair Roger Stevens's term of appointment to expire despite a broad base of support for reappointment. Apparently, after learning that Stevens had once raised money for the Democratic Party, Nixon wished to replace him with a loyal Republican.[6]

Throughout most of 1969, while the search for an appropriate successor to Stevens languished, Nixon drew criticism from arts supporters. Speaking out on behalf of the federal arts program that he had worked so diligently to help create, Senator Claiborne Pell made a well-publicized statement on the Senate floor. Pell acknowledged that the president faced many awesome problems and responsibilities. "It is also important," Pell declared, "that the quality of American life, as well as its protection, should be of great concern to us." Continuing in partisan terms that Pell usually avoided in arts policy discussions, he charged, "the White House is now searching for a person suitably acceptable to the world of arts but who presumably has also a high Republican profile. Perhaps such a combination is hard to find. . . . I do wish that the White House would hurry up."[7]

Some weeks later Pell's outcries were joined by those of Republican senator Jacob Javits and former Kennedy arts consultant August Heckscher. In a speech titled "What Ever Happened to the Arts?" Heckscher declared, "We are today worse off than any of us could have conceived. The Arts Foundation is a ship in irons, without a head, and there is no move from the White House."[8] Heckscher's focus on both the difficulties of "guns and butter" policy, which maintained heavy spending on defense and stretched spending on social programs, and the need for federal support for the arts elicited praise from a *Washington Post* reporter covering the meeting. The reporter agreed that national priorities favored spending on the war in Vietnam over all other considerations but "this does not mean that the feeding of the body somehow cruelly requires the starving of the spirit."[9]

Other media outlets joined in the criticism, as did many on the NEA staff and the National Council for the Arts. According to one news report, "less than 24 hours after they fired [Stevens], the Republicans were admitting they had made a mistake." The story also quoted NEA staff member Charles Mark as saying that "Nixon people called [the Endowment] because they were worried about what the press was saying [about Stevens' departure]. . . . Mind you, they were not worried about the Endowment. They told us to assure the press that they were looking hard for a replacement."[10] Council member Richard Diebenkorn resigned his Council membership in protest of Stevens's mistreatment;[11] Henry Geldzahler left his post as Visual Arts Program Director; and Minoru Yamasaki and Helen Hayes also resigned from the Arts Council that year. Finally, Deputy Chair Livingston Biddle left the NEA to develop a new arts administration program at Fordham University, leaving the agency in the hands of Douglas MacAgy, who served as acting chair in the interim period.[12]

Meanwhile, internal complaints reinforced the barrage of criticism from beyond the walls of the White House. The State Department and the USIA appealed to the new president to continue cultural programs and appropriations and to resolve the search for a new NEA chair.[13] Carol Hartford, a cultural affairs employee at the USIA, argued for prompt action on arts policy and sent a list of suggestions for the NEA chair position.[14] She asserted that inaction was nothing less than an "international embarrassment" of "sensitive proportions" to U.S. delegates at the U.S. National Council on the Arts and Canadian Arts Council meeting in 1969.[15] She also expressed impatience with Nixon for not moving forward with creating a cultural affairs office in his White House—a proposal that she had worked to prepare with Herbert Klein and Leonard Garment earlier that year.[16]

While delay and criticism mounted, the Nixon administration reconsidered its arts policy, undertaking a long search for a new NEA chair and reviewing potential institutional and policy initiatives. Nixon considered several people to head the NEA: John Hightower, of New York State art project fame; John Walker of the National Gallery; Ralph Burgard of the Associated Councils on the Arts; Leslie Cheek, former director of the Virginia Museum of Fine Arts; George Irwin; John D. Rockefeller III; Phil Hanes, who was serving on the National Council on the Arts; McNeil Lowry of the Ford Foundation; Arnold Gingrich of the New York Board of Trade and *Esquire* magazine; and Joseph Pulitzer of the *St. Louis Post Dispatch*.[17] After a time, the leading candidate appeared to be Morton May, a prominent businessman and head of the May Company department stores. May expressed his willingness to take on the job but argued that his business activities would only allow him to do so on a part-time basis. This annoyed Senator Pell, who as head of the Senate Special Subcommittee on the Arts maintained the power to influence any NEA appointment. Senator Pell ultimately blocked May's nomination in favor of a full-time chair for the Endowment, prompting the Nixon administration to continue the search.[18]

John McFadyen, an architect and a leader in New York State arts activities, was also in contention for the post. At one point he believed himself in such good standing that he attended a meeting of the National Council on the Arts and announced that he would be the next chair. Shortly afterward he learned that he, too, was out. "It was embarrassing," remembers Ana Steele, "I mean 'Hi! I'm your new Chair' and then a month later. . . . We only ever found out by reading the newspapers."[19]

In August 1969, the *New York Times* issued a surprising announcement that the long search had apparently ended. Nixon would name Michael Straight to the post.[20] Straight had worked as a writer and researcher for President Franklin D. Roosevelt's cabinet and served as an economist for the State Department in the early 1940s. He was also editor of the *New Republic*, a liberal magazine founded by his father. Straight was well connected in many influential circles. He was an avid art collector and president of the Whitney Foundation in New York and had personally contributed artworks to the White House, National Gallery, Cleveland Museum, and Cornell University.[21]

The *Times* announcement shocked and angered many Republicans on Capitol Hill, who complained to Nixon officials, "Do you mean to tell us that you've fired a Democrat, you've searched for seven months, and the best you can come up with is another Democrat?" By most accounts Senator Javits joined those who balked in a manner uncharacteristic for him, since he had long been working for the arts on a bipartisan basis. In fact, Javits stonewalled the appointment because he favored John Walker.[22] Straight's nomination quickly unraveled. It was rumored that he was rejected because he had been a member of the Communist Party while a student in England and, later, a suspected spy. Although Straight eventually revealed his past affiliations and insisted that he had never been a spy, his story was not made public at the time of his nomination.[23] After Straight's rejection for the chairmanship, Nixon continued to support him and eventually secured him a post as deputy chair at the NEA.[24]

★ Nancy Hanks

Finally, Nancy Hanks, a name that had circulated on White House short lists for some time, floated to the top. By 1969 Hanks, a registered Republican, was a well-known arts supporter associated with the Rockefeller brothers.

After graduating from Duke University in 1949, she had worked in Washington at the Office of Defense Mobilization. There, she first met Nelson Rockefeller, with whom she would maintain a longtime working relationship and a well-known affair.[25] She became a member of his staff on the President's Committee on Government Organization in 1953, then worked as his assistant from 1955 to 1959, when he became a special assistant in the President Eisenhower's Special Projects Office. From 1959 to 1969 she continued as Rockefeller's assistant and also began to work as executive secretary for the Rockefeller Brothers Fund, where she helped to compose *The Performing Arts: Problems and Prospects*, the report that drew so much attention in 1965. Hanks assumed the presidency of the Associated Councils on the Arts in 1968.[26]

Although Hanks's name had appeared on several White House memos regarding leadership of the NEA, she had not received serious consideration because she was a woman.[27] Wearied of the search for an Endowment chair, arts supporters welcomed the news of Hanks's appointment, which Nixon announced in San Clemente, California, on September 3, 1969 (fig. 6.1). Nixon affirmed that in "the further advance in the cultural development of our nation . . . [Hanks] has my full confidence and will have my full cooperation."[28] Her gender ultimately worked in her favor, as Garment convinced Nixon he should expand his appointments to the NEA and the National Council on the Arts specifically to include more women and minorities.[29] Nixon concluded that appointing a woman would gain positive publicity in a realm that had recently warranted so many complaints. News that a woman had won the post captured the attention of the American media. Headlines such as "Woman gets US Arts Council Post" and "Lady of the Arts" were splashed across newspapers that day.[30] The *New York Times* reported that as head of the National Endowment for the Arts, "Miss Hanks will be one of the highest-ranking women in the Nixon Administration."[31] The *Washington Evening Star* noted that she would soon come to the capital to preside over the next meeting of the National Council on the Arts and "for the next four years, this youthful Miami Beach–born career woman should be quite an ornament to the nation's Capital."[32]

Although public reaction to Hanks was overwhelmingly favorable, it revealed that many would take a female leader of a federal agency less seriously than a male. Indeed, the arts were a realm of culture traditionally fostered by women but headed by male presidents and directors of museums and cultural institutions.[33] Ultimately, Hanks proved to be far more than an "orna-

6.1. *President Nixon with* NEA *chair Nancy Hanks.*
(Photo courtesy of the National Archives and Records Administration)

mental" head for the Endowment. Her appointment as chairman (she did not wish to be called a Chairperson or Chairwoman) gently broke with tradition and allowed Nixon to obtain good press and amend for his tardiness on arts policy. Hanks sailed through Senate confirmation in early October after hearings that resembled a reception more than an assessment of her qualifications.

★ Cultural Policy under Nixon: New Directions

In addition to naming a new NEA chair, the Nixon administration pursued new arts policies on a number of fronts in 1969 and 1970. Key advisers began to reevaluate cultural affairs and urge greater action by the president soon after he took office. Apparently the initial delay occurred not only because

Nixon was preoccupied with Vietnam, domestic upheaval, and establishing "law and order" but also because the administration was searching for a cultural strategy that would herald a new Nixon agenda rather than borrowing policies set up by his Democratic predecessors. Galled by the admiration Kennedy had won, undeservedly in Nixon's opinion, the president determined to make his own mark.[34] One Nixon adviser summed up the approach matter of factly:

> Instead of this lets-invite-Pablo-Casals-to-play-his-fiddle while the folks watch television, or the I-promise-you-a-new-paradise-of-art-creation which was the minor theme of the Great Society approach, here is a middle way: the acknowledgement of the President of the United States of the importance of art . . . [and teaching] the young that art is worthy of the attention of the great . . . Roger Stevens called for a new partnership [with business]. . . . Isaac Stern gives government hell for not giving 'money to people' in the arts. . . . They are establishmentarian figures who, whatever their great love for the arts, seem to be irrelevant to what I feel to be the only facet of the artistic complexity worthy of a President's attention: emphasizing the importance of the creation and enjoyment of art in the lives of Americans.[35]

The memo signaled important hallmarks of Nixon's art policy. Like Kennedy and Johnson, Nixon would stage artistic and musical events in the White House and would use his office to lend support to American culture. On the other hand, he did not wish to promise increases in government involvement on arts policy. He hoped to move away from establishment control and strictly elite involvement in the art world and to enhance common citizens' enjoyment of the arts. These initial aspirations would not all bear fruit. Yet Nixon soon increased federal support for the NEA as the president's desire to improve his public image became more pressing. Even while Nixon's staff sneered at what they dubbed "phony Kennedy stuff" with regards to cultural affairs in the Kennedy White House, Nixon himself was sowing the seeds of his own brand of image creation.[36]

Initially, Nixon flirted with establishing a Ministry of Culture, but he never followed through on the idea.[37] After reviewing the state of arts policy, he concluded that the NEA was doing a fine job and that such a ministry was unwarranted. Certainly, establishing another high-profile federal institution would have countered what was becoming a growing demand for smaller government—a conservative political movement that Nixon did not wish to alienate. Instead, he would develop a White House cultural affairs office, which gave him the appearance of moving forward on arts policy while essentially maintaining the same structures already set in place by Presidents Kennedy and Johnson.

Much of Nixon's art policy followed the path laid down in a 1969 memo by Leonard Garment, Nixon's special adviser on civil rights, his primary adviser on culture, and the head of the White House Office of Cultural Affairs. Garment's initial memo brought to Nixon's attention the work of the National Endowment for the Arts. Summarizing the agency's achievements, Garment highlighted the matching grant requirements, especially their success in garnering state and private funds for arts project beyond federal appropriation. Garment also underlined the nonpolitical nature of art grants and the great respect the agency had gained with a host of groups—including politicians of all stripes, established cultural leaders, and the avant-garde.

Garment also sketched out a budgetary outlook for the Endowment, noting that more would need to be done to maintain the agency at its current level of activities by countering inflation's tap on the budget.[38] Greater allocations fell within congressional authorization for the agency and would further stimulate matching grants.[39] Thus, expanded arts funding dovetailed with the administration's overall policy of encouraging private initiative and decentralization and appealed to Nixon's interest in winning friends for his administration not just among fiscal conservatives but democratic arts supporters and cultural magnates at the same time.

Garment also encouraged Nixon to attend arts events and continue international cultural exchanges. Hanks declared that public reaction to positive reports of national leaders going off to the theater was wonderful because people were delighted to "have something on the front page that wasn't gloom and doom, something that didn't go on to dwell on the problems of the city, the antagonism between the two political leaders, etcetera." She might well have included the Vietnam War among those dark clouds that the administration wished to dispel. Furthermore, she added, "our image abroad will most significantly be effected in my judgement by the strength of the arts in this country and how we view them as a society. However there is no question that exporting our cultural resources has its role." She recommended that the NEA be given a greater role in developing cultural programs abroad, in lieu of dividing arts activities between it and the State Department.[40] Garment concurred that this was the best assessment of political goals and social implications of an expanded arts program worthy of the President's personal attention.

Nixon also initiated new White House policies on art displays. Several letters between the president and his staff to noted art museums and collectors indicate that Nixon began gathering art to exhibit in the White House during his administration. These included primarily traditional paintings representing scenes of American history and portraits of famous Americans. Nixon was delighted by the loans of *The Spirit of '76*, by Archibald Willard; *Oklahoma Land Rush*, by John Steuart Curry; *Mt. Vernon*, by George Ropes; and *Charge of the Rough Riders up San Juan Hill*, a sculpture by Frederic Remington. He also obtained work by muralists Diego Rivera and José Clemente Orozco; impressionists Maurice Utrillo, Claude Monet, and Camille Corot; and a portrait of Eisenhower by Andrew Wyeth, which he displayed in the "western White House" in San Clemente. Nixon admired realist painting, although a White House rule disallowing the collection of works by living American artists also curtailed displays of modernist works.[41] However, the "living artists" rule did not prevent his staff from gathering a preponderance of contemporary works in their offices. Photos of Garment's, Klein's, and Kissinger's White House offices show modernist paintings displayed prominently.[42] In fact, their tastes more closely reflected those of the culture brokers and arts institution leaders of the 1950s and 1960s who were instrumental in arts policy development and actual NEA grant selections. Nixon indulged their interests in modern art more often at the very beginning of his administration before he attempted to establish more inclusive federal arts policies.

Documentation on the government's Art in the Embassies Program also shows a keen interest by Nixon administration officials in displaying excellent examples of American achievement in painting and sculpture in U.S. embassies throughout the world, as had been the case during previous administrations during the post–World War II period. Nixon was particularly interested in cultural exhibitions in Eastern Europe and "battleground countries," indicating the continued waging of the cultural Cold War.[43] Catalogs and photographs of art in certain target areas, such as Kuala Lumpur, New Delhi, and Moscow, illustrate that for the most part modernist pieces adorned the walls and pedestals of the American embassies.[44] One photograph captured Kenneth Keating, U.S. ambassador to India, admiring the New Dehli residence displays of Dan Christensen's *Cygnus*, Milton Avery's *Lone Cow in Landscape*, and Karl Knath's *Dunes*. The catalog for the Moscow embassy depicted works by the most famous American abstractionists, including Jackson Pollock, Hans Hofmann, Sam Francis, and Alexander Calder.[45]

In one, more detailed example, illustrations in the catalog of American art in the U.S. embassy in Jidda, Saudi Arabia, also reveal a preponderance of abstract works. The text accompanying the illustrations, which was penned by Henry Geldzahler himself,asserts that American art had truly come of age and that contemporary New York had become as important an art center as Paris once had been. Geldzahler maintained that in the modern age, the entire world was "becoming a single artistic community [where] differences persist, but through exhibitions and photographs of paintings these [were] being minimized."[46] Geldzahler expressed the prevailing American belief that American art (read modernist abstraction) embodied American achievement and best displayed American freedom to the world. Showcasing such art in the embassies brought this message into foreign capitals with the hope that viewers would be attracted by American culture. Nixon condoned the goal and initially went along with the display of modernist art, although he later complained that too many abstract works decorated the American embassies and greater balance of art genres should be sought.[47]

In keeping with previous modernist displays, the first public exhibit of art at the Nixon White House was a showing of David Smith sculptures on the White House grounds the summer of 1969. At that time, the Corcoran Gallery was mounting a major retrospective to honor the late sculptor, but the gallery could not accommodate many of Smith's monumental works in its limited space. Nixon agreed that several of the large pieces from the *Cubi* series (see fig. 4.6), among others, could be placed opposite the gallery on the White House lawn, and his staff arranged for the National Park Service to grant such permission.[48] According to one White House memo, Smith's works were appropriate for display not only because of the sculptor's aesthetic excellence but also because of his role "in creating a new freedom for art throughout the world."[49] Smith was admired for his work on the National Council on the Arts and for the example he set as a common man who rose to prominence by breaking new artistic ground and through public service. Nixon could appreciate Smith the man, and, although Smith the sculptor's aesthetic style was not his favorite, he was willing to compromise his own taste for the benefit of White House guests and the enjoyment of the public.[50] In this respect Nixon followed a tradition set by Kennedy—one that he would not maintain as his term proceeded, however.

In October of 1969, Garment urged a new assault on the arts front. With a minuscule amount of expenditure Nixon could "demonstrate dramatically [his] commitment to 'reordering national priorities'" in the face of war and inflation by *doubling* the NEA's budget. Garment proposed that such a move was justified since the arts and humanities budget was "completely inadequate." More importantly, he argued that if Nixon took this course of action it would have a great impact on public opinion: "support for the arts is increasingly good politics. . . . And this administration should be the first to pay real attention to the importance of communications in the foreign and domestic realm."[51] (Never mind that these international and domestic goals were long part of both Kennedy's and Johnson's policies.)

Charles McWhorter of the Department of State had also encouraged high-level increases for cultural activities, urging "at least" a doubling of the NEA budget. Interestingly, he did not propose such a large increase for his own State Department cultural affairs budget, as he likely believed the public emphasis on domestic expenditure would be of greater benefit to the administration. He posited that the impact would be quite sensational and beneficial to the president at a time when the administration was being heavily criticized on Vietnam. This would provide the president with the "opportunity to demonstrate a deep personal concern with improving the quality of living here at home and his determination to present a better image of America abroad." Then he went on to propose an increase in State Department funds also (by half) to indicate the importance of "letting other people around the world know of the other side of American life as reflected by our . . . artistic activities."[52]

Garment advised the president to consider the long-range planning implications of his policies instead of following a piecemeal approach. This included taking into consideration intellectual and cultural critics' arguments that American leaders be wary of America's tendency toward fostering unlimited growth and material consumption at the expense of long-range growth and goals. One memo concluded that there "could be a good deal of drama to announcing a new approach of controlled growth and . . . a reemphasis on the quality of life as a criterion whereby to guide, stimulate, and inhibit growth of specific areas of society. It would appeal to some values that are presently surfacing, particularly among the young," including New Left criticism of the military-industrial complex fueling the war in Vietnam, student protest against the war, and young people's increased concern with peace, social justice, and personal growth. Moreover, Garment argued that as long as security was maintained, the Nixon administration "might find it stimulating to seek leadership on something other than *solely* economic and military power."[53] These ideas essentially reiterated Kennedy and Johnson policies of advancing art and culture as part of a "fourth dimension" in international affairs in addition to military, economic, and political measures.[54] However, in the turmoil of the late 1960s the idea took on another meaning in domestic politics. Nixon advisers saw arts policy as a vehicle to accentuate the positive and appeal to those tired of American displays of military might and material consumption.

Nixon took this advice to heart, as illustrated in his major address on art policy in December of 1969. Similar to both his predecessors' remarks, his speech to Congress opened with reference to the importance of dedication to "added meaning to our leisure time." Nixon argued that

> [The] attention and support we give the arts and humanities—especially as they effect [*sic*] young people—represent a vital part of our commitment to enhancing the quality of life for all Americans. The full richness of this nation's cultural life need not be the province of relatively few citizens centered in a few cities; on the contrary, the trend toward a wider appreciation of the arts . . . should be strongly encouraged, the diverse culture of every region and community should be explored. . . . There is a growing need for federal stimulus. . . . I propose that Congress approve new funds for the National Foundation . . . [that] will virtually double the current year's level. . . . Few investments we could make would give us so great a return. . . . The arts have a rare capacity to help heal divisions among our own people and to vault some of the barriers that divide the world.[55]

Nixon's request for a doubling of NEA funds in 1971 surprised some, but the language he employed sounded very familiar. His speech indicated the lasting intellectual concern with "the quality of life" in the United States during the post–World War II period and the issue of "redress[ing] the imbalance between the sciences and the humanities." It also echoed a great deal of the populist rhetoric first employed by Lyndon Johnson, as Nixon called for encouraging a wider appreciation of arts, exploring diversity, and using art for social "uplift." Nevertheless, Nixon outdid liberals' support for increasing the federal budget for the arts, taking great pleasure in surprising those who considered him a cultural Philistine.[56] At the same time he also managed to imbue his message on arts policy with his greater concerns for limiting federal involvement by asserting that the government could not substitute public money for private funds and encouraging increased input from state and local agencies. He declared, "the federal role would remain supportive rather than primary."[57] Nixon called this arts policy part of his total program of priorities for the next decade.

★ NEA Budget Increases

In January 1970 Nixon's State of the Union address reiterated his support for the arts and concern with enhancing the quality of life in the United States. Sent to Congress shortly thereafter, Nixon's budget included the significant increases for the National Endowment for the Arts. Nixon not only backed a financial increase for the arts, but he also confirmed a direct link between his overall administration plans and those that would be carried out by the NEA. He demonstrated a high level of interest in the arts budget by later authorizing his aid John Ehrlichman to pave the way for Nancy Hanks's discussion of the budget with Caspar Weinberger at the Office of Management and Budget (OMB).[58] Upon hearing the request, Weinberger noted that at a time when the OMB was "trying to reduce expenditure of most agencies in order to meet the ceilings desired by the President . . . this kind of process usually precludes doubling the budget of any agency." However, he agreed that "a most persuasive case" had been made, and he and the OMB would "certainly do our best."[59]

The reaction to Nixon's arts budget proposal was very positive in the national press. The *New York Times* called the increase "one of the most significant he is making this year in his budget deliberations" and suggested surprise that this would occur in a time of "economic stringency, when many government budget requests are likely to be cut back."[60] The *Evening Star* in Washington, D.C., stated that the administration's culture budget was "heartening" and reflected "a sense of the nation's feeling on the question."[61] The *Minneapolis Tribune* argued that it hoped Congress would appropriate the full amount and "any tendency to dismiss the arts as an expendable luxury will be overcome. . . . Healthy cultural institutions and events are an important part of quality of life."[62] This report illustrates how the "quality of life" phrase had become part of the American vocabulary on cultural progress.

Congress also responded favorably. Rep. John Brademas (D-Ind.), who had long supported arts policy, praised the president's message as a "constructive and encouraging response to the nation's need for greater support of our cultural resources."[63] As chairman of the House subcommittee on education, which had jurisdiction over the arts and humanities, Brademas introduced the administration's bill and promised his weighty support. He was joined by many in the Senate, including Javits, Pell, and Sen. Edward Kennedy (D-Mass.), and by Rep. Richard Ottinger (D-N.Y.), who told the House, "While I have not found it possible to support the President's Vietnam policy or his overall thrust of emphasis on military expenditures . . . I am pleased to be able to support enthusiastically the priority he recently placed on obtaining more funds to support the arts."[64]

Expenditures requested for the NEA under the Nixon administration skyrocketed. By the midpoint of Nixon's tenure, the NEA budget rose to a total of more than ten times the original 1966 budget for the arts of $2.5 million, and by 1974 it had blossomed to almost twenty-five times its original amount. During the Johnson administration between 1967 and 1969, the NEA budget hovered between $7.2 and $8 million. Under Nixon appropriations grew steadily ($8.2 million in 1970, $15 million in 1971, $29.7 million in 1972, $38.2 million in 1973, and $60.7 million in 1973).[65]

Increased budget appropriations for the arts would have been conventional had they merely reflected a normal rise in federal expenditures across the board. However, this was not the case. During the Nixon administration costs were slashed for most federal programs. Within such a stringent economic environment the NEA budget increases were all the more striking. Indeed one report underscored that by 1974 only two federal departments were experiencing funding growth—the NEA and the Department of Defense.[66] This link between cultural funding and defense illustrates the importance American leaders placed on the arts as part of an overarching national and international program designed to uphold American power and prestige.

During his first year in office, Nixon began to indicate that he wished to include the entire government structure in his arts policy plans. In December 1969, he asked all federal agencies to submit a report to the White House on what their agency or department was currently doing for the arts and how they could propose to increase such support. A memo to this effect was sent out from the White House on the same day that Nixon gave his message on the arts to Congress, signifying that a coordinated effort on behalf of the arts was indeed underway at the Nixon White House. In his directive Nixon reminded agency leaders of his concern about the arts and of the recent NEA budget increase; yet he noted that each agency had a role to play in contributing to the arts.[67] Nancy Hanks and Leonard Garment were to report on the responses within the next few months.[68] The results of this federal coordination led to new guidelines on federal art and architecture enhancement and increased use of professional artists for graphics and publications printed by the federal government. Once again, these were measures that had previously been encouraged by President Kennedy after the receipt of August Heckscher's report on the arts and national government.

A more important development would be an increased use of the NEA to coordinate federal uses of and support for the arts and the establishing of a federal Design Assembly, an office specializing in modern design information for the use of administrators and artists employed by the federal government. Nixon argued that improved design quality and superior building presentations would show a "marked improvement in our surroundings and in our ability to communicate." In other words, it was hoped that the rejection of visual mediocrity in government design standards would also improve the image of the America government in the public eye. The NEA oversaw the organization of such a program, although the Design Assembly later became a separate entity.

In addition, President Nixon began to show his support for the arts in another way. In April of 1969, the president announced that he would host a White House dinner and celebration in honor of jazz artist Duke Ellington. The event was scheduled shortly after the publication of a *U.S. News & World Report* magazine article that described a more sedate social atmosphere in the Nixon White House, where formality and propriety were "in," and colorful informality was "out." According to the author, "The marine band now plays only sedate fox trots and waltzes, leaving out the jazz and rock music. . . . So far, Mr. Nixon has not danced at all. . . . Op art has vanished from office walls. Traditional landscapes and portraits now hang where the cubes and swirls and dots used to be. . . . [For State Dinners,] the small round tables that were favored by the Kennedys and the Johnsons [are to be abolished]. One large, U-shaped table is suggested to reestablish protocol and mark quite clearly who is, and who is not, 'above the salt.' "[69]

An even less flattering account of Nixon administration culture, entitled "The Square Elephant at Work and Play," proclaimed, "White House reporters think social secretary Lucy Winchester is deliberately planning dull parties. Cabinet members have been sneaking out of State Dinners. . . . Gone are the scenes from the Broadway shows, the performances by top ballet companies or appearances by musicians such as Van Cliburn. . . . Tapioca is out, cottage cheese with ketchup is in. Living on a welfare budget for a week is *très chic.* . . . Black businessmen are in, but black friends are out, not because the Republicans are prejudiced; they just don't have any colored friends.

Forgotten White Americans are in."[70] In the face of such blatant criticism, Nixon officials welcomed the opportunity to counter allegations of lackluster White House entertainment, bad taste, and apparently racist social practices and prove they could deliver a good show. Inviting a renowned jazz musician like Ellington would help dispel a dour image of Nixon White House entertainment while also demonstrating that black entertainers were welcome and lively music was appreciated.

Ellington was graciously introduced by President Nixon on April 29, 1969, and played before a large audience of Washington dignitaries, many of who enjoyed dancing to the excellent jazz. The *Washington Post* reported Ellington's concert as "a jam session such as the old mansion has never known."[71] Furthermore, the evening elicited the desired reaction from one black musician who commented that "Nixon did something no one else has ever done— this is the first time an American black man was honored in the White House."[72] Nixon officials widely publicized the event, even in international broadcasts and at American embassies around the world. They underscored the event's illustration of progressive cultural programs in the Nixon White House and used it abroad to demonstrate the inclusiveness of American democracy and to enhance world youths' appreciation of American culture.[73]

Early in 1970 Nixon also opened the White House for an exhibit of paintings and a special dinner celebrating artist Andrew Wyeth. Alternately borrowing from precedents set by Kennedy and Johnson, Nixon personally telephoned Wyeth to extend the invitation and invited members of Congress and other officials for special viewings of the works once they were installed.[74] Twenty-two paintings were loaned to the Nixons and displayed in a temporary gallery of specially designed velvet panels in the White House East Room (fig. 6.2). The show included the painting *My Young Friend*, which was completed by Wyeth just in time for the White House exhibit and praised in a *Time* magazine article reporting on the display.[75] Guests and the public were invited to view the exhibit over a five-week period following the dinner.

Although the dinner was for Wyeth personally, the White House made it clear that it was meant to honor all American arts, not merely one artist. One letter written about the Wyeth exhibit explained how Nixon was able to highlight the traditional art form that he personally preferred while avoiding any negative insinuations on his part regarding more abstract genres. The letter explained to a constituent that Nixon meant for the exhibit to acknowledge the significance of all the arts and that President and Mrs. Nixon "have a feeling for the particular value of visual arts of all schools and a sensitive

6.2. *The White House East Room serving as a gallery for Andrew Wyeth paintings in 1970.*
(Photo courtesy of the National Archives and Records Administration)

understanding of the work of realists."[76] Nixon advertised that he was the first president to formally honor an American painter in the White House.[77]

Nixon also used the dinner as an occasion to host a black-tie affair and to demonstrate his concern for American culture through a press conference scheduled that afternoon. For the formal occasion, 110 guests dined on a menu of pheasant and filet of sole, then were joined by an additional 100 attendees to savor the after-dinner entertainment provided by renowned pianist Rudolf Serkin.[78] That evening, Nixon toasted Wyeth as a great individual who had "contributed something special to American life, something that cannot be contributed by our great military strength and our economic wealth, a quality of spirit, a quality of beauty which only the greater civilizations can leave to posterity."[79] The president thus invoked the ideal of American cultural prestige that his predecessors had also employed the arts to secure.

★ *Adjusting NEA Policy and Programs*

The celebration of Wyeth foreshadowed a shift in stylistic preferences that would soon grow beyond the confines of the Nixon White House. The influence of Nixon cultural priorities affected NEA policy and demanded an alteration of programs and grant-making procedure, including those related to the visual arts. Although international programs continued to celebrate modernist abstract art, which by then had long been considered the best symbol of American freedom of expression, Nixon soon began to impose his own taste for traditional styles onto his art policy. In international programs of art exchange, he desired that more figurative and realist works should be included in exhibits. White House files on art exchanges reveal that art shows began to include more traditional paintings and sculptures for exhibits sent abroad, although traditional works by no means replaced the modernist forms that continued to hang alongside them. Nixon also expanded the international exchanges to include the People's Republic of China when he and Chinese premier Chou En-lai issued the Joint Communiqué in 1972, agreeing that "such contacts will make a major contribution over a period of time to the reduction of misunderstanding and tension between our two countries."[80]

Nixon's policies had a greater impact on the domestic art programs, although grassroots interests generated many changes to which the NEA responded favorably. One of Nixon's responses to art policy was an expression of dissatisfaction with the weighting of NEA grants toward artists who worked in abstract forms. The president agreed with numerous complaints sent to NEA chair Nancy Hanks, NEH chair Wallace Edgerton, and the White House about funds supporting "unintelligible art."[81] Hanks defended the nature of NEA grant-making by announcing time and again that grants were neither awards for past work nor commissions for specific works to be produced—they were awards for the artists to use as they saw fit. The policy was meant to safeguard individual artists' creative freedom and ensure that no political control would constrain the freedom of the arts programs. Tension began to develop between White House wishes and those of NEA officials over the nature of the arts to be celebrated by the federal government. Although none of the officials wished to advocate censorship, several changes did occur with the blessing of Nixon and many in Congress who preferred more traditional representational forms and art that their constituents "in Peoria" would appreciate.

Nixon quietly refused to allow any further displays of modernist art near the White House during his administration. When asked by the Corcoran Gallery to approve another use of White House grounds for an art exhibit similar to the David Smith show in 1969, Nixon declined. He instructed Garment to explain that the Smith show was to be considered an extraordinary and "infrequent" use of White House grounds. Nixon later extended this policy beyond the White House when he ordered a display of Alexander Lieberman sculptures removed from the Mall to a location out of his view from the White House. Nixon detested the large red tubular metal sculpture by Lieberman named *Adam*, which he claimed distracted him whenever he noticed it looming outside the presidential offices. Administration documents suggest that Nixon aides considered secretly paying either the NEA or an agreeable Corcoran board member to "donate" the funds for shipping the sculpture to a new and "better" location.[82] Although following Nixon's orders, cultural leaders took great care to cover up the president's explicitly anti–modern art actions with a plan that would make the removal of the sculpture seem positive. Under Garment's insistence that the White House stay out of the search, Nancy Hanks and the NEA sought a new location for the sculpture.[83] It was agreed that the National Park Service would place the sculpture on park property, and the move would be advertised as yet another new means of federal government support for the arts and a response by the Park Service to Nixon's request for increased activity by federal agencies to display quality American art. Ironically, the ruse added to Nixon's reputation as a grand federal patron of the arts, even as he began to undermine what had been federal support for modernist art at the highest levels.

Despite Nixon's newly voiced complaints about avant-garde art, NEA leaders continued support for modernist art while moderating their program development to include greater representation of other forms. As demonstrated in Chapter 5, the preponderance of grants to individual artists under the auspices of the NEA's Visual Arts Program continued to be awarded to abstract modernist painters and sculptors. The NEA was left to pursue its own course more and more after the Watergate break-in in 1972 and investigations between 1973 and 1974 consumed Nixon officials' attention. Yet, during the 1970s, the NEA began to expand its programs to include other aesthetic forms.

During the Nixon administration, cultural officials called for arts programs to reflect more inclusiveness and to address the needs of youth. Such goals won support from ostensibly conflicting elements of American society. On the one hand, civil rights activists of the 1960s advocated greater inclusion of minorities, women, and those representing popular American values and attitudes in federal programs. On the other hand, Nixon administration officials expressed hostility to entitlement programs and minority activism and saw the arts as a positive, uncontroversial, and inexpensive means of promoting diversity. They also began to tailor the NEA programs to the interests of the "forgotten" Americans and the needs of American youth. Ultimately, Nixon officials employed the language of democracy and inclusion while generally addressing the needs of white, rural Americans more than inner-city minorities and youth.

Other studies have noted the pluralistic nature of NEA programs during the 1970s and 1980s. But few have recognized that this expansion occurred under Nixon because he was interested in polishing America's image abroad and his own at home, especially after the Watergate affair spun out of his control and generated increasingly negative opinions of him and his administration in 1973 and 1974.[84] Even after the administration accepted ethnic and regional diversity, it still shied away from the most avant-garde forms of art—steering clear of pop art and the feminist, black, and Chicano arts of the 1970s that held more political and critical messages.

★ *Crafts, Folk Arts, and Expansion Arts*

Expanded NEA budgets fueled the creation of programs for crafts, "expansion arts" (a term referring to community and ethnic arts), and eventually folk arts, although these programs remained rather small and isolated by comparison to the major emphasis on dance, theater, opera, literature, museums, and visual arts. Ignored by the NEA in its early years, crafts and folk arts began to receive some consideration in the 1970s because of Hanks's personal interest. According to Ana Steele, then the NEA's budget and research office director, Hanks took a particular interest in creating a niche for crafts because "her tastes were very catholic . . . [and] she had an understanding of the grass roots."[85] Hanks also recognized that crafts seemed to reach out to common artisans and redress what many considered the NEA's elitist bias. In 1973, the visual arts program awarded the first individual grants to craftspeople.

Still, the program remained small. The NEA awarded 34 crafts fellowships in 1973, 50 in 1974, and 47 in 1975. By comparison, 45 painters and sculptors received individual fellowships (of $4,500 more than the crafts grants) in 1973, 144 in 1974, and 135 in 1975. During this three-year period, craftspeople received a total of $487,000 in grants, while painters and sculptors divided $1,017,500.[86]

Folk arts did not garner attention until even later. After the National Council on the Arts tabled their discussion of the folk arts, the NEA offered no program to handle such grants until 1975—after Nixon had left the White House. The NEA developed an interest in folk arts when Hanks learned that Congress was considering the establishment of a Folklife Center as a third endowment. Hanks feared such a center would become a competitor to the NEA and grew alarmed when Rep. George Mahon (D-Tex.) explained to the House that the "Arts Endowment would cater to the well-educated while the Folklife Center served the people."[87]

To prevent the creation of a folk arts program outside of the NEA, which would heighten the perception of the NEA as an institution catering to more elite art forms, Hanks invited folk art leaders to a meeting at the Endowment in December 1973. Alan Jabbour, head of the Library of Congress Archive of Folk Song, recalled, "It started off very politely, then Larry Reger (the NEA's director of programs and planning) told us what the NEA was doing for folk arts, and the gathering just sat there. They thought it was just a drop in the bucket, and one by one they got up and tore Larry apart. Nancy was not present initially but came into the room in the middle of it and sat down next to me and listened. She didn't know what she was going to do, but she knew she had to do something!"[88] Hanks was shocked by the reaction but immediately decided to create a Folk Arts Program in the NEA. A few days later she invited Alan Jabbour to head it. He came to the NEA in 1974 and oversaw the birth of the program, which he recalled "was initially very small in comparison to the other NEA programs, and perhaps other programs did not take it as seriously." According to Jabbour, the Council was "initially leery of folk arts, but [it] came around." He credited Hanks with embracing what she thought was a good idea and expanding the Endowment.[89]

Despite Jabbour's gracious interpretation of the NEA's motives, the agency in fact shunned folk arts throughout its first ten years, embracing it only as a defensive maneuver in a bureaucratic turf struggle.[90] In its early stages the Folk Arts Program remained an ad hoc collection of grants from other NEA programs that could be grouped under the label "folk." In fact, although Hanks's introduction to the Endowment's 1975 annual report announced the new folk arts initiative, no such program appeared anywhere in the report. Instead, folk arts was relegated a subsection of special projects, with a total of $497,111 going to major American art organizations and universities to develop emerging folk arts projects in music, performances, and the visual arts.[91] Visual arts in the folk classification received even less attention than crafts as part of the overall NEA budget. Moreover, even though the folk arts and crafts programs opened up new categories of aesthetics, they continued to serve primarily white artists.

Another NEA program emerged during the 1970s to address the development of art from minority communities. Roger Stevens and the Art Council had explored working with inner-city youth early in the agency's history, creating 116 art workshops under direction of city mayors in 1968. The grants generally funded inner-city murals and public art projects aimed at social uplift. Despite good intentions such programs remained low priority pilot projects, poorly coordinated with the city administrators. They received limited funds, and the programs fizzled by 1969. In 1971 Nancy Hanks looked anew at community-based organizations and considered doing something to provide training that would enable local communities to express themselves through art. Plans for "developing arts" focused on the black community at a time when the civil rights movement had not only generated increasing celebration of racial and ethnic pride but also taken a turn toward militancy. Organizations such as the Black Panthers were forcing Americans to consider dealing with the needs of inner-city youth in more positive ways.

At the Endowment, the NEA annual report for 1971 quoted from a Junius Eddy article in the July 1970 issue of *Public Administration Review*, which argued that ethnic arts were to help minorities "assert a new-found historical identity, and to reflect the new sense of ethnic pride and awareness they believe is essential to their survival in white America." Eddy called old government programs of cultural enrichment "a kind of loosely organized exposure of poor youngsters (mainly nonwhite) to enriching experiences from the Western middle class cultural tradition, intended to compensate for presumed deprivation in their own lives and backgrounds." He believed another approach was necessary to allow minorities to take greater control of their own cultural expression.[92]

Hanks recognized that the federal government needed to respond to minority concerns not just in terms of social uplift. Therefore, she hired Vantile Whitfield, a prominent leader in the black community with various experiences in cultural programs to lead a new Endowment effort to encourage minority arts. Whitfield had worked as a set designer, actor, television producer, and counselor of juvenile programs in Los Angeles. At the time of his appointment, Whitfield was the artistic director of the Performing Arts Society of Los Angeles. Under his guidance the NEA's Expansion Arts Program was created in 1971. It awarded its first 27 grants that December, mostly to cultural centers of national renown, although the program later extended it reaches to smaller community art programs. Expansion Arts ran into jurisdictional conflicts with state art agencies, conflicts that only intensified as Whitfield argued that his job was to step in where state agencies had failed. The program grew over the years, providing funding to 68 programs in 1972, 194 in 1973, 293 in 1974, and 466 in 1975.[93] Nonetheless, it remained separate from other NEA programs, and its staff had less than the usual interaction with the rest of the Endowment.

If Expansion Arts proved somewhat segregated, it also practiced its own form of exclusion. Its mandate to develop arts programs for minorities did not generally extend to include the increasing numbers of Native American, Puerto Rican, and Chicano artists whom art historians have argued were increasingly important in the developing ethnic arts of the 1970s.[94] Hanks acknowledged complaints from other communities, conceding in one 1977 letter that the "suggestion that more should be done for the Spanish speaking citizens of the state [of Texas] is most valid, and one we are constantly working on. . . . I will discuss this with Van Whitfield."[95] Her note demonstrated that Hispanic artists were still left out more often than not as late as 1977.

The marginalization of minority arts by the NEA during the late 1960s and early 1970s not only reflected a cultural bias in favor of more established white, modernist (generally male) artists in this period, but also the Endowment's policy of funding politically neutral aesthetics. It should come as no surprise that the Nixon administration and, by extension, the Endowment avoided support for openly political and critical art forms. Many of the minority arts produced during the 1970s were overtly political expressions, often not friendly to the Nixon administration and critical of U.S. involvement in Vietnam or American race relations. On such example was a work in East Los Angeles, *Black and White Moratorium Mural*, by Willie Herrón and Gronk, which contained numerous scenes in a collage of black and white sections. The upper-left corner illustrated racist notions by juxtaposing an image of a dark-skinned man with that of a monkey. The prominent middle section of the work depicted white police arresting a black man in a riot scene. Other sections throughout portrayed distraught individuals, barbed wire, prison inmates, and soldiers or police with tear gas (fig. 6.3). The images were less than flattering social commentary on American race relations in the

6.3. *Willie Herrón and Gronk,* Black and White Moratorium Mural, *Los Angeles.*
(Courtesy of the artists)

early 1970s. The artists did not apply for or receive federal support. Nixon
abhorred such aesthetic commentary and wanted to promote more positive
artistic expressions to reveal American cultural development to the world.

★ *Emphasis on "Real Youth"*

The Nixon administration demonstrated an interest in supporting the
cultural activities of American youth in an attempt to promote what they
considered "proper" forms of cultural expression and, increasingly, forms
that would reflect positive images of the Nixon administration and of America. Leonard Garment, Nixon's cultural adviser, has acknowledged that the
president hoped his support for culture would appease antiwar activists.[96]
Moreover, one of the earliest memos on cultural affairs in the Nixon White
House noted that the president should emphasize "average" Americans and
youth in his arts activities and policies.[97] Government officials hoped their

support would generate a future audience for the arts—and enhance the Nixon administration in the public eye.

Upon whom the spotlight should rest to achieve these goals became increasingly clear over the course of Nixon's presidency. One letter to Nixon praised a youth choir that performed at a White House worship service in 1971, positing that the president and Mrs. Nixon would "be impressed with this display of the *real* American youth—as opposed to the small minority we hear so much about on television and in the press."[98] Indeed, Nixon often lauded the clean-cut silent majority and reacted strongly against young protesters who demonstrated on college campuses against the Vietnam War. Nixon ordered Attorney General John Mitchell not to back off from those "stupid kids" and later called both protesters and victims of the shootings at Kent State "bums."[99] He tried to crush the antiwar movement by authorizing wiretaps, grand jury investigations, and felony prosecutions against those involved and by encouraging tactics of intimidation by local police and the FBI, as well as by planting agents provocateurs to incite violence and, by so doing, discredit moderate protesters. To keep himself at a reasonable distance from the harshest denunciations of the antiwar movement, Nixon assigned Vice President Spiro Agnew to unleash the most forceful rhetoric against the antiwar demonstrators. During the October 1969 Moratorium Against the Vietnam War gathering in Washington, D.C., Agnew argued that if challenging the protesters divided the country, then he considered it "time for a positive polarization . . . a constructive realignment" of the American people.[100]

At the same time that he harassed those who opposed his politics, Nixon also courted the opinion of American youth. He supported the lowering of the voting age from 21 to 18, and he instituted the draft lottery, which moved the country toward the all-volunteer army that became the standard by 1973. The president theorized that removing the personal fear of war from two-thirds of those eligible for the draft and allowing youth a greater voice in politics would dispel much of their criticism of his administration and extract a measure of support for his policies. Young Americans welcomed the changes.[101]

Nixon wished to encourage lawful and conservative behavior among American youth and to elicit from them what he considered the more positive forms of cultural expression that a "responsible majority" practiced.[102] As demonstrated above, although the administration proposed rewarding young Americans who turned to art to cultivate quality leisure time rather than wasting it on less admirable pursuits of crime, drugs, or protest, little money was actually expended for inner-city youth art centers. Nonetheless, Nixon took advantage of opportunities to promote examples of "correct" behavior and thinking among young Americans.

One such occasion was orchestrated when the State Department sponsored a tour of communist countries in Eastern Europe by rock group Blood, Sweat and Tears in 1970. It was reported that audiences' reception to the group was "outstandingly favorable" as the concerts highlighted "the American establishment and its youthful opposition getting together to present a very bright aspect of the quality of present-day American life to peoples whose own media have been enjoying a field day coloring it all horrible. The audiences got the message. The ovations they thundered forth were . . . unprecedented, and they were for America as much as for the band as the Bucharest audiences made clear by greeting the conclusion of the last encore with a chant of 'USA, USA' that went until the police stopped it."[103] The positive reaction of the communist audiences to the concert and to American culture illustrated to Nixon that foreign touring of American arts and culture was well worth the effort.

Another equally worthwhile reaction to the tour came from the band itself. Prior to their travels, the band members indicated that they, like many young Americans, were against U.S. participation in the Vietnam War and believed that communism was not as evil as the American government had portrayed it. Then the band returned and announced that "Communism is a stone drag." "I could never live that way," they declared. "I wish that everyone in America . . . could go over there and see what it's like. . . . The positive things that we do really are worth it—compared to what's happening in the rest of the world. . . . It was great to see everyone [in Bucharest] that enthusiastic. . . . It meant something to us there because they could see the freedom we had on the stand."[104] The band's turnaround from an antiadministration, antiwar stance to one more celebratory of the United States was hailed by the Nixon administration as a new "constructive" attitude.[105] Nixon would have been pleased to count among "responsible youth," who were generally defined as young, clean-cut Republicans who supported administration views and activities, more young Americans from among those longer-haired critics. Supporting artistic activities for young Americans was a means of encouraging constructive and responsible behavior, just as supporting job programs and recreational activities for youth was meant to provide a chance for "useful work" and to keep them off the streets and out of trouble.[106]

★ *State and Local Arts Programs*

The NEA also moved toward greater dispersal of funds to state and local agencies. Spreading the arts to Americans throughout the country had always been a fundamental part of the Endowment's overall mission, but during the Nixon administration, the NEA emphasized state arts programs in response to pressure from the Nixon White House and its policy of new federalism. In the 1971 State of the Union address, Nixon asserted that "the time has now come in America to reverse the flow of power and resources from the States and communities to Washington, and start power and resources flowing back from Washington to the States and communities and, more important, to the people all across America."[107] Nixon proposed to allocate money to the states to spend as they desired rather than earmark dollars for programs favored on the federal level. On another occasion the president applied this policy directly to the arts, arguing that government must accept "support of the arts as one of its responsibilities, not only on the Federal level but on the State and local levels as well."[108]

Over the next five years, state and local arts programs grew dramatically in strength. In 1970 the Federal-State Partnership Program staff consisted of two people, and each state was allotted $36,363. By 1975 each state received $200,000. There were also thousands of dollars available through additional funds distributed to states.[109] The idea of federal-state partnership appealed to congressional leaders who supported the program changes as a means to benefit their own states and districts.[110]

State and local arts programs essentially developed separately from the administration of the Visual Arts Program, although they emphasized visual arts in several ways. Art programs in small communities and schools began to spring up in new locations and to grow. As state arts agencies and community arts projects multiplied, access to the arts became possible for more people. Also, importantly, new federalism reinforced the emphasis on distributing funds to a wider geographical area of the United States.

Although the mandate of the NEA specifically demanded that the arts be made available to more of the American public, the distribution of visual arts grants did not always live up to such a goal. The earliest grants were highly concentrated in New York State (57 percent in 1967 and 93 percent in 1969, almost exclusively to artists in New York City), followed by somewhat lesser allotments to a few other metropolitan areas, including Chicago, Washington, D.C., and Los Angeles. Throughout the first ten years of the Visual Arts Program's history, artists in the East received on average more than 50 percent of the awards; artists in the West received approximately 30 percent. After some criticism of this focus and the new accent on reaching out to all areas, the Visual Arts Program staff and panels began to consider geographic location more carefully when awarding fellowships. The distribution, although still concentrated in major cities, began to reflect slightly more inclusion of regions in the Midwest and South. Out of the total percentage of grants, artists in the Midwest received 1 percent in 1969, 10 percent in 1971, 7 percent in 1973, 10 percent in 1974, and 14 percent in 1975, while artists in the South received no grants in 1969 and fewer than 10 percent in subsequent years.[111]

Another method to encourage more involvement in the arts by a greater number of people around the country was a renewed interest in the touring of art through numerous cities and various regions. In some of its first meetings, the National Council on the Arts had discussed ways of touring art exhibits, although little had come of their ideas. During the early 1970s, with increased funds and national interest, NEA chair Nancy Hanks was determined to see the success of a plan called Art Fleet.

Art Fleet was meant to be a permanently touring art gallery. Designs were made of four dome-shaped, environmentally controlled rooms mounted on mobile trailers that could be separated for travel then reassembled into a large, four-room gallery. Such a structure would enable the NEA to realize its goal of bringing fine art to more of the American public. However, fabricating modules that would house and transport precious art objects required a foolproof security system, sensitive environmental controls, and an extremely stable mounting structure that would maintain the stability of the artworks while the vehicles were in motion. Achieving this construction proved impossible. Planners faced with one design flaw after another eventually convinced Hanks that Art Fleet would never sail as it was originally conceived.

Eventually the concept was transformed into a smaller scale project, dubbed Artrain, undertaken by the Michigan State Arts Council. Artrain became a traveling railway composed of a train engine, four gallery cars, and a caboose. The cars housed slides, films, photography, sculptures, paintings, prints, and some crafts. Local artists were invited to display works near Artrain when it arrived in their locale. It toured in twenty Michigan cites in

1971, according to the NEA annual report for that year, and it became so popular that it began to tour in other states by the mid-1970s as well.[112]

Artrain's tours symbolized an achievement for the NEA in partially fulfilling its mission of bringing quality art to more of the American public. Its success in the early 1970s was aided by President Nixon's attention to arts policy expansion and his interest in encouraging initiative by state and local areas as much as (if not more so than) the federal government. This notwithstanding, Nixon's enlargement of the NEA budgets allowed the Endowment to greatly expand federal support for the arts. Although it was not initially clear that President Nixon would prove so surprisingly liberal a patron of the arts, once he was convinced to act on behalf of federal arts policy, he supported a rapid expansion of the NEA budget at an unprecedented rate from just over $7 million in 1968 to over $64 million in 1974. He also oversaw the development of more inclusive programs that allocated greater portions of the NEA's funds to state and local areas, to community-oriented art programs that benefited more minorities and common folk, and to a larger number of figurative artists, even though the Visual Arts Program continued to favor abstract modernists. After Nixon left the White House, the NEA would continue its expansion in these directions, garnering for itself a reputation as a well-respected federal agency that responded to the nation's aesthetic needs by promoting artistic excellence in a variety of forms.

However, what has been perceived as a pluralistic expansion of the NEA in the 1970s in fact harbored more conservative aims. Arts policy expansion during the Nixon administration continued previous policies of U.S. posturing and maneuvering to win the respect of friends and foes alike through whatever means necessary during the Cold War. Just as Kennedy and Johnson had done, Nixon employed the arts to display American cultural achievement. Yet, this goal became more difficult as the Vietnam war spilled over into other locales and Americans began to question and abandon their previously unswerving beliefs in Cold War urgency and U.S. aims. Increasingly, what many had considered the necessary export of American democracy was replaced by distaste for unnecessary bloodshed and American "imperialism." As protests spread, Nixon turned to arts policy to mitigate what he perceived as undesirable cultural outbursts in the United States and to instill more conservative aims in domestic cultural programs. Behind this approach was also the hope of projecting an uplifting image of American society and culture in an anxious time. Ironically, Nixon carried on war in Vietnam, Cambodia,

Laos—and against his perceived enemies at home through the Watergate break-in—at the same time that he projected the film *2001* to demonstrate American achievements and provide an example of what peaceful attitudes and creative minds could attain. At home his goal was less one of social uplift through the arts for underprivileged and undereducated Americans and more one of image enhancement for his own administration—with which he became increasingly concerned in the aftermath of the Watergate investigations. He eschewed modernism as the high-art form that previous leaders and cultural heads thought should be used to instruct Americans in cultural greatness in favor of more common, realist forms. Moreover, he hoped his patronage of the arts would win support among those "forgotten Americans" who longed for peace and private pursuits of pleasure and would provide a positive alternative to what he considered discordant and unflattering youthful protests. In essence, Nixon used arts policy as he had other federal programs, to undercut liberal (Democratic) programs and reassert a conservative political agenda and politically conservative aesthetics.[113]

In retrospect, it would seem that whatever his goals were, Nixon succeeded in garnering a great deal of support for his arts policies as a positive program to enrich the quality of life and in winning the approval of world leaders for his cultural outreach. The significant support for and advances in arts policy under this conservative administration in later years slowly faded from Americans' memories and were generally forgotten by the 1980s as the Cold War rationale lost its force and the arts became labeled ultraliberal by social and fiscal conservatives who rose in opposition to federal support for the arts.

The Pluralist Seventies

We find words like "elitism" and "populism" being used to support a
polarization of the arts. . . . I am convinced a very different approach
is needed, a different means of defining our cultural goals. It seems to
me that "elitism" can indeed mean quality, can indeed mean "the
best"—that is a proper dictionary definition for the word. And
"populism" I would suggest can mean "access." Access to the arts all
across the land. Why not bridge these two words . . . and simply say
that together they can mean "access to the best"? I believe that's what
the arts and humanities legislation intended to convey from the very
beginning—the encouragement of the best, the development of
quality, and the availability of that quality to the greatest possible
numbers of our people.
—Livingston Biddle, NEA *Annual Report, 1978*

★ ★ ★ ★ ★ ★ ★ ★ ★ ★ ★ ★ ★ ★ ★ ★ ★ ★ ★ ★

Excellence and access—such was the promise of Chair Living-
ston Biddle when he took the NEA's helm in 1977.[1] Yet these objectives hardly
broke new ground; the Endowment had struggled to reconcile these two goals
throughout its history. During its early years, NEA leaders seemed elitist—
defining excellence primarily as modern art and developing the means to
expand its reach. By the mid-seventies, however, the political and cultural
context had changed with the breakdown of the Cold War political consensus
in the aftermath of Vietnam and the rise of multiculturalism. The NEA responded by diversifying its definitions of excellence (thus widening access to
funding for a greater variety of artists) and heightening its focus on access to
the arts for all Americans. During the late 1970s, the Endowment achieved its
greatest degree of success fostering cultural democracy.

The seventies marked the heyday of pluralism for the Endowment. While
maintaining support for the arts, President Jimmy Carter slowly reassessed
the agency's activities. Carter indeed proved to be a harbinger of the political
conservatism that would emerge in force during the 1980s to threaten the
NEA's future. Leadership within the agency also changed. Carter replaced
Nancy Hanks with a new chair, Livingston Biddle, to oversee the agency as
a whole. Moreover, the Visual Arts Program acquired new director James

Melchert, after Brian O'Doherty moved to direct a new media arts program; and Alan Jabbour turned over his post in folk arts to Bess Lomax Hawes. Finally, pluralism in the visual arts began to appear more clearly in NEA grants. While not abandoning its old patterns of support for high modernism, the NEA began to open its doors to more diverse groups of artists and art genres.

The 1970s truly marked a golden age for the Endowment. In this period the NEA received its greatest support from political leaders both in the White House and on Capitol Hill. Gone were old questions about the agency's legitimacy that had peppered congressional authorization debates. Instead, everyone from Richard Nixon to Edward Kennedy agreed that the federal government should support the arts. Artists and art institutions that had feared the heavy hand of the government now welcomed NEA's "no strings attached" grants and the mark of approval that they bore. Liberals and conservatives, abstractionists and representationalists, all found favor with the agency. Sadly, this golden age would prove short-lived as economic and political tides shifted.

★ *Holding the Course*

In 1974 Gerald Ford succeeded Nixon as president. Although experienced as a congressman, majority leader, and vice president, Ford's swift and shocking rise to power left him somewhat ill-prepared to plan and execute his own clear policy initiatives. His pardon of Nixon, while intended to move the nation beyond the "American tragedy" of Watergate, eroded his popularity and support.[2] After the pardon, Ford had difficulties with Congress, which saw him more as Nixon's crony than as one of its own. In the 1974 midterm elections, Democrats gained seats in both the House and the Senate, making things more difficult for the Republican president. Congress sat in the nation's driver's seat more often than Ford during his short tenure.

During the Ford years, the Arts Endowment maintained a relatively stable position. Despite Ford's setbacks, the Endowment benefited from Nelson Rockefeller's appointment as vice president, the adept leadership of NEA chair Nancy Hanks, and the continued support of congressional arts advocates.

Gerald and Betty Ford had become allies of the Endowment, especially after its Art in Public Places Program sponsored the installation of Calder's *La Grand Vitesse* sculpture in Grand Rapids, Michigan, their home state and the center of Ford's congressional district. The atmosphere of public support for the arts that developed out of Calder's project won Ford over from his prior skepticism regarding the value of government patronage for the arts. By the time he became president, Ford pledged his support for the arts and promised to aid in their expansion, writing to Hanks that his administration applauded NEA efforts and hoped to aid in garnering more support for the multifaceted cultural expressions America had to offer.[3] Betty Ford was even more favorably inclined toward the arts and the NEA. She had once been a dancer and had worked with Martha Graham's dance company.[4] While serving as first lady, she consciously attended cultural events to show her appreciation for the arts in general and NEA-sponsored activities in particular. She also discussed with NEA staff how to bring arts and crafts into the White House to display their beauty and utility.[5]

Ford's selection of Nelson Rockefeller as vice president proved just as significant as the first family's support for the arts. Rockefeller's long history of arts patronage and his relationship with Nancy Hanks served the Endowment well. Early in his administration, Ford designated his new vice president head of the Domestic Council and charged him with overseeing the domestic legislative package. In his new role, Rockefeller would have a position of power from which to advance his pet causes and further his own presidential ambitions in the future.

However, during their administration Ford and Rockefeller faced serious economic setbacks. By 1974 rampant inflation afflicted the United States. Oil prices, consumer prices, the trade deficit, and unemployment were rising, while the GNP, housing starts, and the Dow-Jones average were falling. Ford hoped to deal with the economy rather conservatively by proposing a 5 percent ceiling on the growth of entitlement programs, budget cuts, and tax increases, and by asking American businesses to voluntarily help in keeping prices down. When his policies did not produce significant results and a recession hit in the fall, Ford altered his course and called for a tax cut and fewer controls on prices. Congress supported Ford's tax cut proposal but continued to pass more spending bills, which angered the president as he tried to limit government expenditures. As the economic crisis continued, Congress agreed to work with Ford toward a rollback of the federal budget for fiscal year 1976.[6]

Until the mid-1970s, the National Endowment for the Arts had enjoyed continuing, substantial expansions in its appropriations, and Ford had followed Nixon's lead in boosting the arts budget each year. Thus, NEA appropriations for 1975 amounted to approximately $86.9 million (a 43 percent increase over the 1974 budget of $60.7 million).[7] As the nation's economic woes deepened, however, Ford proposed cuts in Endowment funds. He also demanded that the agency augment its partnership with business and corporate sponsors to raise matching grants to supplement federal dollars.[8] With the president's blessing, Congress established a challenge grant program for the NEA beginning in 1976. This program awarded one-time project grants and challenged recipients to match each NEA dollar with at least three more dollars from other sources. The NEA promoted this as a means to encourage cultural organizations to achieve financial stability with support from the Endowment, yet beneath this rosy explanation lay a clear directive from the president and Congress for the agency to locate more private funds for matching grants as federal dollars might diminish. Ultimately, budget appropriations for 1976 amounted to approximately $95.6 million, a more modest growth of 10 percent over 1975 levels, but an increase nonetheless.[9]

With economic pressure mounting and all signs pointing to another cutback for the following year to a budget of perhaps eighty million dollars, Hanks appealed to the vice president for assistance. She met with Rockefeller and sent him numerous letters over the following months encouraging him to use his leverage with Ford to preserve the Endowment's funds.

To show his support, Rockefeller also attended the first quarterly meeting of the National Council on the Arts in 1976 and addressed the Council in a speech outlining new ideas for federal arts support under the Ford administration. He reiterated his support of federal funding for the arts but also warned that federal money alone was insufficient and could lead to government control over which kinds of arts would receive national attention. He believed free expression would best be achieved through encouraging more public and private cooperation. Therefore, he supported Ford administration proposals for tax credits to encourage businesses' contributions to the arts. He argued that the Council should work to ally the NEA firmly with business sponsorship as well. He promised to act as a liaison and to take specific initiatives to the president from the NCA when members developed further proposals.[10]

At Hanks's insistence, Rockefeller also intervened with Ford regarding the budget proposals for 1977. Believing that it would carry more weight coming from the vice president than from herself, Hanks drafted a memo to the president from Rockefeller appealing for more funds for the NEA. It asserted that while private funds were important, federal leadership remained more significant. To achieve this an additional twenty million dollars should be added to the budget for 1977.[11]

Hanks also joined forces with NEH chair Ronald Berman, whose appropriations were similarly threatened, and both solicited the president to restore higher funding levels to the NEA and NEH. Hanks's entreaty argued that cutting the agencies' funds would "undermine one of the most successful initiatives of Republican administrations . . . and dangerously impair the only federal encouragement of the nation's cultural and intellectual life at the very time when such encouragement may be most needed."[12]

Ultimately, their efforts shielded the agency from the larger decreases Ford had originally planned, although they did not prevent cuts altogether. Rockefeller informed Hanks that "the best we could do was 94+ million."[13] Although it was not the advance for which she had hoped, Hanks accepted that the amount was ten million more than Ford had first proposed and thanked Rockefeller for his help.[14] Overall budget figures for 1977 rested at $94,644,000—the only slight dip in NEA funds throughout a decade of unprecedented growth. As chair of the NEA, Hanks proved invaluable in defending the Endowment's turf and securing White House support for greater expansion. Yet the agency's success also depended on the secure backing of congressional arts advocates.

While struggles over the budget generally resulted in cuts or slowed expansion for federal agencies during the 1970s, key arts supporters in Congress shielded the NEA, enabling it to grow at a rate 490 percent higher than that for the federal government as a whole.[15] As head of the subcommittee of the arts and humanities within the Senate's Labor and Public Welfare Committee, Sen. Claiborne Pell steadfastly marshaled increases for the NEA. While in the House, Rep. John Brademas paralleled those efforts as chair of the subcommittee on post-secondary and select education, a branch of the House Education and Labor Committee. Brademas fought a tougher battle as House members more often challenged the NEA's appropriations and attempted, unsuccessfully, to keep levels lower than did their Senate counterparts. The Senate offered more support because it was generally more open to large national projects, and senators, unlike congressmen, often sat on both authorization and appropriations committees at the same time. Both Pell and Brademas were aided by the NEA's campaign to secure countless letters from state arts agencies, museums, symphonies, and the public to lobby Congress for higher budgets. The NEA's achievement, as political scientist Matthew Moen has shown, relied on a highly organized "subgovernment" in the 1970s—congressional committees, arts interest groups, and the executive agencies of the White House and NEA developing mutually beneficial arrangements in arts policy.[16] This vigorous subgovernment flourished through the seventies and would later help the NEA to survive the assault mounted against it during the 1980s.

★ 1976: The Bicentennial Bonus

In 1976 the United States celebrated its bicentennial. As the nation's preeminent cultural institution, the NEA became heavily involved in orchestrating America's two-hundredth anniversary. The Arts Council viewed bicentennial celebrations as an especially important means to enhance the Endowment's objectives and implement White House policy goals. Organization of the celebration spanned the Nixon and Ford administrations and both leaders used the bicentennial to emphasize their aim of supporting art forms representing all of the American people.

Nixon launched the American Revolution Bicentennial Commission and appointed former National Council on the Arts member James Johnson Sweeney as its head. Nixon charged the commission to organize the national celebration, to reaffirm the spirit of '76, to recall Americans to our "common purposes," and to unite them "in purpose and dedication to the advancement of human welfare." A memo announcing the commission to Congress resounded the "quality of life" theme so often found in cultural policy statements, as Nixon reiterated that Jefferson's dream of a "pursuit of happiness" rather than material needs "expressed the fundamental theme for our commemoration."[17] Moreover, Nixon pointed to the divisions in American society as something that national bicentennial celebrations could help to heal and suggested that "the creative forces of our national diversity" could strengthen American unity and display American values to the international community.[18]

Ford reinforced much of Nixon's program, reasserting that the "National Council and the National Endowment for the Arts [have been] a great addition to our society. . . . And we shall need the creative gifts of our artists and the capabilities of our cultural institutions to help us celebrate this great anniversary."[19] Ford also extended some previous policy areas. During the bicentennial year, he issued a statement on the arts that supported their expansion but also outlined specific areas in which he wished to include more of the arts of the "many cultures represented in America . . . and increase opportunities for the refinement and presentation of the folk arts and crafts of both rural and urban America."[20] By 1976, the NEA was already moving to adopt these objectives as it expanded its definition of aesthetic excellence and strove to bring quality arts to more Americans. Not only did such actions bring the NEA closer to its professed policy of fostering excellence and access but they also proved good politics. Hanks and other Endowment leaders realized that for the NEA to survive and flourish in a period of budget limitations and increasingly conservative politics, it would have to adjust and put its most positive spin on decentralization. The agency complied at once with presidential goals of federalism and pleased more liberal members of Congress who supported the national arts agency by giving arts grants to their regional constituents.

The Bicentennial Commission's plans included coordinated activities in each state and major city plus national fairs and celebrations in the historic cities of Boston, Philadelphia, and Washington, D.C. The idea was that the commemorations be at once national and local, akin to new federalism policies, as Nixon proposed to "emphasize the local nature of American life and American government" and give individual Americans a greater sense of involvement.[21] The NEA received additional funds specifically to enhance arts organizations' readiness for the national birthday celebrations. It allocated forty million dollars in 1974 and 1975 largely to renovate museums, enhance collection conservation, and aid production of arts performances, festivals, and exhibitions during the bicentennial year.[22] In keeping with the policy goals of decentralization, much of the NEA funds were directed to state arts agencies to administer, with the Endowment itself overseeing national goals and quality.

The National Council on the Arts promised to meet three major objectives: improving the quality of life in the United States through the arts, bringing the talents of American artists to as many people as possible to enrich their lives, and fostering community participation in arts festivals and events across the country. The NEA would provide professional direction for the states and cities and encourage their use of local arts resources ranging from community theater and regional symphonies to the traditional arts and crafts of ethnic and cultural groups in their geographic areas.

In their report on bicentennial planning the Council argued that the arts were too often seen as "privileges" but should be viewed as "rights" of the people "to appreciate and to participate in the creation of beauty."[23] To fulfill its responsibilities in enhancing Americans' rights to art and culture, the Council proposed expanded touring to bring benefits of the arts within the range of everyone in the country. The NEA funded traveling performance companies and museum exhibitions to major cities (both in the United States and abroad) and increased its use of Artrain and Art Fleet (a group of trailer trucks adapted as visual and performing arts exhibition spaces) in small communities and rural areas. The Endowment also stepped up the Works of Art in Public Places Program to assure that each state would have at least one major public art project by 1976.

The Council asserted that the "success of the Celebration can be assured only if it embraces and involves all Americans."[24] With this goal in mind, the NEA strengthened cultural activities involving multicultural and multiethnic communities and traditional arts. These areas included jazz, folk, and ethnic music; folk arts and crafts; and expansion arts, directed at minority and ethnic groups. The bicentennial spurred the NEA toward greater pluralism in arts support during the later part of the 1970s.

★ The Carter Years

As the bicentennial celebration wound down, the election of James Earl Carter to the presidency marked another important political shift. Carter arrived in Washington as an outsider and a new Democrat determined to bring fresh ideas to a Capitol and country still reeling from the debacle of Watergate, defeat in Vietnam, and downturns in the economy. Appealing to Americans as a centrist, Carter was a Democrat who supported aid to cities, youth training and employment, education, environmental protection, civil rights, and women's rights. Yet at the same time, Carter's fiscal conservatism and suspicion of government action alienated many liberals who hoped he would return America to Great Society politics. Democratic Party leaders complained, "We've got this Democrat who's not doing what Hubert Humphrey or Lyndon Johnson would have done."[25] Rather, Carter pledged to balance the federal budget, bring down deficits, and reduce inflation through a "national austerity" program that meant cutting many social programs and deregulating industries. In his inaugural address, he announced, "We have learned that 'more' is not necessarily better, that even our great Nation had its recognized limits."[26] Indeed, he launched a policy of fiscal conservatism that would later be most identified with Ronald Reagan and other Republican conservatives during the 1980s.[27] Carter's promise of open and honest government that would discard the old ideological politics of both liberals and conservatives to meet each problem with practical, if apolitical, solutions appealed to Americans in the post-Watergate years of the late 1970s.

On arts policy, Carter offered a typically neoliberal approach. He promised to continue support for the NEA as had his predecessors, but he also planned to reassess the agency's efficiency, along with all other government agencies. During his first months in office Carter was preoccupied with matters more pressing, yet hints of his inclinations toward the arts gradually emerged.

Dispelling Washingtonians' fears that they were Georgia "crackers" who would eliminate standards and cultural style, the president and first lady Rosalyn Carter displayed keen interest in a variety of arts. Classical music stood first among their favorites, and Carter was known to play it loudly on the Oval Office's stereo system, prompting his personal secretary Susan Clough to remark, "It's debatable whether I'm his secretary or the White House deejay."[28] At their first state reception for Mexican president José López Portillo, Bach orchestral suites accompanied the dinner, and Rudolf Serkin performed Beethoven and Mendelssohn concertos. The Carters also frequented the Kennedy Center and the National Gallery of Art. Roger Stevens, former NEA chair and then head of the Kennedy Center, noted that Carter attended more performances in his first two months in office than all previous presidents combined.[29]

Carter also continued the practice of adorning the White House with American paintings, specifically asking for more impressionist and historical works depicting American scenes. Such paintings as John Twachtman's *Niagara Falls*, Childe Hassam's *Flag Day*, and Butler Brown's *The Brown Farm* were prominently displayed in or near the Oval Office. Although both the president and the first lady were quite knowledgeable about and appreciative of abstract genres, Carter preferred realistic landscapes and traditional styles rather than the avant-garde. Mrs. Carter also enjoyed folk arts and crafts.[30]

Vice President Walter Mondale and his wife, Joan, provided even more liberal support for the arts in general and modern art in particular. The vice president, like Carter, gravitated toward more traditional, realistic works; yet at their residence in Washington, the Mondales exhibited numerous modern works. On the front lawn stood a David Smith steel sculpture that the vice president admired for its strength, and throughout the mansion hung abstract works by Willem de Kooning, Hans Hofmann, Sam Francis, and Mark Rothko and pop art by Andy Warhol, Claes Oldenburg, and Jasper Johns, among others. Joan Mondale had been trained in history and art education and had worked for nine years as a docent at the National Gallery. She loved the clear, simple shapes and sense of color in abstract art and the humor of pop.[31] She was also enthusiastic about crafts and dabbled in pottery when she had the opportunity. During the Carter administration, she became so active in publicizing the benefits of federal arts policy and lobbying for the needs of artists and art organizations that she earned the title "Joan of Art" from the press corps.[32]

The Carters and Mondales expressed similar concerns about arts policy from the earliest days of their administration. They believed that the arts were good for people and art education should be expanded. Carter promised increased appropriations for the National Endowment for the Arts, yet remained vague about exactly what level of support he would seek until he assessed the agency's operations. He offered three main goals for arts policy: He pledged to widen the availability of the arts to all Americans, to put unemployed artists back to work, and to reorganize and decentralize the federal role in cultural endeavors.

In promising to pursue broader access to the arts, Carter vowed to "turn around what's been called an elitist attitude at the Endowment." His administration would work toward more diversity in federal arts support. Carter and his appointees planned to ensure that artists working in many genres would be considered for grants, that more women and minorities would be included among the awardees, and that greater efforts would be made to celebrate the arts with people in their local communities.[33]

Joan Mondale voiced the administration's position specifically, proposing that the NEA and General Services Administration focused too much on modern abstraction and should include more traditional arts in their offerings. "There are so many things we can do besides monumental sculpture," she argued, "Why not tapestries, wall hangings, [and] ceramics" in addition to fine art? When her comments prompted some art purists to express concern to Carter that such a move might lower the standards for art, Mondale defended the administration position. She maintained that it was not a matter of crafts over high art but of crafts *and* high art. "If elitism means that we nourish excellence and cherish creativity, then I'm an elitist," she said, "and if you're talking about populism meaning accessibility, then I'm a populist. Quality of art is not lowered because you have a larger number of participants."[34] Thereafter, this embrace of excellence and access, while always part of the NEA philosophy, would be applied more vigorously to Endowment activities during the late 1970s with greater encouragement from Carter officials and new Endowment leaders.

As part of his reassessment of government efficiency, Carter ordered Stuart Eizenstat to spell out the administration's position on each major domestic policy issue, with the goal of identifying and eliminating overlap in government agencies' workloads and budgets. Senator Claiborne Pell suggested that Carter reactivate the dormant Federal Council on the Arts and Humanities to oversee culture in the same way. Thus, leaders of all federal cultural agencies, including the NEA, NEH, Library of Congress, Smithsonian, and National Archives, would coordinate and streamline their policies. Carter approved the plan and named Joan Mondale the honorary chairperson of the Federal Council (since she was barred from holding an official appointment).[35] Once reformed, the Federal Council moved to determine the scope of all federal agencies' cultural activities, study art education initiatives in each agency, and improve U.S. representation in international cultural events. The NEA served as the principal adviser to other government organizations and facilitated their connections to artists. The streamlining of federal arts policy across the board reinforced Carter's commitment to efficiency and his assertion that sometimes "less is more."

Satisfied that the expansion of arts policy was following a healthy course, Carter acted upon his pledge to augment NEA appropriations. Indeed, budget figures for the Endowment marched progressively upwards each year under Carter. The Endowment received $114.6 million for fiscal year 1978 (an increase of 21 percent over the last Ford budget), $150 million for 1979 (a 31 percent increase), and $154 million for 1980 (a 3 percent increase).[36]

Remarkably, arts appropriations grew while many other federal agencies suffered the brunt of Carter's national austerity program. Expanded arts spending complemented Carter's initial neo-Keynesian economic policy that focused on growth to combat recession. This policy seemed to work as the economy grew during Carter's first three years in office, and the NEA budget continued to flourish. However, the plague of inflation kept ahead of growth, causing a decline in the dollar and a recession. Carter's second economic strategy shifted toward more conservative ideas of fiscal restraint, deregulation, tax relief, and tight monetary policy to manage inflation. By 1980 Carter touted the value of private initiatives and stressed the limits of government action.[37] Yet even as Carter moved closer to supply-side economics, he maintained support for several traditionally liberal spending programs, including the Arts Endowment. In so doing, Carter was less interested in continuing

1960s-style liberalism (evidenced by his rejection of large-scale job creation, welfare, and health programs) as he was in moving toward a more conservative role for the federal government. By expanding arts funds, he hoped to reap symbolic benefits from a small, cheap program with lots of state and local control.[38] Thus, Carter walked a fine line between liberalism and conservatism, resembling Nixon, Reagan, and Bush more than Kennedy and Johnson in his emphasis on decentralization and federal limits.

By 1979 Carter faced not only economic problems but also mounting challenges in foreign policy. The Soviet invasion of Afghanistan; revolutions in Nicaragua, Rhodesia, and Iran; and the hostage crisis in Tehran all consumed Carter's time and attention.[39] While managing these hot spots and battling inflation, the president ultimately relegated domestic policy to the back burner. In light of these developments, art policy became only a minor issue; the NEA budget increase of 3 percent for 1980 seemed as much a victory as a rollback from its previous, more dramatic growth.

Art policy during the Carter years largely followed Nixon's and Ford's models, emphasizing expansion but simultaneously moving more funds to state and local areas and increasing support for traditional and representational arts. Still, Carter pressed harder than Nixon or Ford to include more women and minorities in the grant selections and to widen the availability of the arts to Americans in all regions. Like Nixon, Carter was able to influence the Endowment by appointing a new chair.

★ Changes in NEA Leadership

With Nancy Hanks's second term as NEA chair set to expire in the fall of 1977, President Carter began to consider new leadership for the agency. Hanks remained under consideration, but Senator Pell and other congressional leaders believed that a chair should not serve more than two four-year terms. Pell feared a permanent chair, however popular and successful, might lead to domination of the agency by one person with the power to advance his or her particular preferences over the desires of others on the Council, in panels, and in the public.[40] Additionally, Carter wished to appoint a person of his own choosing. Although everyone acknowledged that Hanks had served the agency brilliantly, Carter and many Democratic congressmen hoped to secure a Democrat in the post rather than continue with Hanks, who had a long history of Republican patronage in government work.

Carter set up a committee to review potential nominees for the arts post,

7.1. *President Carter with Livingston Biddle at the White House.*
(Photo courtesy of the Jimmy Carter Library)

and Vice President Mondale, along with his wife Joan, oversaw its work. Among the candidates were Michael Straight, deputy chair of the NEA; Mc-Neal Lowry, former vice president for the arts and humanities at the Ford Foundation; Roger Kennedy of the Ford Foundation; Seattle mayor Wes Uhlman; Peggy Cooper, the founder of Workshops for Careers in the Arts and one of the developers of Duke Ellington High School for the Arts in Washington, D.C.; and Livingston Biddle, then a staff member for Pell after having served as deputy chair and congressional liaison for the NEA.

Carter summoned Biddle to the White House for a meeting and soon after presented him as the new chair. Distinguished by his valuable experience as a writer and administrator with knowledge of the intricacies of NEA functions, Biddle had the backing of Pell and congressional leaders. The Senate immediately confirmed the appointment. On November 7, 1977, in a ceremony at the Old Executive Office Building, John Brademas swore Biddle into office (fig. 7.1).[41]

As chair, Biddle reiterated his philosophy that the Endowment's purpose was to support arts and artists of the highest quality and make their work available to the greatest number of people for their enjoyment and enrichment—excellence and access. He asserted, "Access was the populist side of the coin, elitism the other—but elitism in its best sense, not as exclusivity, but as the selection of excellence. It was the same coin. It was not two philosophies at odds with each other. . . . The mission had been clear from the word go."[42] As the NEA chair, Biddle dedicated himself to the realization of these two ideals.

Biddle oversaw several important changes in Endowment practices, including greater rotation of NEA program leaders, increased focus on minority concerns, and diversification of programs. Biddle believed that the NEA had reached a size and influence that required structural change. In addition, he hoped to foster greater balance in the agency's support for noteworthy, "elite" art genres as well as more "populist" aesthetic styles.

Biddle immediately implemented a new policy of rotating program directors at least once every five years. Program leaders held the most sensitive positions at the Endowment, working directly with panels of experts to review all grant applications. While Biddle recognized that program directors and panelists took great care to protect the essential elements of objectivity and fairness in their decisions, he also realized the danger that "if the same minds deal continually with the same problems and the same people, there may be a tendency toward perpetuating the status quo."[43] Indeed, stasis prevailed in grant selections. Henceforth, Biddle announced, one-third of the panels would change every two years. He also made program director positions subject to a five-year benchmark (flexible rather than absolute).

Biddle's pronouncement initially engendered a stunned silence from the program directors, who feared that their jobs were on the line. Many objected. Some of them complained that Biddle was simply pushing them out to bring in his own political cronies. When word of the shake-up circulated, groups in certain disciplines rallied around the program leaders who had served the Endowment since its inception and were marked for rotation. When Biddle attended the Theater Communications Group conference, the hostile audience indicated its continuing support for NEA Theater Program director Ruth Mayleas.[44] The negative reaction only convinced Biddle that his new policy was warranted, since he believed no one individual should be perceived as indispensable to a program. Others agreed with Biddle on this point, and some program directors soon left for other positions, making way for new voices at the Endowment.

The policy precipitated a change in leadership in the Visual Arts Program. Brian O'Doherty moved his office a few doors down the hall as he became the director of a newly formed Media Arts Program at the Endowment. James Melchert took over the Visual Arts Program. Melchert, like O'Doherty before him, was an artist who had found his calling after a roundabout career. He studied art at Princeton, then taught English and poetry in Japan, where he began painting. By 1957 he returned to the University of Chicago to pursue an M.F.A. in painting and pottery. Two years later he received an M.A. in decorative arts from the University of California, Berkeley, where he worked under ceramicist and sculptor Peter Voulkos. After his education, Melchert taught ceramics at the San Francisco Art Institute then moved to Berkeley, where he worked as a sculptor and taught in the art department at the University of California. By the time he arrived at the Endowment in 1977, Melchert had exhibited his work at national and international art shows and received critical acclaim as a versatile artist and art educator.[45]

Like Biddle, Melchert hoped to diversify the Endowment's grant-making activities. He asserted, "one of the things that the Endowment is charged with is stimulating activity—which is the opposite of superimposing taste." He also hoped that he could help Congress and the public to see "the brilliance—the range and diversity—of work being done" including alternative arts, women's arts, and crafts.[46] While the NEA had begun to widen its offerings to these areas earlier in the decade, more work was needed to balance these aesthetic styles with the tried-and-true abstract modernism that dominated NEA grants. As the new Visual Arts Program director, Melchert endeavored to fund more diverse art genres by a broader spectrum of artists.

The departing Brian O'Doherty had outlined this path for him before going on to blaze new aesthetic trails in the Media Arts Program. While Biddle's directive to limit program directors' tenures hastened his move, O'Doherty had apparently grown somewhat restless within the visual arts parameters and welcomed the chance to branch out. He had been the driving force behind including greater recognition of up-and-coming conceptual, minimalist, and performance art in visual arts grants, although recognition of such genres remained rather limited during the early years.

Not everyone at the NEA appreciated the new directions. Most opposed was Deputy Chair Michael Straight, who had never fully embraced abstract art and worried that introducing too many new areas and artists would dilute the NEA's aesthetic standards. As early as 1971, he questioned O'Doherty's more inclusive efforts, asking, "is it our role to reinforce 'current ideas and emerging concepts' or . . . to support 'exceptional talent' which may or may not be in conformity with 'current ideas and emerging concepts.' . . . Choices are going to be arbitrary." Not only did Straight oppose new art styles, he also objected to what he considered the application of affirmative action standards to NEA grantees. His memo to O'Doherty heatedly went on to argue, "your note about the necessity of making more grants to women and to minority artists in itself runs contrary as we all know to the standards set for the program. . . . Is the panel to be shown slides or other examples of the works of applicants, and asked to consider them as works or it [sic] the panel to be told that some slides are to be seen with special standards because the artist is female or black or both?"[47] The clash between Straight and O'Doherty permeated their correspondence within the agency, and other Endowment employees still remember their tense relationship.

In the long run, Hanks mediated between the two and eventually accepted that the Endowment needed to respond to the tenor of the times and pursue more inclusive policies. Hanks allowed O'Doherty to outline new ideas for his program. By 1973 the National Council on the Arts and Hanks approved new guidelines for the Visual Arts Program stating that funds would be available not only for painting, sculpture, and printmaking but also for "artists engaged in conceptual, performance and video work in a visual arts context."[48] The following year O'Doherty presented further proposals to Hanks and Straight in a policy meeting where he argued for expansion of nontraditional aesthetics. He pointed out that the art community, with whom he maintained close contact, expressed interest in loosening traditional boundaries defining visual arts and asserted that "in order for the Endowment to be responsive to the realities existing . . . funding across loose boundaries . . . was legitimate and necessary." In addition to the new areas allowed by the Council in the 1973 guidelines for visual arts, O'Doherty thought the NEA should fund more performance work, environmental art, video, and conceptual work that cut across program areas. The initial lack of funding for such new, interdisciplinary fields made sense while they first developed; but these activities had flourished since the late 1960s, and museums and art historians had codified them as sanctioned genres. O'Doherty believed they were ripe for NEA recognition.[49] Yet, it was not until 1976 that the Visual Arts Program officially condoned the funding of conceptual, performance, and video arts and organized panels to review the growing numbers of applications in each specific category.[50]

Meanwhile O'Doherty remained frustrated at the slow pace of change. At one NEA meeting during this period he complained that abstract expression-ism was dead and that he wanted to leave the Visual Arts Program for another job that would allow him to encourage more avant-garde aesthetics.[51] (That he made no reference to representational art reinforces his already long-held belief that that genre was passé as well.) Fortunately, he was able to do just that in the new Media Arts Program, while Melchert strove to manage the Visual Arts Program.

★ NEA Visual Arts, 1976–1980

During the late 1970s, the Endowment expanded both the number and the scope of its visual arts offerings. While increased grants corresponded to the growth of the agency as a whole, the greater variety among them indicated NEA leaders' increased attention to diversity and inclusiveness. Their goals reflected wider political and social trends as the American public and its leaders turned toward greater acceptance and encouragement of pluralism in American life. Nonetheless, visual arts grants shifted quite slowly. The overall pattern continued to follow practices set earlier in the agency's history, gener-ally rewarding the tried-and-true over the avant-garde.

The individual artist's grants to painters and sculptors in the period from 1976 to 1980 resemble previous awards in several ways (see Chapter 5). First, the largest number of grants, 58 percent, were presented to abstract, modern-ist artists. Individuals who included figuration in their work, even though it remained primarily abstract, received approximately 24 percent of the awards. Realists received only 12 percent of these grants overall.[52] In this breakdown each of the three categories appears in the same order as they did in the period from 1967 to 1975. However, a comparison of each area in both time periods indicates that overall awards decreased by approximately 10 percent for abstract genres, while they increased by 6 percent for figurative and 4 percent for realist styles. Thus, although the balance remains tilted toward abstraction, improvement did occur over time.

Individual grants once again rewarded a very distinguished group of widely acclaimed artists. They included Joan Brown, Ron Bladen, Joe Goode, Hans Haake, Patrick Hogan, Donald Judd, Alan Kaprow, Ed McGowin, Nam June Paik, Cynthia Sherman, and Peter Volkous. Several of the artists also received more than one award from the NEA during this period.

In the Art in Public Places Program the old favoritism for abstract mod-ernism stood out even more starkly, yet a current of subtle change also emerged. The majority of grantees continued to work within the abstract monumental style, while the minority executed figurative or realist works. Nevertheless, compared to the 1969–1975 period, the pattern in the late 1970s clearly shows that more figurative and realist artists received funds, especially those working on murals. In addition, the Art in Public Places Program increased its attention to environmental and earthworks artists and even to some notable pop artists.

★ Abstraction, Figuration, and Realism

One example of the abstraction that continued to dominate NEA visual arts awards could be seen in Ilya Bolotowsky's art. In 1977 the Art in Public Places Program and the New York Port Authority commissioned Bolotowsky to create a work of art for the departure lounge of the New York–New Jersey Ferry Terminal. In 1979 he completed *Marine Abstraction*, a forty-foot long, ceramic tile mural featuring geometric squares and lines in brightly colored hues (fig. 7.2). His work stressed abstractionists' long-held concern for light, space, and color in simplified form and as a means for an individual to express the universal. The artist also compared his work to more traditional styles, noting that "if you remove [the lines], it becomes just stripes, and stripes after a while look like a landscape," or in this case a seascape stressing marine colors appropriate for its location.[53] For its dedication ceremony, Joan Mondale and the director of the New York Port Authority joined Bolotowsky to celebrate the successful connection of federal patronage and local sponsorship of art for the public. Bolotowsky spoke of the important impetus of federal arts policy under the WPA (which employed him in the 1930s), State Department–sponsored touring, and then the NEA in elevating American artists and New York to the pinnacle of the art world by the post–World War II period. He encouraged the NEA to continue its support.[54] Although the use of ceramic tile materials was somewhat unique in this mural, its abstract execution again underscored the NEA's preference for modernism, a preference that continued into the late 1970s.

Other Art in Public Places commissions in this period reinforced this trend. Familiar abstract artists received the bulk of awards, including Lloyd Hamrol (five awards), Mark di Suvero (four additional awards), Robert Irwin (four awards), Tony Smith (three awards), Richard Serra (three awards), Nancy Holt (three awards), and Isamu Noguchi, Alexander Lieberman, Rich-

7.2. *Ilya Bolotowsky,* Marine Abstraction, *1979. (© Estate of Ilya Bolotowsky/Licensed by* VAGA, *New York, N.Y.; photo courtesy of the Estate of Ilya Bolotowsky)*

ard Hunt, Michael Heizer, and Mary Miss (each with one or two awards).[55] All of these sculptors created monumental, abstract pieces for their commissions.

Among the abstractionists who received individual artist awards was Joan Brown, one of the best-known painters from San Francisco and a member of the California school of abstract expressionists during the late 1950s and early 1960s. Critics praised her as one of the most prominent women artists in America and compared her to Georgia O'Keeffe, Louise Nevelson, and Claire Falkenstein.[56] Art critic Philip Leider dubbed her "everybody's darling" and argued that her work epitomized and marked the nationwide success of the California School of Fine Arts style developed by Clyfford Still, Elmer Bischoff, Frank Lobdell, and Hassel Smith, Brown's former teachers.[57] Brown

7.3. *Joan Brown*, Girl on a Chair, *1962. (Courtesy of the Estate of Joan Brown; Los Angeles County Museum of Art, Gift of Mr. and Mrs. Robert H. Ginter; photo © 2000 Museum Associates/LACMA [M.64.49])*

herself went on to teach at the California School of Fine Arts and the University of California at Berkeley.

Brown's painting displayed the thick, textured brush strokes typical of abstract expressionism. For example, in her 1962 painting *Girl on a Chair*, she created a provocative nude woman (fig. 7.3). The abstractly painted fig-

ure leans back with her arms behind her head, breasts and thighs prominently exposed, and her legs slightly spread. Her large eyes gaze directly at
the viewer. The chair and background almost blend together as the boldly
painted strokes envelope the rest of the canvas. The figure and style in this
work resembled those of Willem de Kooning's women, although Brown's girl
seemed more in control, relaxed, and less frightening.

Despite her success as an abstract expressionist, Brown had changed her
style by the 1970s. After her divorce from Manuel Neri, another abstract
expressionist, she began to seek a new vision for her work. This resulted in a
break with her art dealer, George Staempfli, who pressed her to continue with
her known style. Rejecting that pressure, Brown returned to art school and
then began to paint bright dreamlike images that included more realistic-
looking representational figures but remained conceptually abstract. For instance, in 1971 she painted *The Bride*, which depicted a female body with a
cat's head in a wedding dress surrounded by colorful fish on the blue upper
half of the canvas and flowers on the black lower portion. The figure held a
rat on a leash in the lower foreground.

Many in the art world found Brown's new direction disconcerting, yet she
never hesitated. She commented to *Artweek* magazine that she painted for
herself alone.[58] She also noted that she most prized the freedom that pursuing her own aesthetic afforded her.[59] While her commitment to this new
figurative/abstract style did not win her the same acclaim in galleries and art
shows that her prior work had, Brown did achieve success. In fact, she seemed
ahead of her time, for by the mid-to-late 1970s other artists were exhibiting
similar tendencies as a new generation emerged and broke with the older
abstract modernist tradition.

The National Endowment for the Arts recognized Brown on more than
one occasion, awarding her an individual artist's fellowship both in 1976 and
1980. These awards illustrated the shift that took place within the Visual Arts
Program at that time. Just as Brown made the transition from abstract modernism to a fresh aesthetic, so too did the program under the direction of
James Melchert. It still granted a disproportionate number of awards to
abstract art, but it gradually began to branch out as well.

In addition to Joan Brown, other NEA grantees also manifested a figurative/
abstract aesthetic, including Deborah Butterfield, who received grants in 1977
and 1980. Her work depicted recognizable forms in abstract construction,
often made from junk, discarded material, or organic fragments. Her series
of horses exemplified her style of drawing both from an older modernist

7.4. *Deborah Butterfield,* Horse, *1985. (Courtesy of the artist; Hirshhorn Museum and Sculpture Garden, Smithsonian Institution, Thomas M. Evans, Jerome L. Greene, Joseph H. Hirshhorn, and Sydney and Frances Lewis Purchase Fund, 1985 [85.11])*

sculptural tradition and from abstract expressionist technique and incorporating new environmental, feminist, and "postmodern" influences. Several of the horse sculptures pieced together steel fragments, once brightly painted but now rusting, as illustrated in *Horse*, 1985 (fig. 7.4). Butterfield described her work as a visual and kinetic process, "I don't know what it is I'm doing until I'm in my studio moving around . . . and then as I do things I react to them. I suppose it would be almost an Abstract Expressionist way of working; I act, and I react to that action." She also described her method as creating forms that were frozen in a moment, more like a painting than a sculpture.[60] Her artistic process and use of industrial material often seemed to mirror other modernist sculptors such as David Smith or Richard Serra. However,

Butterfield's horses suggested not a celebration of the modern but its decay. Rather than the polish and promise of technology, her steel revealed wear and breakdown.

In fact, Butterfield's work departed from the tradition of modernist abstract sculpture that the Endowment had previously favored. She constructed many of her horse sculptures from natural materials, including wood, straw, mud, and paper. Butterfield saw them as literally inseparable from their environment and symbolic of freedom, strength, and nurturing.[61] Critic Donald Kuspit has argued that these horses tapped into people's imagination as living animals, powerful, even though domesticated, irrepressibly vital, and "agent[s] of organic revolt against the inorganic world of technology," which suggested that "we can hold out against technological control of our individuality." Although the fragmented pieces, sometimes of industrial material, of which the horses were composed also seemed to accept that a pure, wholehearted return to nature may not be achieved.[62] Butterfield's work embraced the environmental art movement, which gained in strength throughout the 1970s as part of a larger environmental movement in American culture. She was one of many artists echoing "the national preoccupation with returning to the land" and stressing the temporal nature of art and life.[63]

Her work also projected a feminist quality since Butterfield maintained that many of her horses were fecund mares rather than the powerful war horses usually found in art history. She produced several in a reclining position, deliberately drawing on the art historical tradition of female nudes to project an image of vulnerability coupled with security (since healthy horses only lie down when they feel safe).[64] Moreover, she also created figures of pregnant mares during the early 1970s, which she proposed as her political statement "against war [in Vietnam and in general] . . . and about the issues of procreation and nurturing rather than destruction and demolition."[65] In this expression, her style again differs from the classically masculine abstract modernist sculpture with its emphasis on power and virility.

Beverly Pepper also embodied the new breed of environmental and feminist artists winning Endowment support. In 1975, she received a $20,000 commission from the Art in Public Places Program to create a sculpture for Dartmouth College. *Thel* continued in the monumental abstract style, while incorporating environmentalist elements (fig. 7.5). Pepper designed the sculpture of white, enameled-steel triangular sections descending from a height of eighteen feet to less than one foot. Viewed from one side, the work followed a typical abstract modernist style, displaying large sections of

7.5. *Beverly Pepper*, Thel, *1975–77. (Courtesy Marlborough Gallery, New York;*
Hood Museum of Art, Dartmouth College, Hanover, New Hampshire, purchased through
the Fairchild Art Fund with a matching grant from the National Endowment for the Arts,
Washington, D.C.; © 1977 Jeffrey Nintzel Photography, Grantham, New Hampshire)

industrial material in sharp geometric shapes. However, sod covered sections
of the work even on the steel side and served as the dominant material in the
opposite view. Grass on the sculpture blended the work into the surrounding
lawn, making it appear as though it had grown up out of the ground like a
living entity. At its dedication in May of 1978, Dartmouth Museum and
Gallery director Jan van der Marck and Joan Mondale celebrated *Thel* as an
important advance in bringing real art to the public.[66] Van der Marck even
noted that opposition by some students, who resented the work's taking up a
favorite lounging spot, was desirable because it illustrated that superior art
could not always be popular but should provoke discussion. Only with exposure would more of the public accept new aesthetics.[67] While van der
Marck was defending the modernist aspects of the art, it seemed the public
preferred its environmentally friendly aspects and welcomed more art that
they could interact with and understand. It was exactly this sentiment that

the NEA began to accommodate more frequently in its visual arts grants during the 1970s.

Butterfield and Pepper exemplified the NEA's success in widening its recognition of women artists during the 1970s. They stood among many more women granted awards, including such notables as Eleanor Antin, Judy Chicago, Janet Fish, Nancy Holt, Faith Ringgold, Miriam Shapiro, and Cindy Sherman. Women accounted for 36 percent of the total individual grants in this period (up from only 19 percent between 1967 and 1975).

While abstraction generally continued to win the bulk of NEA awards, realism also received slightly greater attention. This style, too, had undergone some changes during the later 1970s. NEA visual arts grants reflected panelists' acceptance of a broader aesthetic turn toward neorealism or hyperrealism. Realism became more popular as many artists in the 1970s rejected the pure abstraction that had so dominated the art world since 1945. Younger artists returned to depictions of real life, although not necessarily in the traditional sense. Rather than romantic painting or social realism (often with an overt political message), their works usually reflected more gritty subjects in ordinary life or realistic fantasy images. Some neorealists also drew from abstraction by concentrating on details of real objects that appeared as abstract in their painting (a close-up section of a window frame, for example).

The NEA recognized such realist artists as Richard Estes, Janet Fish, Richard Haas, Marilyn Levine, Ed Ruscha, and Terry Schoonhoven. Estes, Fish, and Levine exemplified the hyperrealist genre, painting real life urban (Estes) or landscape (Levine) scenes and contemporary still lifes (Fish) in sharp detail. Hass often painted murals on outdoor structures that illustrated how the building might appear if it continued into the painted space or what landmarks might be visible if the building were removed. Ruscha became well known for his depictions of the urban landscape of Los Angeles and his textually based or word images.

Terry Schoonhoven's painting and murals blended real life scenes with dreamlike images. In *Downtown Los Angeles Underwater*, 1979 (fig. 7.6), Schoonhoven depicted realistic city buildings, streets, and automobiles in an eerie undersea environment. Some buildings listed slightly to the left. Others emitted bubbles that rose toward an unseen surface. Kelp appeared to grow out of the sunken parking lots, and schools of fish swimming between the structures were the only sign of life. The painting evoked a dreamlike or nightmarish quality and played on people's inability to control the environment. Jamie Hoover likened Schoonhoven's work to film noir in its use of

7.6. *Terry Schoonhoven,* Downtown Los Angeles Underwater, *1979. (Courtesy of the artist; Los Angeles County Museum of Art, Janet and Morley Benjamin Fund; photo © 2000 Museum Associates/LACMA [M.81.100])*

illusion and irony to portray modern people as unable to control the forces around them.[68] The work illustrated the breakdown of conventional images and ideas, reflecting the mind-set of many post-1960s artists who had grown disillusioned with modernism and sought new forms of expression. Artists like Schoonhoven also used their work to express their contemporary social and political views of respect for the environment and their rejection of humankind's air of superiority and decadent commercialism.

★ Conceptualism, Video, and Performance Arts

Although NEA painting and sculpture grants continued to favor abstraction, the Visual Arts Program gradually moved toward more pluralist aesthetics. The works of Joan Brown and Deborah Butterfield revealed this subtle shift in the abstract and figurative work, and Terry Schoonhoven's fantasy painting did the same within the realist category. Yet the aesthetic shift appeared far more dramatically in the works of conceptual, video, and performance artists. Between 1976 and 1980 conceptualists received approximately 11 percent of Visual Arts grants, video artists 10 percent, and performance artists 3 percent.[69] Because many artists worked in more than one of these three categories, the percentages probably underrepresent actual funds granted in each area. Even so, these percentages mark a substantial increase for each genre over the 1967–1975 grants.

Conceptual and performance art developed alongside happenings and pop art during the 1960s when Sol LeWitt first worked with language to connect art and life in new ways, and Alan Kaprow combined painting, sculpture, and music into performances. Conceptual, performance, and video art became major movements of the 1970s as other conceptualists expanded its linguistic dimensions and incorporated real objects into their pieces, and more artists engaged in performance or process art and used new video technology. The first NEA visual arts director, Brian O'Doherty, was very interested in these movements, within which he himself worked as conceptual artist Patrick Ireland; however, he generally upheld the modernist framework of the Visual Arts Program between 1967 and 1975 and awarded few grants to artists working within the new aesthetics. Conceptual, performance, and video art received slightly more attention from the NEA in the late 1970s. Funding for these styles increased only after they were well established in the art world and embraced by art critics and culture brokers. This pattern mirrors that of NEA awards to modernist abstraction well after that genre had received acclaim, although conceptual, performance, and video art never received the overwhelming support that abstraction did (because they had not achieved a comparable level of popularity and success).

Roland Reiss was one of the conceptual artists to receive multiple awards from the Endowment. He began as a landscape and abstract painter, heavily influenced by abstract expressionist art in the 1950s and minimalism in the 1960s. By the 1970s, though, Reiss rejected the formalism and reductionism of modernist abstraction. "I dumped less is more for more is more," he reflected, and began to incorporate real objects and contexts into his work.[70] He turned toward conceptual art focusing on semiotics, the study of signs, and created work that played on people's perceptions of words and objects from everyday life. In *Amuse and Amaze*, 1975 (fig. 7.7), for example, he constructed a wooden box spelling out the word "muse" and serving as a maze filled with miniature everyday objects including, furniture, clothing, food, pets, and home electronics. The items are not arranged in a particular order but are meant to be experienced by the viewer "as the unpredictable variety of events you encounter in the course of a day . . . and spin off different meanings and require different solutions to the problems they present."[71] Reiss's play on language reflected his interest in the "word work" of the early conceptualists combined with real objects and situations that connected art with everyday life. This particular piece launched Reiss on a series of miniature conceptual works that he completed in the later 1970s and 1980s. The artist himself credits his NEA grants with allowing him to delve into this new aesthetic. He acknowledged that although his work "was not mainstream at the time, I felt very supported by the NEA as an artist who was allowed to

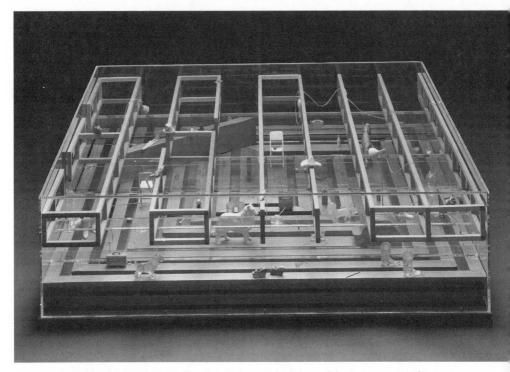

7.7. *Roland Reiss,* Amuse and Amaze, *1975–76. (Courtesy of the artist; Los Angeles County Museum of Art, purchased with funds provided by Richard Shepherd, Burt Kleiner, Purchase Award, Mr. and Mrs. Hart Isaacs, Mr. Keith Wellin, Mr. and Mrs. Herman H. Stone, Mr. and Mrs. Irving Stone, Mr. and Mrs. Albert Newman, Anton G. Roland, Ansley K. Saltz, Anonymous, Harold Diamond, Mr. and Mrs. Milton Sperling, Mr. and Mrs. Taft Schreiber, and Mr. and Mrs. Pierre Sicard; photo © 2000 Museum Associates/LACMA [M.81.93])*

pursue my own course."[72] Thus, the NEA not only reflected but also helped shape aesthetic developments in this area.

Significantly, Reiss departed from the path of the older modernist aesthetic to develop a postmodern one. Like other artists of the period, Reiss was influenced by French theorists Jacques Derrida and Michel Foucault, and by Umberto Eco, whose *A Theory of Semiotics* discussed signs and symbols. Reiss was interested in Eco's notion of "unlimited semiosis," a process of using signs to clarify meanings, which leads people to replace one sign with another sign, picture, or association. As words in a dictionary lead to more words, so signs lead to further signs. Moreover, signs serve as indexes representing concepts or feelings, as a safe indicates wealth and a need for security. Such concepts appear regularly in Reiss's art and encourage the viewer to decipher the multiple meanings of each work.[73] This new postmodern aesthetic was an attempt to represent the complexity of life in a historical period marked by the breakdown of consensus politics and increased acceptance of multicultural and multidimensional points of view. Video art paralleled conceptualism in this regard.

Video art proved to be one of the most avant-garde genres to flourish during the 1970s. It encompassed a host of works involving video tools— video tape recorders and projectors, television cameras and sets, and other processing and viewing devices—and embodied artists' fascination with new technology and its relationship to people. Some of the works concentrated on the images on the tapes and viewing screens. Other pieces used the video equipment as sculptural forms (indeed, many artists who were primarily painters and sculptors experimented with video works). While still others incorporated video with performance art. Video art was part of a larger movement away from the making of art objects per se as well as another aesthetic attempt to communicate more directly with audiences. Ironically, while video works challenged the necessity of museums and curators to mediate their messages, they were generally noncollectible pieces, like performances or conceptual art, that relied upon museums and galleries for exhibition.[74]

Nam June Paik was the best-known artist working within this genre who received a visual arts award from the NEA. Born in Korea, Paik studied music and art history in Japan and Germany during the 1950s. In Germany, he met American avant-garde composer John Cage, who influenced Paik to experiment with musical sound, performance, and sculptural elements. Cage, of course, was involved in the happenings movements, and Paik went on to work with Fluxus, an art movement that paralleled happenings in its rejection of high-art conventions and its new experimentations with music, action, performance, and publication. In the early 1960s, he also began to dabble with electronics and moved to New York, where he collaborated with other Fluxus artists and Charlotte Moorman, another advocate of new music. In 1965 he purchased one of the first portable video cameras and began to create pioneering video tapes and installations. His reputation as "the dean" of art video was well established by the mid-1970s.[75]

Paik's works covered all three types of video art, including video tapes shown on television screens, video sculptures, and video performances. *Video Flag* (fig. 7.8) is an example of an assemblage or video "painting" Paik created

7.8. *Nam June Paik*, Video Flag. *(Courtesy of the artist and Holly Solomon Gallery, New York, N.Y.; Hirshhorn Museum and Sculpture Garden, Smithsonian Institution, Holenia Purchase Fund in Memory of Joseph H. Hirshhorn, 1996; photograph by Lee Stalsworth [96.4])*

by organizing several television screens into a rectangular display resembling the American flag. The television screens representing the stripes of the flag simultaneously played videos of trucks driving in a convoy with the number 110 superimposed on each screen, while at the same time different videos combining images of George Bush and other American leaders before a field of stars played in the upper left corner of the flag. At short, timed intervals, the panels in the star and the stripe areas switched to alternate videos of unrelated images. These television images are less informative than they are decorative and seem to comment on the nature of modern society and on the media as less communicative and more entertainment oriented. Wulf Herzogenrath has called Paik's message "anti-technological."[76] Yet Paik's work undoubtedly embraced technology, albeit with his stated goal to "humanize electronics and technology" and find new and imaginative ways to use it to soothe people's tension in an age when electronic mediums were progressing "too rapidly."[77]

Paik's message appears even more clearly in his video sculpture and performance works. First, in his most obvious method of humanizing technology, Paik created numerous video robots. They were assemblages of television sets, tubing, antennae, and in some cases radio parts, designed to appear like human figures. Some robots could speak through megaphones or speakers on their heads, while others could walk through the use of remote control devices. Second, Paik collaborated with cellist Charlotte Moorman to design and perform works such as *Concerto for TV Cello* and *TV Brassiere for Living Sculpture*. In *Concerto*, Moorman plays a cello made out of three television sets projecting images of her performance. In *TV Brassiere*, she wears a bra composed of two small video screens while playing a real cello. Paik and Moorman asserted that "by using TV as bra . . . the most intimate of belongings of human beings, we will demonstrate the human use of technology, and also stimulate for viewers . . . their fantasy to look for the new, imaginative, and humanistic ways of using our technology."[78]

Endowment recognition of Roland Reiss, Nam June Paik, and many other conceptual, video, and performance artists illustrated the agency's turn toward a more pluralistic vision by the late 1970s. Although a preponderance of visual arts grantees continued to work within the realm of abstraction, most pursued new styles that broke from the purely expressionist, geometrical, or color-field abstraction of the past. Many of the awardees also incorporated figurative and realist elements into their work, and growing numbers embraced more avant-garde genres. By the end of the 1970s, the Endowment as a whole and the Visual Arts Program in particular seemed to adjust to many new aesthetic trends that reflected a more multidimensional image of American art and society, although its acceptance of these styles sometimes lagged behind that of the art world's.

Even the art forms most marginalized by the NEA in the past began to receive greater recognition in this period. Pop, feminist, and ethnic art appear in the grants more regularly by the late 1970s, though still in smaller percentages than other forms. Pop artists received approximately 2 percent of individual awards, while professed feminist and ethnic artists received between 2 and 3 percent each.[79] Moreover, pop art began to receive additional attention through the Art in Public Places Program. Pop art great Claes Oldenburg received five commissions during the late 1970s, for which he designed the classically oversized, whimsical *Crusoe Umbrella* for the Des Moines, Iowa, Civic Center Plaza; *Flashlight* for Las Vegas; and *Button* for the University of Pennsylvania, among other works.

Of course, for all their newfound openness to aesthetic pluralism, Endowment leaders also understood how to protect the agency from criticism. The NEA shied away from promoting artists who produced overtly political critiques of American government and society. It is no coincidence that NEA artist grantees remained primarily abstractionists whose work was politically safe. Nonabstract artists who received awards generally created benign figures or representations. Furthermore, by the time the NEA gave greater consideration to populist, representational artists, that too was a politically advantageous adjustment. The Endowment went along with the more conservative political tides during the 1970s and funded more representational and traditional arts so as to protect itself from charges of elitism and to protect its budget in an age of limits.

★ Folk Arts Program

During the late 1970s when the Endowment widened its doors to greater aesthetic diversity, it paid greater attention not only to contemporary art but also to traditional folk art. After being criticized for ignoring populist art forms and recognizing only elitist ones, the NEA formed a pilot program for the folk arts. It was not a full-fledged program, like those for theater, dance, or visual arts, but functioned as a "special project" within other programs, including those for music and visual arts. During his tenure from 1974 to 1977 as the NEA's director of these projects, Alan Jabbour struggled to guide the programs and increase respect for the folk arts even within the Endowment. By the late 1970s, the NEA widened its acceptance of the genre, creating a Folk Arts Program in its own right and hiring noted folklorist Bess Lomax Hawes to head it. This Endowment action again reflects the desires of the Carter administration, congressional leaders, and much of the public to see the Endowment embrace more populist arts along with high-art forms.

It was not initially clear that the folk projects would survive, let alone flourish. Part of the problem was timing. These pilot projects were in their early stages of development while Ford was reducing NEA allocations for 1976 and 1977. As all programs moderated their plans in the face of budget cuts, Jabbour feared that folk projects would suffer. He complained to Hanks that "other programs, in a pinch, will be tempted to sacrifice their folk compo-nents first." The Music Program was giving serious consideration to omitting the jazz/folk/ethnic segment from its 1976 budget, and the Education Pro-gram was not likely to fund folk projects either. Such changes would result in a serious cutback to what was meant as start-up monies for folk projects and the NEA's backpedaling on its pledge to develop a full-fledged folk art pro-gram. Jabbour encouraged Hanks to restore the budget, thereby sending the message that "you don't regard folk arts components as perfect sacrificial lambs when the gods of austerity frown."[80]

In response, Hanks stepped up her support of the folk programs. Indeed, she understood their public relations impact during the bicentennial year and the support such traditional arts found in the halls of Congress and the White House. When Hanks was challenged by Arts Council member Richard Brown not to budget for "crowd-pleasing projects at the cost of retaining high quality standards," Hanks defended the folk arts projects. She suggested that "many people feel the budgeting in this area is too low, including staff and council members, and members of Congress." Indeed, the NEA should make jazz/folk/ethnic projects a priority for 1976 and provide more grants to the many qualified applicants who could not currently be helped.[81]

Aided by Hanks's and Jabbour's efforts, the fledgling folk programs began to blossom after 1976. In 1975 Endowment staff had solicited applications, and most grants went to documentary and festival support. The following year as word got out of the NEA's growing interest in folk, applications began pour-ing in from folk artists and organizations around the country. For 1976, the Endowment received almost three times more applications for folk projects than it had the previous year. To respond, budget levels for "special projects" in folk were raised to $768,069 (a healthy 49 percent increase over the 1975 figure of $513,911).[82] Other programs also budgeted a portion of their funds for folk, thus the overall funds for folk were actually larger.

By 1977, the NEA's folk arts divisions saw even more dramatic change. Alan Jabbour left at the end of 1976 to head the new Folklife Center at the Library of Congress, and the Endowment hired Bess Lomax Hawes to replace him as its director of folk projects. Hawes was the daughter of famed ethnomusicol-ogist Alan Lomax and herself trained as a folklorist. She had served as an expert adviser on the NEA Music Program's jazz/folk/ethnic panel from time to time and had also worked with the Smithsonian Institution to organize the Bicentennial Folk Festival in the summer of 1976. Her primary employment, however, was as an anthropology and folklore instructor for California State

University at Northridge. Hawes remembered an odd warning in her inter-view with NEA deputy director Michael Straight that she should hang on to her good job, because the NEA folk projects might not continue for long. Nevertheless, she accepted the position because Hanks expressed consider-able enthusiasm and Hawes was herself committed to expanding the recogni-tion of folk arts.[83] She took over the Folk Program in January of 1977 just as Jimmy Carter was inaugurated president.

About the same time that Hawes came to the Endowment, its staff ques-tioned the overlap between the folk projects and the other programs' folk initiatives. Hawes joined their chorus of concern. She pointed out to Hanks that the Music Program's jazz/folk/ethnic segment and the Folk Program had enormous overlap, which caused confusion among applicants. Moreover, the appearance of duplication seemed to let the other programs off the hook, and their folk areas were "showing signs of deterioration." She recommended a clearly organized Folk Program in its own right.[84] She was supported by Walter Anderson of the Music Program, who also told Hanks that while he had been happy to fund indigenous, grassroots arts within his program, he now thought it appropriate to give full staffing, monies, and support to building a full-fledged program for such endeavors.[85]

Hawes was effective in building awareness within the Endowment that relegating folk to uncoordinated, minor-status projects within several other programs was no longer sufficient. In addition to outlining the procedural deficiencies of such a policy at the NEA, she also marshaled significant evi-dence of outside support. Endowment leaders had already seen the success of both the Smithsonian's Folklife Festival and the Library of Congress's Folklife Center. Hawes documented the rising interest in folk arts throughout the country, an interest that had now extended beyond the national bicentennial celebration and was manifested in the ever-growing numbers of applications for folk grants. Even more astutely, she argued that "In view of Congressional interest in the folk arts and other activity on the grassroots level, a more visible . . . Folk Arts program might well be advantageous to the Endowment as a whole."[86] Endowment leaders understood that both the White House and Congress had been calling for and would be pleased with NEA recognition of more traditional arts. By the end of the year, both Nancy Hanks and Michael Straight were persuaded to develop a separate folk program.

In early 1978, the National Council on the Arts and new NEA chair Living-ston Biddle approved a new Folk Arts Program and named Hawes its direc-tor. The Music Program transferred its funds and panel responsibilities from its jazz/folk/ethnic segment to the new Folk Program, and other programs followed suit. Visual Arts drew distinctions between contemporary craft, which it continued to fund, and traditional arts, which it designated to Folk Arts.[87] The Folk Arts Program budget climbed to $1,550,000 for 1978, and then $2,400,000 for both 1979 and 1980.[88]

In a revised statement on policy and goals, the Arts Council charged the new program "to preserve the artistic birthright of present and future generations of Americans by supporting the survival of the best art forms which reflect the American Heritage in its full range of cultural and ethnic diversity."[89] The chair of its folk arts panel congratulated Biddle on inaugurating the Folk Program, stating "this will no doubt help to overcome the sense of distance and elitism in the arts formerly registered by many."[90] Biddle and Hawes concurred that the new program would be politically popular and help to fulfill the Endowment mission to expand access for all Americans to the best arts of all genres. It complemented the NEA's general shift toward a more pluralist vision during the 1970s.

The Folk Arts Program grants between 1978 and 1980 might be classified primarily as awards for festivals, films, and fiddling. The bulk of grants went to music and dance performances, film and slide documentation, and training of young artists by folk master artists, who were usually musicians. Only a small percentage of awards went to visual folk artists, such as potters, quilters, or painters. In 1978, approximately 85 percent of Folk Arts Program funds went to festival planning and programming, organizational support for institutions promoting folk arts, and documentation of traditional arts and music. Nine percent of awards went to organizations working primarily with visual arts genres in this field. Five percent of the total grants were awarded to individual folk artists, primarily traditional music performers. In subsequent years this breakdown of awards remained essentially the same, with 9 percent of awards going to visual folk arts and the remainder to other genres.

By 1979 and 1980 the awards to individuals disappeared while an "apprenticeship" category appeared. This section covered awards for young artists to train with renowned professionals in traditional folk arts and crafts. Like the awards to individuals, it remained the smallest portion of the program totals, receiving 1 percent and 2 percent of 1979 and 1980 budget totals respectively. Eventually the State Program, a division within the NEA designed to allocate funds to state art agencies, rather than the Folk Arts Program would manage these apprenticeship awards. Folk Arts director Bess Lomax Hawes commented that she did not believe in supporting individual artists in the same way that the Visual Arts Program did. Rather than provide a few "high class" grants to single artists, Hawes worked to fund the folk arts "community." She argued that "folk arts had a huge and diverse constituency spread across the United States. . . . Our goal was to keep a community doing folk art and make sure that traditions could be passed down to the next generations." Of course that meant funding individuals in some cases, but the award was aimed at a larger public. Hawes maintained that this method of community support involved far more people and resulted in fewer individuals being passed over for personal grants as the Folk Arts Program announced its very limited awards.[91]

The Folk Arts Program awards to visual folk arts included a wide array of aesthetic types and styles, which was also typical of its other grants. Among the awards in 1979, for example, were two awards totaling $40,000 to the Burk Foundation of San Francisco, California, for a traditional quilt exhibit and film documenting the lives and work of the quilters; a $29,820 award to the El Centro Cultural y Museo el Barrio of Taos, New Mexico, to photograph work of *enjaradora*, the women who traditionally do the final sculpting and plastering of fireplaces in adobe homes; $17,770 to the Kotzebue Teen Center of Kotzebue, Arkansas, to showcase Inupiat tribal skills of skin sewing, the construction of traditional clothing, and sled building; $9,000 to the Utah Arts Council for demonstrations of Navajo weaving, basket making, and silversmithing in local schools; and $8,000 to the Hellenic American Neighborhood Action Committee in New York for an exhibition of Greek embroidery, rug weaving, and traditional needlework.[92]

Daniel Sheehy, deputy director of the Folk Arts Program (and later its director), estimated that by the 1980s the program funded artists from 139 different ethnic groups across all regions of the United States and its territories. Hawes noted her program's success in aiding arts groups and helping to preserve folk traditions in so many communities, usually with a one-time only grant. Indeed, the Folk Arts Program had an unmatched record of giving awards to some of the most widespread and diverse arts organizations, with fewer repeat grants than any other program within the Endowment. Hawes suggested that this record of achievement attracted much support from Congress, where representatives could see the benefit of arts programs for constituents in their home states and local communities.[93] Many in Congress also appreciated the traditional rather than modern nature of the arts funded by Hawes's program. Thus, despite its small size, the Folk Arts Program was politically popular. Endowment leaders understood and publicized its attractive qualities to its advantage, successfully enlarging the Folk Arts Program and using it in part to portray the NEA as an agency supporting access to the best in a plurality of art genres for all Americans.

During the 1970s the National Endowment for the Arts came of age and realized a more pluralist vision. The agency and its programs responded to a variety of changes taking place in both the aesthetic and the political arena. In the art world, modernism had passed its prime, and postmodernist and multidimensional arts rose to prominence during the 1970s. Under the new leadership of chair Livingston Biddle and program directors James Melchert and Bess Lomax Hawes, the NEA began to adjust the focus of its visual arts awards. While modernist abstraction continued to garner Endowment support, other genres including neorealist, conceptual, performance, video, and folk arts all received greater recognition, as did women and minority artists. Thus, by the end of the 1970s, the NEA grants parameters reflected a somewhat more representative, diverse image of American arts and society.

Presidents Ford and Carter, while maintaining high levels of support for the Endowment, extended the trends toward inclusiveness (especially of traditional arts and of women and minority artists) and demanded greater state and local access to arts activities and funding. Both also moved toward the possibility of downsizing the NEA budget as the American economy took a turn for the worse. While Ford did so for one budget cycle and then restored and raised NEA appropriations, Carter displayed greater determination to streamline government responsibilities and scale back in national cultural policy. In the long run, although he continued to pledge support for the NEA, Carter anticipated the conservative rhetoric and rollbacks that the Reagan administration promised in the 1980s.

Congress ultimately proved the NEA's most consistent champion. Arts advocates in the House and Senate wedded to a more liberal tradition of government continued to press for increased appropriations and to defend the agency against cuts. They also responded to the added political utility of the NEA's broadening aesthetics. Liberals and conservatives alike found it easier to justify guarding the agency when more of its funds flowed to their states and local districts and more of the art supported represented American tastes.

Ironically, some of the very changes that the NEA embraced in this pluralist era would backfire in the next decade. Greater allocations of funds to state and local arts organizations grew in popularity and ultimately undermined government leaders' commitment to the Endowment as a national agency.

Conservatives looking for more ways to reduce government expenditure would argue in the 1980s that federal government support was not needed if states and private organizations were already supporting the arts. Cultural conservatives also dismissed the agency's efforts to include more diversity among its grantees as "political correctness" rather than arts support. Even the seemingly widely accepted trend toward more representational aesthetics would haunt the NEA by the end of the 1980s. It was not modernist abstraction but representational photography by Robert Mapplethorpe that doomed the NEA to criticism and cutbacks. In the final analysis, although it was most appropriate as the arts policy of a democracy, pluralism proved divisive and destructive when distorted by those who opposed it.

Conclusion

Our cultural institutions are an essential national resource; they must be kept strong. While I believe firmly that the federal government must reduce its spending, I am nevertheless sympathetic to the very real needs of our cultural organizations and . . . plan to make better use of existing federal resources and to increase the support for the arts and humanities by the private sector.

—Ronald Reagan, "Statement by the President on Task Force for the Arts and Humanities," May 6, 1981

★ ★

On June 5, 1981, President Ronald Reagan signed Executive Order 12308, which established a presidential task force on the arts and humanities to advise him on policy for his administration. At its head stood Charlton Heston as cochair for the arts. Although a former member of the National Council on the Arts, Heston was better known as an actor and spokesman for conservative ideology. Like his friend Reagan, Heston believed in limited government, backed right-wing politicians, and supported the National Rifle Association (of which he later became president). Reagan's selection of Heston for the arts task force paralleled his leadership choices for other federal departments for which he had little regard and foreshadowed what he had in mind for the NEA. Just as Interior Secretary James Watt cast aside environmental protections and opened national parks to more mining, drilling, and logging, and Labor Secretary Raymond Donovan undermined unions and eased industrial regulations, Heston advocated downsized federal arts management and increased private support for the arts and humanities.[1]

The task force revealed that federal support for the arts was no longer the fait accompli that it had been during the NEA's golden years. Once Reagan announced, "government is not the solution. Government is the problem," the very idea of federal arts policy was loudly challenged not only by political conservatives but also by scores of so-called arts advocates who sided with the president's conservative agenda and recommended phasing out federal funding for the arts.[2] This point of view mirrored Reagan's "new federalism." Borrowing the term from and extending its meaning beyond that of Richard Nixon, Reagan promised that his new federalism would not only shift greater responsibilities to state and local government but also slash the size and scope of the federal government. He vowed to cut both the government's national supervisory role and its budget, while states, cities, and private enterprise were to take up the slack and the costs.

Reagan's task force revealed how federal support for the arts had come full circle. From pre-1960s suspicion and zero funding, it had turned to unquestioning backing of the NEA during the late 1960s and 1970s. In the 1980s, it then returned to promises to keep up the Endowment while undermining its very foundation by refocusing efforts away from federal leadership toward private control. The task force report argued that the private sector should "fulfill and extend its traditional role as the principal benefactor of America's cultural heritage."[3] Its emphasis on private support followed a larger pattern of privatization under Reagan that opened the door for the federal government to step back and eventually remove itself from the arena of arts and humanities funding.

The task force on the arts and humanities cited the nation's economic woes to justify its recommendations. It asserted, "inflation imperils America's economic vitality and the health of our cultural institutions. We recognize that the best remedy for the serious financial condition of the arts and humanities is the reestablishment of a sound non-inflationary economy." It also acknowledged that the president's "efforts to assist the recovery of the economy and the restoration of fiscal stability [were] critical to the health of the nation and its cultural heritage."[4] The task force thus embraced Reagan's fiscal conservatism and exacted it upon the Endowments.

The group recommended several steps to reduce federal expenditures and stimulate greater private support for the arts and humanities. First, it called for maintenance of the structures of the NEA and NEH, finding them and the peer panel review system sound because they placed "judgment in the hands of those outside the federal government."[5] Second, it demanded greater cooperation and coordination between federal, state, and local cultural agencies, with a view toward shifting greater fund-raising responsibilities to the state and local agencies. The task force also emphasized adjusting federal tax codes to stimulate philanthropy (across the board, not only for the arts and humanities). Finally, it suggested revitalizing the Federal Council on the Arts and Humanities, adding private citizens to its ranks, and charging it with overseeing the president's cultural policies. The Federal Council, led by a private citizen (perhaps a corporate leader and cultural institution board member) would essentially take over the cultural lead—although not the funding—that had been the purview of the NEA since its inception.

The task force also pressed for greater assistance to the arts from private individuals and institutions. Ironically, task force members noted that "augmenting private sector support in the wake of Federal budgetary reductions for the arts and humanities [was] a difficult task." Nevertheless, they urged the private sector "to meet its responsibility to support those activities so central to the nation's cultural health."[6] They also suggested that President Reagan take an active role in celebrating the arts and persuading the private sector to expand its initiatives. Members commented that with his unique background as an actor and good relationship with corporate leaders, Reagan occupied a particularly strong leadership position. They recommended that he promote the arts by attending cultural events and opening the White House for publicized arts performances, exhibits, and award ceremonies. Such activity would provide symbolic support without requiring funding. Reagan could then urge private sector leaders to bequest more to the arts and humanities, and he could reward their efforts with invitations to White House cultural affairs and other special acknowledgments of their contributions.

These recommendations did not meet unanimous approval. The task force included former NEA chairs Roger Stevens and Nancy Hanks and former Visual Arts Program director Henry Geldzahler, each of whom had championed the role of federal arts support and shaped the NEA into a successful government agency. The task force's final report relegated their opposition to a footnote, however, with only a bland acknowledgement that while "not every member subscribes to every view or recommendation in this report, it reflects the substantial agreement of the members."[7]

Reagan welcomed the task force recommendations and implemented them during his administration. In June of 1982, Reagan established the President's Committee on the Arts and the Humanities, superseding the Federal Council on the Arts and Humanities.[8] He then introduced the National Medal of the Arts in 1983 to recognize artistic achievement. The first White House ceremony to honor the medalists served more aptly as an inexpensive means to attract attention to the president and his winners. Those awarded included architect Philip Johnson, arts educator Elma Lewis, novelist James Michener, poet Czeslaw Milosz, modernist painter Frank Stella, playwright Luis Valdez, mezzo-soprano Frederica von Stade, and violinist Pinchas Zuckerman. In addition to the expected array of artists, guests included representatives of the Cleveland Foundation, the Dayton Hudson Foundation, Philip Morris, and Texaco. Reagan specifically used the occasion to reward private philanthropy in the arts, which he argued was responsible for "a much broader cultural base" in the United States than that provided by federal funds.[9] Reagan further expanded the power of corporate contributions through tax policies that allowed larger deductions for "charitable contributions." Private enterprises could at once claim greater tax write-offs and advertise themselves in museums and arts venues across the nation.

To administer his new policy initiatives at the NEA, Reagan also appointed Frank Hodsoll its new chair. Hodsoll had no arts background. He had been trained as a lawyer and previously worked in the Foreign Service and for the Commerce Department. More tellingly, he had worked on the Reagan campaign and served as deputy to the president's chief of staff, James Baker.[10] As a loyal servant of Reagan, Hodsoll presided over a three-pronged revamping of the arts agency. First, he worked to streamline the NEA's administration. The new chair reviewed staff activities and oversaw a major shift in the make-up of the Arts Council. Reagan's appointees to that body included fewer artists and more representatives of the corporate world—museum trustees, board of directors' members, and corporate sponsors—who were inclined to follow the president's lead rather than assert their aesthetic opinions. Chair Hodsoll also questioned staff grant recommendations and rejected some for the first time. For example, he refused to fund art critic Lucy Lippard's political documentation/distribution organization. Although he did not cite any specific problem with the proposal, his administration conceivably worried that a left-wing feminist's political documentation might portray the Reagan administration in a negative light. Anticipating later anti-Endowment rhetoric, he opined to Lippard that such action was within his authority as chair "in order to assure accountability for expenditures of the taxpayer's money."[11] Hodsoll's second policy change was to preside over the scaling back of the agency's budget and to roll back the NEA's expansion in programs. A 10 percent decrease in funds for fiscal year 1982 signaled further cuts in the future. Finally, while downsizing federal support, Hodsoll simultaneously expanded the challenge grant program to enlist greater private funds for arts projects and propelled the Endowment to increase funds for local arts programs with the addition of a test program of support for local arts agencies in 1983.[12] His actions prompted critics to label him the "James Watt for the arts."[13]

Reagan's policy reversals marked both a triumph for conservative politics and a beginning of the end for NEA programs. Under Reagan's new federalism, federal allocations to state and local governments actually fell. State costs rose, in some cases precipitating further cuts in services at the state level and/or increases in state taxes to offset federal rollbacks.[14] When tightening their belts across the board, states did not generally increase cultural budgets, nor for that matter did private enterprise. Following cuts in federal support, businesses also watered down their philanthropic and cultural endeavors. Furthermore, recognizing their signal from the president, conservative ideologues joined the attack to end federal arts funding altogether. Arts controversies offered further justification for a plan already set in place. The right wing of the Republican Party used the Mapplethorpe and Serrano controversies to brand the NEA as morally lax and a waste of federal funds. However, the arts agency served merely as a pawn in the conservatives' broader battle against their actual target—the moderate wing of the Republican Party.

In the 1992 presidential race, right-wing Republican challenger Pat Buchanan used the NEA art controversies to attack moderate incumbent President George Bush's handling of the NEA. Charging Bush as remiss in his defense of Republican values, Buchanan hoped to gain support for his more conservative style of leadership in the New Hampshire and Georgia primaries. His charges prompted Bush to defensively fire NEA chair John Frohnmayer, who had approved grants to the museums that exhibited the Mapplethorpe and Serrano art.[15] Although Buchanan lost his bid for election, right-wing conservatives (especially the religious Right) successfully used the hot press issue of "degenerate" arts to consolidate their power in government—culminating in the election of 1994 and the Republican "Contract with America," which included Newt Gingrich's pledge to eliminate the National Endowment for the Arts.

Ultimately, the NEA was a victim of the broader political battle. In 1995, Congress slashed budget allocations for the National Endowment for the Arts by 40 percent for 1996 and cut funding for individual artists. In the aftermath of budget reductions, the NEA was forced to eliminate thirteen of its seventeen programs, including the Visual Arts Program. No longer would painters and sculptors be recognized for their work and granted funds to develop and exhibit their aesthetics. Today the NEA is a shadow of its former self, merely adding small amounts of federal money to an arena of cultural philanthropy dominated by private institutional patronage. Reagan's federalism—giving more funds to states and local groups and pressing for increased private sector management—halted federal leadership in the arts.

The ideal of a federalized muse had been conceived during a specific historical period and by the 1980s no longer held sway over the political leadership in the United States. In 1965, the National Endowment for the Arts emerged as a result of the joining of powerful intellectual, political, and cultural forces during the crisis of the Cold War. The establishment of the NEA marked an unprecedented shift in U.S. government arts policy, because while the federal government has commissioned artists' work throughout American history, it had opposed full-fledged federal sponsorship of the arts on a national scale until the late twentieth century. One famous exception was the 1930s WPA federal art projects, which served essentially as an employment program. In contrast, the establishment of an official national arts institution in 1965 developed out of a very different rationale. With the culture of the Cold War and the new economic stability of the early 1960s, Presidents John F. Kennedy and Lyndon Johnson did not need to be concerned with providing relief for artists as did President Franklin Roosevelt in the 1930s; rather, they sought to provide a national and international example of American cultural freedom and social uplift. They successfully forged new ideological connections between fundamental foreign and domestic policy issues and the need for a U.S. arts policy.

In the Cold War era Americans defined themselves as uniquely democratic and free, particularly in contrast to communist oppression. From this mindset arose an official art policy designed to celebrate American art as symbolic of American freedom. Presidential reports and speeches from both the Kennedy and the Johnson administrations illustrated these administrators' desire to exhibit America's superior democratic leadership not only in science and technology but in art and culture as well. Kennedy hoped to "win the hearts and minds" of other peoples contemplating democratic forms of government over communism and employed the arts to achieve this end. Johnson's supporters shared this belief, and LBJ, the ever-capable politician, was able to push through Congress and sign into law the bill establishing the National Endowment for the Arts in 1965.

Kennedy and Johnson's ideological commitment to the promotion of freedom, both domestically and internationally, led to their endorsement of limited federal involvement in the selection of any specific art form over another for recognition. Presidential papers demonstrate that both the Kennedy and the Johnson administrations advocated a wide range of arts support; nevertheless, government funding did favor high art forms. Ultimately, the definition of aesthetic excellence became linked primarily with abstract modernism in the visual arts. Much like their efforts on behalf of civil rights or Medicare, which did not overturn the prevailing institutional dominance, Kennedy's and Johnson's organization of the NEA embraced culture brokers' established ideals.[16] Instead of supporting avant-garde or radical art, the NEA embraced the tried-and-true. The National Council on the Arts and Visual Arts Program leaders supported the ideals of free expression and social uplift through the arts and ultimately chose to fund artists who followed a well-established, high modernist tradition.[17] Because it was abstract, this aesthetic was unlikely to be interpreted in ways potentially disrupting to the political and cultural consensus.

In this fashion, NEA standards evaded engagement with many of the social, cultural, and aesthetic developments of the 1960s. The more militant aspects of the civil rights movement and its offspring feminist, racial, ethnic, and sexual revolutions, the rise of the New Left, and the expansion of the Vietnam War all contributed to a new generation of aesthetics reflective of more inclusive postmodern trends. Pop, feminist, ethnic, and racial arts produced work aesthetically more figurative and politically more critical of American life than modernist abstract art. Herrón and Gronk's mural *Black and White Moratorium* reflected this new aesthetic, while older forms of abstract expressionism, such as those found in Motherwell's *Elegies*, had become the accepted cannon but were no longer on the cutting edge. Juxtaposed against these alternative developments, the aesthetically high modernist and politically consensus-oriented underpinnings of the Endowment stand out as older, more conservative, and ultimately out of step with contemporary changes.

This tradition continued to drive NEA policies during the 1970s. A cold warrior and politician in many ways similar to Kennedy and Johnson, Nixon, ironically, proved to be quite liberal in his expansion of NEA funding. However, his generosity grew less out of his love of modern art and more out of his desire to capture the issue of art funding from liberals (both Democrat and Republican) and to bolster his image as a leader and a benefactor of the American public, particularly those he described as forgotten Americans. Nixon won approval from Democrats and Republicans for his actions, ushering in a golden age for the arts endowment.

At the same time, Nixon plotted to change federal arts policy. In the turmoil of the late 1960s and early 1970s, the Cold War consensus began to break down in the minds of the general public as a result of its negative perceptions of Vietnam and Watergate. Most Americans became more cynical in their views of politics, and many artists became more critical of the U.S. government.[18] However, Nixon dismissed these increasing expressions of discontent, and under his administration the NEA virtually ignored their challenges. While Nixon expanded funding, he also imbued art policy with more conservative aims. Guided by his new federalism, he shifted more funds to state and local areas and away from the national agency. He also pursued greater funding of representational aesthetics, and under his guidance the NEA enlarged its percentage of grants to artists who created figurative, folk, and other more populist forms of art. These trends continued under the Carter administration. Vowing to make the arts agency more reflective of American society as a whole, Carter pressed the NEA to pursue pluralistic goals. Between 1976 and 1980 larger percentages of funds were awarded to representational, realist, feminist, ethnic, and folk artists. Nevertheless, the changes were subtle. Neither Nixon nor Carter was able to fully overcome the modernist aesthetics entrenched in the NEA Visual Arts Program.

In theory, the state was not to control artistic production, as many in the 1950s and 1960s had feared would happen and as several historians have argued was the case under European state arts patronage.[19] Rather, in the United States, the state was supposed to enable the blossoming of a creativity reflective of American democratic society. The original NEA mission included implementing such high ideals. Paradoxically, the political and cultural elite who oversaw the arts agency's development imposed a traditional vision of culture. Although they were somewhat removed from the selection of grants because of the institutionalized hierarchy of the National Council on the Arts and the individual arts programs, presidents and their cultural advisers were able to control appointments of NEA chairs and Arts Council members. In this manner they imposed a specific aesthetic and political vision that curtailed pluralist tastes on the Council and in the NEA programs. More work remains to be done on the multifarious activities of the NEA in other areas besides the visual arts, yet I believe my argument will stand.[20]

In the final analysis, the NEA mission to promote the best art and make it accessible to the most people did not prove fully attainable. Nevertheless, the NEA accomplished a great deal. It stimulated the growth of state arts agencies from five in 1965 to fifty-six in 1995 (in all fifty states plus U.S. territories and Washington, D.C.); awarded over 100,000 grants to artists and art organizations; generated matching grants from private institutions estimated at a ratio of eleven dollars for every federal dollar spent; placed over 14,000 practicing artists in 4,700 schools to work with children on art education; and, most importantly, provided artists with recognition that what they do is positive and valuable to American society.[21] Political leaders and arts supporters who worked together to build the foundation for the NEA deserve applause for their unswerving beliefs in excellence and achievement—even if they were not able to satisfy everyone's definitions of those standards. At first this was because the NEA began with a rigid view of modernism as the aesthetic standard. Moreover, the NEA started with limited funding as an experimental agency and could not fund every genre. To its credit, as appropriations increased, the agency expanded its definition of excellence to include more pluralist art forms.

Despite his largesse with arts funds, Nixon shifted NEA policy in a way that began to undermine the agency, and Reagan finished the task. Nixon orchestrated a transformation from the pursuit of artistic excellence as defined by master artists to the pursuit of images acceptable to the public. Later President Reagan populated the Arts Council with more bureaucrats and fewer artists, and the NEA began to lose its voice as the determiner of aesthetic merit.[22] This opened the door for opposition in Congress to attack the agency as unsound and to return to arguments that arts policy was fiscally unnecessary. As conservatives gained ground during the 1980s, they tapped into Americans' frustrations with economic hardship to create a growing anti-tax, antigovernment constituency. In such an environment, the NEA was no longer viewed as a necessary recipient of public money. In addition, conservative antielitism stung the NEA. Many in Congress agreed that the NEA was no longer needed to tell the public what kind of art was best. Thus, Congress expressed not only fiscal conservatism but also cultural conservatism—criticizing the NEA first as elitist, then, during the Mapplethorpe and Serrano controversies, as corrupt.[23] It finally succeeded in reducing budgetary allocations to the point of rescinding the Endowment's ability to function in a meaningful fashion.

The Cold War rationale for founding the National Endowment for the Arts had been lost by the late 1980s. After the collapse of the Soviet Union and communist governments across Eastern Europe, American leaders celebrated the victory of freedom and democracy (and capitalism) over communism. Triumphant America no longer saw a need to justify itself to the world as the best culture. Many perceived the U.S. "win" in the Cold War as already having proven American superiority. Unfortunately, such thinking left little room for an agency designed to promote and display cultural excellence.

However, while government leaders lost their taste for arts policy, the American public did not. Amid the debate about the NEA's alleged indiscretions, a 1992 Harris poll revealed that most Americans support federal arts funding without content restrictions.[24] The conservative agenda that gripped Congress in the 1980s and 1990s pushed its members out of touch with public interest in the arts. Its continuing hold in American politics precludes a return to robust federal support for the arts in the near future. Yet the federal muse may rebound in the twenty-first century.

Rebuilding the NEA would require some changes in current thinking about arts policy: First, the history of the NEA and its achievements must be better understood. The agency did not misspend taxpayer's money on questionable art but admirably performed its mission to support artistic excellence across a broad spectrum and to ensure that the American public had access to such creativity. Its measure of excellence was tilted toward abstract modernism, but the Visual Arts Program moved to correct this imbalance. Unfortunately, it was not allowed the time to fully adjust before its budget was slashed. (Ironically, it was representational art in the form of Mapplethorpe's photography rather than abstract art that launched the conservative attack on the NEA in general and the visual arts in particular.) The agency was even more successful in widening access to the arts. When the Endowment began, few state or regional arts organizations existed, and artists and their audiences alike were confined primarily to New York and a few other cities. By the 1980s every state and region had an arts organization; the National Assembly of State Arts Agencies lobbied for greater power and funding for all.[25] The NEA earmarked 20 percent of its funds for the states, and by the 1980s Congress had mandated an additional 5 percent. NEA funds for state arts programs increased from approximately $2 million in 1967 to over $22 million in 1980.[26] Correspondingly, audiences also expanded as artistic displays and performances became more accessible to them. Historically, the American public has been sympathetic to Endowment activities, and greater knowledge of the NEA's history and accomplishments should only enhance their appreciation.

Second, arts must be depoliticized. The National Endowment for the Arts needs presidential and congressional backing of a bipartisan nature if it is to survive and rebuild. As mandated by the NEA's authorizing legislation, the president appoints the agency's chair and council, and Congress must provide an annual budget and oversight in the form of reauthorization every five years. In early years, the executive and legislative branches placed highly qualified artists and arts administrators in charge of the NEA and provided the agency with a reasonable operating budget. Reauthorization followed upon the assumption that the arts were a vital element in a free society and that the NEA remained true to its mission of pursuing excellence and access. Unfortunately, in the 1980s American leaders lost this broader perspective. They focused on the bottom line, and the agency became a political football tossed about by conservatives and liberals.

The only way to solve the problem of politicization is to form a true endowment structure to remove the agency from reliance on an elected Congress for operating funds. The president and Congress would have to muster the necessary leadership and foresight to authorize an arts and humanities endowment in the first place. But once established, such an endowment would operate from its own funds rather than begging to Congress each year. This would be a bold step for the U.S. government, and no doubt politicians would fear rejection by their backers. Yet cultural endowments have proved remarkably successful in the private sector. The Carnegie Corporation of New York, founded in 1911 with a $135 million donation is now worth almost $2 billion. The Rockefeller Foundation, chartered in 1913 with a $100 million donation counted over $3.5 billion in assets in 2000.[27] Neither figure includes the very generous amounts already awarded by both of these organizations to researchers, scholars, and artists. The National Endowment for the Arts would add to these cultural endeavors the recognition and approval of the federal government and the American people—who have already expressed a clear desire for federal arts funding free of political control. Leaving arts support entirely up to the private sector favors commercially viable art alone. In contrast, Endowment support (determined by artists' peer panels) also aided promising new artists and public art, which engaged the American public to a greater degree in debates about art, culture, and national policy.

Finally, political leaders and NEA staff must rededicate themselves to the original mandate of state noninterference based upon the First Amendment right to freedom of speech. Once funds are provided to begin the endowment, artists should simply be asked to pursue excellence. This policy would require Americans to place their trust in art rather than politics—a worthy goal, and one that history has shown to be difficult but attainable.

NOTES

Four appendixes containing details on the membership and activities of some of the organizations discussed herein are available on-line at <http://www.ibiblio.org/uncpress/binkiewicz/>.

Abbreviations

AR	Arts
Cong. Rec.	*Congressional Record*
FA	Federal Aid
FG	Federal Government
JFK Library	John F. Kennedy Library, Boston, Mass.
LBJ Library	Lyndon Baines Johnson Library, Austin, Tex.
NARA	National Archives and Records Administration
NCA	National Council on the Arts
NEA	National Endowment for the Arts
OMB	Office of Management and Budget
Public Papers	*Public Papers of the President of the United States*
RG	Record Group
SF	Subject Files
SMOF	Staff Member Office Files
WHCF	White House Central Files

Introduction

1. Haithman, "Studying the Politics."

2. Honan, "Congressional Anger Threatens Arts."

3. The law generated another series of battles. In 1990 four artists (Karen Finley, John Fleck, Holly Hughes, and Tim Miller—called the "NEA Four") whose grants were denied under the "decency clause" sued the NEA, claiming that the policy constituted censorship and was in violation of the First Amendment protection of free speech. While two lower courts ruled in their favor, in 1998 the Supreme Court upheld the decency clause. Fiore and Savage, "Ruling Restores Decency Clause."

4. According to a Harris Poll in 1992, the majority of Americans did not believe that the NEA had gone too far, and 75 percent of those polled opposed government restrictions on art content such as those later imposed by Helms. See Arthurs and Davis, "News Flash to Washington: Americans *Like* the Arts." (Emphasis in original.)

5. Advocating a larger role for the federal government, modern "left" liberalism broke with the tradition of classical liberalism, which emphasized laissez-faire government and a free-market economy. This change accompanied the New Deal, although

Progressives had begun to shift toward government activism even before then. Those who still favored classical liberalism became the modern Right. See Weir, Orloff, and Skocpol, *The Politics of Social Policy*, 54−55, 435.

6. Because these recent controversies have been well documented and debated, I have chosen not to rehash them here. Rather, in keeping with my historic approach, I remain focused on the pre-Reagan era when the NEA experienced unprecedented support.

7. Works by art historians and arts managers have covered only certain elements of NEA history, focusing on public art funding in the 1970s and 1980s. For example, Edward Arian's study begins its analysis of the theater, music, and museum programs in 1978, thus missing the crucial formative years of the agency. See Arian, *The Unfulfilled Promise*. Wyszomirski's and Mulcahy's study includes more historical material, but it is written by political scientists and arts managers who provide little analysis of major historical trends influencing the agency. See Mulcahy and Wyszomirski, *America's Commitment to Culture*. More background, albeit very brief, is provided in Taylor and Barresi, *Arts at a New Frontier*.

Art historians have covered visual arts developments by focusing on the pluralist nature of arts funding, largely overlooking the more conservative tendencies that my historical context teases out. See Galligan, "National Endowment for the Arts"; King, "Pluralism in the Visual Arts"; McCombie, "Art and Policy"; and Wetenhall, "Ascendency of Modern Public Sculpture."

The recent historical writing on the NEA began with a wide-ranging, polemic monograph that draws upon secondary sources to give a sweeping, if less than substantive, history of the entire agency and its controversies. See Marquis, *Art Lessons*. More thoughtful recent works have also concentrated on political debates, leaving out much detail and attention to art. For example, see Levy, *Government and the Arts*; and Kammen, *In the Past Lane*, Chapter 2.

Michael Brenson's recent publication, *Visionaries and Outcasts*, examines both political history and the NEA's visual artist's fellowships, yet it falls short of thoroughly historical and objective analysis. Brenson's work was originally commissioned by the NEA itself and presents an overly positive evaluation of the agency based not on archival research but primarily contemporary interviews and sources. My work presents a more complete assessment of the history of arts policy and the NEA visual arts program.

8. Silverman, *Art Nouveau*.

9. Schorske, *Fin-de-Siècle Vienna*; and Paret, *The Berlin Secession*. Other very useful studies include Adamson, *Avant-Garde Florence*; and Silver, *Esprit de Corps*.

10. Kozloff, "American Painting"; Cockcroft, "Abstract Expressionism"; and Guilbaut, *How New York Stole*.

11. In many scholarly works the generational conflict has been broadly depicted in terms of Freudian conflicts between fathers and sons. Some historians have applied this concept more specifically to artists and intellectuals. For example, Carl Schorske explains that both Gustav Klimt and Sigmund Freud himself reacted to personal conflicts by breaking free from the past. Schorske also has proposed that Viennese Secessionism expressed a wider generational reaction against bourgeois liberalism. See Schorske, *Fin-de-Siècle Vienna*. Similarly, in *The Shock of the New*, Robert Hughes examines genera-

tional breaks between avant-garde artists and their predecessors demonstrated in movements by constructivists, dadaists, expressionists, surrealists, and American abstract expressionists. See also Robert Wohl, *The Generation of 1914*.

12. American art historians and critics have become especially interested in the nuances of linguistics and the representations of cultures—both dominant and pluralist. The works of conceptual, postconceptual, ethnic, and feminist artists and critics represent this postmodern trend. See Bois, "Hans Haacke's Critique"; Buchloh, "Conceptual Art 1962–1969"; Chave, "Minimalism"; Lippard, "Sweeping Exchanges"; Robbins, *The Pluralist Era*; del Castillo, McKenna, and Yarbro-Bejarano, *Chicano Art*; and Cockcroft and Barnet-Sanchez, *Signs from the Heart*.

13. See, for example, Bourdieu, "Cultural Reproduction and Social Reproduction" and *Distinction*; Foucault, *The Foucault Reader*; Gramsci, *Selections from the Prison Notebooks*; and the works of historians Hunt, *The New Cultural History*, and Toews, "Intellectual History."

14. Cultural critics have frequently focused on elitism as a negative theme in the implementation of arts policies by museums and other cultural institutions. Works by T. J. Jackson Lears and Serge Guilbaut apply Gramsci's idea of cultural hegemony to U.S. art and cultural history. I propose that elites in the federal government also demonstrated a hegemonic tendency through arts policy. This is clear in presidential and NEA records, especially as they are contrasted with more popular trends. Casey Nelson Blake's analysis of the controversy surrounding corporate and federal collaboration in erecting Richard Serra's abstract sculpture, *Tilted Arc*, has shown that the interests and tastes of the general public have not always corresponded to those of federal administrators. Nevertheless, as Joan Shelley Rubin has shown to be true in the literary world, high culture and popular culture have coexisted. I present American political and cultural ideals juxtaposed with the practices of the endowment, while examining what this reveals about American culture being elitist or representative and democratic. See Lears, "The Concept of Cultural Hegemony"; Guilbaut, *How New York Stole*; Blake, "An Atmosphere of Effrontery"; and Rubin, *The Making of Middlebrow Culture*, 32.

15. My work gives New Frontier and Great Society programs a more positive review that those presented by Allen Matusow or Godfrey Hodgson, which consider liberalism's ultimate failure in the 1960s. I stand closer to Bruce Schulman's assessment of the positive as well as negative impacts of the Great Society of which the NEA was a part. See Matusow, *The Unraveling of America*; Hodgson, *America in Our Time*; and Schulman, *Lyndon B. Johnson*.

16. Reeves, *President Kennedy*.

17. My study draws on Hoff, *Nixon Reconsidered*.

18. Arian, *The Unfulfilled Promise*.

Chapter 1

1. Livingston Biddle studied international arts funding while preparing legislation for the establishment of an American arts foundation. His figures were widely quoted in the *Congressional Record* during the 1960s. Biddle, *Our Government and the Arts*; and author's interview with Biddle, November 7, 1996.

2. For more on colonial views on art, see Harris, *The Artist in American Society*.

3. More background on U.S. attitudes toward the arts is discussed in Taylor and Barresi, *Arts at a New Frontier*, 3–6.

4. Adams, "Letter to Abigail Adams, 1780."

5. Harris also presents an excellent discussion of American fears of luxury and corruption, which, he argues, stemmed not only from Puritan values but also from republican philosophy, with its belief in virtue required by citizens in a democratic republic. These ideas contributed to biases against the arts and inhibited arts policy. See Harris, *The Artist in American Society*, Chapter 2.

6. Although Jefferson enjoyed art and architecture, he preferred simple classical styles, which he deemed more suited to the American republic. See Berman, *Thomas Jefferson among the Arts*; Shackelford, *Jefferson's Travels in Europe*; and McDonald, *The Presidency of Thomas Jefferson*.

7. Early American attitudes toward art are presented in Levy, *Government and the Arts*, 18–19; and Weinberg, *The Lure of Paris*, 20, 37.

8. For a more complete discussion of paintings and sculptures in the Capitol building, as well as their representation of American imperialism and subjugation of Native Americans, see Fryd, *Art and Empire*.

9. Greenough was delighted with his government commission because he considered not the money itself but the "consideration and weight" most important. Harris has shown that artists eagerly sought government commissions because they "conferred a distinction which the artist could never receive from private clients." Harris, *The Artist in American Society*, 83.

10. Fryd, *Art and Empire*. In Chapter 3, "Horatio Greenough's *George Washington*," Fryd asserts that Greenough had employed widely accepted classical and neoclassical sculptural techniques in his depiction of Washington and aimed to represent him as an exemplary republican rather than an authoritarian figure. Nevertheless, most Americans were not fully cognizant of Greenough's artistic symbols (such as the sword held with its hilt toward the people to indicate Washington's service to them), and congressional patrons did not appreciate the artist's vision.

11. This incident is also recounted by Myron and Sundell, *Art in America*, 67–68. The statue is now on view in the Smithsonian Institution.

12. Samuel Cox's initiative appears in House proceedings, *Cong. Rec.*, 43rd Cong., 1st sess., 2078; and House proceedings, *Cong. Rec.*, 46th Cong., 2nd sess., 21.

13. *U.S. Statutes at Large* 26, 1093.

14. See Taylor and Barresi, *Arts at a New Frontier*, 7. This notwithstanding, Americans enjoyed the arts in private collections. Major American museums, including the Boston Museum of Fine Arts and New York's Metropolitan Museum of Art, opened their doors in the late nineteenth century. Moreover, many Americans frequented Europe's art galleries and art institutions. For more on American artists' and patrons' travels to France see Weinberg, *The Lure of Paris*. American travels became the basis for works by several novelists, including Henry James, Edith Warton, and William Dean Howells, who provided numerous accounts of characters' journeys to Europe to "see all the great things, and do what the clever people do," in the words of Christopher Newman from

James's *The American*. This character acquires an "aesthetic headache" while at the Louvre trying to absorb so many works of art previously unfamiliar to him. Yet he intends to collect a great many fine works for his American home, even purchasing a copy of the *Mona Lisa* from a Parisian art student. James used Newman to represent late nineteenth-century Americans who believed they needed to learn of and obtain European art to become cultured. See James, *The American*, 55, 33–39. Howells's characters were depicted more often as decadent materialists, as seen in *The Rise of Silas Lapham*.

15. Cooper, *The Warrior and the Priest*, 86–87.

16. In the 1910s and 1920s, American elites were interested in showing that American culture could be both democratic and civilized and that a consumer culture could also maintain integrity and cultural standards. Organizations such as the Book of the Month Club, founded during this period, appealed directly both to the elite's mission of social and cultural uplift for the masses and to popular desires for guidance and serviceable commodification. Rubin, *The Making of Middlebrow Culture*, 98–102.

17. Levy, *Government and the Arts*, 41.

18. *U.S. Statutes at Large* 36, 371; and House proceedings, *Cong. Rec.*, 61st Cong., 2nd sess., 45:1671, 5708.

19. For a detailed account of Roosevelt's presidency and New Deal programs see Leuchtenburg, *Franklin D. Roosevelt*. For more discussion of U.S. economic policy under Presidents Hoover and Roosevelt and concerns with balanced budgets versus Keynesian economics see Garraty, *The Great Depression*.

20. O'Connor, *Federal Support*, 16. Of course, artists have always had to make difficult choices between their art and practical employment, but this was exacerbated during the Great Depression. General information on the federal art projects also appears in McKinzie, *The New Deal for Artists*; Matthews, "Arts and the People"; and Monroe, "The 1930s."

21. Garraty, *The Great Depression*, 112.

22. O'Connor, *Federal Support*, 19.

23. Ibid., 43, 102. Also see Garraty, *The Great Depression*, for discussions of prevalent fiscal restraint.

24. Matthews, *The Federal Theatre*, 64, 120; and McKinzie, *The New Deal for Artists*, 106.

25. See the discussion of congressional opposition to this program in Matthews, *The Federal Theatre*, 5, 260.

26. McKinzie, *The New Deal for Artists*, 181. Richard Candida Smith explained that artist Clay Spohn, who worked for the WPA in California, hated the bureaucracy that he was forced to wade through in order to complete a project. The process included submitting plans to county committees made up of politicians and some other artists not employed by the WPA who then reviewed the project's topic and style according to the local community's taste. Once the project was approved, any further changes had to be resubmitted for approval. Spohn considered this procedure dulling to his creative process and argued that his work for the WPA was not "painting" but simply "illustration" for his "clients." Spohn as cited in Smith, *Utopia and Dissent*, 74.

27. O'Connor, *Federal Support*, 25.

28. Marling, *Wall-to-Wall America*, 8.

29. Ibid., 326, 293.

30. Refregier's mural depicted radical labor violence. The artist himself was considered a leftist. Arnautoff's work illustrated a street scene filled with working-class people reading papers at a newsstand selling communist and leftist journals such as the *Daily Worker* and *Masses*. See Marling, *Wall-to-Wall America*, 45–49.

31. Lorser Feitelson as quoted in Smith, *Utopia and Dissent*, 28.

32. Jonathan Harris goes a step further to assert that the Federal Art Project, "through its various programs and discourses . . . produced a particular 'national-popular' rhetoric supporting Roosevelt's reformist policies." In essence Harris argues that by using art as part of his populist appeal to the American people, Roosevelt projected the idea that the New Deal would be able to resolve economic, political, and ideological conflicts at a time when American capitalist society was in crisis. Drawing heavily upon Antonio Gramsci's concept of cultural hegemony, Harris proposes that the utopian view offered by Roosevelt and the WPA artists was employed to maintain the capitalist hegemony in the United States during the Great Depression. See Harris, *Federal Art and National Culture*, 7–8.

33. Matthews, *The Federal Theatre*.

34. O'Connor, *Federal Support*, 28; and Matthews, *The Federal Theatre*, 300.

35. McKinzie, *The New Deal for Artists*, 169.

36. Ibid., 50; and O'Connor, *Federal Support*, 23, 28.

37. Gestural and color-field paintings were two distinct branches within the genre of abstract expressionism. For a detailed discussion of the genre and its powerful connections to broader American cultural concerns at midcentury, see Leja, *Reframing Abstract Expressionism*.

38. Harold Rosenberg coined the term "action painting" to describe Jackson Pollock's style of abstract expressionism. See Rosenberg, "The American Action Painters." Pollock had also worked for a time as a WPA artist producing more figurative work under the direction of Thomas Hart Benton. He learned new painting techniques in Marxist David Alfaro Siqueiros's Experimental Workshop in New York City in the 1930s. See Hurlburt, *The Mexican Muralists*, 221.

39. Jackson Pollock, "Interview with William Wright (1958)," in Stiles and Selz, *Theories and Documents*, 22–24.

40. For more details on abstract expressionism and Jackson Pollock, see Ashton, *The Life and Times*; Geldzahler, *New York Painting and Sculpture*; Guilbaut, *Reconstructing Modernism*; and Leja, *Reframing Abstract Expressionism*.

41. Greenberg, "Avant-Garde and Kitsch" and *Art and Culture*; Rosenberg, "The American Action Painters" and *The Tradition of the New*; and Sandler, *The Triumph of American Painting*.

42. "Jackson Pollock."

43. Cockcroft, "Abstract Expressionism"; Guilbaut, *How New York Stole*; and Kozloff, "American Painting." Larson documented that Sen. Hubert Humphrey (D-MN), Rep. Frank Thompson (D-NJ), and Rep. Philip Hart (D-MI) supported U.S. government exhibits of modernist abstract art in the 1950s, see *The Reluctant Patron*, 139, 144, and 255.

44. Quote by Alfred Barr of the Museum of Modern Art in the introduction to the catalog for "The New American Painting" exhibition shown in Europe in 1958 and 1959. See Stiles and Selz, *Theories and Documents*, 42.

45. Rockefeller as quoted in Reich, *Life of Nelson A. Rockefeller*, 407. See 215 for Rockefeller's work during the New Deal period.

46. Eisenhower's conservative stance on fiscal and social policy is discussed in Greenstein, *The Hidden-Hand Presidency*, 49–52.

47. "Ike Sets His Course."

48. Reich, *Life of Nelson A. Rockefeller*, 628. For more on Rockefeller's political leanings and Republican suspicion of his liberal tendencies see 689, 708, and 719.

49. *New York Times*, October 7, 1956; Larson, *The Reluctant Patron*, 249; and "Ike Likes the Arts." See also U.S. Senate, *International Cultural Exchange and Trade Fair Participation Act of 1956*.

50. Eisenhower signed the bill for the building of a national cultural center in 1958 and entertained the idea of further arts support suggested to him by August Heckscher in the report by the President's Commission on National Goals completed in 1960. However, the president did not act. See Heckscher, "The Quality of American Culture."

51. For more on the impact of the Cold War and McCarthyism in the United States see Fried, *Nightmare in Red*; and Griffith, *The Politics of Fear*.

52. Stalin and Hitler both considered abstract art debased. See Lindey, *Art in the Cold War*, Chapter 6; and Barron, *Degenerate Art*.

53. *Cong. Rec.*, 81st Cong., 1st sess., 3234–35.

54. *Cong. Rec.*, 82nd Cong., 2nd sess., 2423–27.

55. George Biddle is a member of the Philadelphia Biddle family and the uncle of later NEA chair Livingston Biddle. George Biddle was the first to approach FDR with the idea of a federal arts project. He worked for the Treasury Section of Painting and Sculpture during the 1930s and tried to propose new art policy ideas to American presidents after the WPA's and Section's demise. For greater depth on art policy during the 1940s and 1950s, see Larson, *The Reluctant Patron*.

56. Moe, "Government and the Arts."

57. More detailed accounts of WPA art projects and issues of control appear in Harris, *Federal Art and National Culture*; McKinzie, *The New Deal for Artists*; and Marling, *Wall-to-Wall America*.

58. Portner, *Washington Post and Times Herald*, July 15, 1956.

59. For a brief background of Thompson and his work in Congress see Wilson, *Liberal Leader in the House*. Thompson later became embroiled in controversy and little historical writing details his demise in Congress after the 1960s.

60. Thompson, "Are the Communists Right," 5.

61. For an account of Javits's life see Javits and Steinberg, *Javits*.

62. This liberal style of government activism and cold warrior internationalism adopted by members of both political parties has also been called "pragmatic liberalism" because of its emphasis on pragmatism more than political ideology in the post–World War II period. See Underwood and Daniels, *Governor Rockefeller of New York*, Chapter 1 (10); and Reich, *Life of Nelson A. Rockefeller*.

63. See Cockcroft, "Abstract Expressionism," for a well-rounded discussion of the U.S. State Department and USIA programs for touring American art abroad during the 1950s. Cultural advocates who later became prominent in NEA policy formation supported these efforts.

64. *New York Herald Tribune*, June 3, 1958.

65. Quoted in U.S. House, *Federal Grants to Fine Arts Programs and Projects*, 29. The list of bills covered in these hearings represents the bulk of the efforts undertaken by arts supporters during the 1950s. I have condensed these efforts into a broader discussion of major trends rather than exploring the path of each bill individually. For a more detailed account see Larson, *The Reluctant Patron*; or Mark, *Reluctant Bureaucrats*.

66. Canby saw his editorial post at the Book-of-the-Month Club as "professorial" and thought an aristocratic impulse should assert itself over the democratic masses (or lowbrow culture). See Rubin, *The Making of Middlebrow Culture*, 115.

67. Humphrey, *Education of a Public Man*. A more recent view of Humphrey may be found in Garrettson, *Hubert H. Humphrey*.

68. The Humphrey and Johnson relationship would prove a long and mutually beneficial one, as Johnson helped Humphrey gain acceptance in a Senate dominated by the southern Democratic establishment during the 1950s, and Humphrey became a liaison between Johnson and the northern liberals. See Schulman, *Lyndon B. Johnson*.

69. Humphrey's remarks in U.S. Senate, *International Cultural Exchange and Trade Fair Participation Act of 1956*, 28. Humphrey also criticized the USIA for its timidity on this matter. See Senate proceedings, *Cong. Rec.*, 84th Cong., 2nd sess., 10918–20.

70. Pell aide Livingston Biddle attests to the close ties between the Kennedy family and Pell. The two families often dined together, and Kennedy and Pell often sailed together unaccompanied by the usual entourages. Author's interview with Biddle, November 7, 1996.

71. *New York Times*, September 29, 1960, 22; *New York Times*, September 30, 1960, 16; and *Current Biography*, 1972.

72. Author's interview with Pell.

73. Pell was appointed chair of the subcommittee in 1962. According to Livingston Biddle, Sen. Lister Hill initially balked at what he considered an outrageous request for chairmanship from junior senator Pell. But Hill ultimately decided to grant Pell the position because he thought that the new subcommittee would lack political relevance, while Pell would owe him a favor. Author's interview with Biddle, January 5, 1994.

74. Pell speaking on behalf of a bill to establish a national arts program, Senate proceedings, *Cong. Rec.*, 88th Cong., 1st sess., 25263–64.

75. Senate proceedings, *Cong. Rec.*, 88th Cong., 1st sess., 25269–70.

76. House proceedings, *Cong. Rec.*, 87th Cong., 1st sess., 20499.

77. Ibid. Of course, the jet bomber cost is measured by 1961 standards.

78. House proceedings, *Cong. Rec.*, 87th Cong., 2nd sess., 4040.

79. Senate proceedings, *Cong. Rec.*, 87th Cong., 2nd sess., 5224.

80. House proceedings, *Cong. Rec.*, 87th Cong., 2nd sess., 13825.

Chapter 2

1. Kennedy, "Letter to Theodate Johnson."

2. For the visual arts this included the abstract painting and sculpture that were then champions of the New York and international art scene. Kennedy respected the discipline and free expression of the modernist genre, although his own stylistic preference was for representational painting and classical artworks.

Art historians generally agree that American modernism, particularly abstract expressionist painting, had achieved prominence in the world art market after World War II. Cockcroft and Guilbaut have argued that it became the darling not only of art critics but also of political figures interested in exporting the ideals of American cultural freedom. See Guilbaut, *How New York Stole*; and Cockcroft, "Abstract Expressionism." Kennedy himself was schooled in cultural appreciation and encouraged in the area of modern art by his wife, Jacqueline, and close friend and painter Bill Walton.

3. "Babbitt" was a code word among Europeans for American banality. Kennedy's point was aimed as much at them as at American audiences. See Pells, *Not Like Us*, 20.

4. Kennedy, "Letter to Theodate Johnson."

5. Ibid.

6. Kennedy, "Letter to Irving Kolodin."

7. Reeves, *President Kennedy*, 54.

8. Kennedy as quoted in Matthews, *Kennedy and Nixon*, 192; "Behind Closed Doors: The Private Life of a Public Man," in White, *Kennedy*, 268–69.

9. New Deal Works Progress Administration arts projects were not meant to be lasting programs. Rather, they were designed to provide temporary relief for unemployed artists and were quickly dismantled at the end of the 1930s.

10. Macdonald, *Memoirs of a Revolutionist*, 236.

11. "USA v. USSR," in ibid., 312. The essay originally appeared in *Partisan Review*.

12. Schlesinger, *The Vital Center*.

13. Lasch, *The New Radicalism in America*, 308–11.

14. The CIA had funded the congress with laundered money. Schlesinger was only involved in the initial conference at a time when it had a great deal of support among American intellectuals. However, he was aware and supportive of the CIA's cultural endeavors. The congress continued to meet well into the 1960s; however, it lost the support of artists and intellectuals as U.S. involvement in Vietnam escalated and became less accepted and once its CIA funding source became widely known. Schlesinger noted that the Ford Foundation later picked up funding for the congress. Author's interview with Schlesinger; Pells, *The Liberal Mind*, 128–29; Saunders, *The Cultural Cold War*, 91; and Coleman, *The Liberal Conspiracy*.

15. Galbraith, *American Capitalism*.

16. Critics' fears in the 1950s parallel those of the 1910s and 1920s as well. Joan Rubin has documented how cultural elites used the Book-of-the-Month Club, outline texts, great books serials, and literary radio programs to try to instill genteel values into American popular culture and combat the standardization and consumerism of the modern era. See Rubin, *The Making of Middlebrow Culture*.

17. Whyte, *The Organization Man*, 362, 404.

18. Riesman, *The Lonely Crowd*, 21, 131.

19. Ibid., and Whyte, *The Organization Man*.

20. Whyte, *The Organization Man*, 65.

21. Galbraith. *The Affluent Society*, 4.

22. Ibid., 192.

23. Galbraith, *The Affluent Society*.

24. Ibid., 273.

25. Social scientists became more active in public policy and foreign policy initiatives during the 1950s and 1960s, as many saw it their duty to aid the American government and the advance of American ideology during the Cold War. See Latham, *Modernization as Ideology*, 22, 53.

26. Schlesinger, "The Challenge of Abundance." Also see discussions of Schlesinger in Pells, *The Liberal Mind*, 131–146; and Matusow, *The Unraveling of America*, Chapter 1.

27. Author's interview with Schlesinger. Schlesinger's support for the arts was not necessarily for one specific genre. In his memoir, he noted that he was not in favor of abstract expressionism per se, as Serge Guilbaut concluded. Schlesinger, *A Life in the 20th Century*, 520.

28. Greenberg, "Avant-Garde and Kitsch"; "Work and Leisure under Industrialism"; and "The Plight of Our Culture."

29. "Masscult and Midcult," in Macdonald, *Against the American Grain*, 34.

30. Goodman, *Growing Up Absurd*, 109.

31. McDougall, *The Heavens and the Earth*, 199.

32. Johnson is quoted in Halberstam, *The Fifties*, 625. The reference to *Life* appears on 626. Also integral to this discussion of American know-how are Flesch, *Why Johnny Can't Read*; and Trace, *What Ivan Knows*. These texts gained notoriety for their comparisons of American students' academic laziness to the prowess of their Russian counterparts in literature, history, and foreign languages. They also enlivened cultural policy debates over the benefits of Ivan's exposure to opera, theater, and art versus Johnny's intake of American television. Speaking for the establishment of a National Arts Foundation, Representative Kearns quotes from the Trace book. See House proceedings, *Congr. Rec.*, 87th Cong., 2nd sess., 5201.

33. Latham, *Modernization as Ideology*, 57 and 115.

34. Schlesinger as quoted in Decter, "Kennedyism," 20.

35. Frost, "The Next Augustan Age"; also see notes on Frost's inaugural participation in Schlesinger, *A Thousand Days*, 671.

36. "Inaugural Address," January 20, 1961, in *Public Papers: Kennedy*, 15.

37. Von Eckhardt, "Oral History Interview with August Heckscher," 3. Also see listings of the invitees in August Heckscher Papers, box 40, folder 8, JFK Library.

38. Kennedy, "Letter to Theodate Johnson."

39. Memo, January 1961, Heckscher Papers, box 40, folder 8, JFK Library. For a discussion of those involved in drafting the list of invitees, see Von Eckhardt, "Oral History Interview with August Heckscher," 6. Pièrre Salinger later solicited comments

and suggestions from these artists on arts policy; the comments were delivered to art consultant Heckscher.

40. Papers for *A Thousand Days*, Arthur Schlesinger Papers, box W-3, JFK Library.

41. There are other important instances in which Kennedy deliberately disregarded the social taboo on fraternizing with those deemed enemies of the United States for their communist sympathies or general criticisms of the government. For instance, the president-elect and his brother Robert crossed an American Legion picket line in 1960 to see *Spartacus*—the film based on a novel by former communist Howard Fast (who had won the Stalin Peace Prize in 1954), with a screenplay by former Hollywood Ten convict, Dalton Trumbo. Kennedy also intended to resurrect the reputation of J. Robert Oppenheimer by bestowing upon him the Fermi Prize for his achievements in nuclear energy. Johnson presented this award in December of 1963, removing the pall cast over the celebrated physicist when the Eisenhower administration revoked his security clearance in 1953 and the Atomic Energy Commission declared him a security risk because of his opposition to the development of the hydrogen bomb. See Whitfield, *Culture of the Cold War*, 181, 211, and 219.

42. Von Eckhardt, "Oral History Interview with August Heckscher." 3.

43. Ibid.

44. Kennedy to Professor Jacques Barzun, September 13, 1961, Heckscher Papers, box 40, folder 12, JFK Library.

45. More critical views of Kennedy's cultural activities are expressed in White, *Kennedy*.

46. For comments on John Kennedy's artistic tastes, see, for example, "Oral History Interview with Jacqueline Kennedy," JFK Library; Fey, *The Pleasure of His Company*, 181.

47. Gelb, "Culture Makes a Hit," 64–66.

48. Author's interview with Salinger. Numerous memos in the Heckscher Papers at the JFK Library also point to a prominent role by the first lady in cultural policy.

49. See Gelb, "Culture Makes a Hit", 66; Thayer, *Jacqueline Kennedy*; and Thayer, *Jacqueline Bouvier Kennedy*.

50. Thayer, *Jacqueline Kennedy*. According to Doris Kearns Goodwin, it was Jacqueline Kennedy's idea to invite Frost to read at the inauguration. See Goodwin, *The Fitzgeralds and the Kennedys*, 813.

51. It has been widely quoted that John Kennedy's father, Joseph Kennedy, had frequently stated to his son that "image is everything" in public life. See Goodwin, *The Fitzgeralds and the Kennedys*; and Reeves, *A Question of Character*, 252.

52. Schlesinger, *A Thousand Days*, 672.

53. Lincoln, *The Kennedy White House Parties*, 57.

54. *New York Times*, November 1961.

55. Jacqueline Kennedy as quoted in Salinger, *P.S.*, 104.

56. Hall and Pinchot, *Jacqueline Kennedy*, 151; and Thayer, *Jacqueline Kennedy*, 31.

57. Jacqueline Kennedy accepted the generally held belief that woman's place was in the home rather than the public sphere. For discussion of the conventional depictions of women in the 1950s to which she conformed, see May, *Homeward Bound*.

58. McCarthy, *Women's Culture*; and Blair, *The Torchbearers*.

59. "A Tour of the White House."

60. Lincoln, *The Kennedy White House Parties*, 112–25; and Thayer, *Jacqueline Kennedy*, 183–84.

61. See Thayer, *Jacqueline Kennedy*, 196. Kennedy remarks at French embassy.

62. The American activity in the Venice Biennale and French opposition to American "cultural imperialism" are documented by Monahan, "Cultural Cartography," 369–416.

63. "A Strategy for Cultural Advancement," Heckscher Papers, box 35, folder 10, JFK Library.

64. Ibid., 1.

65. Ibid.

66. For an account of the Berlin Crisis, see Reeves, *President Kennedy*, 185–208; and Schlesinger, *A Thousand Days*, 353–70.

67. Schlesinger, *A Thousand Days*, 286. For a detailed discussion of the Bay of Pigs see 219–49; and Reeves, *President Kennedy*, 88–106.

68. Schlesinger, *A Thousand Days*, 362.

69. The policies of massive retaliation and flexible response are detailed by Gaddis in *Strategies of Containment*.

70. Phillip Coombs discussed cultural aspects of this all-encompassing international policy and detailed international education programs in his book. Coombs, *Fourth Dimension of Foreign Policy*.

71. Heckscher, *The Public Happiness*.

72. Schlesinger to JFK, "Moving Ahead on the Cultural Front," November 22, 1961, Schlesinger Papers, box 16, folder 3, JFK Library.

73. JFK to August Heckscher, "Role and Assignment," December 5, 1961, Heckscher Papers, box 6, folder 15, JFK Library.

74. Von Eckhardt, "Oral History Interview with August Heckscher." 48.

75. "The Arts and the National Government," report to President Kennedy, May 28, 1963, Heckscher Papers, box 40, folder 2, 1–9, JFK Library.

76. "The Challenge of Ugliness," Address at the Conference on Aesthetic Responsibility, New York Chapter of the American Institute of Architects, April 3, 1962. Reprinted in *Cong. Rec.*, 87th Cong., 2nd sess., 8910–12.

77. "The Arts and the National Government," report to President Kennedy, May 28, 1963, Heckscher Papers, box 40, folder 2, 27–28, JFK Library.

78. Ibid., 28.

79. Schlesinger believes that Kennedy intended to appoint Richard Goodwin to the post. *A Thousand Days*, 675.

80. Kennedy to Heckscher, June 10, 1963, Heckscher Papers, box 40, folder 2, JFK Library.

81. Kennedy's references to the American pursuit of happiness and a discussion of Jeffersonian ideals in which the arts would combat accumulation of the wealth that might encourage "course and vicious habits" can be found in JFK's "Remarks at the National Cultural Center Dinner," November 29, 1962, Heckscher Papers, box 40, folder 4, 3, JFK Library.

82. Galbraith, *The Affluent Society*.

83. JFK, "The Arts in America," draft article for *Look*, Heckscher Papers, box 40, folder 4, 8, JFK Library.

84. JFK, "Special Message to the Congress on Education," February 6, 1962, Heckscher Papers, box 35, folder 1, JFK Library.

85. *Executive Order 11112*, June 12, 1963, WHCF, box 122, folder 4, JFK Library.

86. "Statement by the President Establishing the President's Advisory Council on the Arts," June 12, 1963, WHCF, box 122, folder 4, JFK Library.

87. Kennedy biographers, such as Reeves and Schlesinger, concur that JFK was unwilling to jeopardize his primary foreign policy objectives by antagonizing conservative legislators on domestic issues such as civil rights or the arts, which he deemed less imperative. Nevertheless, it is also recognized that he did promote the arts in new ways, see Wetenhall, "Camelot's Legacy to Public Art," 303–8.

88. Schlesinger, *A Thousand Days*, 710.

89. Author's interview with Pell. Also see Stewart, "Interview with Senator Claiborne Pell," 15; and a letter from Pell to Mrs. Kennedy attached to the interview transcript. See also letters from Rep. Frank Thompson to Mrs. Kennedy, WHCF, box 40, JFK Library.

90. During the 1950s, congressional arts supporters attempted to pass bills that would establish an advisory council on the arts (S. 741 and H.R. 4172), provide aid to state arts projects (S. 785), and establish a U.S. arts foundation (S. 936, S. 1250). These measures were combined in S. 2379 and H.R. 9586 in 1963.

91. Senator Humphrey speaking on the National Arts and Cultural Development Act, Senate proceedings, *Cong. Rec.*, 88th Cong., 1st sess., 266, 25268.

92. "The Foundation is authorized to establish and conduct a program of grants-in-aid in a manner consistent with the declaration of policy set forth in the National Arts and Cultural Development Act of 1963. . . . The amount of any grants allotted to any group pursuant to this subsection shall not exceed 50 per centum of the total cost of such project or production." As set forth in the National Arts and Cultural Development Act of 1963, Senate proceedings, *Cong. Rec.*, 88th Cong., 1st sess., 25272.

93. House proceedings, *Cong. Rec.*, 88th Cong., 1st sess., 18276.

94. House proceedings, *Cong. Rec.*, 87th Cong., 2nd sess., A1902.

95. Senate proceedings, *Cong. Rec.*, 87th Cong., 2nd sess., 17231.

96. "Remarks at Amherst College upon Receiving an Honorary Degree," October 26, 1963, in *Public Papers: Kennedy*, 817.

97. Senate proceedings, *Cong. Rec.*, 87th Cong., 2nd sess., 5222.

98. Kennedy, Statement Accompanying the Executive Order 11112, WHCF, box 122, folder 4, JFK Library.

99. Senate proceedings, *Cong. Rec.*, 88th Cong., 1st sess., 266.

100. Senate proceedings, *Cong. Rec.*, 88th Cong., 1st sess., 25263.

101. Senate proceedings, *Cong. Rec.*, 87th Cong., 2nd sess., 2111, 10948. My estimation of percentage is based on a detailed analysis of the *Congressional Records* between 1960 and 1963. This tactic illustrates a common strategy in Congress whereby members link issues in an effort to achieve the passage of one on the coattails of the other. See Light, *The President's Agenda*.

102. Senate proceedings, *Cong. Rec.*, 87th Cong., 1st sess., 1546–1547.

103. Ibid., 2062.

104. House proceedings, *Cong. Rec.*, 87th Cong., 1st sess., 18279.

105. Ibid., 18278.

106. Wagnleitner, "The Irony of American Culture," 293. For a more detailed study see Wagnleitner, *Coca-Colonization and the Cold War*.

107. House proceedings, *Cong. Rec.*, 87th Cong., 1st sess., 20497.

108. References to these books appear numerous times in the *Congressional Record* and in intellectual and cultural writings, such as Goodman's *Growing Up Absurd*, for example, which reveals a widespread American concern about falling behind the Soviets.

109. House proceedings, *Cong. Rec.*, 87th Cong., 2nd sess., 5201.

110. Senate proceedings, *Cong. Rec.*, 88th Cong., 1st sess., 266.

111. Ibid., 25265.

112. Ibid., 25266.

113. "Remarks at Amherst College upon Receiving an Honorary Degree," October 26, 1963, in *Public Papers: Kennedy*, 815.

114. Wetenhall, "Ascendancy of Modern Public Sculpture," 306.

115. See Canaday, "Art in the Soviet." Also "Khrushchev Scolds Abstract Painters"; and "Soviet Orders Disciplining for Cultural Avant-Garde."

116. Javits and Steinberg, *Javits*, 313.

117. Roger Hilsman, Kennedy's assistant secretary of state for Far Eastern affairs, scoffed that "Camelot was an invention of my good friend Teddy White, using Jackie's romanticism after the president's death. If Jack Kennedy had heard this stuff about Camelot he would have vomited." Hilsman as quoted in Matthews, *Kennedy and Nixon*, 244.

Chapter 3

1. Goldman, *The Tragedy of Lyndon Johnson*, 27–28.

2. Whitfield, *The Culture of the Cold War*, 181, 211, and 219.

3. Johnson historians agree that the president carried on many of the initiatives first outlined under the Kennedy administration, yet Johnson also desperately wanted to emerge from under Kennedy's shadow and achieve his own measures of success. See Kearns, *Lyndon Johnson and the American Dream*; and Schulman, *Lyndon B. Johnson*.

4. "Address before a Joint Session of the Congress," November 27, 1963, in *Public Papers: Johnson*, 10.

5. Goldman, as quoted in "Unpaid Brain Trust."

6. Kalman, *Abe Fortas*, 218.

7. For a complete list of those intellectuals who worked with Goldman, see Goldman, *The Tragedy of Lyndon Johnson*, 130. All accepted their assignment and were approved by President Johnson.

8. Ibid., 139–40.

9. Riesman, *The Lonely Crowd*; Whyte, *The Organization Man*; and Galbraith, *The Affluent Society*.

10. Barbara Tuchman as quoted in Goldman, *The Tragedy of Lyndon Johnson*, 139.

11. "Address at the Centennial Commencement of Swarthmore College," June 8, 1964, in *Public Papers: Johnson*, 1:756.

12. Heckscher to Fortas, cc to Schlesinger, "The Arts," January 7, 1964, Schlesinger Papers, box W-3, folder 3, JFK Library.

13. Javits to Johnson, December 5, 1963, WHCF, FG 712, "President's Advisory Council on the Arts," box 396, folder 2, LBJ Library.

14. Lawrence O'Brien to Javits, December 17, 1963, WHCF, FG 712, "President's Advisory Council on the Arts," box 395, LBJ Library.

15. Abe Fortas to Johnson, March 10, 1964; and Fortas to Jack Valenti, December 6, 1964; as quoted in Kalman, *Abe Fortas*, 221. Apparently, Fortas was worried that the tension between President Johnson and Robert Kennedy, a Kennedy Center Board leader, over who would get the most credit for the nation's cultural programs would overshadow the progress of Johnson's arts policies. See also Kalman, *Abe Fortas*, 223.

16. Roger Stevens to Jack Valenti, March 25, 1965, WHCF, FG 11–12, "National Council on the Arts," box 123, LBJ Library.

17. According to Kalman, Fortas was shocked at an early Johnson White House function by a group of French singers doing a "kind of third-rate boogie-woogie performance of Bach" and asked Bloom to "do me, the nation, and the cause of culture a favor" by developing the list of musicians for the White House. See Kalman, *Abe Fortas*, 220.

18. Bornet, *The Presidency of Lyndon B. Johnson*, 113–14.

19. Douglas Cater to Johnson, November 21, 1964, WHCF, AR-Arts, box 1, folder 1, LBJ Library. Kay Halle, who had been involved with the artist invitations for the JFK inaugural, was influential in encouraging Cater to request similar action from Johnson. Halle to Cater, July 27, 1964, WHCF, AR-Arts, box 1, folder 5, LBJ Library.

20. Johnson's views were well articulated in his memoir. He asserted that anyone who believed that the communists were not working to conquer other nations was simply naive. Johnson never abandoned the attitude prevalent among the World War II generation that totalitarian regimes should not be appeased but rather should be forcefully stopped from spreading their influence. This attitude and his belief in consensus politics contributed to his commitment to countering the spread of communism and to winning the war in Vietnam. See Johnson, *The Vantage Point*. Historians have also noted that Johnson worked within established systems and, despite his liberal programs, slowly reformed (rather than completely changed) social policies in ways that did not challenge previous federal policies of working with big businesses and more conservative constituents. For example, when establishing Medicare and antipoverty legislation, Johnson did not upset the American Medical Association or challenge the control of local politicians and institution leaders. See, for example, Schulman, *Lyndon B. Johnson*, 95.

21. "Remarks at the University of Michigan," May 22, 1964, in *Public Papers: Johnson*, 704–7.

22. "Annual Message to Congress on the State of the Union," January 4, 1965, in *Public Papers: Johnson*, 7–8.

23. Ibid.

24. Siegel, "Johnson," 138–42.

25. Johnson, *The Vantage Point.*

26. Light, *The President's Agenda*, 39, 45.

27. For a more detailed look at the substantive legislative accomplishments Johnson achieved under his Great Society, consult Schulman's, *Lyndon B. Johnson.*

28. "What's Ahead." Historians have also discussed the growth of the American economy in the post–World War II period. For example, see Stephen K. McNees, "A Brief Overview of the Post–World War II Expansions," in Vatter and Walker, *History of the U.S. Economy*, 48–51.

29. "Letter to the Speaker in Support of the Establishment of a National Council on the Arts," August 18, 1964, in *Public Papers: Johnson*, 983. This was written on the day that McCormack was scheduled to report on the bill H.R. 9586, and is thus a fine example not only of Johnson's interest in art legislation but his shrewd political timing.

30. *Public Papers: Johnson*, 1624–26.

31. Humphrey discussed his enlarged role as vice president in an interview appearing in *Fortune*, August 1965.

32. House proceedings, *Cong. Rec.*, 88th Cong., 2nd sess., 20646.

33. House proceedings, *Cong. Rec.*, 89th Cong., 1st sess., 23946.

34. Ibid., 23966.

35. Ibid., 23954.

36. House proceedings, *Cong. Rec.*, 88th Cong., 2nd sess., 20663.

37. House proceedings, *Cong. Rec.*, 89th Cong., 1st sess., 7257.

38. A copy of the bill including the humanities is dated January 5, 1965. WHCF, FG 11–12, "National Council on the Arts," box 123, LBJ Library. Also see memo from Douglas Cater to Bill Moyers, January 18, 1965, WHCF, FG 266, "National Foundation on the Arts and Humanities," box 298, LBJ Library.

39. A copy of this statement may be found in WHCF, Bill Moyers Papers, "Arts and Humanities," box 5, LBJ Library.

40. Passage of the bill is noted in Senate proceedings, *Cong. Rec.*, 88th Cong., 2nd sess., 20923. Johnson signed it on September 3, 1964, see p. 22394. Ryan's remarks may be found in House proceedings, *Cong. Rec.*, 88th Cong., 2nd sess., 20662.

41. House proceedings, *Cong. Rec.*, 89th Cong., 1st sess., 36.

42. Pell to Jack Valenti, January 5, 1965, WHCF, LBJ Library. The letter notes that including the humanities would attract "a much wider segment of support." According to a discussion with Livingston Biddle by Louann Temple, Pell did not ask the White House for a bill. The Johnson administration solicited recommendations and submitted its own bill a month later. See Temple, "Pathfinders for the Imagination," 88.

43. Senate proceedings, *Cong. Rec.*, 89th Cong., 1st sess., 380–83. For the House bills refer to p. 413.

44. WHCF, "Legislative Background. Arts and Humanities Foundation," LE/AR Arts, box 1, LBJ Library; and "Statement by the President on the Proposed National Foundation on the Arts and Humanities," March 10, 1965, in *Public Papers: Johnson*, 273–74.

45. Conte, "Congress," 41.

46. House proceedings, *Cong. Rec.*, 89th Cong., 1st sess., 23937, 23952.

47. House proceedings, *Cong. Rec.*, 89th Cong., 1st sess., 23944.

48. Ibid. Representative Thompson is the speaker.

49. Snow argued that at one pole were "the literary intellectuals—at the other scientists. . . . Between the two exists a gulf of mutual miscomprehension—sometimes . . . hostility and dislike, but most of all a lack of understanding." C. P. Snow, "The Two Cultures."

50. Tichenor's comments in the *MIT Technology Review*, March 1955, are cited in Whyte, *The Organization Man*, 90–91.

51. *Public Papers: Johnson* (1965), 1022.

52. Remarks by both Seaborg and Haworth appear in Conte, "Congress," 40–42.

53. Statement by the president to the first meeting of the National Council on the Arts at the White House, April 9, 1965. WHCF, Harry McPherson Papers, "Arts—National Council on the," box 4, LBJ Library.

54. Robert Lowell to President Johnson, May 30, 1965, WHCF, AR-Arts, box 2, "11/23/63–6/4/65," LBJ Library.

55. Memos from Goldman to Moyers; letter from Goldman to Lowell, June 2, 1965, WHCF, AR-Arts, box 2, "11/23/63–6/4/65," LBJ Library.

56. The Lowell letter aroused much debate, prompting artists and intellectuals to vie for positions on either side of the controversy. John Steinbeck, among others, wrote to Jack Valenti asking him to assure the president that although he would not attend the festival, this was not for lack of support for the administration's policies. On the other hand, Robert Silvers and Stanley Kunitz sent a telegram to Johnson with twenty signatures of those supporting Lowell's position against Johnson's foreign policies. Their text read, "[We] hope that people in this and other countries will not conclude that a White House arts program testifies to approval of administration policy by members of the artistic community." Much of this correspondence may be found in GEN AR, box 2, WHCF, LBJ Library. For an overview of the festival, see also Goldman, *The Tragedy of Lyndon Johnson*, Chapter 16.

57. A complete list of artwork on display at the White House festival of the arts may be found in WHCF, AR-Arts, box 2, LBJ Library. Emphasis was placed on contemporary work.

58. "Remarks at the White House Festival of the Arts," June 14, 1965, in *Public Papers: Johnson*, 659–60.

59. *New York Times*, June 15, 1965, 1.

60. *New York Times*, June 20, 1965.

61. See Johnson's remarks as quoted in the *New York Times*, June 15, 1965, 1.

62. "Remarks to Members of Bakersfield College Choir on the Creative and Performing Arts in America," August 4, 1965, in *Public Papers: Johnson*, 832–34.

63. See Johnson's dealing with the 89th Congress in the *Congressional Quarterly Almanac*, 89th Cong., 1st sess., 302–3. See also descriptions of Johnson's record in Bornet, *The Presidency of Lyndon B. Johnson*, Chapter 10. For Johnson's own views on the need to proceed quickly, see Johnson, *The Vantage Point*.

64. This rule was first put into effect in 1949 and then reinstated in 1965 and 1966. It

states that if the Rules Committee does not release a bill within twenty-one days, the speaker may recognize a member of the committee that reported the bill to invoke a rule permitting House action. Thus, with a majority vote the bill is freed for debate.

65. Livingston Biddle recalled that Roger Stevens petitioned Smith to release the bill but was unsuccessful. See Biddle, *Our Government and the Arts*, 168–69. See also Mark, *Reluctant Bureaucrats*, 115.

66. The vote showed 360 in favor, 114 against, and 57 abstaining or absent. Senate proceedings, *Cong. Rec.*, 89th Cong., 1st sess., 13110; for passage in the House, see p. 23980. The "yeas" and "nays" of the roll call vote on September 13 may be found on p. 23620. On September 15, a measure to return the bill to committee was finally rejected.

67. "Remarks at the Signing of the Arts and Humanities Bill," September 29, 1965, in *Public Papers: Johnson*, 1023.

Chapter 4

1. "Policy Statement of the National Council on the Arts," 1966, Roger Stevens Files, Eckington Warehouse, box 15–21, folder #8, NEA.

2. Lynn Hunt's analysis of political rhetoric explains how the creation of a "unity" factor provides a force of positive identification to bring people together but delineates divisions as well. Her thesis illuminates the discourse surrounding American arts policy formation, as the political and cultural elite joined together to create a national art program and set a standard for the arts that was clearly termed "classical, excellent, and fine." These terms were not meant to describe the best expression of any art form but of specific classical genres, such as opera, classical music, and, in the visual arts, abstract expressionism. Government officials used these terms to rally support for American art programs because they believed that championing these elite art forms would demonstrate the superiority of American culture and the political and economic systems that allowed it to flourish. This goal was especially prized in the context of the Cold War. Ironically, as the NEA records illustrate, such a bias usually resulted in the exclusion or marginalization of nontraditional, avant-garde art and older realist traditions as well. Thus, discourse was used to signify specific aesthetics and ideologies and, as Hunt argues, language "could actively be an instrument of power," not merely reflecting actuality but also as an "instrument for transforming reality." See Hunt, *The New Cultural History*, 17.

3. The Commission of Fine Arts, established in 1910, was only responsible for overseeing architectural development in Washington, D.C., and the WPA was a temporary work program despite its unprecedented aid to the arts during the 1930s.

4. Mark, *Reluctant Bureaucrats*; and Larson, *The Reluctant Patron*, 205.

5. Initially, the Council was forced to proceed tenuously, as the original legislation had left out the words "per annum" for its budget, thus threatening to defund the body and render it impotent after one year. After causing a limited financial crisis for the staff, this oversight was soon rectified by Frank Thompson in new legislation passed in time for the Council meeting at the White House. Larson, *The Reluctant Patron*, 271.

6. *National Arts and Cultural Development Act of 1964*, 2.

7. Francis Biddle, who was Livingston Biddle's uncle, had also worked as a muralist for the WPA.

8. *National Arts and Cultural Development Act of 1964*, 1.

9. "Resolution on Education in the Arts," National Council on the Arts, June 24–25, 1965, Stevens Files, box 18/21, folder 10, NEA.

10. "Policy Statement of the National Council on the Arts, 1966," Stevens Files, box 15/21, folder 8, NEA.

11. Devon Meade to Roger Stevens, "Five Year Program for the Visual Arts," September 9, 1966, Stevens Files, box 18/21, folder 10, NEA.

12. Historian Alice Golfarb Marquis has belittled this as a "firehose approach" to art policy, but the apparent lack of pattern to the Council's initial actions was to be expected, since Council members were creating an original program through their own innovative ideas. Marquis, *Art Lessons*, 80.

13. In *The Unfulfilled Promise*, Arian argues that the Music, Opera, Theater, and Museum Programs were highly conservative.

14. Cockcroft, "Abstract Expressionism"; Guilbaut, *How New York Stole*; and Kozloff, "American Painting during the Cold War."

15. WHCF, Schlesinger Papers, box 1, "Advisory Council on the Arts," folder 2, 3c, JFK Library. Shahn's name is also highlighted as a possible selection in an October 30, 1963, memo in folder 12.

16. McCord, *Andrew Wyeth*.

17. Shahn is discussed in Jonathan Harris's excellent work on the New Deal art projects. Harris notes that Geldzahler considered social realist art formally banal. See Harris, *Federal Art and National Culture*, 161–62.

18. Arnason, *The History of Modern Art*, 375.

19. Schlesinger Papers, box 1, JFK Library.

20. Guston is discussed in Stiles and Selz, *Theories and Documents*, 172, 249–53.

21. "Modern Sculpture and Society," in McCoy, *David Smith*, 43.

22. Memo, March 22, 1963, Heckscher Papers, box 29, folder 7, JFK Library. Richard Diebenkorn's name appears on a list dated October 3, 1963, Schlesinger Papers, box 1, folder 12, JFK Library.

23. WHCF, FG 11–12, "National Council on the Arts," box 123, LBJ Library.

24. De Kooning is discussed as one of the founders of abstract expressionism in Ashton, *The Life and Times*.

25. Belz, *Frankenthaler*; and Goossen, *Helen Frankenthaler*.

26. Frankenthaler later wrote an article contending that serious problems underlay the National Council on the Arts's "censorship" of controversial artists in the 1980s after the Mapplethorpe exhibit. She argued that, in contrast to the Soviet Union and China, "We must not smother the expression of art any more than we should suppress or annihilate protests and parades, all part of our unique and precious democracy." Although she also stated that she was concerned that the NEA was losing its ability to endorse "quality" art and supporting more mediocre enterprises, such as Mapplethorpe's work. "Raise the level," she concluded. Her comments seem to suggest that she

endorsed the 1950s generation's views that the ideals of artistic freedom and political support for the arts were best found in abstract expressionism and color-field art. See Frankenthaler, "Did We Spawn an Arts Monster?"

27. The titles of Motherwell's "Elegy to the Spanish Republic" and his "Irish Elegy" series honored those who struggled for democracy and self-rule during the Spanish Civil War and in the Irish Republic. This indicated his support of freedom and democracy for all peoples—a sentiment that permeated American political rhetoric at a heightened level during the Cold War. For more on Motherwell see Ashton, *The Life and Times*, and Terenzio, *Collected Writings of Robert Motherwell*.

28. Motherwell in Johnson, *American Artists on Art*, 29. Motherwell's comments on the need for artists' control of university, museum, and art institutions may be found in Terenzio, *Collected Writings of Robert Motherwell*, 61.

29. Biddle told an entertaining tale of the painting donation. By Biddle's account, on a visit to Stevens's office Motherwell suggested that the NEA should display some art, at which point he was immediately solicited to donate one of his works. He agreed and sent a painting to the endowment. When he returned at a later date, Stevens asked how he liked the display of his work. Replying that the place was suitable, Motherwell then walked over to rehang the painting right side up. Apparently, Stevens was not enough of an abstract art aficionado to recognize the proper position for the artwork. Thus, it became important to garner advice and recommendations for the visual arts by modernist experts such as Motherwell. Author's interview with Biddle, November 7, 1996.

30. Terenzio, *Collected Writing of Robert Motherwell*, xxiii.

31. Hunt as quoted in "Art since 1950, Richard Hunt."

32. Hunt noted that "now sculpture can now be its own subject, and its object can be to express itself, by allusion to its traditions, involvement with its new means, and interactions with its environment." Lieberman, *The Sculpture of Richard Hunt*, 14.

33. Johnson adhered to long-accepted parameters in politics, just as he upheld Cold War policies set in place by his predecessors and argued that anyone who thought that "communists were not a threat to the United States was naive." He believed in abstract art's ability to showcase American freedom, an opinion generally held among politicians and cultural leaders during the 1950s, as both Cockcroft and Guilbaut have shown. Essentially, Johnson was pragmatic in working with the system and cooperating with powerful figures in Congress and the private sphere to achieve his goals. For example, in securing the passage of Medicare legislation, he did not challenge the American Medical Association; nor did he challenge the art establishment in establishing the NEA.

34. More than other Council nominees, Sontag accepted both high and low art forms, modernism and pop. She wrote about multiple aesthetics and interactions between them and argued that critics needed to be more open to the possibilities in aesthetics beyond high modernism. See *Against Interpretation* (1964) and "The 'Salmagundi' Interview" (1975), in Sontag, *The Susan Sontag Reader*, 97, 335−36.

35. An August 5, 1965, memo lists Sontag as Stevens's choice for the Arts Council, although she was considered controversial. A subsequent list of possible Arts Council members includes a request for an FBI background check next to Sontag's name and notes that she has been "vehement on Vietnam." This memo also indicates that the

Johnson White House wanted to populate the Council with more women and African American representatives of the art world, as well as with someone from the labor movement, whom Herman Kenin ultimately represented. See WHCF, John Macy Office Files, "National Endowment for the Arts," box 841–42, folders 3 and 6, LBJ Library.

36. René d'Harnoncourt is mentioned in Guilbaut, "The New Adventures," 247–48. Also see *Current Biography*, 1952, 145–47.

37. *New Yorker*, December 3, 1949.

38. Scavullo, "Interview with Henry Geldzahler."

39. Henry Geldzahler, *Current Biography*, 1978, 148–52.

40. Scavullo, "Interview with Henry Geldzahler."

41. Geldzahler, "Interview with Helen Frankenthaler."

42. Although he enjoyed pop and has been considered one of its major promoters, Geldzahler argued in 1969 that "Pop Art was an episode, an interesting one that has left its mark on the decade, and will continue to affect the future, but not a major modern movement which continues to spawn new artists. In fact, just about everything new and original in Pop Art was started by a few artists in the first years of its existence." Geldzahler, *New York Painting and Sculpture*, 37.

43. Godsmith, review of "New York Painting and Sculpture: 1940–1970"; Genauer, review of "New York Painting and Sculpture: 1940–1970."

44. Council member biographies, Stevens Files, NEA; and *Current Biography*, 1961.

45. On Oliver Smith, see "Elephant's Eye," 33.

46. Norris Houghton in *Theatre Arts*, February 1946.

47. Smith in de Kooning, "David Smith Makes a Sculpture."

48. "Introduction" and Smith's formal writings, speeches, and notes, in McCoy, *David Smith*; and "David Smith" in Arnason, *The History of Modern Art*, 409–10.

49. Greenberg, "David Smith"; and "David Smith: Comments on His Latest Works," in *Clement Greenberg*, 279, 228.

50. Smith, "Statements, Writings," in *Theories and Documents of Contemporary Art*, ed. Stiles and Selz, 37.

51. Smith, "The Sculptor's Relationship to the Museum, Dealer, and Public," Address at the First Woodstock Conference of Artists, N.Y., August 29, 1947, reprinted in *David Smith*, ed. McCoy, 59.

52. Diebenkorn said that at first he wanted it both ways: "a figure with a credible face—but also a painting wherein the shapes, including the face shape, worked with the all-over power I'd come to feel was a requisite of a total work . . . so the face had to lose a measure of its personality. . . . This compromise . . . was a large one . . . one that perhaps undermined my figurative resolve in the long run." Diebenkorn as quoted by John Elderfield in "Figure and Field," 21.

53. "A Personal Expression," in Terenzio, *Collected Writings of Robert Motherwell*, 59–62.

54. "Meeting of the National Council on the Arts, May 12–14(?), 1967, Tarrytown, New York," NEA, 50.

55. Devon Meade to Roger Stevens, "Panel Members," October 4, 1966, Stevens Files, box 18/21, folder 10, NEA.

56. Meade to Stevens and Livingston Biddle, "Resume of Programs in the Visual Arts," July 15, 1966, Stevens Files, box 18/21, folder 1, NEA.

57. Meade to Stevens, "Five Year Program for the Visual Arts," September 9, 1966, Stevens Files, box 18/21, folder 10, NEA.

58. "Status Report of Current Museum Programs," November 3, 1967, Stevens Files, box 18/21, folder 1, 2, NEA.

59. Prints, lithographs, drawings, and slides that could be sent to schools and smaller museum facilities for educational purposes were considered optimum "didactic materials." Meade to Stevens and Biddle, "Three Year Program for the Visual Arts," May 3, 1966, Stevens Files, box 18/21, folder 10, 5, NEA.

60. Discussion of the slide project, "Fifth Meeting of the National Council on the Arts, May 15, 1966," 20, NEA.

61. Meade to Stevens, "Five Year Program for the Visual Arts," September 9, 1966, Stevens Files, box 18/21, folder 10, 1, NEA.

62. The Museum Purchase Plan is discussed and the Gemini Print Workshop is listed as grant number A68-I-15, at $20,000, in "Meeting of the National Council on the Arts, May 12–14, 1967," NEA. Later mention of the prints appears in "Meeting of the National Council on the Arts, May 22–24, 1969," NEA.

63. "Status Report of Current Museum Programs," November 3, 1967, Stevens Files, box 18/21, folder 1, 2, NEA.

64. James Sweeny and René d'Harnoncourt, "Second Meeting of the National Council on the Arts, November 14, 1965," microfilm, roll 1, 230, LBJ Library.

65. "Status Report on the Visual Arts," March 28, 1967, Stevens Files, box 18/21, folder 10, NEA.

66. D'Harnoncourt, "Second Meeting of the National Council on the Arts, November 14, 1965," 410, NEA; and "Fifth Meeting of the National Council on the Arts, May 13, 1966," microfilm, roll 1, 138–150, LBJ Library.

67. Sarah Knott to Roger Stevens, February, July 17, and October 14, 1965, Stevens Files, box 12/21, folder 5, NEA.

68. Meade to Stevens, "Five Year Program for the Visual Arts," September 9, 1966, Stevens Files, box 18/21, folder 10, 2, NEA.

69. This conversation is related by Biddle in *Our Government and the Arts*, 230–33.

70. Robert Motherwell considered Calder an internationally accomplished master because of "his native American ingenuity (a preference for tools, rather than the brush), leading in turn to a fresh discovery (an art of motion), coupled with the advances of . . . art (abstract forms) and European thought (the surrealist understanding of the desirability of the object of pleasure)." Terenzio, *Collected Writings of Robert Motherwell*, 26.

71. Richard Diebenkorn's *Ingleside* was installed in the Grand Rapids Art Museum as part of the Grand Rapids/NEA project. See Visual Art Program, Public Art Files, NEA.

72. Gerald Ford as quoted in Beardsley, *Art in Public Places*, 17.

73. A staunch endowment supporter, Senator Pell was one of those who asked for such lists of art genres. Author's interviews with both Biddle and Pell. Michael Faubian of the NEA Visual Arts Program confirmed this.

74. Roger Stevens admitted in a Senate subcommittee hearing that the NEA did fund more abstract than representational artists, but he also noted the public acceptance of abstract arts, including the Picasso sculpture unveiled in Chicago's Civic Center Plaza on August 15, 1967. See "Aid for Artists." Later NEA chair Nancy Hanks also provided information to Congress on the genres of visual arts funded by the NEA, though sources at the NEA assert that she fudged the data by employing a very liberal definition of "representational." Discussions with NEA staff.

75. Hunt, *The New Cultural History*, 17.

Chapter 5

1. D'Harnoncourt, "Challenge and Promise."

2. See Greenberg, *Art and Culture*; Sandler, *The Triumph of American Painting*; Guilbaut, *How New York Stole*; and Cockcroft, *Abstract Expressionism*.

3. Art historical monographs on the NEA have tended to focus on a later period or on only one part of the NEA spectrum, and no work has been done covering the whole of the Visual Arts Program. Edward Arian's study of the NEA focused on the Music (classical), Dance, Opera, Theater, and Museums Programs, but did not include the Visual Arts Program. See Arian, *The Unfulfilled Promise*.

4. Roger Stevens's files and Johnson's *Public Papers* contain numerous examples of such requests, such as a letter by William Phillips and reply by Roger Stevens, dated March 10, 1966, in Stevens Files, box 3/21, folder 3, NEA.

5. Straight, *Nancy Hanks*, 285; interviews with Biddle; and discussions with NEA staff.

6. Motherwell, Frankenthaler, and NEA grantees George Sugarman, Tony Smith, and Ray Parker had been at the Hunter Art College in the late 1950s and early 1960s. See Goossen, *Artists at the Hunter*.

7. Individual painter's and sculptor's awards are listed in the NEA *Annual Report, 1967*. The artists' styles have been compiled from *Artforum*; *Art in America*; *Art News*; numerous museum catalogs; Bénézit, *Dictionnaire Critique et Documentaire*; Cummings, *Dictionary of Contemporary American Artists*; and Fielding, *Dictionary of American Painters*.

8. These percentages are based conservatively on calculations from the database I compiled on visual artists' awards, which can be found in on-line Appendix 3. Other sources have determined that the percentage of grants to abstract artists was even higher. Frank Wright, president of the Council of American Artists Societies, complained to Congress that of all sixty awards granted in 1967, only eight went to representational painters. He is quoted in Taylor and Barresi, *Arts at a New Frontier*, 97.

9. For a more detailed account of Goodnough's work and career, see Bush and Moffett, *Goodnough*.

10. *Newsweek*, March 1962.

11. Sandler, "Reviews: Robert Goodnough."

12. Greenberg, "Post-Painterly Abstraction," in *Clement Greenberg*.

13. Gene Davis as quoted in Rose, "Conversation with Gene Davis." Also see Wall, *Gene Davis*.

14. Hess, "All's Well That Ends Well."

15. The Salmagundi Club membership consisted of artists who were more traditionalist in style, and the Hotel des Artistes was a housing complex on the Upper West
Side of Manhattan that housed recognized artists, many of whom were also representational and traditionalist painters.

16. Rep. Theodore R. Kupferman (R-N.Y.), speech in the House of Representatives,
November 9, 1967, *Cong. Rec.*, 90th Cong., 1st sess., 10415.

17. For example, Martin Hannon of the Salmagundi Club, who wrote to President
Richard Nixon in 1969 to complain about the dominance of modern abstract forms in
NEA Visual Arts grants. Nixon Papers, WHCF, SF, AR-Arts, box 1, NARA.

18. Author's interview with Biddle, November 7, 1996.

19. That this was the common practice has been verified by several NEA staff members and in an interview with Livingston Biddle, although I have not discovered any such
lists.

20. For example, *Artforum*, September 1972, 57. Although since this ad is from a later
date, it is a more detailed announcement including application availability not only for
individual fellowships and art in public places, but also art critics' fellowships, artist-in-
residence programs, services in the field, visual arts in the performing arts, and exhibition aid.

21. Devon Meade to Roger Stevens, "Panel Members," October 4, 1966, Stevens Files,
box 18/21, folder 10, NEA. Walker Art Center director Martin Friedman later served on
the Arts Council beginning in 1978. After the early criticism of NEA grants expressed by
Michael Werboff, Stevens invited realist artist Andrew Wyeth to serve on one of the
regional panels, but Wyeth's name does not appear in later NEA reports. Stevens's
actions are noted in a letter from Stevens to Richard Diebenkorn, January 22, 1968,
Stevens Files, box 18/21, NEA.

22. I attended such a closed visual arts panel meeting in 1993 while an NEA fellow. I
found it a grueling process wherein panelists were bombarded with hosts of slides and
application details over four days of extremely long meetings with very little break time;
evenings were filled with gatherings at each others' hotels or at program members'
homes, where discussion of the applications undoubtedly continued. Panel members
were directed to narrow the field of applications from thousands to hundreds, and then
to the final group of artists to be recommended to the Council. The finalists would have
been viewed three or four times in the process. But trying to reconcile short meeting times with the abundance of applications forced panelists to make their decisions
quickly, which likely pressed them to select artists who displayed those aesthetics that the
panelists considered the best among their own preferences.

23. Panelists are listed in NEA *Annual Reports, 1969–1975*. See on-line Appendix 2. In
1977, Livingston Biddle instituted a policy to rotate individuals and avoid stagnation on
panels by requiring change in panelists approximately every five years and by moving
program directors or removing them after six-year terms. See Biddle, *Our Government
and the Arts*, 383–85.

24. Several NEA staff members explained in interviews that when congressional
members questioned the individual grants, Hanks devised this change to sidestep potential conflict over specific grants and to defend the artists' right to freedom of expression.

Her plan worked quite well in preventing criticism while allowing the NEA to fund hundreds of artists for their future work. The individual awards were later brought into question again in the 1980s after the negative publicity over Mapplethorpe, Serrano, and the NEA Four. With the downsizing of the NEA in 1995, the individual grants were eliminated. See "GOP Foes of Tax-Financed Arts"; and "NEA Plans Nearly 50% Cut."

25. Author's discussion with O'Doherty.

26. O'Doherty posited that the aesthetic pluralism of the 1970s that attempted to circumvent the gallery space and capitalist process of art was doomed to failure because it was seen as dangerous and intolerable to dealers, artists, and viewers who relied on the art institutions and market to survive. A moment of possible change was abandoned as purists maintained the institutional system and an aesthetic appropriate to it. See O'Doherty, *Inside the White Cube*, 79, 89–90. Essays first appeared in *Artforum* in 1976.

27. Author's discussion with O'Doherty.

28. Ak, *Rope Drawings of Patrick Ireland*.

29. Individual painter's and sculptor's awards are listed in the NEA *Annual Reports, 1967–1975*. The artists' styles are noted in *Artforum*; *Art in America*; *Art News*; museum catalogs; Bénézit, *Dictionnaire Critique et Documentaire*; Cummings, *Dictionary of Contemporary American Artists*; and Fielding, *Dictionary of American Painters*.

30. Geldzahler singled out Richard Pousette-Dart, Robert Goodnough, Jack Youngerman, Al Held, Friedel Dzubas, Edward Avedisian, Darby Bannard, and Ron Davis as such noteworthy artists. Geldzahler, *Making It New*, 106.

31. See Wood, *Six Painters*.

32. Geldzahler, *Making It New*, 106.

33. Fry, "The Mind Behind the Art: Recent Painting of Richard Pousette-Dart," in *Richard Pousette-Dart*, 6.

34. Fry calls Pousette-Dart's work transcendental, ibid., 7. See also Ratcliff, "Concerning the Spiritual in Pousette-Dart"; and for a discussion of the spiritual aspects of Mark Rothko, Hughes, *The Shock of the New*, 320–23. Art critics hailed abstract expressionism for this ability to express universal human concerns in the Cold War era, as has been noted by Cockcroft in "Abstract Expressionism: Weapon of the Cold War," and Guilbaut in *How New York Stole the Idea of Modern Art*.

35. Tuchman, *Mark di Suvero*, 1–2.

36. Di Suvero response to NEA questionnaire, August 1970, as quoted in NEA *Annual Report, 1970*, 51.

37. Lloyd, "Gazed into Like Crystal."

38. "C'est la prise de conscience de la capacité de donner des formes aux émotions, c'est la prise de conscience que l'art est une manière de dire ce qui nous touche le pas." Mark di Suvero also stated that architectural principles were more important to him than to many and that he believed in using minimalism in expressing human connections across time and space, particularly in an age when he believed mankind could create a new human community if they followed the right path. "Je suis un enfant d'Einstein, comme nous tous. Je ne peux voir l'espace sans temps. Je voudrais donner aux hommes le sens de leur capacité d'aller beaucoup plus loin. . . . Je voudrais donner le sens de la capacité humaine. . . . Nous sommes à un moment où nous pourrions créer

une nouvelle espèce humaine. Le problème est le but, la cible que nous choisissons . . . . L'architecture est plus importante pour moi que tout le reste. Le Post-modernisme est réducteur. Avec les techniques que j'utilise, j'aimerais aller au-delà. Il y a encore des possibilités d'espace à explorer." Di Suvero as quoted in Perlain, "Entretien avec Mark di Suvero," 21, 24.

39. For a more comprehensive look at artists' participation in creating the Peace Tower, see Schwartz, "The Politicalization of the Avant-Garde." At the time of this article's publication, Brian O'Doherty was both the head of the NEA's Visual Arts Program and the editor of *Art in America*. As did others at the NEA, he supported the antiwar movement while working under Richard Nixon.

40. Excerpted from Donald Judd, "Specific Objects," Arts Yearbook (1965), as quoted in Johnson, *American Artists on Art*, 105–8.

41. Judd, as quoted in Bruce Glaser, "Questions to Stella and Judd," in Johnson, *American Artists on Art*, 115.

42. John Cage experimented with musical forms in the 1940s, including uses of minimal notes, discordant sounds, and audience participation. See Stiles and Selz, *Theories and Documents*, 681.

43. Allan Kaprow as quoted in Arnason, *The History of Modern Art*, 472.

44. "Push and Pull: A Furniture Comedy for Hans Hofmann," 1963, in Kaprow, *Assemblage, Environments and Happenings*, 20–21.

45. Heizer received NEA awards in 1974 and 1975 for works of art in public places. Serra received a public art award in 1972 and an individual fellowship in 1974. Miss was awarded individual fellowships in both 1974 and 1975. Holt received an individual fellowship in 1975 and two public sculpture grants after 1975.

46. Pop artist Claes Oldenburg, who had also worked in happenings and developed widely acclaimed pop forms, was, like Kaprow, ignored by the NEA until 1973, when he was commissioned under the Art in Public Places Program to create a monumental public sculpture, *Flashlight*, for the city of Las Vegas.

47. LeWitt, "Paragraphs on Conceptual Art."

48. See Cockcroft and Barnet-Sanchez, *Signs from the Heart*; Geldzahler, *Making It New*; and Haskell, *Blam!*

49. See NEA *Annual Reports, 1973–1976*.

50. Galligan, "National Endowment for the Arts"; and King, "Pluralism in the Visual Arts."

51. Brenson, *Visionaries and Outcasts*, 30–32.

52. Guilbaut has argued that even artists who might not have believed in this expression of their artwork allowed others to represent their art in this manner because it was beneficial to their careers. See Guilbaut, *How New York Stole*; and Cockcroft, *Abstract Expressionism*.

53. Individual painter's and sculptor's awards and the artists' residences are listed in the NEA *Annual Reports, 1967–1975*.

54. National Council on the Arts meeting records, 1966; and Meade to Stevens, "Five Year Program for the Visual Arts," September 9, 1966, Stevens Files, box 18/21, folder 10, 2, NEA. The NCA's Visual Arts Committee was made up of René d'Harnoncourt, Henry

Geldzahler, David Smith, Oliver Smith, James Johnson Sweeney, and Richard Dieben-korn and frequently included artist Robert Motherwell.

55. Visual Arts Program guidelines, NEA.

56. This information was compiled from NEA *Annual Reports, 1967–1975*; and Beardsley, *Art in Public Places*. The artists' styles are noted in Bénézit, *Dictionnaire Critique et Documentaire*; Cummings, *Dictionary of Contemporary American Artists*; Fielding, *Dictionary of American Painters*; and in *Artforum, Art in America*, and *Art News*. See on-line Appendix 4 for more complete information.

57. Noguchi, "Meanings in Modern Sculpture," in Apostolis-Cappadona and Alt-shuler, *Isamu Noguchi*, 35–36.

58. Greenberg, "Art"; Kramer, "The Purest of Living Sculptors."

59. Geldzahler, *Making It New*, 217.

60. Nancy Hanks to Seattle mayor J. Bruman, 1969, Visual Arts Program, Public Art Projects Files, NEA.

61. Beardsley, *Art in Public Places*, 20–22.

62. James Haseltine, executive director of the Washington State Arts Commission, to Brian O'Doherty, October 14, 1969, Visual Arts Program, Public Art Projects Files, NEA.

63. See on-line Appendix 3 for information on regional distribution of NEA funds.

64. Noguchi, "Towards a Reintegration of the Arts," in Apostolis-Cappadona and Altshuler, *Isamu Noguchi* 26.

65. See NEA *Annual Reports* and information in on-line Appendix 4.

66. Boston Foundation grant applications and report, 1970, Visual Arts Program, Public Art Projects Files, NEA.

67. "Report on Grant to Summerthing 1970 Mural Program," Visual Arts Program, Public Art Projects Files, NEA.

68. The NEA's Music Program supported opera at twice the rate it supported classical music until 1970, when support for classical music surpassed that for opera. Opera became its own program. Jazz and folk music were excluded from NEA support until 1969, when they began receiving very small proportions of Music Program funds. The rates at which classical forms outpaced jazz and folk music are astounding. Classical music was funded at rates approximately seventy-two times higher than jazz, and folk music was listed in its own category only once in 1969. Figures for 1969 are typical of the first years of Music Program funding: classical music, $259,770; opera, $525,000; jazz, $25,500; and folk, $15,700. In the 1970s a new Jazz, Folk, Ethnic Program was formed to fund not only music, but dance, literature, visual arts, and performances in these categories. This program was funded at rates significantly lower that those for the Music, Opera, Theater, and Dance Programs.

Theater Program statistics are similar to those for the Music Program. Classical theater works and Shakespeare plays received the bulk of NEA funds, while contemporary theater programs lagged behind. In 1969 Theater Program funds were broken down as follows: Shakespeare, $345,000; classical, $282,500; American classics, $314,000; and contemporary, $135,000.

Dance Program funding also follows the same pattern, with classical ballet receiving the highest level of funding. Again using 1969 as a typical year, dance grants were distributed in the following way: ballet, $400,000; modern $200,000; other, $35,000. There was no folk dancing category that year.

For further statistics on NEA funding by program see the NEA *Annual Reports, 1966–1975.*

69. Arian, *The Unfulfilled Promise*, 8.

Chapter 6

1. Straight, *Twigs for an Eagle's Nest*, 115.

2. Straight's membership in the group is noted in a memo from Leonard Garment to Caspar Weinberger, "RE: FY 1972 Budget Request for International Cultural Activities," October 27, 1970, Nixon Papers, WHCF, SF, FG OMB, box 1, NARA; and Straight's participation in, as well as the success of, the film festival are also noted in a biographical memo, Nixon Papers, SMOF, Garment Papers, "Cultural Affairs" box 177, "Michael Straight" folder, NARA.

3. To date, scholarly and popular writings about Nixon have examined his personal and political histories, assessed his psychological profile, exhausted leads on the Watergate break-in and cover-up, debated his Vietnam War and peace strategies, and hailed his successes in foreign affairs. See, for example, Ambrose, *Nixon*; Ambrose, *Ruin and Recovery, 1973–1990*; Colodny and Gettlin, *Silent Coup*; Emery, *Watergate*; and Schurmann, *Foreign Politics of Richard Nixon*. More recently, Joan Hoff has argued that the primarily Watergate-centered discussions have obfuscated Nixon's place in history as someone who could at once be both "the best and the worst" of presidents. She has helped to launch a new and more balanced interpretation of Nixon's administration as one more complex than first meets the eye, advancing the position that scholars should reprioritize their analyses to give proper credit to Nixon's achievements in domestic policy. I agree with her approach. See Hoff, *Nixon Reconsidered*.

4. As quoted in Matthews, *Kennedy and Nixon*, 58.

5. Chapter 1, "Down to the Nut-Cutting: Richard Nixon and the Assault on Public Life," in Schulman, *The Seventies*, affirms my view of Nixon as "Trickster."

6. This view is supported by a variety of sources on the NEA, including Mark, *Reluctant Bureaucrats*, 179; Taylor and Barresi, *Arts at a New Frontier*, 121; and Biddle, *Our Government and the Arts*, 278.

7. Statement by Sen. Claiborne Pell to the Senate, April 22, 1969, Nixon Papers, SMOF, Garment Papers, box 200, NARA.

8. Heckscher, "What Ever Happened to the Arts?" as quoted in Hume, "The Arts in Trouble."

9. Hume, "The Arts in Trouble."

10. *Milwaukee Journal*, March 30, 1969.

11. Mark notes that Diebenkorn issued a statement saying forthrightly that he could no longer work for the present administration. See Mark, *Reluctant Bureaucrats*, 180.

12. MacAgy had been the director of the California School of Fine Arts in the late 1940s and was instrumental in transforming it into an institution devoted to experimentation in modern abstract art. He hired abstract expressionists and color-field artists to

join the school faculty, including Edward Corbett, David Park, Hassel Smith, Clay Spohn, Elmer Bichoff, Clyfford Still, and Richard Diebenkorn. Mark Rothko, Mark Tobey, and Ad Reinhardt were also asked to teach individual classes at the school. For more on MacAgy's tenure at the California School of Fine Arts, consult Smith, *Utopia and Dissent*, Chapter 4.

13. For example, see letter to Leonard Garment from John Richardson Jr., assistant secretary for educational and cultural affairs, Department of State, October 27, 1969, Nixon Papers, SMOF, Garment Papers, box 43, NARA.

14. Carol Harford to Herbert Klein, June 26, 1969, "RE: My Memos of March 18, 1969; March 10, 1969," Nixon Papers, SMOF, Herbert Klein Papers, box 2, NARA.

15. Ibid.

16. Harford to Klein, "The Nixon Administration and the Arts," May 23, 1969; and the cultural affairs proposal, February 17, 1969, Nixon Papers, SMOF, Herbert Klein Papers, box 2, NARA.

17. Harford to Klein, June 26, 1969, Nixon Papers, SMOF, Klein Papers, box 2, NARA; and Garment to Flanigan, July 10, 1969, Nixon Papers, SMOF, Garment Papers, box 199, NARA.

18. Author's interviews with Pell and Biddle.

19. Author's interview with Steele.

20. *New York Times*, August 22, 1969.

21. Biography in Nixon Papers, SMOF, Garment Papers, box 150, "Straight" folder 2, NARA; also, *Who's Who in Government* and *Current Biography*, 1972.

22. Quote in Taylor and Barresi, *Arts at a New Frontier*, 123.

23. Straight's past spy affiliations were still discussed by NEA staff members when I served as an arts administration fellow in 1993. Straight himself acknowledged that he did affiliate with communists in the 1930s at a time when many others had done the same. However, he attested that despite occasional visits from party members, he refused to spy for them after he returned to the United States and began working for the federal government during the 1940s. He eventually broke off all relationships with his one-time acquaintances. Moreover, Straight had revealed his former associations with communists to Kennedy officials and the FBI in 1963 when he had been considered by Kennedy to head the Arts Council. He declined the post to avoid groundless publicity and criticism for Kennedy, and the information did not become public until a 1981 newspaper report in Britain named his connections to Anthony Blunt, who did, indeed, spy for the Soviets in England. Nixon could certainly have looked into Straight's background and been made aware of his former affiliations, but Straight's past was not public knowledge in the 1970s. See Straight, *After Long Silence*, 61, 102, 130, 157, 167, 319, 332.

24. See Eugene Cowen to Peter Flanigan, September 10, 1969; Hartford to Garment, October 7, 1969, noting "*RN* wants *MS*"; and October 29, 1969, noting clearance for Straight; Nixon Papers, SMOF, Garment Papers, box 150, "Straight" folder 2, NARA.

25. Hanks's love affair with Rockefeller, a married man, has long been hinted at but is noted openly in Reich, *The Life of Nelson Rockefeller*, 473 and 548; and Marquis, *Art Lessons*, 96.

26. *Current Biography*, 1971, and NEA staff biographies, in National Endowment for the Arts, Papers of the Chairman, Nancy Hanks. For a comprehensive biography see Straight, *Nancy Hanks*.

27. Interview with Biddle.

28. Press Release, "Statement by the President on the Appointment of Nancy Hanks as Chairman of the National Endowment for the Arts," September 3, 1969, Nixon Papers, SMOF, Garment Papers, box 200, NARA.

29. Memos from Garment to Harford and later to Hanks, September 1970, noting "President Nixon should not nominate nine white citizens to the nine vacancies on the Council," Nixon Papers, SMOF, Garment Papers, box 198, NARA.

30. *Baltimore Evening Sun*, September 3, 1969, and newspaper of unknown title, copies in Nixon Papers, SMOF, Garment Papers, NARA.

31. *New York Times*, September 3, 1969, copy in Nixon Papers, SMOF, Garment Papers, NARA.

32. Lowens, "Organizing for the Arts"

33. McCarthy, *Women's Culture*; and Blair, *The Torchbearers*.

34. Nixon seemed obsessed at times with outmaneuvering the Kennedys and, understanding this, his White House advisers sometimes used comparisons to the Kennedys as a sure way to get the president to take certain actions such as scheduling more press conferences. Nixon took great pleasure in being the one who succeeded in doing more for culture, presiding over the moon landing, and accomplishing anything that had been a Kennedy goal. For a detailed account of the Nixon-Kennedy competition, see Matthews, *Kennedy and Nixon*, 257, 275–79, and 300.

35. Memo from Jim Keogh to the President, February 6, 1969, Nixon Papers, WHCF, AR (Arts), box 1, NARA.

36. Ibid.

37. See letter to Mrs. Jean R. Jenkins, October 16, 1972, Nixon Papers, WHCF, SF, AR (Arts), box 1, NARA; and Nixon Papers, WHCF, SF, FG, 999 Proposed Departments, Agencies, Boards, and Commissions, NARA.

38. Inflation had become a major problem by the late 1960s, and the phenomenon of stagflation (increased inflation coupled with a slowed economy) would preoccupy economic advisors in the years ahead. See Vatter and Walker, *History of the U.S. Economy*, 11, 294.

39. Leonard Garment to H. R. Haldeman, May 14, 1969; and Hanks (to Garment-?), February 28, 1969, Nixon Papers, WHCF, SF, AR (Arts), box 1, NARA.

40. Hanks to Garment, February 28, 1969, Nixon Papers, WHCF, SF, AR (Arts), box 1, NARA.

41. See letters from Nixon to John Ward of Remington Art Memorial Museum, March 17 and April 22, 1969; Nixon to Leonard Firestone of the Los Angeles County Museum of Art, September 12, 1969; William Campbell of the National Gallery to Peter Flanigan, May 25, 1970; and GSA memo from E. B. Stillwell to Daniel Patrick Moynihan on art in California White House in Nixon Papers, WHCF, SF, AR (Arts), box 4, NARA.

42. The paintings in Kissinger's office look like works by Mark Rothko and Josef

Albers. See official photographs taken during the Nixon administration, including batch 9075 (2–9); 1517 (18, 21, 28); 9373 (4A and 10A) at the National Archives.

43. This quote is taken from John Ehrlichman, "Notes of Meetings with the President," November 25, 1969, Nixon Papers, box 3, NARA.

44. India became a serious area of contention during the Nixon administration as that nationwarred with Pakistan and the Soviet-Indian Friendship Treaty was signed in 1971. Nixon resented and feared the relationship and sided with Pakistan because he believed that it had closer ties to China and that such a move would benefit his triangular diplomacy. See Ambrose, *Nixon*, 483.

45. Dan Christensen was among the first modernist abstract artists to receive an individual fellowship from the NEA in 1969. The American embassy in Moscow also displayed works by Sam Gilliam, Adolph Gotlieb, Charles Demuth, Stuart Davies, Paul Jenkins, Jasper Johns, John Marin, Louise Nevelson, Lowel Nesbitt, Barnett Newman, Chuck Prentiss, William T. Williams, Lorser Feitelson, Ralph Humphrey, Charles Sheeler, and Milton Avery in addition to those named above. Only four of the paintings could be classified as figurative works, of which only one is realist. See Nixon Papers, SMOF, Garment Papers, box 190, "Art in the Embassies" folder, NARA.

46. Geldzahler, *Contemporary American Art in the American Embassy, Jidda, Saudi Arabia*, catalog, in Nixon Papers, SMOF, Garment Papers, box 190, NARA.

47. Memo to the president from Henry Loomis, acting Director of USIA, January 13, 1970, Nixon Papers, WHCF, SF, AR (Arts), box 1, NARA.

48. Letter of September 7, 1969, Nixon Papers, WHCF, SF, AR (Arts), box 4, NARA.

49. Memo for Connie Stuart from Carol Harford, November 12, 1969, Nixon Papers, SMOF, Garment Papers, box 180, NARA.

50. A memo on White House entertainment also notes that Nixon did not care for modern dance but was willing to schedule such performances for guests who enjoyed it. Memo for Dwight Chapin to Constance Stuart, November 19, 1969, Nixon Papers, SMOF, Garment Papers, box 180, NARA.

51. Emphasis in original. Memo from Garment to Nixon, October 23, 1969, Nixon Papers, SMOF, Garment Papers, box 201, "National Endowments for the Arts and Humanities," NARA.

52. Charles McWhorter to Leonard Garment, October 22, 1969, Nixon Papers, SMOF, Garment Papers, box 204, "Department of State," NARA.

53. Emphasis in original. These ideas were presented to Garment in a memo by Raymond Bauer, December 9, 1969, Nixon Papers, SMOF, Garment Papers, box 43, NARA.

54. Coombs, *The Fourth Dimension of Foreign Policy*, 6–7.

55. Nixon, "Arts, Humanities Text," December 10, 1969, in *Nixon: The First Year of His Presidency*, 119–20A.

56. Stephen Ambrose describes Nixon's deriving great enjoyment from confounding those who characterized him in rigid terms. In this respect his increase of NEA funds to show his support for the arts resembles his drive to "open" China and to achieve detente with the Soviet Union despite his strident anticommunism. See Ambrose, *Nixon*, 439.

57. Nixon, "Arts, Humanities Text," December 10, 1969, in *Nixon: The First Year of His Presidency*, 119–20A.

58. See Garment to Ehrlichman, October 19, 1970; Garment to Haldeman; and Garment to Weinberger, October 27, 1970, Nixon Papers, WHCF, SF, FG OMB, box 1, NARA; and Weinberger to Garment, December 4, 1972, Nixon Papers, WHCF, SF, FG OMB, box 4, NARA.

59. Caspar Weinberger to Leonbard Garment, November 2, 1970, Nixon Papers, WHCF, SMOF, Garment Papers, box 177, NARA.

60. Taubman, "Nixon to Seek Full $60 Million."

61. *Washington Evening Star*, January 26, 1971.

62. "Support for the Arts No Luxury."

63. Brademas as quoted in "Brademas Lauds Nixon."

64. Ottinger as quoted in House proceedings, *Cong. Rec.*, 91st Cong., 1st sess.

65. Memo on NEA budget, October 31, 1973, Nixon Papers, WHCF, SF, Federal Aid, FA (Arts), box 2, NARA. The figures for 1974 are estimates. The greatest increases reflected Nixon's prioritizing of federal spending for the arts, as indicated by spending increases after 1971 that were generated by Nixon's budget requests beginning in 1970 for expenditures in the following fiscal year. The Nixon budgets were appropriated nearly in full by Congress and show dramatic percentage increases in the arts budget over a five-year period. The arts budget grew by 83 percent between 1970 and 1971, 98 percent by 1972, 29 percent by 1973, and 59 percent by 1974. Although the 1973 expansion was the smallest by percentage, it nevertheless reflected an increase in actual funds of $8.5 million—a raise higher than the entire budget for the NEA for each of its first five years.

66. Newspaper article on Nixon's budget priorities found in Nixon Papers, WHCF, SMOF, Garment Papers, box 28, NARA.

67. Garment to the heads of departments and agencies, December 10, 1969; and Nixon, "Memorandum to the Heads of Departments and Agencies," May 26, 1971, Nixon Papers, WHCF, SF, FG AR (Arts), box 1, NARA.

68. Nancy Hanks reported a brief summary of results from the polling of federal agencies to a meeting of the Associated Council of the Arts. See Nixon remarks to the Associated Council of the Arts, May 16, 1972, Nixon Papers, WHCF, SF, AR (Arts), box 1, NARA.

69. "A New Way of Life."

70. Crawford, "The Square Elephant."

71. *Washington Post*, April 30, 1969.

72. Unknown speaker as quoted in Ambrose, *Nixon*, 247.

73. Nixon Papers, WHCF, SMOF, Garment Papers, box 190, "Art in Embassy Program" folder, NARA. Ehrlichman also mentions that U.S. culture should be emphasized particularly in battleground countries and Eastern Europe, 11-25-69, "Notes of Meetings with the President," November 25, 1969, Nixon Papers, SMOF, Ehrlichman Papers, box 3, NARA.

74. It was brought to Nixon's attention that Kennedy had personally invited Wyeth to the White House, although the artist never accepted. Nixon called Wyeth to avoid appearing less gracious than Kennedy. See Constance Stuart to Dwight Chapin, Novem-

ber 17, 1969; and William Timmons to Sen. George Aiken,March 3, 1970, Nixon Papers, WHCF, SF, FG AR (Arts), box 4, NARA.

75. "President's Choice."

76. Carol Harford to Margaret E. Stucki, September 2, 1970, Nixon Papers, WHCF, SF, FG AR (Arts), box 4, NARA.

77. White House press release, February 12, 1970, Nixon Papers, SMOF, Garment Papers, box 180, NARA.

78. See press releases, schedule, and menu in Nixon Papers, WHCF, SMOF, Garment Papers, box 206, "Wyeth Dinner" folder, NARA.

79. Nixon remarks at the Wyeth dinner, White House press release, February 19, 1970, Nixon Papers, WHCF, SMOF, Garment Papers, box 206, NARA.

80. The Joint Communiqué is quoted in a letter from John Holdridge of the National Security Council to Rexford Stead of the Los Angeles County Museum of Art, April 18, 1972, regarding the exchange of arts with China, Nixon Papers, WHCF, SF, AR-(Arts), box 2, NARA.

81. For example, see letter from Manuel Tolegian to Wallace Edgerton and Nixon, March 19, 1971, complaining of "unintelligible art"; and reply by Edgerton, April 9, 1971, Nixon Papers, WHCF, SF, AR-(Arts), box 1, NARA.

82. For Garment's reply to the Corcoran, see letter to Aldus Chapin from Garment, April 7, 1970. The memo regarding paying for removal of the sculpture notes that "needless to say, whatever we do, we have to be sure to protect our source of information." See Harford to Garment, April 23, 1971, Nixon Papers, WHCF, SMOF, Garment Papers, box 213, "Corcoran Gallery" file, NARA.

83. Handwritten notes by Garment to Carol Harford appear in the margins on a White House memo, reading "Carol—I do *not* want the Lieberman relocated on the Mall *under any circumstances!!*" and, "This has been handled so far by Nancy Hanks. I want the W.H. To stay out of it!" See memo "to Len..RE: Lieberman sculpture," June 11, 1971, Nixon Papers, WHCF, SMOF, Garment Papers, box 182, NARA. (Emphasis in original.)

84. Opinion polls show a 63 percent disapproval rate for Nixon in January of 1974 and three out of four Americans believing that the president knew about the Watergate break-ins and cover-up. For an account of Watergate and its impact on the Nixon White House, see McQuaid, *The Anxious Years*; the Gallup poll results appear on p. 250.

85. Author's interview with Steele. This is supported by Straight in *Nancy Hanks*, 274.

86. See NEA *Annual Reports, 1973–1975*.

87. See Straight, *Nancy Hanks*, 275. Hanks probably believed the Folklife Center would be competitive and detrimental to her expansionist plans for the NEA because the NEH and NEA had become increasingly estranged as a result of their struggles over museum funding—resulting when Hanks tried to take over history and culture museum funding under the auspices of the NEA's museum programs. She lost that battle. See Straight, *Nancy Hanks*, Chapter 31.

88. Author's interview with Alan Jabbour.

89. Ibid.

90. I disagree with art historians Ann Galligan and Elaine King, who have celebrated the NEA as a democratic and pluralist art institution, echoing Jabbour's positive re-

action to the NEA's advancement of the folk arts. Galligan, "The National Endowment"; and King, "Pluralism in the Visual Arts."

91. See NEA *Annual Report, 1975,* 5 and 88.

92. Junius Eddy as quoted in NEA *Annual Report, 1971,* 33-34.

93. See NEA *Annual Reports, 1972-1975.*

94. One such argument about the emerging Chicano arts movement may be found in Cockcroft and Barnet-Sanchez, *Signs from the Heart. Art in America* also indicated the importance of ethnic arts in the early 1970s by devoting the entire July/August 1972 issue to Indian artists and representations of Native Americans and by featuring African American artists in the September/October 1970 issue.

95. Nancy Hanks to Mrs. Roy Riddell of the Texas Art and Humanities Commission, August 1, 1977, Records of the NEA, Nancy Hanks Files, RG 266, box 1, NARA.

96. Garment's comments were addressed to future NEA chair Jane Alexander. See Alexander, *Command Performance,* 77.

97. Jim Keogh to Nixon, February 6, 1969, Nixon Papers, WHCF, SF, AR (Arts), box 1, NARA.

98. Emphasis in original. Letter from Charles H. Crutchfield, President of the Jefferson Standard Broadcasting Company, to Nixon, November 9, 1971, Nixon Papers, WHCF, SF, AR (Arts), box 3, NARA.

99. Ambrose, *Nixon,* 351, 375-77; and Gitlin, *The Sixties,* 409. Nixon himself claimed later that he was only referring to riotous protestors, not all students, as bums. See Nixon, *RN,* 456-57. After the Kent State shootings, Nixon's attorney general Mitchell stated that the demonstrators were "inviting violence." A few days later, youths in New York marched to the mayor's mansion demanding that the flag be lowered to half-mast to honor those slain at Kent State. When construction workers nearby heard about the incident, they marched against the students with clubs and demanded the flag's return to its proper place—to them, the demonstrators at Kent State had only gotten what they deserved. After this episode, the term "hard hat" (referring to the hats worn by constructions workers) began to be applied to mean a working-class backlash against left-wing demonstrators and liberal politics in general. Nixon identified with the construction worker and invited New York City construction union representatives to the White House, where they presented the president with his own hard hat. See McQuaid, *The Anxious Years,* 160.

100. Vice President Spiro Agnew as quoted in McQuaid, *The Anxious Years,* 377-79.

101. McQuaid, *The Anxious Years,* 156.

102. Ambrose, *Nixon,* 375-77.

103. Ira Wolfert of the *Reader's Digest* to Assistant Secretary John Richardson, July 28, 1970, as quoted in memo to Nixon from William Rogers, secretary of the Department of State, August 14, 1970, Nixon Papers, WHCF, SF, Department of State, box 203, NARA.

104. "Lessons for a Rock Group"; and *New York Post,* July 10, 1970.

105. Memo from Secretary of State William Rogers to President Nixon, August 14, 1970, Nixon Papers, WHCF, SF, Department of State, box 203, NARA.

106. Nixon encouraged expanded youth opportunities in federal government jobs

and through the National Alliance of Businessmen. In 1971 he announced increases in government jobs in the Federal Summer Employment Program for Youth and the Youth Conservation Corps. See "Statement about Summer Job and Recreation Opportunities for Youth," June 2, 1971, in *Public Papers: Nixon*, 697.

107. *Public Papers: Nixon*, 53.

108. "Remarks at the Annual Conference of the Associated Councils of the Arts," May 26, 1971, in *Public Papers: Nixon*, 676.

109. NEA, *Federal-State Partnership Program*, 176–89.

110. NEA *Annual Reports*.

111. These percentages are drawn from the author's database documenting all visual arts fellowships between 1967 and 1980. See on-line Appendix 3.

112. NEA *Annual Report, 1971*, 69. Today Artrain is directed by the Michigan State Arts Council and is still touring the United States. See *Smithsonian*, August 1996, 76–80.

113. I am referring to Nixon's subtle but nevertheless powerful moves to establish more conservative aims and dismantle the liberal thrust of many federal programs. For example, Nixon's housing policies shifted support from public housing to rent subsidies, thereby preserving federal spending while at the same time circumventing local city government officials who worked with the Great Society programs, civil rights groups, and labor unions who had overseen building contracts for public housing. The idea of Nixon as the Trickster is supported by several historical accounts, including Matusow, *The Unraveling of America*; and McQuaid, *The Anxious Years*.

Chapter 7

1. Biddle as quoted in NEA *Annual Report, 1978*, 7.

2. Ford as quoted in Greene, *The Presidency of Gerald R. Ford*, 52.

3. "White House policy statement on vocations and arts," November 1976, Records of the NEA, Hanks Files, box 27, "White House Correspondence" folder, NARA.

4. Greene, *The Presidency of Gerald R. Ford*, 33; and Biddle, *Our Government and the Arts*, 324.

5. Barbara Otis to Nancy Hanks, November 7, 1974, Records of the NEA, Hanks Files, box 28, "Mrs. Ford" folder, NARA.

6. Greene, *The Presidency of Gerald R. Ford*, 68–80.

7. NEA *Annual Report, 1975* and *1976*.

8. Ford argued that challenge grants would broaden the base of ongoing financial support for the arts from nonfederal sources and enhance the public and private sector partnership. Copy of Ford speech, October 14, Records of the NEA, Hanks Files, box 27, "Ford" folder, NARA.

9. NEA *Annual Report, 1976*.

10. Rockefeller remarks to the National Council on the Arts, February 6, 1976, Records of the NEA, Hanks Files, box 31, "White House, Rockefeller" folder, NARA.

11. Draft of memo from Rockefeller to Ford, in Hanks letter to Rockefeller, December 1, 1976, Records of the NEA, Hanks Files, box 31, "White House, Rockefeller" folder, NARA.

12. Hanks to Ford, December 1976, Records of the NEA, Hanks Files, Box 33, NARA.

13. Rockefeller to Hanks, December 15, 1976, Records of the NEA, Hanks Files, box 31, "White House, Rockefeller" folder, NARA.

14. Hanks to Rockefeller, December 16, 1976, Records of the NEA, Hanks Files, box 31, "White House, Rockefeller" folder, NARA.

15. Moen, "Congress and the National Endowment," 188.

16. Ibid., 189–90.

17. "Bicentennial Transmittal Letter to the Congress," First, September 11, 1970, Nixon Papers, SMOF, Garment Papers, box 36, "Bicentennial" files, NARA.

18. Nixon, "Suggested Remarks at Appearance with Bicentennial Commission," October 8, 1969, 2, in Nixon Papers, WHCF, SF, "American Bicentennial Service Commission," box 2, NARA.

19. Ford, Statement on Transmitting the Annual Report of the National Endowment for the Arts to Congress, NEA *Annual Report, 1975,* iv.

20. Ford, "White House Policy Statement on Vocations and Arts," November 1976, Records of the NEA, Hanks Files, Program Files -W-, "White House Correspondence" folder, box 27, NARA.

21. Ibid., 3.

22. "Bicentennial Plans Announced," NEA press release for April 3, 1974, in Nixon Papers, WHCF, SMOF, Garment Papers, "Bicentennial" files, box 36, NARA.

23. NCA, "Report on Bicentennial Planning," August 4, 1972, 7, 26th Meeting of the National Council on the Arts, August 10–11, 1972, Records of Meetings of the NCA, box 8, NARA.

24. Ibid., 22.

25. Hamilton Jordan as quoted in Dubofsky, "Jimmy Carter and the End of the Politics of Productivity," in Fink and Graham, *The Carter Presidency,* 97. See also Chapter 5, "Jimmy Carter and the Crisis of Confidence," in Schulman, *The Seventies.*

26. "Inaugural Address," in *Public Papers: Carter,* 1:2.

27. Leuchtenburg, "Jimmy Carter and the Post–New Deal Presidency," in Fink and Graham, *The Carter Presidency,* 7–28.

28. Clough, in Kadis, "Jimmy Carter," 51.

29. Ibid.

30. P. M. K., "The First Family at the Corcoran"; and Diamonstein, "Jimmy, Jody, Zbig and Ham."

31. Kotz, "Washington's 'Joan of Art.' "

32. Ibid., 49.

33. Kadis, "Jimmy Carter," 53.

34. Joan Mondale as quoted in Kotz, "Washington's 'Joan of Art,' " 52. Emphasis in original.

35. Ibid., 54. The Federal Council on the Arts and Humanities was originally set up in the National Arts and Humanities Act of 1965. That law outlined its membership as including the NEA chair, chair of the Commission on Fine Arts, head of the GSA, librarian of congress, archivist of the United States, director of the National Park Service, director of the National Science Foundation, director of the International Communica-

tions Agency, secretary of the U.S. Senate, secretary of the Smithsonian Institution, and a member of the House of Representatives. Traditionally, the chair of the Federal Council is rotated between the chairs of the NEA and NEH.

36. NEA *Annual Report* appropriations figures 1978–80.

37. Schulman, "Slouching toward the Supply Side," in Fink and Graham, *The Carter Presidency*, 54.

38. Thomas J. Sugrue, "Carter's Urban Policy Crisis," in Fink and Graham, *The Carter Presidency*, 149–50.

39. Kaufman, *The Presidency of James Earl Carter*, 151–66.

40. Biddle, *Our Government and the Arts*, 345–46.

41. Ibid., 365.

42. Ibid., 359.

43. Ibid., 381–83; and author's interview with Biddle, November 7, 1996.

44. Ibid., 383.

45. Geracimos and Marzorati, "The Artocrats," 107.

46. Melchert, as quoted in ibid.

47. Straight to O'Doherty, November 26, 1971, Records of the NEA, Hanks Files, box 11, "Visual Arts" folder, NARA.

48. NEA, Visual Arts Guidelines, 1974; NCA Meeting Records, 1973, NARA.

49. Julie Moore, "Memorandum for the Record, RE: Individual Fellowships (Visual Arts Program)," July 19, 1974, Records of the NEA, Hanks Files, box 11, "Visual Arts" folder, NARA.

50. 1976 advisory panels list for visual arts, Records of the NEA, A-03-81, RG 288, box 3, "Panelists" folder, NARA.

51. Author's interview with Alan Jabbour.

52. Percentages have been rounded up. Individual painter's and sculptor's awards are listed in the NEA *Annual Report, 1976–1980*. On-line Appendix 3 includes more details. The artists' styles have been compiled from *Artforum*; *Art in America*; *Art News*; numerous museum catalogs; Bénézit, *Dictionnaire Critique et Documentaire*; Cummings, *Dictionary of Contemporary American Artists*; and Fielding, *Dictionary of American Painters*.

53. Bolotowsky, "On Neoplasticism," 221–30. See also Ellis, *Ilya Bolotowsky*.

54. Andrew Bolotowsky, letter to the author, November 19, 2000.

55. See on-line Appendix 4 for more details on the Art in Public Places awards.

56. Willard, "Women of American Art."

57. Leider, "Joan Brown."

58. CNM, "Joan Brown's Neo-Naives."

59. Karlstrom, "Tape-Recorded Interview with Joan Brown," 25.

60. Butterfield as quoted in Tucker, "An Interview with Deborah Butterfield," 19, 37.

61. Ibid., 44.

62. Kuspit, "The Horse in the Industrial Age," 58–61.

63. Robins, "Earth Sculptures, Site Works, and Installations," Chapter 4, in *The Pluralist Era*, 76.

64. Butterfield as quoted in Tucker, "An Interview with Deborah Butterfield," 17–18, 44.

65. Ibid., 19.

66. Van der Marck, "Looking Back on Four Years," 26.

67. Van der Marck, "Sculpture around Campus."

68. Hoover, "The Mirrored Image of the Silent City," in Glenn and Bledsoe, *Vapor Dreams in L.A.*, 24–27.

69. Percentages have been rounded up. More contemporary artists working in these styles received NEA grants in the late 1970s than previously, although they remained a minority within the overall pattern of grants. Individual painter's and sculptor's awards are listed in the NEA *Annual Report, 1976–1980*. The artists' styles have been compiled from *Artforum*; *Art in America*; *Art News*; numerous museum catalogs; Bénézit, *Dictionnaire Critique et Documentaire*; Cummings, *Dictionary of Contemporary American Artists*; and Fielding, *Dictionary of American Painters*.

70. Reiss as quoted in Smith, "How Does an Object Tell? The Semiotic Dimension of Roland Reiss' Sculpture," in Brown, *Roland Reiss*, 26.

71. Brown, *Roland Reiss*, 40.

72. Author's interview with Reiss.

73. Eco, *A Theory of Semiotics*. Other postmodern theorists and works that influenced this generation of artists include Derrida, *Writing and Difference*; Foucault, *The Order of Things* and *Power/Knowledge*; and Jurgen Habermas, "Modernity vs. Postmodernity," *New German Critique*, 22 (Winter 1981). For a good overview, see Harvey, *The Condition of Postmodernity*.

74. David Ross, "A Provisional Overview of Artists' Television in the U.S.," and Mona Da Vinci, "Video: The Art of Observable Dreams," in Battcock, *New Video Artists*, 138–65, 11–23.

75. Gregory Battcock, "Disaster in New York," in Paik and Moorman, "Videa, Vidiot, Videoogy," in Battcock, *New Artists Video*, 137. Originally printed in *Domus* (1976). Also see Drew, *Nam June Paik, Video Works*.

76. Herzogenrath, "The Anti-Technological Technology of Nam June Paik's Robots," in Drew, *Nam June Paik, Video Works*, 6.

77. Paik and Moorman, "Videa, Vidiot, Videology," in Battcock, *New Video Artists*, 129.

78. Ibid.

79. These figures may undercount such styles, since individual artists did not always identify themselves as feminist or ethnic artists. See NEA *Annual Reports 1976–1980* and on-line Appendix 3 for details.

80. Jabbour to Hanks, "Memo RE: FY 1976 Budget," January 26, 1975, Records of the NEA, Hanks Files, box 5, "Folk Arts—Jabbour" file, NARA.

81. Minutes of the 42nd Meeting of the National Council on the Arts, November 21–23, 1975, NCA Meeting Records, box 15, 42–43, NARA.

82. Memo from Hawes to Hanks, March 25, 1977, NEA Records, "Folk Arts" files, box 1, A-05-80, 6, NARA.

83. Author's interview with Hawes.

84. Memo from Hawes to Hanks, March 25, 1977, NEA Records, "Folk Arts" files, box 1, A-05-80, 8–10, NARA.

85. Memo from Anderson to Hanks (via Hawes), March 11, 1977, NEA Records, "Folk Arts" files, box 1, A-05-80, NARA.

86. Memo from Hawes to Hanks, March 9, 1977, NEA Records, "Folk Arts" files, box 1, A-05-80, 6, NARA.

87. Memos from Hawes to Tighe, April 3, 1978; and memo from Tighe to Keith Stevens, director of Budget Division, May 22, 1978, NEA Records, "Folk Arts" files, box 1, A-05-80, NARA.

88. "Folk Art Program Guidelines for FY 1980," in Minutes of the 59th Meeting of the National Council on the Arts, February 9–11, 1979, NCA Records, box 21, NARA.

89. Ibid.

90. Letter from Barre Toelken to Biddle, August 30, 1978, NEA Records, "Folk Arts" files, box 1, A-05-80, NARA.

91. Author's interview with Hawes.

92. Folk Arts Program awards in NEA *Annual Report, 1979,* 87–99.

93. Author's interview with Hawes. Hawes also said that she specifically informed congressmen about the Folk Arts Program grants in their local districts.

Conclusion

1. Dallek, *Ronald Reagan,* 88–92; Switzer, *Green Backlash,* Parts 2 and 3.

2. "Inaugural Address," January 20, 1981, in *Public Papers: Reagan,* 1. Livingston Biddle recalled that the task force was dominated by those who objected to the concept of federal support for the arts, Biddle, *Our Government and the Arts,* 503.

3. *Report to the President,* 1.

4. Ibid., iii.

5. Ibid., 2.

6. Ibid., 3.

7. Ibid., ii.

8. The Committee was headed by Chair Andrew Heiskell and Vice Chairmen Armand S. Deutsch and W. Barnabas McHenry and included a membership of up to thirty-four federal and private institution leaders. Several of those who had worked on the Presidential Task Force on the Arts and Humanities also served on this committee. NEA, *A Brief Chronology,* 42, 52.

9. Ibid., 52; Reagan, as quoted in Molotsky, "Reagan Calls for Medal."

10. Taylor and Barresi, *Arts at a New Frontier,* 239.

11. Hodsoll as quoted in Marquis, *Art Lessons,* 186.

12. Hodsoll, "Chairman's Statement," NEA *Annual Report, 1983,* 3.

13. As quoted in Marquis, *Art Lessons,* 165.

14. Schaller, *Reckoning with Reagan,* 71.

15. Levy, *Government and the Arts,* 124.

16. In part, this corresponds to the critical appraisal of Kennedy and Johnson that appears in Matusow, *The Unraveling of America.*

17. This reflects Bourdieu's argument that elite taste and power are perpetuated through the education and institutional orders controlled by the elite. See Bourdieu, *Distinction.*

18. McQuaid, *The Anxious Years*; and Harrison and Wood, *Art in Theory, 1900–1990.*

19. Silverman argues that the French state worked with artists to promote art nouveau in the late nineteenth century, while Silver asserts, similarly, that political leaders with a nationalist ideology influenced aesthetic styles after the turn of the century. See Silverman, *Art Nouveau*; and Silver, *Esprit de Corps*. Marling and Harris have explained how American political leaders conrolled WPA arts. See Marling, *Wall-to-Wall America*; and Harris, *Federal Art and National Culture.*

20. Arian's assessment of recent trends in the Opera, Theater, Music, and Museum Programs confirms that traditional arts were overwhelmingly supported in these fields. See Arian, *The Unfulfilled Promise.*

21. The accomplishments of the NEA are documented in the agency's annual reports and have been listed in NEA promotional material. For the matching funds figures, see "Celebrate the Arts," a brochure published by the NEA and Borders Bookstores, 1995; Proffitt, "Jane Alexander" and "NEA."

22. For lists of Arts Council members and their occupations, see NEA *Annual Reports*. Former Council member and artist Helen Frankenthaler expressed her trepidation over the falling quality of art grants in the late 1980s due to weakening definitions of quality. While she did not say so outright, I attribute the problem in part to the lack of artistic leadership on the Council after it was filled with bureaucrats. See Frankenthaler, "Did We Spawn an Arts Monster?"

23. Schulman discusses the emerging New Right in the 1970s forming an agenda around defense, antielitism, and family values and ultimately touching off a tax revolt and antigovernment movement. Schulman, *The Seventies*, 199–201. Also Crawford, *Thunder on the Right*; and Edsall and Edsall, *Chain Reaction.*

24. The Harris Poll revealed that Americans want continued federal support for the arts without any content restrictions. See Arthurs and Davis, "News Flash to Washington."

25. Regional arts agencies included: Arts Midwest in Minneapolis, Mid-Atlantic Arts Foundation in Baltimore, Mid-America Arts Alliance in Kansas City, New England Foundation for the Arts in Boston, Southern Arts Federation in Atlanta, and Western States Arts Federation in Santa Fe.

26. NEA *Annual Report, 1980*, 361–67.

27. "A History of the Rockefeller Foundation," <www.rockfound.org>; "Historic Note" under Corporate Archives section of <www.carnegie.org>; and *Foundation Directory 2002* for current assets.

BIBLIOGRAPHY

RESEARCH COLLECTIONS

Austin, Texas
Lyndon Baines Johnson Presidential Library
    Diary Collection
    Entertainment Files
    National Council on the Arts Meeting Records (microfilm)
    Oral History Collection
    White House Central Files
        James Gaither Papers
        Richard Goodwin Papers
        Charles Horsky Papers
        Harry McPherson Papers
        Bill Moyers Papers
        Henry Wilson Papers

Boston, Massachusetts
John F. Kennedy Presidential Library
    Entertainment Files
    Oral History Collection
    White House Central Files
        August Heckscher Papers
        Pièrre Salinger Papers
        Arthur Schlesinger Jr. Papers
        Theodore Sorensen Papers

San Marino, California
Archives of American Art, Smithsonian Institution, West Coast Branch,
    Huntington Library
    Oral History Collection

Washington, D.C.
National Archives and Records Administration
    Richard M. Nixon Presidential Papers
        White House Central Subject Files
        White House Staff Member Office Files
            John Ehrlichman Papers
            Leonard Garment Papers
            Herbert Klein Papers
            Susan Porter Papers

Social Affairs Files
Records of the National Endowment for the Arts
Livingston Biddle, Administrative Files
Nancy Hanks, Administrative Files
Records of the National Foundation for the Arts and Humanities
National Council on the Arts, Meeting Notes and Files
National Endowment for the Arts
Annual Reports, 1965–1993
National Council on the Arts, Meeting Records
Research Division Notes 1–53
Research Division Reports 1–31
Roger Stevens, Administrative Files
Visual Arts Program Files
Art in Public Places Files
Photography Files

INTERVIEWS

Interviews Conducted by the Author
Biddle, Livingston. Washington, D.C., November 7, 1996, and January 5, 1994.
Faubian, Michael. Washington, D.C., October 9, 1993.
Hawes, Bess Lomax. Northridge, Calif., August 23, 2000.
Heckscher, August. New York, N.Y., January 2, 1997.
Jabbour, Alan. Washington, D.C., September 12, 1995.
Pell, Claiborne. Washington, D.C., September 21, 1995.
Reiss, Roland. Los Angeles, Calif., December 5, 2000.
Salinger, Pièrre. Los Angeles, Calif., November 1, 1995.
Schlesinger, Arthur, Jr. New York, N.Y., September 19, 1995.
Steele, Ana. Washington, D.C., November 24, 1993.

Discussions with NEA Staff
Carlson, Paul. Washington, D.C., November 1993.
Jacobs, Edythe. Washington, D.C., October 1993.
Kubli, Bert. Washington, D.C., October 1993.
Larson, Gary O. Washington, D.C., November 1993.
Lim, Silvio. Washington, D.C., November 1993.
O'Doherty, Brian. Washington, D.C., January 4, 1994.
Sheehy, Daniel. Washington D.C., December 1993.

Archival Interviews
Cummings, Paul. "Interview of Henry Geldzahler." January 27, 1970, Archives of
American Art, Huntington Library.
Frantz, Joe B. "Oral History Interview with Arthur M. Schlesinger, Jr." November 4,
1971, LBJ Library.
Greene, Roberta. "Second Oral History Interview with Senator Jacob Javits." April 10,
1973, JFK Library.

Heuvel, William vanden. "Oral History Interview with Senator Jacob Javits." June 19, 1970. JFK Library.

Karlstrom, Paul. "Tape-Recorded Interview with Joan Brown, Session #3." 1973, Archives of American Art.

"Oral History Interview with Jacqueline Kennedy." Conducted by the LBJ Library, 1974, JFK Library.

Stewart, John. "Interview with Senator Claiborne Pell." February 6, 1967, JFK Library.

Von Eckhardt, Wolf. "Oral History Interview with August Heckscher." December 10, 1965, JFK Library.

GOVERNMENT DOCUMENTS

Congressional Quarterly Almanac. 89th Cong., 1st sess. Washington, D.C.: Congressional Quarterly, Inc., 1965.

Congressional Record. 43rd Cong., 1st sess. Washington, D.C.: U.S. Government Printing Office, 1874.

Congressional Record. 46th Cong., 2nd sess. Washington, D.C.: U.S. Government Printing Office, 1879.

Congressional Record. 61st Cong., 2nd sess. Washington, D.C.: U.S. Government Printing Office, 1910.

Congressional Record, 81st Cong., 1st sess. Washington, D.C.: U.S. Government Printing Office, 1949.

Congressional Record, 82nd Cong., 2nd sess. Washington, D.C.: U.S. Government Printing Office, 1952

Congressional Record. 84th Cong., 2nd sess. Washington, D.C.: U.S. Government Printing Office, 1956.

Congressional Record. 86th Cong., 2nd sess. Washington, D.C.: U.S. Government Printing Office, 1960.

Congressional Record. 87th Cong., 1st sess. Washington, D.C.: U.S. Government Printing Office, 1961.

Congressional Record. 87th Cong., 2nd sess. Washington, D.C.: U.S. Government Printing Office, 1962.

Congressional Record. 88th Cong., 1st sess. Washington, D.C.: U.S. Government Printing Office, 1963.

Congressional Record. 88th Cong., 2nd sess. Washington, D.C.: U.S. Government Printing Office, 1964.

Congressional Record. 89th Cong., 1st sess. Washington, D.C.: U.S. Government Printing Office, 1965.

Congressional Record. 90th Cong., 1st sess. Washington, D.C.: U.S. Government Printing Office, 1967.

Congressional Record. 91st Cong., 1st sess. Washington, D.C.: U.S. Government Printing Office, 1969.

National Arts and Cultural Development Act of 1964. Public Law 88–579. 88th Cong., 2nd sess. H.R. 9586, September 3, 1964. Washington, D.C.: U.S. Government Printing Office, 1964.

National Endowment for the Arts. *A Brief Chronology*. Washington, D.C.: U.S. Government Printing Office, 1985.

——. *Federal-State Partnership Program and Funding Information Booklet*. Washington, D.C.: NEA Office, 1976.

Nixon: The First Year of His Presidency. Congressional Quarterly. Washington, D.C.: U.S. Government Printing Office, 1970.

The Public Papers of the President of the United States: Jimmy Carter. Washington, D.C.: U.S. Government Printing Office, 1977–1981.

The Public Papers of the President of the United States: John F. Kennedy. Washington, D.C.: U.S. Government Printing Office, 1961–1963.

The Public Papers of the President of the United States: Lyndon Baines Johnson. Washington, D.C.: U.S. Government Printing Office, 1963–1969.

The Public Papers of the President of the United States: Richard Nixon. Washington, D.C.: U.S. Government Printing Office, 1969–1974.

The Public Papers of the President of the United States: Ronald Reagan. Washington, D.C.: U.S. Government Printing Office, 1981–1988.

Report to the President. Presidential Task Force on the Arts and Humanities. Washington, D.C.: Task Force, 1981.

U.S. Congress. House. *Federal Grants to Fine Arts Programs and Projects. Hearings before a Special Subcommittee of the Committee on Education and Labor on H.R. 452, 5136, 5330, 5397, 7106, 7185, 7192, 7383, 7433, 7533, 8047, and 9111*. 83rd Cong., 2nd sess. Washington, D.C.: U.S. Government Printing Office, 1954.

——. *National Arts and Cultural Development Act of 1963. Hearing before the Special Subcommittee on Labor of the Committee on Education and Labor on H.R. 9587*, 88th Cong., 2nd sess. Washington, D.C.: U.S. Government Printing Office, 1964.

——. *National Arts and Humanities Foundations. Hearing before the Special Subcommittee on Labor of the Committee on Education and Labor on H.R. 334, H.R. 2043, H.R. 3617, and Similar Bills to Establish National Foundations on the Arts and Humanities*. 89th Cong., 1st sess. Washington, D.C.: U.S. Government Printing Office, 1965.

——. *Federal Advisory Commission on the Arts. Hearings before a Subcommittee of the Committee on Education and Labor on H.R. 2569 and Related Bills to Provide for the Establishment of a Federal Advisory Commission on the Arts to Assist in the Growth and Development of the Fine Arts in the United States*. 86th Cong., 1st sess. Washington, D.C.: U.S. Government Printing Office, 1959.

——. *Hearings before a Subcommittee of the Committee on Education and Labor on H.R. 3541, 1089, 1945, 6374, 6642, and 7076*. 85th Cong., 1st sess. Washington, D.C.: U.S. Government Printing Office, 1957.

——. House and Senate. National Arts and Humanities Foundations. *Joint Hearing before the Special Subcommittee on the Arts and Humanities of the Committee on Labor and Public Welfare, U.S. Senate, and the Special Subcommittee on Labor of the Committee on Education and Labor, House, on Bills to Establish National Foundations on the Arts and Humanities*. 89th Cong., 1st sess. Washington, D.C.: U.S. Government Printing Office, 1965.

——. Senate. Federal Advisory Council on the Arts. *Hearings before a Subcommittee of the Committee on Labor and Public Welfare on S. 3054, a Bill to Provide for the Establishment of a Federal Advisory Commission on the Arts, and for other Purposes, and S. 3419, a Bill to Provide for the Establishment of a Federal Advisory Committee on the Arts, and for other Purposes.* 84th Cong., 2nd sess. Washington, D.C.: U.S. Government Printing Office, 1956.

——. Senate. *International Cultural Exchange and Trade Fair Participation Act of 1956. Hearing before the Committee on Foreign Relations on S. 3116 and S. 3172, Bills to Provide for the Promotion and Strengthening of International Relations through Cultural and Athletic Exchanges and Participation in International Fairs and Festivals.* 84th Cong., 2nd sess. Washington, D.C.: U.S. Government Printing Office, 1956.

U.S. Statutes at Large 26 (1891).

U.S. Statutes at Large 36. (1911).

PERIODICALS

Artforum, January 1964–December 1975

Art in America, January 1966–December 1980

Art News, January 1966–December 1980

BOOKS AND ARTICLES

Aarons, Leroy. "Arts Festival Fever Grips White House." *Washington Post*, June 14, 1965, B1.

——. "Festival of Arts at White House: Today is Pure Culture, Not Politics." *Washington Post*, June 15, 1965, 1.

Adams, John. "Letter to Abigail Adams, 1780." In *Letters of John Adams Addressed to His Wife*, edited by C. F. Adams, 2:68. Boston: Charles C. Little and James Brown, 1841.

Adamson, Walter. *Avant-Garde Florence: From Modernism to Fascism*. Cambridge: Harvard University Press, 1994.

"AHR Forum on Popular Culture." *American Historical Review* 97 (1992).

"Aid for Artists: But Is It Really Art?" *U.S. News & World Report*, August 28, 1967, 11.

Ak, Edit de, ed. *Rope Drawings of Patrick Ireland*. La Jolla, Calif.: La Jolla Museum of Contemporary Art, 1977.

Alexander, Jane. *Command Performance: An Actress in the Theater of Politics*. New York: Public Affairs, 2000.

Ambrose, Stephen. *Nixon: The Triumph of a Politician 1962–1972*. New York: Simon and Schuster, 1989.

——. *Ruin and Recovery, 1973–1990*. New York: Simon and Schuster, 1991.

Anderson, Patrick. *The Presidents' Men*. New York: Doubleday, 1968.

Apostolis-Cappadona, Diana, and Bruce Altshuler, eds. *Isamu Noguchi: Essays and Conversations*. New York: Harry N. Abrams, 1994.

Appleby, Joyce. "One Good Turn Deserves Another: Moving Beyond the Linguistic." *American Historical Review* 97 (December 1989): 1326–32.

"Arguing the Case For Being Panicky." *Life*, 1957.

Arian, Edward. *The Unfulfilled Promise: Public Subsidy of the Arts in America*. Philadelphia: Temple University Press, 1989.

Arnason, H. H. *The History of Modern Art*. New York: Harry N. Abrams, 1986.

"Art and Politics." *Newsweek*, June 17, 1963, 85.

"Art since 1950, Richard Hunt." *National Museum of American Art Research Bulletin* 1, no. 1 (1996): 32.

Arthurs, Alberta, and Douglas Davis. "News Flash to Washington: Americans *Like* the Arts." *Los Angeles Times*, January 1992.

"Arts and the Man—and the State." *Newsweek*, June 28, 1965, 22–24.

Ashton, Dore. *The Life and Times of the New York School*. New York: Viking, 1972.

Barron, Stephanie, ed. *Degenerate Art: The Fate of the Avant-Garde in Nazi Germany*. Los Angeles: Los Angeles County Museum of Art, 1991.

Battcock, Gregory, ed. *New Video Artists: A Critical Anthology*. New York: E. P. Dutton, 1978.

Beardsley, John. *Art in Public Places: A Survey of Community Sponsored Projects Supported by the National Endowment for the Arts*. Washington, D.C.: Partners for Livable Places, 1981.

Belz, Carl. *Frankenthaler: The 1950s*. Waltham, Mass.: Rose Art Museum, 1981.

Benedict, Stephen, ed. *Public Money and the Muse*. New York: W. W. Norton, 1991.

Bénézit, Emmanuel. *Dictionnaire Critique et Documentaire des Peintres, Sculpteurs, Dessinateurs et Graveurs de Tous les Temps et de Tous les Pays*. Paris: Grund, 1976.

Berman, Eleanor. *Thomas Jefferson among the Arts, An Essay in Early American Esthetics*. New York: Philosophical Library, 1947.

Biddle, Livingston. *Our Government and the Arts: A Perspective from the Inside*. New York: ACA Books, 1988.

Blair, Karen. *The Torchbearers: Women and Their Amateur Arts Associations in America, 1890–1930*. Indianapolis: Indiana University Press, 1994.

Blake, Casey Nelson. "An Atmosphere of Effrontery: Richard Serra, 'Tilted Arc,' and the Crisis of Public Art." In *The Power of Culture*, ed. Richard Wightman Fox and T. J. Jackson Lears, 247–89. Chicago: University of Chicago Press, 1993.

Bois, Yve-alain. "Hans Haacke's Critique of Multinational Corporations." *October* 39 (1986): 129–44.

Bolotowsky, Ilya. "On Neoplasticism and My Own Work: A Memoir." *Leonardo* 2 (July 1969): 221–30.

Bonaventure, Paul, and Catherine Lampert, eds. *Richard Diebenkorn*. London: Whitechapel Art Gallery, 1991.

Bond, Constance. "Artrain: A Museum That's Right on Track." *Smithsonian*, August 1996, 76–87.

Bornet, Vaughn Davis. *The Presidency of Lyndon B. Johnson*. Lawrence: University Press of Kansas, 1983.

Bourdieu, Pièrre. "Cultural Reproduction and Social Reproduction." In *Power and Ideology in Education*, ed. Jerome Karabel and A. H. Halsey. New York: Oxford University Press, 1977.

———. *Distinction: A Social Critique of the Judgement of Taste*. Translated by Richard Nice. Cambridge: Harvard University Press, 1984.

"Brademas Lauds Nixon." *South Bend Tribune*, December 11, 1969.

Brenson, Michael. *Visionaries and Outcasts: The NEA, Congress, and the Place of the Visual Artist in America*. New York: New Press, 2001.

Brown, Betty Ann, ed. *Roland Reiss: A Seventeen Year Survey*. Los Angeles: Fellows of Contemporary Art, 1991.

Buchloh, Benjamin. "Conceptual Art 1962–1969: From the Aesthetic of Administration to the Critique of Institutions." *October* 55 (1990): 105–43.

Bush, Martin H., and Kenworth Moffett. *Goodnough*. Wichita, Kans.: University Art Museum, Wichita State University, 1973.

Canaday, John. "Art in the Soviet: Review of a Paradox." *New York Times*, September 30, 1963.

———. "Khrushchev Scolds Abstract Painters." *New York Times*, December 2, 1962.

———. "Soviet Orders Disciplining for Cultural Avant-Garde." *New York Times*, December 4, 1962.

Cater, Douglas. "The Kennedy Look in the Arts." *Horizon*, September 1961, 8–17.

"Celebrate the Arts." Borders Bookstore and the National Endowment for the Arts, 1995.

Chave, Anna. "Minimalism and the Rhetoric of Power." *Arts* 64 (1990): 44–63.

Chipp, Herschel B., ed. *Theories of Modern Art: A Source Book by Artists and Critics*. Berkeley: University of California Press, 1968.

CNM. "Joan Brown's Neo-Naives." *Artweek* 2 (July 10, 1971): 3.

Cockcroft, Eva. "Abstract Expressionism, Weapon of the Cold War." *Artforum* 12 (June 1974): 39–41.

Cockcroft, Eva Sperling, and Holly Barnet-Sanchez. *Signs from the Heart: California Chicano Murals*. Los Angeles: Social and Political Art Resources Center, 1990.

Coe, Richard. "Artist and Patron Meet in Unique White House Fete." *Washington Post*, June 15, 1965, 1.

———. "State of the Arts: Johnson Administration Setting Record for Cultural Activity." *Washington Post*, January 15, 1967, G1–3.

Coleman, Peter. *The Liberal Conspiracy: The Congress for Cultural Freedom and the Struggle for the Mind of Postwar Europe*. New York: Free Press, 1989.

Collins, Bradford. "Clement Greenberg and the Search for Abstract Expressionism's Successor: A Study in the Manipulation of Avant-Garde Consciousness." *Arts* 61 (1987): 36–43.

Colodny, Len, and Robert Gettlin. *Silent Coup: The Removal of a President*. New York: St. Martin's Press, 1991.

Conte, Luther. "Congress: Birth of NSF Recalled as New Foundation Established to Strengthen Arts, Humanities." *Science*, October 1, 1965, 40–42.

Coombs, Phillip. *The Fourth Dimension of Foreign Policy: Educational and Cultural Affairs*. New York: Harper and Row, 1964.

Cooper, John Milton, Jr. *The Warrior and the Priest: Woodrow Wilson and Theodore Roosevelt*. Cambridge: Harvard University Press, 1983.

Corn, Wanda. "Coming of Age: Historical Scholarship on American Art." *Art Bulletin* 70, no. 2 (1988) 188–207.

Crawford, Clare. "The Square Elephant at Work and Play." *Washingtonian*, October 1969.

Crawford, Alan. *Thunder on the Right: The "New Right" and the Politics of Resentment.* New York: Pantheon, 1980.

Crow, Thomas. "Modernism and Mass Culture in the Visual Arts." In *Modern Art in the Common Culture.* New Haven: Yale University Press, 1996.

"Culture Chief." *New Yorker*, March 1962, 25–26.

Cummings, Paul. *Dictionary of Contemporary American Artists.* New York: St. Martin's Press, 1982.

Current Biography. New York: H. W. Wilson, 1952, 1961, 1972, and 1978.

Dallek, Robert. *Lone Star Rising: Lyndon Johnson and His Times, 1908–1960.* New York: Oxford University Press, 1991.

——. *Ronald Reagan: The Politics of Symbolism.* Cambridge: Harvard University Press, 1999.

Decter, Midge. "Kennedyism." *Commentary* 49 (January 1970): 19–27.

De Kooning, Elaine. "David Smith Makes a Sculpture." *Art News*, September 1951, 38–41.

del Castillo, Richard, Teresa McKenna, and Yvonne Yarbro-Bejarano, eds. *Chicano Art: Resistance and Affirmation, 1965–1985.* Los Angeles: University of California, Wight Art Gallery, 1991.

D'Harnoncourt, René. "Challenge and Promise: Modern Art and Society." *Art News*, November 1948, 252.

Diamonstein, Barbaralee. "Jimmy, Jody, Zbig and Ham & The Art at the Office." *Art News*, March 1978, 36–43.

Doss, Erica. *Benton, Pollock, and the Politics of Modernism: From Regionalism to Abstract Expressionism.* Chicago: University of Chicago Press, 1991.

Drew, Joanna. *Nam June Paik, Video Works, 1963–88.* London: Hayward Gallery, 1988.

Edgar, Natalie. "Noguchi: Master of Ceremony." *Art News*, April 1968, 50–52.

Edsall, Thomas Byrne, and Mary Edsall. *Chain Reaction: The Impact of Race, Rights, and Taxes on American Politics.* New York: Norton, 1991.

Elderfield, John. "Figure and Field." In *Richard Diebenkorn*, edited by Paul Bonaventure and Catherine Lampert. London: Whitechapel, 1991.

"Elephant's Eye." *New Yorker*, September 10, 1955, 33–35.

Ellis, Robert M. *Ilya Bolotowsky: Painting and Columns.* Albuquerque: University Art Museum, 1970.

Emery, Fred. *Watergate: The Corruption of American Politics and the Fall of Richard Nixon.* New York: Touchstone, 1995.

Ermarth, Michael. "Mindful Matters: The Empire's New Codes and the Plight of Modern European Intellectual History." *Journal of Modern History* (September 1985): 506–26.

Fey, Paul B., Jr. *The Pleasure of His Company.* New York: Harper and Row, 1966.

Fielding, Mantel. *Dictionary of American Painters, Sculptors, and Engravers.* Edited by Glenn B. Opitz. New York: Apollo Books, 1986.

Fink, Gary M., and Hugh Davis Graham. *The Carter Presidency: Policy Choices in the Post–New Deal Era*. Lawrence: University Press of Kansas, 1998.

Fiore, Faye, and David Savage. "Ruling Restores Decency Clause for Arts Grants." *Los Angeles Times*, June 26, 1998.

Flam, Jack. *Richard Diebenkorn: The Ocean Park Paintings*. New York: Rizzoli International Publications, 1992.

Flesch, Rudolf. *Why Johnny Can't Read—And What You Can Do About It*. New York: Harper and Brothers, 1955.

Foucault, Michel. *The Foucault Reader*. Edited by Paul Rabinow. New York: Pantheon, 1984.

Frankenthaler, Helen. "Did We Spawn an Arts Monster?" *New York Times*, July 17, 1989.

Frascina, Francis, and Jonathan Harris, eds. *Art in Modern Culture: An Anthology of Critical Texts*. New York: Harper Collins, 1992.

Fraser, Steve, and Gary Gerstle, eds. *The Rise and Fall of the New Deal Order*. Princeton, N.J.: Princeton University Press, 1989.

Fried, Michael. *Three American Painters: Kenneth Noland, Jules Olitski, Frank Stella*. Cambridge: Fogg Art Museum, Harvard University Press, 1965.

Fried, Richard M. *Nightmare in Red: The McCarthy Era in Perspective*. New York: Oxford University Press, 1990.

Frost, Robert. "The Next Augustan Age: For John F. Kennedy/His Inauguration, with Some Preliminary History in Rhyme." In *New Enlarged Anthology of Robert Frost's Poems*, edited by Louis Untermeyer, 276–78. New York: Washington Square Press, 1971.

Fry, Edward. *Richard Pousette-Dart: Recent Paintings*. New York: ACA Galleries, 1991.

Fryd, Vivien Green. *Art and Empire: The Politics of Ethnicity in the U.S. Capital, 1815–1860*. New Haven: Yale University Press, 1992.

Gaddis, John. *Strategies of Containment*. New York: Oxford University Press, 1982.

——. *The United States and the End of the Cold War*. New York: Oxford University Press, 1992.

Galbraith, John Kenneth. *The Affluent Society*. Boston: Houghton Mifflin, 1958.

——. *American Capitalism*. Boston: Houghton Mifflin, 1956.

Galbraith, John, and Russell Lynes. "Should the Government Subsidize the Arts?" *Print* (May 1961): 47–49.

Galligan, Ann Mary. "The National Endowment for the Arts and Humanities: An Experiment in Cultural Democracy." Ph.D. diss., Columbia University Teachers College, 1989.

Garraty, John. *The Great Depression*. New York: Anchor Books, 1987.

Garrettson, Charles. *Hubert H. Humphrey: The Politics of Joy*. New Brunswick, N.J.: Transaction, 1993.

Gelb, Arthur, and Barbara Gelb. "Culture Makes a Hit at the White House." *New York Times Magazine*, January 28, 1962, 64–66.

Geldzahler, Henry. "Interview with Helen Frankenthaler." *Artforum* 4, no. 2 (October 1965): 36–38.

——. *Making It New: Essays, Interviews, and Talks*. New York: Turtle Point, 1994.

——. *New York Painting and Sculpture: 1940–1970*. New York: E. P. Dutton, 1969.

Genauer, Emily. Review of "New York Painting and Sculpture: 1940–1970." *Newsday*, 1969.

Geracimos, Ann, and Gerald Marzorati. "The Artocrats." *Art in America*, July/August 1978, 100–109.

Gitlin, Todd. *The Sixties: Years of Hope, Days of Rage*. New York: Bantam, 1987.

Glenn, Constance W., and Jane K. Bledsoe. *Vapor Dreams in L.A.: Terry Schoonhoven's Empty State*. Long Beach: University Art Museum, California State University, Long Beach, 1982.

Gluck, Mary. *George Lukacs and His Generation—1900–1918*. Cambridge: Harvard University Press, 1985.

Goldman, Eric. *The Tragedy of Lyndon Johnson*. New York: Alfred A. Knopf, 1969.

Godsmith, Barbara. Review of "New York Painting and Sculpture: 1940–1970." *New York*, 1969.

Goodman, Paul. *Growing Up Absurd: Problems of Youth in the Organized System*. New York: Random House, 1956.

Goodwin, Doris Kearns. *The Fitzgeralds and the Kennedys*. New York: Simon and Schuster, 1987.

Goodwin, Richard N. *Remembering America: A Voice From the Sixties*. Boston: Little, Brown, 1988.

Goossen, E. C. *Artists at the Hunter*. New York: Hunter College Art Gallery, 1984.

——. *Helen Frankenthaler*. New York: Frederick A. Praeger, 1969.

"GOP Foes of Tax-Financed Arts Win Victory in House." *Los Angeles Times*, July 14, 1995.

Gorman, Paul R. *Left Intellectuals and Popular Culture in Twentieth-Century America*. Chapel Hill: University of North Carolina Press, 1996.

"Government and the Arts: How Much to Whom?" *Newsweek*, July 18, 1966, 56–60.

Gramsci, Antonio. *Selections from the Prison Notebooks of Antonio Gramsci*. Translated by Quintin Hoare. New York: International, 1971.

Greenberg, Clement. "Art." *Nation*, March 19, 1949.

——. *Art and Culture*. Boston: Beacon Press, 1961.

——. "Avant-Garde and Kitsch." *Partisan Review*, Fall 1939, 34–49.

——. *Clement Greenberg: The Collected Essays and Criticism*. Edited by John O'Brian. Chicago: University of Chicago Press, 1993.

——. "Post-Painterly Abstraction" 1964. In *The Great Decade of American Abstraction: Modernist Art, 1960–70*, edited by E. A. Carmean Jr. Houston: Museum of Fine Arts, 1974.

Greene, John Robert. *The Presidency of Gerald R. Ford*. Lawrence: University Press of Kansas, 1995.

Greenstein, Fred I. *The Hidden-Hand Presidency: Eisenhower As Leader*. New York: Basic Books, 1982.

Griffith, Robert. *The Politics of Fear: Joseph R. McCarthy and the Senate*. Rochelle Park, N.J.: Hayden, 1970.

Guilbaut, Serge. *How New York Stole the Idea of Modern Art: Abstract Expressionism, Freedom, and the Cold War*. Chicago: University of Chicago Press, 1983.

——. "The New Adventures of the Avant-Garde in America: Greenberg, Pollock, or From Trotskyism to the New Liberalism of the 'Vital Center.' " *October* 15 (Winter 1980): 61–78.

——, ed. *Reconstructing Modernism*. Cambridge: MIT Press, 1990.

Haithman, Diane. "Studying the Politics of the Arts." *Los Angeles Times*, October 23, 1995.

Halberstam, David. *The Fifties*. New York: Villard, 1993.

Hall, Gordon Langley, and Ann Pinchot. *Jacqueline Kennedy: A Biography*. New York: Frederick Fell, 1964.

Harris, Jonathan. *Federal Art and National Culture: The Politics of Identity in New Deal America*. New York: Cambridge University Press, 1995.

Harris, Neil. *The Artist in American Society: The Formative Years 1790–1860*. New York: Clarion, 1966.

Harrison, Charles, and Paul Wood, eds. *Art in Theory, 1900–1990: An Anthology of Changing Ideas*. Cambridge, Mass.: Blackwell, 1992.

Harvey, David. *The Condition of Postmodernity: An Enquiry into the Origins of Cultural Change*. Cambridge, Mass: Blackwell, 1990.

Haskell, Barbara. *Blam! The Explosion of Pop, Mininalism, and Performance, 1958–1964*. New York: Whitney Museum, 1984.

Heckscher, August. *The Arts and the National Government*. Washington, D.C.: U.S. Government Printing Office, 1963.

——. "The Central Role of the Arts." *Music Journal*, January 1964, 13.

——. *The Individual and the Mass*. New York: Twentieth Century Fund, 1965.

——. *The Public Happiness*. New York: Atheneum, 1962.

——. "The Quality of American Culture." In *Goals for Americans*, President's Commission on National Goals. New York: Columbia University, 1960.

Hess, T. B. "All's Well That Ends Well." *Art News*, February 1967, 21.

Hodgson, Godfrey. *America in Our Time*. New York: Vintage Books, 1976.

Hoff, Joan. *Nixon Reconsidered*. New York: Basic Books, 1994.

Honan, William. "Congressional Anger Threatens Arts." *New York Times*, June 20, 1989.

Houghton, Norris. Review. *Theatre Arts*, February 1946.

Howells, William Dean. *The Rise of Silas Lapham*. Edited by Walter J. Meserve and David Norhloh. Bloomington: Indiana University Press, 1971.

"Hubert Humphrey Interview." *Fortune*, August 1965.

Hughes, Robert. *The Shock of the New*. New York: Alfred A. Knopf, 1991.

Hume, Paul. "The Arts in Trouble." *Washington Post*, June 29, 1969.

Humphrey, Hubert H. *The Education of a Public Man: My Life and Politics*. New York: Doubleday, 1976.

Hunt, Lynn. *The New Cultural History*. Berkeley: University of California Press, 1989.

Hurlburt, Laurance P. *The Mexican Muralists in the United States*. Albuquerque: University of New Mexico Press, 1989.

"Ike Likes the Arts, So—U.S. May Export Culture." *U.S. News & World Report*, January 28, 1955, 68.

"Ike Sets His Course: Something for All If Congress Goes Along." *U.S. News & World Report*, January 14, 1955, 45–46.

"Jackson Pollock: Is He the Greatest Living Painter in the United States?" *Life*, August 8, 1949, 45.

James, Henry. *The American*. Edited by William Spengemann. New York: Penguin, 1981.

Javits, Sen. Jacob, and Rafael Steinberg. *Javits: The Autobiography of a Public Man*. Boston: Houghton Mifflin, 1981.

Jelavich, Peter. "Popular Dimensions of Modern Elite Culture: The Case of Theater in Fin-de-Siècle Munich." In *Modern European Intellectual History: Reappraisals and New Perspectives*, edited by D. LaCapra and Steven Kaplan, 220–50. New York: Cornell University Press, 1982.

Johns, Elizabeth. "Scholarship in American Art: Its History and Recent Development." *American Studies International* 22, no. 2 (1984): 3-40.

Johnson, Ellen H., ed. *American Artists on Art*. New York: Harper and Row, 1982.

Johnson, Lyndon B. *The Vantage Point*. New York: Popular Library, 1971.

Jonasse, Richard. "The National Endowment for the Arts and the Public Sphere." M.A. thesis, University of Oregon, 1992.

Jumonville, Neil. *Critical Crossings: The New York Intellectuals in Postwar America*. Berkeley: University of California Press, 1991.

Kadis, Phillip M. "Jimmy Carter: A Big Grin for Culture." *Art News*, May 1977, 50–54.

Kalman, Laura. *Abe Fortas: A Biography*. New Haven: Yale University Press, 1990.

Kammen, Michael. *In the Past Lane: Historical Perspectives on American Culture*. New York: Oxford University Press, 1997.

Kaprow, Allan. *Assemblage, Environments and Happenings*. New York: Harry N. Abrams, 1966.

Kaufman, Burton I. *The Presidency of James Earl Carter, Jr.* Lawrence: University Press of Kansas, 1993.

Kearns, Doris. *Lyndon Johnson and the American Dream*. New York: Harper and Row, 1976.

Kennedy, John F. "The Arts in America." *Look*, 1962.

———. "Letter to Irving Kolodin." *Saturday Review*, October 29, 1960, 44.

———. "Letter to Theodate Johnson." *Musical America*, September 13, 1960, 11.

King, Elaine. "Pluralism in the Visual Arts in the United States, 1965–1978: The National Endowment for the Arts, an Influential Force." Ph.D. diss., Northwestern University, 1986.

Kotz, Mary Lynn. "Washington's 'Joan of Art.'" *Art News*, September 1978, 46–55.

Kozloff, Max. "American Painting during the Cold War." *Artforum* (May 1973): 42–54.

Kramer, Hilton. "Art—Richard Hunt." *Nation*, March 23, 1963.

———. "The Purest of Living Sculptors." *New York Times*, May 21, 1978.

Kuspit, Donald. "The Horse in the Industrial Age: Deborah Butterfield's Sculptures." In *Horses: The Art of Deborah Butterfield*. Coral Gables: Lowe Art Museum, University of Miami, 1992.

LaCapra, Dominic, and Steven Kaplan. *Modern European Intellectual History: Reappraisals and New Perspectives*. Ithaca: Cornell University Press, 1982.

Larsen, Neil. *Modernism and Hegemony: A Materialist Critique of Aesthetic Agencies*. Minneapolis: University of Minnesota Press, 1990.

Larson, Gary O. *The Reluctant Patron: The United States Government and the Arts, 1943–1965*. Philadelphia: University of Pennsylvania Press, 1983.

Lasch, Christopher. *The New Radicalism in America, 1889–1963: The Intellectual as Social Type*. New York: Vintage Books, 1965.

Latham, Michael E. *Modernization as Ideology: American Social Science and "Nation Building" in the Kennedy Era*. Chapel Hill: University of North Carolina Press, 2000.

Lears, T. J. Jackson. "The Concept of Cultural Hegemony: Problems and Possibilities." *American Historical Review* 90 (June 1985): 567–93.

Leider, Philip. "Joan Brown: Her Work Illustrates the Progress of a San Francisco Mood." *Artforum* 1 (June 1963): 28–31.

Leja, Michael. *Reframing Abstract Expressionism: Subjectivity and Painting in the 1940s*. New Haven: Yale University Press, 1993.

Lekachman, Robert. *Greed Is Not Enough*. New York: Pantheon, 1982.

"Lessons for a Rock Group." *New York Times*, July 19, 1970.

Leuchtenburg, William. *Franklin D. Roosevelt and the New Deal*. New York: Harper Torchbooks, 1963.

——. "The Pertinence of Political History: Reflections on the Significance of the State in America." *Journal of American History* 73 (1986): 585–600.

Levering, Ralph B. *The Cold War: A Post–Cold War History*. Wheeling, Ill.: Harlan Davidson, 1994.

Levine, Lawrence W. *Highbrow/Lowbrow: The Emergence of Cultural Hierarchy in America*. Cambridge: Harvard University Press, 1988.

Levy, Alan Howard. *Government and the Arts: Debates over Federal Support of the Arts in America from George Washington to Jesse Helms*. Latham, Md.: University Press of America, 1997.

LeWitt, Sol. "Paragraphs on Conceptual Art." *Artforum* (June 1967): 79.

——. *Sol LeWitt Structures 1962–1993*. Oxford, England: Museum of Modern Art Oxford, 1993.

Lieberman, William S., ed. *The Sculpture of Richard Hunt*. New York: Museum of Modern Art, 1971.

Light, Paul. *The President's Agenda: Domestic Policy Choices from Kennedy to Reagan*. Baltimore: Johns Hopkins University Press, 1982.

Lincoln, Anne H. *The Kennedy White House Parties*. New York: Viking, 1967.

Lindey, Christine. *Art in the Cold War: From Vladivostok to Kalamazoo, 1945–1962*. New York: New Amsterdam, 1990.

Lippard, Lucy. "Sweeping Exchanges: The Contribution of Feminism to the Art of the 1970s." *Art Journal* 40 (1980): 362–65.

——. *Tony Smith*. New York: Harry N. Abrams, 1970.

Lipset, Seymour Martin, and Leo Lowenthal. *Culture and Social Character: The Works of David Riesman Reviewed*. New York: Free Press, 1961.

Lipsitz, George. "Listening to Learn and Learning to Listen: Popular Culture, Cultural Theory, and American Studies." *American Quarterly* 42 (1990): 615–36.

Lloyd, Ann Wilson. "Gazed into Like Crystal." In *Mark di Suvero: Retrospective 1959–1991*, 131. Nice, France: Musée d'Art Moderne et d'Art Contemporain, 1991.

Lowens, Irving. "Organizing for the Arts is Nancy Hanks's Specialty." *Washington Evening Star*, September 3, 1969.

Lucie-Smith, Edward. *Movements in Art since 1945*. London: Thames and Hudson, 1984.

Macdonald, Dwight. *Against the American Grain*. New York: Random House, 1956.

——. *Memoirs of a Revolutionist: Essays in Political Criticism*. New York: Farrar, Straus and Cudahy, 1957.

Mamiya, Christin J. *Pop Art and Consumer Culture*. Austin: University of Texas Press, 1992.

Mark, Charles. *Reluctant Bureaucrats: The Struggle to Establish the National Endowment for the Arts*. Dubuque, Iowa: Kendall/Hunt, 1990.

Marling, Karal Ann. *Wall-to-Wall America: A Cultural History of Post Office Murals in the Great Depression*. Minneapolis: University of Minnesota Press, 1982.

Marquis, Alice Goldfarb. *Art Lessons: Learning from the Rise and Fall of Public Arts Funding*. New York: Basic Books, 1995.

Matthews, Christopher. *Kennedy and Nixon: The Rivalry That Shaped Postwar America*. New York: Simon and Schuster, 1996.

Matthews, Jane de Hart. "Art and Politics in Cold War America." *American Historical Review* 81 (October 1976): 762–87.

——. "Arts and the People: The New Deal Quest for Cultural Democracy." *Journal of American History* 62 (September 1975): 316–39.

——. *The Federal Theatre, 1935–1939: Plays, Relief, and Politics*. Princeton, N.J.: Princeton University Press, 1967.

Matusow, Allen. *The Unraveling of America*. New York: Harper and Row, 1984.

May, Elaine Tyler. *Homeward Bound: American Families in the Cold War Era*. New York: Basic Books, 1988.

May, Lary, ed. *Recasting America: Culture and Politics in the Age of Cold War*. Chicago: University of Chicago Press, 1989.

McCarthy, Kathleen D. *Women's Culture: American Philanthropy and Art, 1830–1930*. Chicago: University of Chicago Press, 1991.

McCombie, Mary Eleanor. "Art and Policy: The National Endowment for the Arts's Art in Public Places Program, 1967–1980." Ph.D. diss., University of Texas at Austin, 1992.

McCord, David, ed. *Andrew Wyeth*. Boston: Museum of Fine Arts, 1970.

McCoy, Garnet, ed. *David Smith*. New York: Praeger, 1973.

McDonald, Forrest. *The Presidency of Thomas Jefferson*. Lawrence: University Press of Kansas, 1976.

McDougall, Walter A. *The Heavens and the Earth: A Political History of the Space Age*. New York: Basic Books, 1985.

McKinzie, Richard. *The New Deal for Artists*. Princeton, N.J.: Princeton University Press, 1973.

McQuaid, Kim. *The Anxious Years: America in the Vietnam-Watergate Era*. New York: Basic Books, 1989.

Megill, Allan. *Prophets of Extremity: Nietzsche, Heidegger, Foucault, Derrida*. Berkeley: University of California Press, 1985.

Moe, Henry Allen. "Government and the Arts: A Proposal by George Biddle, with Comment and Criticism by Others." *Harper's*, October 1943, 427–34.

Moen, Matthew C. "Congress and the National Endowment for the Arts: Institutional Patterns and Art Funding, 1965–1994." *Social Science Journal* 34, no. 2 (1997) 185–200.

Molotsky, Irvin. "Reagan Calls for Medal for Leaders in the Arts." *New York Times*, May 18, 1983.

Monahan, Laurie J. "Cultural Cartography: American Designs at the 1964 Venice Biennale." In *Reconstructing Modernism*, edited by Serge Guilbaut, 369–416. Cambridge: MIT Press, 1990.

Monroe, Gerald. "The 1930s: Art, Ideology, and WPA." *Art in America*, November/December 1975, 64–67.

Mukerji, Chandra, and Michael Schudson, eds. *Rethinking Popular Culture*. Berkeley, University of California Press, 1991.

Mulcahy, Kevin V., and Margaret Jane Wyszomirski, eds. *America's Commitment to Culture: Government and the Arts*. San Francisco: Westview, 1995.

Myron, Robert, and Abner Sundell. *Art in America: From Colonial Days through the 19th Century*. New York: Macmillan, 1969.

"National Endowment for the Arts Visual Arts Program, 1972–73." *Artforum* (September 1972): 57.

"NEA Plans Nearly 50% Cut in Staff." *Los Angeles Times*, October 19, 1995.

Netzer, Dick. *The Subsidized Muse: Public Support for the Arts in the United States*. New York: Cambridge University Press, 1978.

Neustadt, Richard. *Presidential Power and the Modern Presidents: The Politics of Leadership from Roosevelt to Reagan*. New York: Free Press, 1990.

"A New Way of Life at the White House." *U.S. News & World Report*. February 24, 1969.

Nixon, Richard. *RN: The Memoirs of Richard Nixon*. New York: Grosset and Dunlap, 1978.

Nodelman, Sheldon. "David Smith." *Art News*, February 1969, 28–31.

Norton-Taylor, Duncan. "Roger Stevens: A Performing Art." *Fortune* 73, no. 3 (1966).

O'Connor, Francis. *Art for the Millions: Essays from the 1930s by Artists and Administrators of the WPA Federal Art Project*. Boston: New York Graphic Society, 1973.

———. *Federal Support for the Visual Arts: The New Deal and Now*. Greenwich, Conn.: New York Graphic Society, 1969.

O'Doherty, Brian. "The Grand Rapids Challenge." *Art in America*, January/February 1974, 78–79.

———. *Inside the White Cube: The Ideology of the Gallery Space*. Santa Monica, Calif.: Lapis Press, 1976.

———. "Public Art and the Government: A Progress Report." *Art in America*, May/June 1974, 44–49.

P.M.K. "The First Family at the Corcoran." *Art News*, May 1977, 52–53.

Paret, Peter. *The Berlin Secession: Modernism and Its Enemies in Imperial Germany*. Cambridge: Harvard University Press, 1980.

Pells, Richard. *The Liberal Mind in a Conservative Age: American Intellectuals during the 1940s and 1950s*. New York: Harper and Row, 1985.

——. *Not Like Us: How Europeans Have Loved, Hated, and Transformed American Culture since World War II*. New York: Basic Books, 1997.

Perlain, Gilbert. "Entretien avec Mark di Suvero." In *Mark di Suvero: Retrospective 1959–1991*, 21–24. Nice, France: Musée d'Art Moderne et d'Art Contemporain, 1991.

——. *Mark di Suvero*. Nice, France: Musée d'Art Moderne et d'Art Contemporain, 1991.

Portner, Leslie Judd. *Washington Post and Times Herald*, July 15, 1956.

"President's Choice." *Time*, February 23, 1970, 62–65.

Proffitt, Steve. "Jane Alexander: Defending the Arts Endowment from the Right—and the Left." *Los Angeles Times*, October 2, 1994.

——. "NEA: Vital Link Between Society and Arts." *Los Angeles Times*, April 27, 1997.

Purcell, Ralph. *Government and Art: A Study of the American Experience*. Washington, D.C.: Public Affairs Press, 1956.

Ratcliff, Carter. "Concerning the Spiritual in Pousette-Dart." *Art in America*, November/December 1974, 89–91.

Reeves, Richard. *President Kennedy: Profile of Power*. New York: Simon and Schuster, 1993.

Reeves, Thomas. *A Question of Character: A Life of John F. Kennedy*. New York: Free Press, 1991.

Reich, Cary. *The Life of Nelson A. Rockefeller: Worlds to Conquer, 1908–1958*. New York: Doubleday, 1996.

Reynolds, Ann. "Reproducing Nature: The Museum of Natural History as Nonsite." *October* 45 (1988): 109–127.

Riesman, David. *The Lonely Crowd*. New Haven: Yale University Press, 1950.

Robbins, Corrine. *The Pluralist Era: American Art 1976–1981*. New York: Harper and Row, 1984.

Rose, Barbara. "Conversation with Gene Davis." *Artforum* (March 1971): 50–54.

Rosenberg, Harold. "The American Action Painters." *Art News*, December 1952, 22–23, 48–50.

——. *The Tradition of the New*. New York: Da Capo Press, 1959.

Rovere, Richard. "Letter from Washington." *New Yorker*, November 30, 1963.

Rubin, Joan Shelley. *The Making of Middlebrow Culture*. Chapel Hill: University of North Carolina Press, 1992.

Salinger, Pièrre. *P. S.: A Memoir*. New York: St. Martin's Press, 1995.

——. *With Kennedy*. New York: Doubleday, 1966.

Sandler, Irving. "Reviews: Robert Goodnough." *Art News*, April 1963, 12.

——. *The Triumph of American Painting*. New York: Praeger, 1970.

Saunders, Frances Stoner. *The Cultural Cold War: The CIA and the World of Arts and Letters*. New York: New Press, 1999.

Scavullo, Francesco. "Interview with Henry Geldzahler." In *Scavullo on Men*. New York: Random House, 1977.

Schaller, Michael. *Reckoning with Reagan: America and Its President in the 1980s*. New York: Oxford University Press, 1992.

Schlesinger, Arthur, Jr. "The Challenge of Abundance." *Reporter* (May 1956).

——. *A Life in the 20th Century: Innocent Beginnings, 1917–1950*. Boston: Houghton Mifflin, 2000.

——. *A Thousand Days: John F. Kennedy in the White House*. Boston: Houghton Mifflin, 1965.

——. *The Vital Center*. Boston: Houghton Mifflin, 1949.

Schorske, Carl. *Fin-de-Siècle Vienna*. New York: Vintage Books, 1961, 1981.

Schulman, Bruce J. *Lyndon B. Johnson and American Liberalism: A Brief Biography with Documents*. Boston: Bedford Books, 1995.

——. *The Seventies: The Great Shift in American Culture, Politics, and Society*. New York: Free Press, 2001.

Schurmann, Franz. *The Foreign Politics of Richard Nixon: The Grand Design*. Berkeley: University of California Institute for International Studies, 1987.

Schwartz, Therese. "The Politicalization of the Avant-Garde." *Art in America*, November/December 1971, 96–105.

Secrest, Meryle. "At 32, the Daddy of the Pop Art Genre." *Washington Post*, January 15, 1967, F1–F12.

Shackelford, George Cohen. *Jefferson's Travels in Europe*. Baltimore: Johns Hopkins University Press, 1995.

Shott, Sarah. *Carl Andre, Dan Flavin, Donald Judd, Sol LeWitt*. London: Waddington Galleries, 1984.

Siegel, Frederick. "Johnson: Triumphant Liberalism." In *A History of Our Time: Readings on Postwar America*, edited by William Chafe and Harvard Sitkoff, 138–42. New York: Oxford University Press, 1991.

Silver, Kenneth. *Esprit de Corps: The Great War and French Art, 1914–1925*. New Haven: Yale University Press, 1981.

Silverman, Debora. *Art Nouveau in Fin-de-Siècle France: Politics, Psychology, and Style*. Berkeley: University of California Press, 1989.

Singal, Daniel, ed. *Modernist Culture in America*. Belmont, Calif.: Wadsworth, 1991.

Skiles, Jacqueline. *Cultural Policy and Social Tradition*. New York: New School for Social Research, 1990.

Skocpol, Theda. "Bringing the State Back In." In *Bringing the State Back In*, edited by Peter Evans, 3–37. New York: Oxford University Press, 1985.

Smith, Richard Candida. *Utopia and Dissent: Art, Poetry, and Politics in California*. Berkeley: University of California Press, 1995.

Snow, C. P. "The Two Cultures and the Scientific Revolution." In *Rede Lectures, 1959*. New York: Cambridge University Press, 1960.

Sontag, Susan. *The Susan Sontag Reader*. New York: Farrar, Straus, Giroux, 1982.

Stevens, Elisabeth. "White House Art Festival Set for Opening." *Washington Post*, June 13, 1965, B1.

Stevens, Roger. "The State of the Arts: A 1966 Balance Sheet." *Saturday Review*, March 12, 1966, 24–25.

Stich, Sidra. *Made in U.S.A.* Berkeley: University of California Press, 1987.

Stiles, Kristine, and Peter Selz, eds. *Theories and Documents of Contemporary Art: A Sourcebook of Artists' Writings.* Berkeley: University of California Press, 1996.

Storey, John. *An Introductory Guide to Cultural Theory and Popular Culture.* Athens: University of Georgia Press, 1993.

Straight, Michael. *After Long Silence.* London: Collins, 1983.

——. *Nancy Hanks: An Intimate Portrait.* Durham, N.C.: Duke University Press, 1988.

——. *Twigs for an Eagle's Nest: Government and the Arts, 1965–1978.* Berkeley, Calif.: Devon Press, 1979.

"Support for the Arts No Luxury." *Minneapolis Tribune*, February 21, 1971.

Switzer, Jacqueline Vaughan. *Green Backlash.* Boulder, Colo.: Lynne Rienner, 1997.

T.B.H. "Artists in the Great Society?" *Art in America*, June 1965.

Taubman, Howard. "Nixon to Seek Full $60 Million to Assist Endowments in Arts." *New York Times*, January 16, 1971.

Taylor, Fannie, and Anthony Barresi. *The Arts at a New Frontier: The National Endowment for the Arts.* New York: Plenum, 1984.

Temple, Louann. "Pathfinders for the Imagination." M.A. thesis, University of Texas at Austin, 1990.

Terenzio, Stephanie, ed. *The Collected Writings of Robert Motherwell.* New York: Oxford University Press, 1992.

Thayer, Mary Van Rensselaer. *Jacqueline Bouvier Kennedy.* New York: Doubleday, 1961.

——. *Jacqueline Kennedy: The White House Years.* Boston: Little, Brown, 1967.

Thompson, Frank. "Are The Communists Right in Calling Us Cultural Barbarians?" *Music Journal* (July–August 1955): 5, 20.

——. "The Arts in Congress." *Music Journal* (September 1964): 27, 77–79.

——. "The Federal Government's Role in Art." *Educational Theatre Journal* (December 1957): 300–305.

Tickner, Lisa. "The Body Politic: Female Sexualtiy and Women Artists Since 1970." In *Looking On: Images of Femininity in the Visual Arts and Media*, edited by Rosemary Betterton, 235–53. New York: Pandora, 1987.

Tissot, Roland. *L'Amerique et Ses Peintres, 1940–1980.* Lyon, France: Presses Universitaires de Lyon, 1990.

Toews, John E. "Intellectual History after the Linguistic Turn: The Autonomy of Meaning and the Irreducibility of Experience." *American Historical Review* 92 (October 1987): 879–907.

"A Tour of the White House with Mrs. John F. Kennedy." Produced by Perry Wolfe, CBS. February 14, 1962. Film and Television Archive, University of California, Los Angeles.

Trace, Arthur S., Jr. *What Ivan Knows That Johnny Doesn't.* New York: Random House, 1961.

Tuchman, Phyllis. *Mark di Suvero: 25 Years of Sculpture and Drawings.* New York: Storm King Art Center, 1985.

Tucker, Marcia. "An Interview with Deborah Butterfield." *Horses: The Art of Deborah Butterfield*. Coral Gables: Lowe Art Museum, University of Miami, 1992.

Udall, Stewart. "The Arts as a National Resource." *Saturday Review*, March 28, 1964, 14–16.

———. "The Quality of Life in This Technological Age." *Music Journal* (February 1964): 19–20, 46.

Underwood, James E., and William J. Daniels. *Governor Rockefeller of New York: The Apex of Pragmatic Liberalism in the United States*. Westport, Conn.: Greenwood Press, 1982.

"Unpaid Brain Trust Taking Form for President Johnson." *Houston Chronicle*, February 23, 1964.

Van der Marck, Jan. "Looking back on Four Years," *Acquisitions 1974–1978*. Hanover, New Hampshire: Dartmouth College Museum and Galleries, 1979.

———. "Sculpture Around Campus: Dartmouth College." *Art Journal* 37, no. 3 (Spring 1978): 248–50.

Vatter, Harold G., and John Walker, eds. *History of the U.S. Economy since World War II*. New York: M. E. Sharpe, 1996.

Von Eckardt, Wolf. "Critics Are Discovering That Stevens Is a Swan." *Washington Post*, October 30, 1966, G9.

Wagnleitner, Reinhold. *Coca-Colonization and the Cold War: The Cultural Mission of the United States in Austria after the Second World War*. Translated by Diana M. Wolf. Chapel Hill: University of North Carolina Press, 1994.

———. "The Irony of American Culture Abroad: Austria and the Cold War." In *Recasting America: Culture and Politics in the Age of Cold War*, edited by Larry May, 285–301. Chicago: University of Chicago Press, 1989.

Wall, Donald, ed. *Gene Davis*. New York: Praeger, 1975.

Weinberg, H. Barbara. *The Lure of Paris: Nineteenth-Century American Painters and Their French Teachers*. New York: Abbeville Press, 1991.

Weir, Margaret, Ann Shola Orloff, and Theda Skocpol, eds. *The Politics of Social Policy in the United States*. Princeton, N.J.: Princeton University Press, 1988.

Wetenhall, John. "The Ascendancy of Modern Public Sculpture in America." Ph.D. diss., Stanford University, 1988.

———. "Camelot's Legacy to Public Art: Aesthetic Ideology in the New Frontier." *Art Journal* (Winter 1989): 303–8.

"What's Ahead in the Stock Market Now, As Experts See It." *U.S. News & World Report*, June 28, 1965, 45.

White, Hayden. *The Content of the Form: Narrative Discourse and Historical Representation*. Baltimore: Johns Hopkins University Press, 1987.

White, Mark J., ed. *Kennedy: The New Frontier Revisited*. New York: New York University Press, 1998.

Whitfield, Stephen. *The Culture of the Cold War*. Baltimore: Johns Hopkins University Press, 1991.

Whyte, William. *The Organization Man*. New York: Simon and Schuster, 1956.

Willard, Charlotte. "Women of American Art." *Look*, September 27, 1960, 70.

Wilson, Augusta E. *Liberal Leader in the House: Frank Thompson, Jr.* Washington, D.C.: Acropolis Books, 1968.

Wohl, Robert. *The Generation of 1914.* Cambridge: Harvard University Press, 1979.

Wood, James N. *Six Painters: Edward Avedisian, Darby Bannard, Dan Christensen, Ron Davis, Larry Poons, Peter Young.* Buffalo: Buffalo Fine Arts Academy, 1971.

INDEX